EDWARD II

THE UNCONVENTIONAL KING

KATHRYN WARNER

AMBERLEY

To my parents, Phil and Elaine

This edition first published 2015

First published 2014

Amberley Publishing
The Hill, Stroud
Gloucestershire, GL5 4EP

www.amberley-books.com

British Library Cataloguing in Publication Data.
A catalogue record for this book is available from the British Library.

ISBN 978 1 4456 5054 8 (paperback)
ISBN 978 1 4456 4132 4 (ebook)

Typeset by Fakenham Prepress Solutions, Fakenham, Norfolk NR21 8NN
Printed in the UK.

Contents

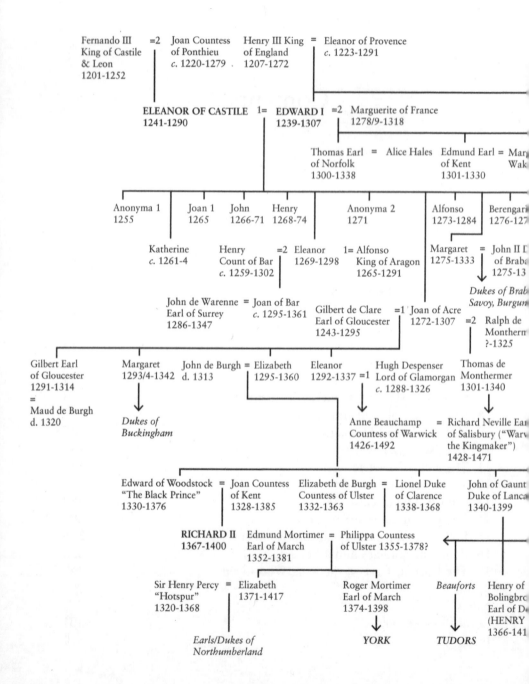

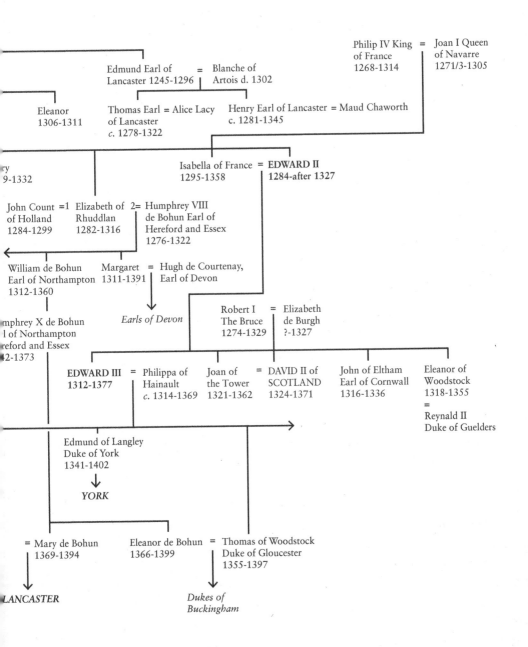

Philip IV King = Joan I Queen
of France   of Navarre
1268-1314   1271/3-1305

Edmund Earl of = Blanche of
Lancaster 1245-1296   Artois d. 1302

Eleanor
1306-1311

Thomas Earl = Alice Lacy
of Lancaster
c. 1278-1322

Henry Earl of Lancaster = Maud Chaworth
c. 1281-1345

Isabella of France = EDWARD II
1295-1358   1284-after 1327

ry
9-1332

John Count =1 Elizabeth of 2= Humphrey VIII
of Holland   Rhuddlan   de Bohun Earl of
1284-1299   1282-1316   Hereford and Essex
                              1276-1322

William de Bohun   Margaret = Hugh de Courtenay,
Earl of Northampton 1311-1391   Earl of Devon
1312-1360

mphrey X de Bohun   Earls of Devon   Robert I = Elizabeth
l of Northampton   The Bruce   de Burgh
reford and Essex   1274-1329   ?-1327
2-1373

EDWARD III = Philippa of   Joan of   = DAVID II of   John of Eltham   Eleanor of
1312-1377   Hainault   the Tower   SCOTLAND   Earl of Cornwall Woodstock
             c. 1314-1369 1321-1362   1324-1371   1316-1336   1318-1355
                                                                       =
                                                                       Reynald II
                                                                       Duke of Guelders

Edmund of Langley
Duke of York
1341-1402

YORK

= Mary de Bohun   Eleanor de Bohun = Thomas of Woodstock
1369-1394   1366-1399   Duke of Gloucester
                                        1355-1397

LANCASTER   Dukes of
                     Buckingham

Acknowledgements

I am very grateful to Ian Mortimer, who suggested that I should write a biography of Edward in the first place, for his support, kindness and help over the years.

Thank you to Nicola Gale and everyone at Amberley.

Thank you to Susan Higginbotham for kindly providing me with helpful documents and for our many fascinating conversations about Edward.

Thank you to the staff of the National Archives, the Society of Antiquaries, Corpus Christi College Cambridge, Warwickshire County Record Office, Gloucester Cathedral, Berkeley Castle and Tewkesbury Abbey for their help.

Thank you to Folko Boermans, Sarah Butterfield, Lisa May Davidson, Jules Frusher, Vishnu Nair, Joe Oliver, Jennifer Parcell, Sami Parkkonen, Sharon Penman, Mary Pollock, Jamie Staley, Gillian Thomson and Kate Wingrove, for all your help.

Everyone who comments on my Edward site, all my history friends in real life and via email, on Facebook and Twitter, all over the world, unfortunately you are far too numerous to name individually, but I thank you all.

Foreword by Ian Mortimer

Primogeniture was a cruel method of selecting a king. The very idea that a man should be given absolute power simply on account of his paternity – with no reference to his father's or mother's qualities, or even his own ability – seems a recipe for disaster. The added notion that his selection was a divine appointment made it impossible for him to refuse, even if he was exceedingly unsuited for political responsibility. At the same time, the dire penalties for failure meant that the throne cast a dark shadow across the consciences of its occupants. Even the most successful English kings had their daunting moments – one thinks of Henry II's war with his sons, the rebellions against Edward I in the 1290s, the parliamentary challenges to Edward III in 1341 and 1376, the attempts on Henry IV's life, and Edward IV's period of exile in the middle of his reign. All in all, it is surprising that so many English princes rose to the challenge of positive kingship: of the nineteen monarchs crowned between the Conquest and the Reformation, perhaps ten emerge with a reputation for successful leadership. As is well known, Edward II was not one of them.

Edward is rather a member of a more select group: a king whose failings were more important than his successes in the history of the realm. This does not make his reign any less significant than those of his predecessors; indeed, England's great traditions of legal freedom and parliamentary representation owe far more to disastrous reigns than magnificent ones. We may look to William II, whose tyranny and 'accidental' assassination paved the way for Henry I's charter of liberties – the first time a king of England was formally bound to the law. There is the even more notable example of King John, without whose ineptitude there would have been no Magna Carta. The divisive rule of his son, Henry III, led to the establishment of the English parliament. And it was the reign of Edward II that brought to the fore the radical notion that Englishmen owed their loyalty to the Crown itself, not its wearer. Even more importantly, Edward II's enforced abdication demonstrated that there were limits to the inviolable status of an anointed, hereditary monarch. From 1327, if a king of England broke his coronation oaths, he could be dethroned by his subjects acting in parliament.

There can be no doubt therefore that Edward II occupies a seminal place in the history of England and, indeed, of the whole of Europe. Moreover, it was not just his reign or a particular series of bad decisions that were important; it was his very personality that was the critical factor. When government was vested in a single individual, its failings were almost entirely personal. As Kathryn Warner makes clear in this book, Edward II's short temper, his overbearing pride, and his refusal to compromise or make allowance for similarly brittle qualities in others, led to a violent clash with his most powerful cousin, Thomas of Lancaster, resulting in the latter's downfall – one of Edward's few triumphs. His personal vindictiveness towards Lancaster and his adherents led to many executions and accusations of tyranny, which ultimately led to Edward's own downfall. Trust Edward to snatch an utter calamity from the jaws of success! Overall, his internal battle to understand his own complex nature meant that he was always trying to have things both ways: to have the dignity and power of a king and yet at the same time the freedom of the common man – to dig ditches, go swimming and give lavish gifts to his friends, if he felt like doing so. The result was the almost inevitable alienation of the nobility, who expected a man to be one thing or the other: either a properly regal king or a plain commoner. And Edward himself could not come to terms with their requirement for him to be both something he was and something he was not. Despite his piety, he was never truly able to resolve the great accident of his own birth – that he, with all his faults and doubts in himself, had been chosen by God to be king.

A new biography of Edward II is thus an important publication. This is all the more the case as Edward II studies in the past have in many respects been lacking. Even at the sharper end of the historiography, academics adopted a sort of 'Edward II routine' in which certain difficult questions were not asked, let alone answered in full. Nowhere is this more in evidence than with regard to his death – the information underpinning which has been shown to be a deliberate lie, carefully designed to conceal the location of his new prison in late 1327. But it also applies to Edward as a man and thus to the entire understanding of precisely why his reign foundered. Scholarly medievalists who, in the twentieth century, favoured objectivity over a sympathetic portrait of the man, simply sat in judgement on him and did not seek to understand why he acted as he did. Thus they missed much of the man's character and failed to understand the reasons for his nobles' actions. Only relatively recently with the publication of Seymour Phillips's Edward II has this generally parlous state of affairs been remedied – but even that book demonstrates its author's inability completely to break away from the 'Edward II routine' in respect of the man's death and possible later life.

Kathryn Warner brings fresh air to the study of this reign. For her no aspect of the 'Edward II routine' can be taken at face value. She re-examines the issues, and criticises and corrects the rest of us fearlessly and tactfully. She understands the limits of historical evidence but she also knows its power, and she revises many distortions that have crept into the traditionally accepted version of events, especially where they are not supported by contemporary sources. But most importantly of all, she understands the importance of the human subject beyond the evidence. After all, the evidence in itself is a matter for antiquaries; the historian has to reach for the vitality that is only touched upon here and there by the documents. In this case the essential things to grasp are the man's personality and his contemporary reputation: what motivated him, what frightened him, and what he perceived to be his worth to others. I was once criticised by an eminent scholar for devoting more pages in a biography to the matter of whether Edward III raped the countess of Salisbury than the parliamentary crisis of 1341. But I still maintain that in a true biography – as opposed to a history book about a reign – it is important to present not only what a man thought of himself but his awareness of what others thought of him. In this context I very much admire Kathryn's concentration on Gaveston at the outset of Edward's reign: some historians would regard the Gaveston episode as a mere distraction, and less important than Edward's governmental crises. However, putting that relationship centre-stage reflects Edward's own priorities. It demonstrates how his whole approach to kingship was secondary to the companionship of his adopted brother. Edward II's personal relationships, and his lack of awareness of how they were seen, lies right at the very heart of his story, along with the contradictions in his nature mentioned above. The more objectively and judgementally you view the man, and ignore the huge distortions of his personal life, which ultimately were his undoing, the further you drift from the truth.

It goes without saying that deliberate attempts to understand a medieval character, and to present his concerns and priorities in proportion, are fraught with difficulty. Too often attempts to write a sympathetic study end in a whitewash. Worse, there is a danger that an emotional credulity may seep into the narrative, and obscure the contradictions of the character. Such romanticism does not affect Kathryn's work. When she says the king 'swooned' at the start of the book it is because she has an early-fourteenth-century source that says Edward 'swooned'. What emerges from her work is an integrity which is both reassuring and refreshing. You know you can trust her because she passionately wants to understand the reality of the man's life.

Edward II's reign will always be regarded as a failure but as a result of studies like this, there is a hope that the man who was the centre of events will emerge in all his complexity, not simply as a weak king. He had his virtues – among them his piety, his loyalty to his friends and his generosity. As Kathryn observes, he was not devoid of strategic ability – I smiled when I read her line that the astuteness he showed when defending his favourites was 'to the intense frustration of his contemporaries'. Reading this book I found myself asking the question, was there ever a ruler of England whose perception of his own virtues differed so much from those of his contemporaries? Where he saw virtue, they saw betrayal. Given that state of affairs, what could he possibly have done to make a success of his reign? He was, it seems, doomed by his inheritance.

Ian Mortimer

A Note on Wages and Prices

Rather than giving modern equivalents of incomes and prices in the early fourteenth century, which are almost impossible to calculate accurately and which, with inflation, date quickly, this page is intended to give an idea of the value of money in Edward II's reign.

The only coin in general circulation in England was the silver penny, which could be broken in two to make a half-penny, or into four to make a farthing. The main unit of currency was the pound, consisting of 240 pence or twenty shillings, though it remained a purely theoretical notion for most people. Large sums of money could only be transported in barrels containing thousands of pennies. The mark was another unit of currency often used in accounting: it equalled two-thirds of a pound, or thirteen shillings and four pence, or 160 pence.

The average daily wage of an unskilled labourer was one or one and a half pence.

Skilled craftsmen of course earned more: Edward II's carpenters were paid three pence a day, and his master carpenters six pence.

In Edward's household, pages earned two pence per day, grooms and archers three pence, squires seven and a half pence, and sergeants-at-arms twelve pence (one shilling). His steward earned 200 marks per year, or £133, six shillings and eight pence.

The minimum annual income to qualify for knighthood was £40.

The annual gross income of the earl of Lancaster, the richest man in England, was £11,000.

A loaf of the cheapest bread cost a farthing (quarter of a penny). A chicken, two dozen eggs and a gallon of ale each cost a penny.

The cost of a trained warhorse was £50 to £80, a cow cost ten or twelve shillings, and a sheep cost twenty pence or less.

Introduction

Kenilworth Castle, Warwickshire, Tuesday 20 January 1327

Edward II wore black and swooned. Pale-faced and surrounded by his enemies, had you not known he was the king you would never have guessed it from his demeanour or that of the bishops, barons, knights, abbots and others who had come to Kenilworth from parliament in London to do what had never been done in England before. Hostile, angry, uneasy, they demanded that the king abdicate his throne to his fourteen-year-old son.

They hurled accusations at Edward. He was incompetent to govern and allowed evil counsellors to rule for him, he had lost Scotland and lands in France and Ireland, he had imprisoned, exiled, killed and disinherited many noblemen and churchmen, he neglected the business of his kingdom and pursued worthless hobbies fit only for peasants. Powerless, in captivity and with his closest friends dead, there was little Edward could do but consent to their demand, and so for the first time in English history, a son succeeded to the throne while his father still lived. In tears, Edward knelt and begged his subjects' pardon for his trespasses.[1] Aghast at what had become of him and his reign, he declared passionately, 'I greatly lament that I have so utterly failed my people, but I could not be other than I am.'[2]

I could not be other than I am. Edward II's entire life was a battle against what was expected of him. Entirely unconventional by the standards of his time, even eccentric, he had neither the temperament nor the ability to fill the position he had been born into, to the great unhappiness of himself and his subjects. His reign of nineteen and a half years, July 1307 to January 1327, was a turbulent history of constant threats of civil war, endless conflicts and quarrels with his barons, failed military campaigns and dependence on male favourites. Before his accession, no English earl had been executed since Waltheof in 1076. During Edward's reign and its immediate aftermath, the regime of his queen and her own male favourite, an earl counted himself lucky to die in his bed. No fewer than six were executed between 1312 and 1330, and two died in battle.

Edward's reign ended in his own wife rebelling and launching an invasion of his country, his forced abdication in favour of his son and, according to traditional accounts, in his atrocious murder. Subject to scathing criticism in his own lifetime, Edward has fared even worse since. 'A more complete ninny than Edward II has seldom occupied a throne'; 'Brutal and brainless ... incompetent, idle, frivolous and incurious'; 'A scatter-brained wastrel'; 'A weakling and a fool'; 'Weak-willed and frivolous'; 'A coward and a trifler'; 'Worthy never to have been born' are just some of the harsh judgements passed on this most maligned of monarchs.[3] That Edward II was an utter failure as a ruler and war leader is very hard to deny. After all, no king ends his reign wandering around Wales with a mere handful of followers, pursued by an army, without making a long series of truly horrible mistakes. However, Edward had the misfortune to be born in the wrong era. Many of the character traits and behaviour that made him such a disastrous king, and were incomprehensible and even shocking to his contemporaries, would be judged differently today. In many ways, Edward was ahead of his time. He was openly a lover of men, he enjoyed the company of his lowborn subjects and their activities such as thatching roofs and shoeing horses, he bought his own fish and bread, he spent much time near the end of his reign living in a cottage rather than in one of his luxurious palaces, he once had to pay compensation to his jester for accidentally injuring him while swimming in the Thames in winter, he went on a swimming and rowing holiday with a large crowd of 'common people', he watched fishermen fishing and ditchers digging and sometimes joined in, he loved the outdoors and physical exercise, he is one of only two people in history to found colleges at both Oxford and Cambridge.[4]

Edward inspired polarised opinions in his own lifetime and afterwards. Many people despised him. A few adored and were passionately devoted to him. Edward was a complex and difficult man, and a bundle of contradictions. Fiercely emotional, he loved and hated to extremes, could nurse a grudge for many years and never forgave a betrayal, though on the other hand he was remarkably generous and kind to people he loved and those who pleased him. Although often amiable and good-natured, with a highly developed sense of humour, he had a vile temper and could be unpleasant and spiteful. He reacted, and frequently overreacted, emotionally rather than with his intellect, and his personal likes and dislikes entirely dominated his policy throughout his reign. He showed little in the way of determination or ambition, except when his male favourites were threatened. Then, he acted with great energy and astuteness, to the intense frustration of his contemporaries; he had plenty of ability when he chose to use it, but directed it to the wrong ends. His indecisiveness was also infuriating, and he had a tendency to believe and act on whatever the last person had said to him. His great-grandson Richard II made unsuccessful attempts to have him canonised as a saint, and the fourteenth-century chronicler Geoffrey le Baker depicted him as a Christlike figure nobly suffering the torments of lesser people. On the other hand, the Westminster chronicler spoke at length of his 'insane stupidity' and his 'wicked fury', and other contemporaries despaired of him and his inability or unwillingness to be what his subjects wanted and needed him to be.

This biography is not intended to whitewash a deeply flawed man or skate over his numerous errors and failings and the miseries heaped on his subjects during his reign, but it is intended to provide a more vivid and personal portrait of Edward than has been seen before, and to demolish some of the myths invented about him which have come to be widely and wrongly seen as historical fact. Edward II was far more than the disastrous king who came between two great ones, his father Edward I and son Edward III, even if many people are only aware of him as the gay foppish prince who was cuckolded by William Wallace in the Hollywood film *Braveheart* and who had a lover named Piers Gaveston, who may or may not have been thrown out of a window by Edward's father. The one thing that almost everyone is sure they know about Edward II is that he died at Berkeley Castle with a red-hot poker thrust inside his anus. It is beyond all reasonable doubt, however, that this story is a myth, and the tale that Wallace slept with Edward's wife and was the real father of his son Edward III is sheer modern invention.

He was passionate, brutal, kind, generous, capricious, indolent, spiteful, obsessive, good-humoured, affable, foolish, erratic, gracious, shy, charming and vengeful. He was Edward II, and this is his life and death.

1

Heir to the Throne and Accession

On Friday 7 July 1307, sixty-eight-year-old King Edward I of England, 'fearless and warlike, in all things strenuous and illustrious', came to the end of his long and eventful life in a remote corner of his kingdom, at Burgh-by-Sands near Carlisle.[1] Appropriately enough for a man known as the Hammer of the Scots, he died with Scotland in sight across the Solway Firth, on his way to yet another military campaign there. Around three in the afternoon, the harsh and terrifying king, survivor of an assassination attempt in the Holy Land, conqueror of North Wales, and father of at least seventeen children, raised himself from his bed to take some food, and fell back dead in his attendants' arms.[2] Messengers set out immediately to inform his successor, and galloped the 315 miles to London in a mere four days.

Lord Edward of Caernarfon, prince of Wales, duke of Aquitaine, earl of Chester and count of Ponthieu, was staying at the palace of Lambeth. Edward had set out in mid-June to join his father in the north, but on reaching Northampton changed his mind and returned to London, apparently in no great rush to help chase Robert Bruce and his adherents around the south-west of Scotland. Before returning to the safety of the capital, he sent his father two barrels of expensive sturgeon, a thoughtful if not terribly useful gift for a man heading into a war zone.[3] On 11 July 1307, Edward heard himself addressed as 'my lord king' for the first time, and although no chronicle or letter records his reaction, we may assume that he was pleased to succeed to the throne for one reason, at least. Ten weeks earlier, his father had sent his beloved friend, the Gascon knight Piers Gaveston, into exile on the Continent. Now free to do whatever he wanted, Edward recalled Gaveston, most probably the very first act he took as king.[4] He thus immediately set out his main priority for the next couple of decades: dedication to his male favourites. Probably the royal messengers told Edward that his father, on his deathbed, had ordered him not to recall Gaveston to England.[5] Edward, missing his friend terribly, took not the slightest notice.

The kingdom rejoiced at the news of Edward II's accession, at least for a while; the new king was young, regal in appearance, a breath of fresh air after the thirty-five-year reign of his father, and 'equal to or indeed more excellent than other kings'.[6] His subjects were to become considerably less enthusiastic when they discovered what he was really like: a man with little desire to rule, finding the grind of government considerably less to his liking than gambling, thatching roofs and swimming, with little aptitude for warfare, and deeply in love with another man and determined to treat him as an equal. In July 1307, Edward II was twenty-three years old, at least the fourteenth and perhaps fifteenth or sixteenth child of Edward I, the fourth but eldest surviving of his six sons. He had been born in Caernarfon, North Wales, on the feast day of St Mark the Evangelist in the twelfth year of his father's reign, 25 April 1284, and was baptised there on 1 May, with nineteen pounds paid out in alms to celebrate his birth and baptism.[7] Edward is one of three kings of England born in Wales, the others being Henry V in 1386 and Henry VII in 1457, and he was the only one close to the throne at the time of his birth.

Edward I was almost forty-five in April 1284, born on 17 June 1239, and had been king of England since the death of his father Henry III in November 1272. Edward of Caernarfon's Spanish mother Queen Eleanor was forty-two at the time of her youngest child's birth; she was born in late 1241 as Doña Leonor de Castilla, twelfth of the fifteen children of the great warrior king Fernando III of Castile and Leon, later canonised as San Fernando.[8] Born the son of a reigning king, grandson of two more kings, Edward of Caernarfon's ancestry was impeccably royal on both sides. His parents had been married for just under thirty years at the time of his birth: their wedding took place in Burgos, northern Spain, on 1 November 1254. Edward was named after his father, who himself was named in honour of his father King Henry's favourite saint, Edward the Confessor. Between 1066 when the Confessor died and Edward I's birth in 1239, the Anglo-Saxon name Edward had fallen out of use in England and by the middle of the thirteenth century probably sounded as old-fashioned as Leofwin, Ethelred and Wulfnoth, but the fact that all the kings of England between 1272 and 1377 bore the name ensured its popularity for evermore.

Edward of Caernarfon was not born as heir to his father's throne. That honour belonged to his ten-year-old brother Alfonso, born in Bayonne in south-west France in November 1273 and named after his uncle and godfather Alfonso X of Castile. Alfonso of Bayonne's sudden death on 19 August 1284, while Edward I was arranging a future marriage for him with Count Floris V of Holland's daughter Margaret, came as a shock to his grieving parents and to the people of England, who for a decade had grown accustomed to the idea that one day a King Alfonso would rule over them. Two other sons of Edward I and Eleanor of Castile, John and Henry, had died in 1271 and 1274 at the ages of five and six respectively. At four months old, Edward of Caernarfon became his father's sole male heir and next in line to the throne, and having lost three boys in childhood, Edward I must have been desperately worried about his remaining son's welfare and the future of his dynasty. Luckily, Edward of Caernarfon was a sturdy, healthy child who is only known to have been ill once in childhood, when he came down with tertian fever shortly before he turned ten.[9] As well as their four sons, Edward I and Queen Eleanor had at least ten daughters, five or more of whom – Katherine, Joan, Berengaria and others whose names are unknown – died in childhood. Five survived: Eleanor, born in 1269 and fifteen years Edward of Caernarfon's senior; Joan of Acre, born in the Holy Land in 1272; Margaret, born in 1275; Mary, born in 1279; and Elizabeth of Rhuddlan, born in August 1282 and only twenty months older than Edward.

Edward left Wales when he was a few months old and didn't return until just before his seventeenth birthday in April 1301. There is no truth to the often-repeated tale that his father tricked the people of North Wales by promising them a prince who spoke no English, then presenting them with his newborn son; this story was invented 300 years later.[10] Edward of Caernarfon was not created prince of Wales (and earl of Chester) until 7 February 1301. He may have been conceived in Caernarfon as well as born there, as his father's itinerary demonstrates that he and the queen spent much of July and August 1283 in the town.[11] Edward's very existence was threatened eight months before his birth in late August 1283 when a fire broke out in his parents' bedchamber one night at Caergwrle Castle, and the royal couple barely escaped with their lives.[12] Even before he was created Prince of Wales and returned there, Edward of Caernarfon was remembered in the land of his birth: in 1290 when he was six, a man from Caernarfon brought him a gift of six herons, and in 1300 the constable of Conwy sent him a gift of two greyhounds.[13] Many of Edward's letters for the years 1304/05, when he was at the beginning of his twenties, fortuitously survive, and a famous one to Philip IV of France's half-brother Louis of Evreux shows him poking gentle affectionate fun at Wales:

> We send you a big trotting palfrey which can hardly carry its own weight, and some of our bandy-legged harriers from Wales, who can well catch a hare if they find it asleep, and some of our running dogs which go at a gentle pace – for well we know that you take delight in lazy dogs. And, dear cousin, if you want anything else from our land of Wales, we can send you plenty of wild lads, if you wish, who will well know how to teach breeding to the young heirs and heiresses of great lords.[14]

This letter has often been misunderstood in modern times, but clearly demonstrates Edward's sense of humour and ability to share a joke with a man he knew well; Evreux was his second cousin and frequent correspondent.

Edward was only two years old when in May 1286 his parents left England and sailed to the king's duchy of Aquitaine, in south-west France. They didn't return until late July 1289, and sixteen months later Queen Eleanor died, at Harby in Nottinghamshire on 28 November 1290, aged forty-nine.[15] Her body was buried at Westminster Abbey and her viscera at Lincoln Cathedral, and her heart was given, with that of her son Alfonso, to the Dominican friars of London. Her grieving husband movingly referred to her in a letter as 'whom in life we dearly cherished, and whom in death we cannot cease to love', and remained a widower for nine years.[16] In her memory, the king built the famous Eleanor Crosses at the dozen places where her funeral procession had rested on the way to Westminster, three of which still survive, and the queen's magnificent brass effigy can be seen to this day at Westminster Abbey. Only six of her fourteen or more children outlived her. Six-year-old Edward of Caernarfon inherited Eleanor's county of Ponthieu, which she had in turn inherited from her mother Joan, Queen of Castile, and became count of Ponthieu, his first title. Ponthieu was a small but strategically important county in northern France bordering Normandy, with its capital at Abbeville, in the modern department of Somme and region of Picardy.

Edward can barely have known his half-Spanish, half-French mother, and seven months after her death his paternal grandmother Eleanor of Provence, widow of Henry III and the only one of his grandparents still alive when Edward was born, also died. Eleanor of Provence was a devoted mother and grandmother who took an interest in Edward's welfare, once asking her son Edward I to allow the boy to remain in the south of England while the king travelled north, on the grounds that his health might be at risk in the bleaker northern climate and its 'bad air'.[17] The lack of a maternal figure as he grew up may well have affected Edward emotionally, and in a 1305 letter to his much older kinswoman Agnes de Valence, he rather poignantly called her his 'good mother' and promised that he would do whatever he could for her, 'as a son who would gladly do and procure whatever could turn to your profit and honour'.[18]

Throughout Edward's childhood, his older sisters also left his company as they married, though he remained on close and affectionate terms with at least some of them into adulthood. Eleanor, although betrothed for many years to the Spanish king Alfonso III of Aragon, wed Henri III, count of Bar in eastern France, and had two children before her death in 1298. Joan of Acre was betrothed in childhood to Hartmann von Hapsburg, son of the German king Rudolf I, but he drowned in 1281 and she married instead Gilbert 'the Red' de Clare, earl of Gloucester, with whom she had four children. She outraged her father in 1297 by secretly marrying a humble squire named Ralph Monthermer, while the king was negotiating for her to marry the count of Savoy, and had another four children with him. Margaret married John II, duke of Brabant in modern-day Belgium and the Netherlands, and had one child, Duke John III. Mary became a reluctant nun at Amesbury Priory in Wiltshire. Elizabeth married firstly John I, count of Holland, who died childless aged fifteen, and secondly Humphrey de Bohun, earl of Hereford, with whom she had ten children. Edward I married his second wife Marguerite of France, half-sister of Philip IV, in September 1299, when he was sixty and she twenty, and Edward of Caernarfon fifteen. Queen Marguerite was the mother of Edward's half-siblings, Thomas of Brotherton, born in 1300 and sixteen years Edward's junior, Edmund of Woodstock, born in 1301, and Eleanor, born in 1306 when their father Edward I was almost sixty-seven, who died when she was five.

Edward of Caernarfon himself was betrothed three times in childhood in furtherance of his father's foreign policy. His first fiancée, when he was five, was his cousin Margaret the 'Maid of Norway', daughter of Erik II of Norway and granddaughter of Alexander III of Scotland. On the death of Alexander – Edward I's brother-in-law – in March 1286, Margaret became queen of Scotland in her own right, but died in September 1290 at the age of only seven. It is fascinating to contemplate how different British history might be if Margaret had lived to adulthood and married Edward, and whether England and Scotland would have been united centuries earlier than really happened. Edward was next betrothed in 1291, when he was seven, to Blanche, another half-sister of Philip IV of France. Philip and Edward I went to war in 1294, and this engagement was broken off and Edward betrothed instead to Philippa, daughter of Edward I's ally the count of Flanders. This in turn was ended in 1297 when Edward I and Philip IV made peace. Edward's fourth betrothal in 1299 was the one which ultimately ended in marriage.

Edward lived at the centre of a large household of many dozens of people, as was appropriate for the heir to the throne. His tutor was Sir Guy Ferre and he may also have been taught by Dominican friars, and although we know little about his education, there is no reason to assume that it was lacking in any way or that Edward was ignorant and stupid.[19] Although we have no direct evidence that Edward could write – the earliest extant example of a king of England's handwriting is his son Edward III's, from 1329 – we may assume that he could. His sisters Eleanor and Mary and his sister-in-law Margaret Wake were able to write, and it would be odd if the future king of England had less education than his sisters and especially if he had less than a woman from the baronial house of Wake.[20] The St Albans chronicler tells a story that in 1317 a woman on horseback placed a letter in front of Edward, who began to read it out loud: proof that he could indeed read, as his powerful chamberlain and 'favourite' of the 1320s, Hugh Despenser, certainly could.[21] Edward's strong interest in the universities of Oxford and Cambridge is hardly the sign of an uneducated man unconcerned with learning, and he also supported the archbishop of Dublin in his creation of a university there, which was formally established in 1312.[22] Edward's native language was French, or rather the version of it used by the medieval English elite, now known as Anglo-Norman. He would have learnt Latin and presumably could also speak fluent English, though as with his ability to write, there is no direct evidence for this.

During his childhood Edward spent the winter at one place, often Langley near St Albans in Hertfordshire, and in spring and summer travelled around the south of England and the Midlands, rarely spending more than a night or two in each town. The size of the future king's household and the amount of food and drink required for them could prove onerous to local inhabitants as he travelled around the country: in 1294, when Edward was ten and had spent a few weeks at Langley and St Albans, the Dunstable annalist complained, 'Two hundred dishes a day were not sufficient for his kitchen. Whatever he spent on himself and his followers he took without paying for it.'[23] Even as a child Edward regularly entertained many magnates and prelates, who visited him with retinues of their own. His extant household accounts of 1292/93 show that, for example, Edward Balliol, son of the king of Scotland John Balliol, visited him on 17 May 1293; a week later, the bishop of Jebail in Syria dined with him; and Edward's sister Mary the nun, his cousins Thomas and Henry of Lancaster (sons of Edward I's brother Edmund) and his brother-in-law John of Brabant (who married Edward's sister Margaret in 1290) arrived in June. The three boys stayed for a few days with large retinues who all had to be provided with food, drink, accommodation, and lodging and fodder for their horses, to the exasperation of Edward's clerk, who recorded their presence daily as 'they are staying', 'they are still here' and 'here they are still. And this day is burdensome.'[24] A few weeks later, the clerk recorded somewhat vaguely that nine-year-old Edward dined with 'a monk and some other monks'.[25] As well as all the relatives, nobles and prelates who regularly visited Edward of Caernarfon, there were highborn children who lived in his household with him, at least for a while. In 1290 when he was six, he had the company of, among others, Maud Chaworth (born 1282), granddaughter of the earl of Warwick, who married Edward's cousin Henry of Lancaster in or before 1297; Eleanor de Burgh, eldest daughter of the earl of Ulster; and Humphrey de Bohun, heir to the earldom of Hereford, who would marry Edward's sister Elizabeth in 1302.[26] In the early 1300s, the earl of Gloucester's nephew Gilbert de Clare, lord of Thomond in Ireland, and

Piers Gaveston from a noble family of Béarn were among the members of Edward's household, and according to the much later chronicler Jean Froissart, Edward's notorious favourite Hugh Despenser also lived in the future king's household as a boy or young man.

Edward of Caernarfon's childhood came to an end and his public life began in earnest in August 1297 at the age of thirteen, when his father departed from the kingdom with an army to campaign against the French and Philip IV in Flanders. Edward was left behind as nominal regent in the king's absence, not an easy position, given the many crises in England that year: defeat by William Wallace at Stirling Bridge and a mighty row between Edward I and the earls of Norfolk and Hereford, among much else.[27] On 7 February 1301, Edward was granted all the royal lands in Wales and the earldom of Chester, and from that point on, was always known as the prince of Wales. A few weeks later he finally revisited the land of his birth – though not, in fact, Caernarfon itself, where he never set foot again – when he travelled there to take the homage and fealty of his Welsh tenants.[28] More lands and titles came on 7 April 1306, when Edward I gave the duchy of Aquitaine to his eldest son.[29] Edward of Caernarfon was now prince of Wales, duke of Aquitaine, earl of Chester and count of Ponthieu, and at Pentecost, 22 May 1306, a month after his twenty-second birthday, he was knighted at Westminster with almost 300 other young men.[30]

The appreciative chronicler Piers Langtoft described the mass knighting and the banquet afterwards as the most splendid sight seen in Britain since King Arthur was crowned at Caerleon.[31] Edward of Caernarfon was knighted by his father in a private ceremony in the chapel of Westminster Palace, and the king then girded his son with the sword-belt, and Henry de Lacy, earl of Lincoln, and Edward's brother-in-law Humphrey de Bohun fastened on his spurs. Then, before the high altar in the abbey church itself, Edward knighted all the other young men, who were supposed to have spent the previous night awake and in prayerful contemplation, but instead filled the New Temple church with the noise of talking, shouting, laughing and trumpet calls. Among the men knighted in May 1306 were Piers Gaveston and Hugh Despenser, Edward's favourites; the earls of Surrey and Arundel; and Roger Mortimer, who twenty years later would bring down the king.[32] To entertain the new knights at a lavish banquet in Westminster Hall afterwards, Edward I hired eighty minstrels, who included Pearl in the Eye, William Without Manners, Reginald the Liar, Edward of Caernarfon's trumpeters Januche and Gillot, his *crwth* (a Welsh stringed instrument) player Nagary and his harper Amekyn, the famous acrobat Matilda Makejoy, and others called Gaunsaillie, Grendone, Fairfax, Mahu of the North and 'the minstrel with the bells'.[33] A list of silk items handed out at this time to some members of the royal family gives an idea of the colourful splendour of Edward's surroundings:

he received five pieces of yellow silk for lining a quilt, one piece of green for lining his cloak, five pieces of red to make a curtain for his bed and ten pieces of various colours to make two mattresses.[34]

Little more than a year later, Edward I was dead. Soon after recalling Piers Gaveston on hearing the news of his father's death on 11 July 1307, Edward II set out from London, and reached Burgh-by-Sands in eight days. There, he viewed the embalmed body of his father, and supposedly wept for him.[35] At about the same time, a letter announcing Gaveston's return to England reached him.[36] This was breakneck speed considering that Edward's messenger had to cross the Channel and find Gaveston, busily covering himself with glory on the jousting fields of the Continent. No doubt he cut a fine figure with the outfits Edward had sent him, one of which was of green velvet decorated with pearls, gold and silver piping, and gold aiguillettes. He was certainly not short of money, as Edward had recently sent him the enormous sum of £260.[37]

Edward's weeping is merely a conventional expression, and it may be that he did not grieve much for Edward I. In 1305, the two men quarrelled, and the king refused to allow his wayward son to enter his presence for much of that summer. Not long before his death, Edward I tore out handfuls of Edward's hair, called him an 'ill-born son of a whore', and perhaps even threw him to the ground, during another dreadful quarrel.[38] On the other hand, disputes between the king and his heir were common in the Middle Ages – as Edward's biographer Professor Seymour Phillips points out, Edward I himself clashed with his father Henry III on occasion – and there is no real reason to suppose that Edward I found his heir particularly disappointing or unpromising; the notion that he did is based on hindsight after Edward's failed reign.[39] Neither, apparently, did anyone else, and the author of the *Vita Edwardi Secundi* comments that Edward as prince of Wales showed considerable promise and raised his future subjects' hopes (but dashed them when he became king).[40]

It can hardly be doubted, though, that in many ways Edward II's character and behaviour were utterly unconventional by the standards of his time and position. Most eccentrically of all, 'from his youth he devoted himself in private to the art of rowing and driving carts, of digging ditches and thatching houses, as was commonly said, and also with his companions at night to various works of ingenuity and skill, and to other pointless trivial occupations unsuitable for the son of a king'.[41] As well as digging, thatching and driving carts, Edward loved building walls, swimming, hedging, working with wrought iron and shoeing horses, and not only did he enjoy such hobbies, he did them well: he was 'very skilful in what he delighted to employ his hands upon'.[42] The contradictory king, 'bountiful and splendid in living', spent vast sums on clothes and jewels and took delight in dressing lavishly, yet was equally happy to go out into the fields or shimmy up a roof, which he would hardly have done while wearing all his court finery.[43] How Edward came to take part in and enjoy such hobbies is not known, but perhaps his interest arose during his childhood at Langley.

Edward revelled in his own enormous strength and excellent health, and was devoted to the outdoors and exacting physical exercise. But whereas nowadays he would no doubt be seen as an excellent role model for a nation with an increasingly sedentary lifestyle, in the fourteenth century Edward's love of rustic pursuits met with a total lack of comprehension from his contemporaries, who entirely failed to see the appeal. Worse, his hobbies attracted scathing contempt from the magnates, chroniclers, his own household and even the pope, in an era when knights and nobles did knightly and noble things like jousting, hunting and fighting, and peasants did peasant things like digging, building and thatching, and never the twain should meet. Edward's great-grandfather Count Raymond-Berenger V of Provence had even passed laws prohibiting the knightly class from undertaking the tasks of villeins.[44] The king's willingness to 'give himself up always to improper works and occupations' was deemed important enough to be mentioned many years later at his deposition as one of the reasons for his unsuitability to be king, not only because such occupations were considered incompatible with his royal dignity, but because they led him 'to neglect the business of his kingdom'.[45] Edward did not only appreciate the pursuits of the lowborn, he also enjoyed their company, and whereas a king with the common touch would be applauded today, the fourteenth-century mind found this fact abhorrent. 'He forsook the company of lords, and fraternised with harlots, singers, actors, carters, ditchers, oarsmen, sailors, and others who practise the mechanical arts,' sniffed the chronicler Ranulph Higden.[46] Edward's enjoyment of the company of his lowborn subjects is almost certainly indirect evidence that he could speak English, as such people would not have spoken French, the language of the elite.

On 20 July 1307, Edward II was proclaimed king of England and lord of Ireland at Carlisle Castle, 'by descent and heritage', and added two more titles to the four he already held.[47] He may not yet have realised it, but his father had left him an extraordinarily difficult legacy: empty coffers, an unwinnable war in Scotland, unfriendly relations with France, dissatisfied, restless magnates.[48] Even a man more suited to the role he had been born into might have struggled to fulfil this position adequately, and Edward II, as he would soon demonstrate, was not suited to the role of king.

2

The New King and His Favourite

In the great hall of Carlisle Castle, Edward II sat in solitary splendour and watched the earls and lords who had attended his father before his death come before him and in order of rank, drop to one knee, kiss his hand, and swear homage and fealty to him as their liege lord. What these men thought of their new king cannot be known. Certainly they knew of his love for Piers Gaveston, almost certainly of his unseemly rustic pursuits, and perhaps felt uneasy about the future. But whatever they, and Edward's subjects, might have thought of his strange hobbies and his abilities, or lack of them, nobody ever criticised his appearance. He was every inch a king. The contemporary author of the *Vita Edwardi Secundi* (Life of Edward II), who knew him well and who criticised him far more often than not, described him as 'tall and strong, a fine figure of a handsome man'. In 1300, aged sixteen, he was said to be 'of a well-proportioned and handsome person', and after his accession, 'handsome in body and great of strength', 'physically he was one of the strongest men in his realm', 'elegant, of outstanding strength', and 'a handsome man, strong of body and limb'.[1] He had a moustache and beard, and fair curly or wavy hair, which he wore parted in the middle, sometimes held in place with a circlet, and falling almost to his shoulders. He must have been about 6 feet or a little more: his father stood 6 feet 2 inches, and his son Edward III's life-sized death mannequin measured 5 feet 10½ inches. Edward II was probably taller than his son, however, as the author of the *Vita* remarked on his height, and the chronicler Thomas Walsingham said that Edward III was 'not excessively tall'.[2]

Around 23 July, the new king supervised the departure of his father's funeral procession as it began its long journey south to Westminster. The procession was led by Anthony Bek, bishop of Durham and the only Englishman in history to hold the title of patriarch of Jerusalem, whom Edward called 'our entire and certain friend'.[3] Edward left Carlisle on 31 July and crossed the Scottish border with his army, or rather his father's army, to march the 30 miles to Dumfries. Prior to his death, Edward I had intended to hunt down Robert Bruce, defeat him utterly, and execute him with all the considerable brutality the age was capable of. In March 1306, Bruce had had himself crowned king of Scots at Scone Abbey, a few weeks after stabbing his greatest enemy and rival John 'the Red Comyn' to death in the Greyfriars church in Dumfries. This act followed a ten-year interregnum in Scotland, and the previous king, John Balliol, removed from the throne in 1296, was still alive in Picardy with his son, another Edward (who had dined with Edward of Caernarfon in 1293). English kings did not claim the throne of Scotland, to which they had no right, but felt entitled to interfere in Scottish affairs and believed that the Scottish kings owed them fealty for their kingdom. Edward I and his son refused to acknowledge Robert Bruce as king of Scots, and neither did the pope, thanks to Bruce's sacrilegious murder of Comyn in church. After his inauguration as king, Bruce fled to the west of Scotland with his only remaining brother – yet another Edward – and his few supporters; most of Scotland was dominated politically by the powerful Comyn faction, who, understandably, were as keen as Edward I to find and execute him. In England, 'King Hob', as Bruce was derisively known, was considered a rebel and a traitor, having previously been an ally of Edward I, and much of Edward II's reign would be taken up with endless campaigns to defeat Bruce and assume what he considered his rightful position as overlord of Scotland.

On 6 August 1307, Edward granted the earldom of Cornwall to Piers Gaveston, possibly without Gaveston's prior knowledge, as Edward would later claim to the pope.[4] Although Edward's earls later complained bitterly about Gaveston's advancement, all but one of them, Warwick, put their seals to the charter, and it is not true, as the *Annales Paulini* claim, that the barons later had the charter burnt: it still exists in the National Archives in Kew.[5] The earldom of Cornwall was Edward's own inheritance: the previous earl, Edmund, nephew of Henry III, died in 1300, and as he had no children, nieces or nephews, the earldom passed to his first cousin Edward I as Edmund's nearest male heir, and thence to Edward II.[6]

Edward and Piers Gaveston were reunited at Dumfries, sometime in August. This must have been an extremely emotional occasion for Edward, who probably loved Gaveston more than he loved any other person in his life. The flamboyant Piers, whose family took its name from the Béarnais village of Gabaston close to the Pyrenees, was of noble birth, the second of the four sons of Arnaud de Gabaston or Gaveston and Claramonde de Marsan, and far from being the low-born nobody he is often made out to be.[7] His father and grandfathers were among the leading barons of Béarn. Gaveston's date of birth is not known, but he was older than Edward, born by July 1283 at the latest and possibly a few years earlier; his parents were married before 30 June 1272.[8] The first known reference to 'Perrot Gaveston' – 'Perrot' or 'Perott' was his nickname – appears in November 1297, when he was a squire of Edward I's household.[9] Edward I sent Gaveston to live in his son's household in 1300 when Edward was sixteen, though it may be that the two young men had met before.

Odd though it might seem from later events, Edward I placed Gaveston, a courageous and excellent soldier and successful jouster *par extraordinaire*, in his son's household with the intention that he should become Edward's role model, which perhaps indicates that he was indeed several years older than Edward. Gaveston served in the king's army in 1297 and impressed Edward I with his military ability, which the king probably hoped would rub off on his son. By 1303, Gaveston was described as Edward's 'companion'.[10] No likeness or physical description of him exists, and contemporary chroniclers were so unremittingly hostile that it is difficult to form a clear picture of his personality, but he was athletic, charming, courteous but sharp-tongued, irreverent, witty, and boundlessly self-confident, even arrogant. A later chronicler – who in fact never saw him – described him as elegant and agile, sharp-witted, refined and well-practised in military matters.[11] Much like Edward himself, Gaveston polarised opinion, and most people hated him. Edward loved him beyond reason, and far beyond sense.

In February 1307, Edward I banished Gaveston from England, a move that, contrary to contemporary chroniclers' beliefs, was not intended to be punitive. The king set the date of departure two months in advance, after Gaveston had competed in a jousting tournament, gave him a generous financial settlement of a hundred marks a year, and ordered him to await his eventual return.[12] None of this suggests that Edward I was angry with Gaveston personally. At that stage in his life, fierce and irascible, his fury would be very apparent, as he demonstrated around this time by tearing out clumps of his son's hair and kicking him. It is highly likely that it was Edward of Caernarfon's own conduct which caused Edward I to order Gaveston out of England, perhaps because Edward had asked his father permission to grant either his county of Ponthieu or the earldom of Cornwall to his friend – though the *Scalacronica* claims that Gaveston 'was accused before the king of diverse crime and vices, which rendered him unfit company for the king's son'.[13] Edward I was probably troubled by the relationship that had developed between the two men and 'the undue intimacy which the young Lord Edward had adopted towards' Gaveston, and deeply concerned that his son's love for the Gascon would create insurmountable problems and divisions in England when he himself was dead and Edward acceded to the throne – correctly, as it turned out.[14]

That Edward II loved Piers Gaveston is beyond all doubt. Precisely how he loved him, however, is a difficult question to answer. There is nothing written by Edward himself that would give us any insight into his feelings for Gaveston, except that, occasionally, he referred to him in official letters as 'our dear and faithful brother', the same address he used for his half-brothers. Five chronicles written during or shortly after Edward's lifetime say that he referred to Gaveston as 'my brother' in speech, the *Vita* calls Gaveston 'a great earl whom the king had adopted as brother', and the *Annales Paulini* also say he was Edward's 'adoptive brother'.[15] For two young men to swear an oath of adoptive brotherhood was usually considered honourable; the problem with Edward naming Gaveston as his brother, as their contemporaries saw it, was the gulf of rank which separated them.[16] Chroniclers also commented on Edward's immoderate, inordinate and excessive love for Gaveston: 'I do not remember to have heard that one man so loved another. Jonathan cherished David, Achilles loved Patroclus. But we do not read that they were immoderate. Our king, however, was incapable of moderate favour,' says the *Vita*, and other chroniclers wrote much the same thing.[17] Edward's behaviour in the first five years of his reign bears out this judgement. We also learn that when Edward first saw Gaveston, 'he fell so much in love that he entered upon an enduring compact with him, and determined to knit an indissoluble bond of affection with him, above all other mortals'.[18] It is important to remember that this did not automatically mean romantic love, as we would understand it. The early fourteenth century was an age when men bandied about declarations of love for other men far more easily than in later eras; the earl of Richmond's chaplain claimed in 1309, for example, that Piers Gaveston loved Richmond 'beyond measure'.[19] A few years later, Edward's cousin the earl of Lancaster, on learning that his friend and confidant Robert Holland had abandoned him during his rebellion against the king, groaned 'How could he find it in his heart to betray me, when I loved him so much?'[20] The usual assumption that Edward and Gaveston's relationship was sexual and erotic owes far more to Christopher Marlowe's *c.* 1592 play *Edward II* and numerous modern productions of it, including Derek Jarman's explicit film version of 1991, than to any fourteenth-century evidence. Although Edward definitely loved Gaveston, Gaveston's feelings for the king are impossible to determine with any certainty. One might be tempted to take a cynical view: Gaveston was a younger son with little chance of inheriting his family's lands, and besides, his father left Gascony for England in the late 1290s in dire financial straits, and had to support himself by entering Edward I's service.[21] Gaveston therefore had few prospects for wealth or advancement in his homeland or in England, and had nothing to lose and everything to gain by courting the favour of the future king. On the other hand, it is entirely possible that Gaveston did genuinely love Edward.

Although Edward II was a man who loved men, we cannot say with any certainty how he loved them, and his sexuality was rather more complex than is often surmised these days. He fathered an illegitimate son, Adam, sometime between 1305 and 1310, when he was in his early to mid-twenties.[22] In the fourteenth century, people were almost invariably named after close members of their family, and as none of Edward's relatives bore the name, this implies that either his son's mother was the daughter or sister of a man called Adam, or that his son's godfather was called Adam. Piers Gaveston also fathered an illegitimate daughter, Amie.[23] Despite some modern speculation to the contrary, there is no reason whatsoever to think that Edward did not father his wife Isabella's children; a comparison of their itineraries proves conclusively that they were together approximately nine months before the births of all their offspring. The true nature of Edward II's and Piers Gaveston's relationship is unknown, and forever unknowable. Whether they were lovers, whether their relationship was romantic, or romantic on one side and calculating on the other, or erotic but unconsummated, or based on an oath of adoptive brotherhood, or the deeply affectionate bond of two men who met in adolescence and formed a close and unbreakable friendship, ultimately matters less than the fact that Edward's excessive favour to Gaveston caused widespread envy and resentment.

At Dumfries, Edward took the homage of the Scottish lords who were loyal to him, and left on 12 August with Gaveston and his army, intending to march north and pursue Robert Bruce. He spent several weeks wandering from Dumfries to Sanquhar and Cumnock, doing and achieving nothing in particular except attending a feast that Gaveston gave on 17 August – where he gave a pound each to the Welsh trumpeters Yevan and Ythel who played for them – and soon gave up the pursuit.[24] In late August he retraced his steps to Carlisle, and from there, travelled to Knaresborough Castle in Yorkshire, which now belonged to Gaveston. For the new earl of Cornwall, the huge costs involved in entertaining the king and his retinue for a few days hardly constituted a problem, as Edward had just made him one of the richest men in the country, with an annual income of about £4,000.[25]

Puzzled by Edward's unwillingness to chase up hill and down dale in pursuit of a fugitive, albeit royal, Scotsman, three fourteenth-century chronicles claimed that he abandoned the war with Scotland because of his desire to marry his fiancée, Isabella of France, as soon as possible.[26] This is extremely unlikely. Isabella was probably only eleven years old in the summer of 1307, and although Edward II had many faults, lusting after prepubescent girls was not one of them. There are no grounds to suppose either that he was desperately keen for his wedding to a girl he had never seen and whom he had to marry for political reasons to go ahead, or that he was trying to get out of it.[27] The real reasons for Edward's departure from Scotland are not hard to find: it was important for him to return south and take over his father's government, and make arrangements for his coronation and wedding. Edward's precipitate departure from Scotland, however, where he didn't return for three years, allowed Robert Bruce the breathing space to consolidate his position and gain allies.

Edward around this time ordered the arrest of Walter Langton, bishop of Coventry and Lichfield, possibly at Piers Gaveston's instigation.[28] In 1305, Edward and Gaveston had entered Langton's lands and stolen his deer, and Edward insulted him with 'certain gross and harsh words', the main cause of his quarrel with his father which ended with the old king refusing to allow his son anywhere near him.[29] Langton remained in prison, accused, among other things, of consorting with the devil and, rather more conventionally, of misappropriating public funds. However, he would be reconciled with the king by early 1312, and served him faithfully until his death in 1321. Edward also asked the pope to restore Robert Winchelsey to the archbishopric of Canterbury, from which he had been suspended the year before at the request of Edward I.[30] Winchelsey returned to England in March 1308, and repaid Edward by becoming one of his and Gaveston's most intractable enemies, a stance he maintained until his death. Edward's dislike of a future ally and trust of a future enemy provide early evidence of his inept judgement of character.

In the early months of his reign, Edward communicated with Philip IV of France about his wedding to Philip's daughter Isabella, which was to go ahead in January 1308 in Boulogne, and set about making arrangements for his trip to France.[31] Edward and Isabella, his fourth fiancée, had been betrothed since 1299, when he was fifteen and she three or four. The reason for their betrothal lay in the rich province of Gascony. Edward's great-great-grandmother Eleanor had brought the duchy of Aquitaine to the English Crown in 1152 on her marriage to the future Henry II. In 1259, in an attempt to end the decades of military conflict between England and France over the vast French territories ruled by England, Henry III and Louis IX signed the Treaty of Paris, which stated that the English king could keep Gascony of the original inheritance, but held it as a vassal of the king of France.[32] This meant that the English kings owed homage to the French king as their feudal overlord, which caused great friction between the two countries. Every time a new king of either country acceded to the throne, the English king had to travel to France and kneel to its king, a situation they found intolerably demeaning and tried to delay as long as possible. The French kings for their part hated that the English Crown ruled such a large area of France. These tensions would erupt into war between England and France in 1294, 1324 and, most notably, the Hundred Years War in 1337. If a vassal did not pay homage within a certain time limit, his overlord had the right to confiscate his estates. Therefore, paying homage to the king of France was a duty

Edward II had no means of escaping, and he was particularly unfortunate that no fewer than four kings ruled France during his comparatively short reign. Philip IV seized an opportunity to confiscate Gascony from Edward I in 1294, and the price of regaining it was a marriage alliance: Edward I would marry Philip's half-sister Marguerite, and his son would marry Philip's daughter, Isabella.

After enjoying Gaveston's hospitality at Knaresborough, Edward travelled to Nottingham, where he spent a week in early September supervising alterations to the castle and paid a pound to his harper Robert Clough for playing for him.[33] He moved on to Northampton, and opened his first parliament on 16 October. Parliament sat for a mere three days, its objectives only to discuss the late king's funeral arrangements and the new king's nuptials and coronation, and to grant Edward expenses for them. At Northampton Edward sent a letter to Oljeitu, 'illustrious king of the Tartars', who was the ruler of the Ilkhanate, part of the Mongol Empire covering much of modern-day Afghanistan, Azerbaijan, Georgia, Iran, Iraq, Pakistan and Turkey, and ordered his falcons and dogs brought to him.[34] His enjoyment of hawking and hunting, far more conventional than his other hobbies, aroused no ire or incomprehension among his contemporaries, though it is notable that unlike his son Edward III he never competed personally in a joust, that sport so beloved of medieval royal and noble men. Perhaps he was simply not interested, or perhaps his father, concerned for the future of his dynasty, forbade it (the earl of Surrey's son and Duke John I of Brabant were killed jousting in 1286 and 1294 during Edward's childhood; it was a dangerous activity).

Edward I's funeral took place at Westminster Abbey three and a half months after his death on 27 October, and he was buried in a simple tomb near his first wife Eleanor of Castile and his father Henry III in the chapel of St Edward the Confessor. A story told much later in the fourteenth century claims that the old king had ordered that his flesh be boiled down and removed and his bones carried before an army to Scotland, but this is unlikely to be true, and even if he had, his son took no notice.[35] Edward II spent £100 on horses for knights to ride in the procession, and gave 100 marks to be distributed to the poor and £2 to William Attefenne, sumpter-man, 'for the great labour he sustained in providing torches and leather for the body of the deceased king'; he spent £453 altogether.[36] His filial duty done, Edward issued an edict ordering everyone to refer to Gaveston by his title, earl of Cornwall, rather than by his name.[37] This probably reflects Edward's determination that Gaveston, only a minor noble by birth, should not be disparaged by the great magnates, rather than being a statement on the formality or otherwise of his court.

Edward was determined that his 'brother Piers' should become a member of the royal family, and arranged a marriage for his friend. Unfortunately, the three of Edward's numerous sisters who were still alive were unavailable: twenty-five-year-old Elizabeth was married to the earl of Hereford; twenty-eight-year-old Mary was a nun; and thirty-two-year-old Margaret was married to the duke of Brabant. There remained his little half-sister Eleanor, Edward I's youngest child, but she was only eighteen months old in the autumn of 1307. Edward, therefore, was forced to make Gaveston his nephew by marriage rather than his brother, by marrying him to one of his nieces. A few of them were already unavailable. His eldest niece, fifteen-year-old Eleanor de Clare, had married Hugh Despenser in May 1306. Eleven-year-old Joan of Bar was married to John de Warenne, earl of Surrey, and ten-year-old Mary Monthermer was betrothed to Duncan MacDuff, earl of Fife. Joan Monthermer was promised to the priory of Amesbury, and Eleanor de Bohun was only three, which left Edward's other Clare nieces, thirteen-year-old Margaret and twelve-year-old Elizabeth. Because sisters usually –though not always – married in birth order, it fell to Margaret, second of the five daughters of Edward's sister Joan of Acre (who had died in April), to marry her uncle's Gascon favourite. Evidently Edward had been planning a Clare-Gaveston match for months; the charter granting his friend the earldom of Cornwall in August 1307 was decorated with the Clare arms as well as Gaveston's own.[38]

On 1 November 1307, only five days after her grandfather Edward I's funeral, Margaret married Gaveston at Berkhamsted Castle, 30 miles from London. Presumably it was attended by Margaret's brother Gilbert de Clare, recently granted his earldoms of Gloucester and Hertford at the age of sixteen, five years before he could normally have expected to inherit.[39] Possibly, Edward offered him this as a sweetener to accept his sister's marriage to Gaveston, but also, an earl was far more use to him politically than an underage ward. Gloucester didn't complain; he now had an annual income of £6,000, which made him one of the richest men in the country, even wealthier than his new brother-in-law. He was Edward's eldest nephew, only seven years younger than the king, and fifteen years older than his aunt, Edward I's youngest child Eleanor.[40] Edward II's stepmother Marguerite of France, dowager queen of England, also attended the wedding. Before his accession, Edward had been on good terms with the stepmother who wasn't much older than he was, and often asked her to intercede with his father on his behalf. Forty years younger than her husband, Marguerite had nevertheless enjoyed a good relationship with him, though she was never crowned as queen. Edward gave jewels worth thirty pounds to the bride and groom, a roan-coloured palfrey horse worth twenty pounds to Margaret de Clare and expensive cloth worked with gold and pearls to her ladies, and provided the generous amount of seven pounds, ten shillings and six pence in pennies to be thrown over the heads of the bride and groom at the door of the chapel.[41] His almoner collected the money, which would comfortably have fed several families for a year, and distributed it to the poor. The king spent an enormous twenty pounds on the minstrels, and evidently it was quite a celebration, as he gave five shillings in compensation to a local resident for 'damage done by the king's party' to his property.[42] Edward also spent fifty-two pounds on two warhorses for himself on 4 November, one a bay and the other 'white spotted'.[43]

And so a thirteen-year-old girl married a man in his mid-twenties or older, who was involved in an intense relationship with her uncle. To modern sensibilities this seems callous, but nobody at the time complained about it in such terms. They did, however, protest that the old king's granddaughter was being disparaged, and that her marriage should be used to further English interests instead. Edward, predictably, ignored them. Given Margaret's youth, it is unlikely that she and Gaveston began cohabiting after the wedding, and Gaveston's marriage made little difference to his relationship with Edward.

After the wedding, Edward returned to his favourite residence of Langley in Hertfordshire, where he had to deal with a difficult situation that had recently arisen: the Knights Templar. The Templars were a military monastic order, extremely rich, and Edward's second cousin and future father-in-law Philip IV of France itched to get his hands on their money. On Friday 13 October 1307, he ordered all the Templars in France to be arrested, accusing them of sodomy, heresy, idolatry and urinating and spitting on the cross. He and Pope Clement V, who resided at Avignon, not Rome, pressed Edward to arrest the Templars in England. Edward refused, telling Philip he found the accusations 'more than it is possible to believe'.[44] This infuriated Philip, who had no mind to allow the young man to defy him and to make him look foolish in the eyes of Europe. Edward's refusal to arrest the Templars speaks well of him, as it was an easy opportunity for him to seize their goods, lands and money, to pay off some of the enormous debts his father had bequeathed him.

On 4 December 1307, Edward wrote to the kings of Sicily, Castile, Portugal and Aragon, the first three of whom were his cousins, telling them that he believed the charges against the Templars were nothing more than 'the slanders of ill-natured men, who are animated ... with a spirit of cupidity and envy', a very daring way to refer to the king of France and his counsellors, asking them to remember the Templars' devotion, honesty and long service to the Christian faith, and saying that belief in the accusations was 'hardly to be entertained'. Edward also sent a letter to the pope on 10 December, saying he had heard 'a rumour of infamy, a rumour indeed full of bitterness, terrible to think of, horrible to hear, and detestable in wickedness' and that 'we are unable to believe in suspicious stories of this kind until we know with greater certainty about these things'.[45]

On 14 December, however, Edward received the papal bull *Pastoralis praeeminentiae*, which ordered all Christian rulers of Europe to arrest the Templars and seize their lands, in the name of the papacy.[46] A papal bull was next to impossible to ignore, and therefore, he issued an order for the Templars to be arrested on 10 January 1308, a few weeks in advance; in France, they had been given no warning.[47] Edward did his best to protect the Templars, and ordered his sheriffs to see that they were honourably housed and 'not to place them in hard and vile prison, and to find them sustenance'.[48] This was a kindness in an age when prisons had no obligation to feed their prisoners. A year later, he ordered the sheriffs to pay the Templars their wages, four pence a day, with arrears from the first day of their imprisonment.[49] It is easy to criticise Edward for caving in to pressure and betraying his principles, but he was young, inexperienced, not yet crowned, and facing the two most powerful men in Europe. Other European rulers also ordered the Templars in their countries to be arrested, despite initial reluctance. In March 1312, Pope Clement V finally disbanded the order.[50]

Edward found time to remember the Welsh woman, Mary or Mariota Maunsel, who had nursed him for a few weeks after he was born, and granted her seventy-three acres of land at Caernarfon rent-free for life. Some years later, he gave her an income of five pounds a year – a generous amount for a woman of her status – and paid for her to travel from Caernarfon to visit him.[51] He sent letters on behalf of the bishop of Lidda to his 'dearest friend' the king of Armenia – not named but either Leo III or his successor Oshin – and Oljeitu, ruler of the Ilkhanate, upgraded in the letter from 'king of the Tartars' to 'emperor' and also not named, presumably because Edward and his advisers were uncertain of the current political situation in distant countries.[52]

While Edward dealt with Templars, Tartars and Welsh nurses, Piers Gaveston held a jousting tournament at his castle of Wallingford near Oxford in honour of his young bride Margaret. Edward encouraged him to hold the tournament, though evidently didn't attend himself, as his itinerary places him at Langley, 45 miles away, and at Reading, 25 miles away, on 2 December.[53] Gaveston and his team of knights defeated the earls of Surrey, Arundel and Hereford, and destroyed their dignity by knocking them off their horses into the mud, to their great humiliation and anger. Indignant commentators said that Gaveston 'most vilely trod under foot' the opposition, and accused him of fielding 200 knights instead of the agreed sixty.[54] Not only did Gaveston dominate Edward's favour to an incredible degree, the earls could match him neither in wit nor in military prowess, and their hostility to him increased as a result of the tournament.[55] Gaveston, secure in Edward's love and favour, cocked a snook at the high and mighty earls, and they found him aggravating and arrogant to an incredible degree: 'his countenance exacted greater deference than that of the king. His arrogance was intolerable to the barons and a prime cause of hatred and rancour'. The earls and other barons did have very good reason to be concerned. Gaveston monopolised Edward's presence; no one could see him without Gaveston's being there, and Edward rudely ignored his barons and talked only to his friend.[56] Chronicler Adam Murimuth wrote that Edward 'was ruled by Piers' counsel, despising the counsel of the other nobles'.[57] Edward's obsession with Gaveston is shown in the numerous favours, lands and gifts of money granted to him and his adherents, to the detriment of others, who believed – correctly – that they had more right than the Gascon to wield so much influence over the king. It was said that Gaveston was 'almost a king', that two kings ruled England, one in name and one in deed, and that Edward did Gaveston great reverence and worshipped him, as though his friend were a god.[58]

Although the *Annales Paulini* claim that Edward and Gaveston spent Christmas together at Wye in Kent, in fact Edward didn't reach Wye until 3 January 1308, and spent the festive season at Westminster, presumably with Gaveston and perhaps with Gaveston's wife Margaret.[59] On 26 December, the king took the extraordinary step of appointing his friend *custos regni*, keeper of the realm, while he travelled to France to marry Isabella.[60] The author of the *Vita* spoke for many when he exclaimed 'An astonishing thing, that he who had lately been an exile and outcast from England should now be made ruler and guardian of the realm'.[61] It would have been far more tactful and acceptable to appoint one of his little half-brothers Thomas or Edmund as regent, a nominal one at least, though they were only six and seven years old. Gaveston, in fact, did little controversial during his regency, and although he was criticised for making the earls kneel to him and for his customary tactlessness, this seems to be insecurity rather than arrogance; he was unsure of himself without the king, and out of his depth.[62]

Edward left London and Piers Gaveston in late December and travelled through Kent towards Dover, which he reached on 13 January 1308, having already ordered numerous provisions, including vast amounts of wood and charcoal and 'ten good leaden cauldrons', to be laid in against his arrival. He also ordered the mayor and sheriffs of London to provide and deliver a ship for his tents for his retinue to sleep in once they reached France, sent his baker ahead to Boulogne 'to make preparations for the reception of the king', and ordered William le Portour to find '300 boards of the longest to be found for making tables'.[63] Edward spent his last few days as a single man at the priory of St Martin with some of the men who were to accompany him to France, including his cousin the earl of Pembroke, brother-in-law the earl of Hereford, nephew-in-law the earl of Surrey, and his friend Anthony Bek, bishop of Durham and patriarch of Jerusalem.

All the barons could do was hope that Edward's impending marriage would distract his attention from Gaveston, and that he would start to rule as a king should. Unfortunately, their hopes were to be dashed. Edward II had neither the ability nor the temperament to fill his difficult role, and in 1308 the unpromising beginning of his reign deteriorated almost to the point of civil war.

3

Exile and Intrigue

Having scandalised his kingdom by appointing Piers Gaveston as regent, Edward left Dover at dawn on 22 January 1308 and arrived in Boulogne on the 24th, where the French king and his retinue were waiting for him. He arrived three days later than he had arranged with Philip, most probably because of bad weather in the Channel.[1] In winter the crossing was particularly treacherous, and could take several days. The following day, Thursday 25 January, Edward saw his long-term fiancée for the first time, when they married before the door of Notre Dame in Boulogne. Isabella, sixth of the seven children of Philip IV and Joan, queen of Navarre in her own right, was probably born in late 1295, so was over eleven years younger than Edward and only twelve at the time of the wedding.[2] Her elder sisters Marguerite and Blanche died very young, in or before 1295; one of them might have married Edward instead if she had lived. Her elder brothers Louis, Philip and Charles all reigned as kings of France, her younger brother Robert died a few months after she married Edward, and her mother Queen Joan I of Navarre had died in 1305 in her early thirties. Isabella was named after her paternal grandmother Isabel of Aragon, the first queen of Philip III of France. Her maternal grandfather King Enrique I of Navarre was said to have suffocated in his own fat in 1274, and her maternal grandmother Blanche of Artois, queen of Navarre and countess of Lancaster, was, in a typically confusing example of royal inter-relations, also Edward II's aunt by marriage.[3] Edward and Isabella were fairly closely related: Edward's grandmother Eleanor of Provence was the younger sister of Isabella's great-grandmother Marguerite, queen of Louis IX, making them second cousins once removed. Isabella had been betrothed to Edward since the Treaty of Montreuil in June 1299 when she was probably three years old, and thus for as long as she could consciously remember would have known that it was her destiny to marry him.

Edward's first reaction to his bride is unrecorded. Isabella was said by several contemporaries to be beautiful, and given that her father and brother Charles were known in their lifetimes as *le Bel* or 'the Handsome', she probably was. Perhaps her loveliness impressed her new husband, or perhaps Edward saw only a girl half his age and of no conceivable interest to him. Whether a pubescent girl, beautiful or not, held much appeal for him is an unanswerable question. Isabella has been unjustly vilified down the centuries as 'the she-wolf of France', and condemned as wicked and unnatural by writers incensed that a woman could rebel against her lawfully wedded spouse. Nowadays, however, she is more often portrayed as a long-suffering, put-upon victim of her callously neglectful husband who is miraculously transformed into an empowered feminist icon, striking a courageous blow for women everywhere by fighting back against marital oppression and finding an opportunity for self-fulfilment by taking a lover. Depictions of her reflect the way society currently views women who step outside the bounds of conventional behaviour rather than the real Isabella, who was neither a modern feminist and believer in sexual equality transplanted to the Middle Ages, nor an evil unfeminine caricature. Like her husband, Isabella was a complex character with qualities both admirable and not. Avaricious and extravagant to a degree extraordinary even by the standards of fourteenth-century royals, she nevertheless had many fine qualities, including compassion, loyalty, piety and courage. For most of her marriage to Edward, until his behaviour alienated her irrevocably in the 1320s, Isabella was his loyal and supportive companion and ally, and their relationship was far more successful than commonly supposed. This says a great deal about Isabella's interpersonal skills, as the fiercely emotional and erratic Edward must have been a difficult man to live with.

Whether Isabella had already heard rumours of her new husband's unsuitable rustic pastimes or about his intense relationship with Piers Gaveston, is not known, and if she had, there was nothing she could do about it. For her wedding, Isabella wore a red cloak lined with yellow sindon, over a gown and tunic in blue and gold; fifty years later, she would be buried with the cloak. Edward wore a satin surcoat and cloak embroidered with jewels, and both wore crowns glittering with precious stones.[4] With these sumptuous clothes and the good looks ascribed to both of them by contemporaries, they must have looked magnificent, and the wedding was a splendid occasion. Not counting the couple themselves, four kings and three queens attended: Philip IV; his eldest son, eighteen-year-old Louis, king of Navarre; Charles 'the Lame', king of Sicily and Naples and titular king of Jerusalem; Marie of Brabant, dowager queen of France and Philip IV's stepmother; her daughter Marguerite, dowager queen of England and Edward II's stepmother; Albrecht of Hapsburg, king of Germany, who attended with his wife Elisabeth of Görz-Tirol and their son Leopold, duke of Austria. Also present were Edward's sister and brother-in-law the duke and duchess of Brabant and the counts of Flanders, Namur, Hainault, Nevers, St Pol, Dreux and Savoy.[5] Edward, as duke of Aquitaine and count of Ponthieu, performed homage for his lands to Philip on 31 January, an unpleasant, albeit essential, duty he hated.

Isabella brought Edward no dowry; Philip IV made it plain that her marriage portion was the duchy of Aquitaine and Edward's other lands in France, which his father Edward I had forfeited to the French Crown in 1294. The French king was magnanimously returning the lands to his new son-in-law because he hoped one day to see a grandchild of his holding them, he told Edward and his advisors.[6] Philip's wedding presents to Edward included a 'ring of his realm' and other jewellery, a bed or couch 'more beautiful than any other' and expensive warhorses.[7] Philip also presented his daughter with a lavish trousseau to take with her to England, including gold crowns, tapestries and seventy-two headdresses, and the twelve-year-old queen probably received a generous gift from her new husband: an illuminated manuscript now known as the Isabella Psalter and held in a library in Munich.[8] Eight days of celebration and feasting followed the wedding ceremony, with the most magnificent banquet of all taking place on 28 January, hosted by Edward. Two days later, he presided over yet another great feast, with his new queen by his side, and the noblemen present also took part in a jousting event. Edward almost certainly didn't participate. He showed no great interest in jousting unless Piers Gaveston was competing, which probably demonstrates an interest in Gaveston rather than in the sport. Perhaps if the inhabitants of Boulogne had needed a new ditch to be dug, or had horses in desperate need of shoeing, he would have been their man. All in all, however, it was a superbly lavish occasion, as befitted the wedding of the king of England and the king of France's daughter, though tensions lurked beneath the glittering surface, as they usually did during Edward's reign.

After the wedding, Isabella shared Edward's accommodation, and although it is possible that they consummated their marriage, to make it valid and binding, it is unlikely that they began regular sexual relations. Although Edward needed a son and heir, like all kings, he waited until his wife was old enough to endure pregnancy and childbirth without causing damage to her developing body, and they conceived their first child four years later, when Isabella was sixteen.

Philip IV took the opportunity to present Edward with a list of his grievances concerning Gascony, which Edward ignored. Soon after, he sent the wedding gifts Philip had given him to Piers Gaveston, an act often seen as the first of many examples of Edward's mistreatment of his wife. Most probably, however, he simply sent them to his friend, whom he trusted more than anyone and who was regent of his kingdom in his absence, to store in a safe place. Sending the gifts to Gaveston does not necessarily imply that Edward intended Gaveston to keep them; the *Annales Paulini* say that Philip IV 'gave' (*dedit* in the Latin original) the gifts to Edward, who 'sent' (*misit*) them to Gaveston. Although a scene where Gaveston flaunts himself in jewels rightfully belonging to the queen has become a staple of novels featuring Edward II, and much modern non-fiction repeats the tall tale that Edward heartlessly gave away his wife's jewellery to his lover, the *Annales Paulini* specify that Philip gave the gifts later sent to Gaveston in England only to Edward, not to Isabella, not even to them jointly.[9] There is of course no possible reason why Philip would have given his daughter warhorses, and the *Annales Paulini* do not even mention her or her possessions at this point. Edward giving his wife's jewels to Gaveston is a modern invention which melts away into nothing in the face of evidence.

While in France, a group of English nobles, including the earls of Pembroke, Lincoln, Surrey and Hereford, put their seals to the Boulogne Agreement or Boulogne Declaration. This document attempted to separate the two sides of kingship: the king as a person, and the Crown, and stated that the barons' loyalty was due less to the current king than to the Crown itself. This theory was to rear its head again during Edward's reign. The Agreement probably demonstrates the enormous concern over Edward's reliance on Piers Gaveston, though it also reflects the conflicts which arose between the king and the barons at the end of Edward I's reign, and Gaveston was not in fact mentioned. Neither does the document show any hostility towards Edward II personally.[10] Roger Mortimer, the man who many years later became Queen Isabella's favourite and invaded Edward's kingdom, was not one of the men who set his seal to the Agreement.[11] Mortimer was then twenty, a long-term and loyal companion of the king and Gaveston, and it speaks volumes about Edward II that he later became the king's most dangerous enemy. The earl of Warwick was another attendee who did not sign the Boulogne Agreement, perhaps rather oddly, as he was shortly to become an enemy of Edward and Gaveston, and had refused to sign the charter granting the earldom of Cornwall to the Gascon.

Edward and Isabella left Boulogne on 3 February and arrived at Dover in mid-afternoon on the 7th, when Isabella got her first look at the country that would be her home for the next half a century.[12] (She never had the chance to meet William Wallace, as shown in *Braveheart*, as he had been executed two and a half years previously on 23 August 1305.) A group of noble men and women was waiting for them, including Edward's sisters Mary the nun and Elizabeth, countess of Hereford; Alicia, dowager countess of Norfolk, whose niece Philippa of Hainault would marry Edward and Isabella's son in 1328; and Earl Thomas of Lancaster's brother Henry, the king's first cousin.[13] The Lancasters were also Isabella's uncles, younger half-brothers of her mother Queen Joan.

She had other relatives in England: the dowager queen Marguerite was her aunt, Edward's young half-brothers Thomas and Edmund her first cousins, and the earl of Richmond another cousin.[14]

When Edward saw Piers Gaveston, he behaved as though the pair had been apart for many months. In front of everybody, Edward demonstrated his 'improper familiarity' with Gaveston, and is reported to have 'run to Piers among them, giving him kisses and repeated embraces; he was adored with a singular familiarity. Which special familiarity, already known to the magnates, furnished fuel to their jealousy.'[15] Edward and Isabella did not travel together, but came ashore separately: 'the king touched at Dover in his barge ... and the queen a little afterward touched here with certain ladies accompanying her,' so it seems unlikely that Isabella saw her new husband's enthusiastic greeting of Gaveston, despite the numerous modern novels depicting her shock and horror at the sight.[16] It was not the kissing and embracing themselves that were the problem – the early fourteenth century was a tactile age and kissing on the lips was a common way even for two men to greet each other, with no necessary implications of sexual desire – but that Edward singled Gaveston out for special attention and kissed and embraced his friend more than he kissed and embraced the other barons.[17]

Edward and Isabella travelled through Kent towards London, spending five days at Edward's palace of Eltham on the way, which Bishop Anthony Bek had given to him in 1305 and which he later granted to Isabella. Edward's treasurer had ordered lampreys from Gloucester for the king to enjoy on his return to England.[18] According to the *Annales Paulini*, Piers Gaveston held a jousting tournament at Faversham to celebrate the king's marriage; whether Edward himself attended is unclear, though his route from Dover and Canterbury to London did take him past or through Faversham.[19] On 21 February, the mayor and aldermen of London rode out to greet the new king and queen, and in great procession, cheered by a crowd of thousands, Edward and Isabella rode through the city to the Tower. London was rather less filthy than usual and the streets had been lavishly decorated, so that the city annalist wrote with pride and enormous exaggeration that it resembled 'a new Jerusalem'.[20]

On 24 February, Edward and Isabella rode to Westminster for their coronation, which should have taken place on the 18th, but was delayed by a week. Some of the barons had already demanded that Gaveston be exiled from England, and threatened to impede the coronation if he were not, forcing a delay.[21] Edward's coronation differed from its predecessors in several respects. Firstly, the wives of peers attended for the first time. Secondly, Edward took his oath in French, not Latin, as his ancestors had done – a fact often unfairly used to condemn him as stupid, lazy and uneducated by some historians.[22] This conveniently ignores the fact that Edward, even if he knew no Latin, which is most unlikely, could easily have learnt the short responses by heart, and that French was the native language of just about everyone who attended the coronation and he surely only intended that everyone present understood what was being said. Thirdly, a fourth and new clause was added to the coronation oath, whereby Edward swore to 'observe the just laws and customs that the community of your realm shall determine'.[23]

On the morning of Sunday 25 February 1308, Edward, barefoot and wearing a green robe and black hose, walked from Westminster Hall to the Abbey with Isabella, along a cloth strewn with flowers. Owing to the enormous crush of spectators, the king and queen had to be led into the abbey by a back door. Above them, the barons of the Cinque Ports carried an embroidered canopy, and before them proceeded the prelates and the barons, six men carrying Edward's gilt spurs, the royal sceptre, the royal rod, and the three royal swords. Roger Frowyk, goldsmith of London, had been paid twenty pounds in late January for repairing the sceptre.[24] Then came four men carrying a board covered with checked cloth, on which the royal robes were placed. They were Hugh Despenser the Elder, Roger Mortimer, Thomas de Vere, son of the earl of Oxford, and Edmund Fitzalan, earl of Arundel. Eighteen years later, one of these men would order the execution of two of the others. Following Despenser and the others came Edward's treasurer Walter Reynolds, bishop of Worcester and later archbishop of Canterbury, carrying the paten of the chalice of St Edward the Confessor. Behind him came the chancellor of England, carrying the chalice of St Edward itself. And finally and controversially, Piers Gaveston, just before the king and queen and therefore in prime position, carrying the royal crown. Gaveston was described as 'so decked out that he more resembled the god Mars than an ordinary mortal'.[25] The other earls wore cloth-of-gold (material shot through with gold thread), as they were entitled to do in the king's presence, but Gaveston, never one to hide his light under a bushel, wore royal purple, of silk, encrusted with pearls. The *Annales Paulini* complained that Gaveston 'sought his own glory rather than the king's' and was 'more splendidly dressed than the king'.[26] Evidently, Edward didn't mind. On the day of his coronation, he banned a jousting tournament at Stepney supposedly at the bidding of Piers Gaveston, who feared for his life if it went ahead.[27]

During the ceremony, Edward allowed Gaveston to put on his right spur, angering many, as these duties were of profound ritual significance, and Edward was publicly placing Gaveston above the rest of the nobility. In the procession back to the palace at the end of the ceremony, Gaveston carried the sword of mercy, which caused more mutterings, or rather shouts, of discontent. Everyone then proceeded to Westminster Hall for a banquet, which Gaveston had organised. Forty ovens were specially constructed and large quantities of wine ordered from Bordeaux, while London merchants supplied ale, 'large cattle and boars', sheep and pigs, three fishmongers received £170 for 'large fish' and pike, and one John le Discher provided salt-cellars, plates and dishes at a cost of twenty pounds.[28] A temporary timber hall at least 500 feet long was built along the river wall by Westminster palace, with fourteen smaller halls crammed in and taking up almost all the space as far as the palace gate, and underground pipes supplied red and white wine and a spiced drink to a fountain which flowed day and night.[29] The parlous state of Edward's finances – his father had left him massive debts of about £200,000 – meant that, despite the money parliament had granted him the previous autumn, he had to pay for the coronation with loans from Italian bankers, the Frescobaldi.[30]

Unfortunately, the banquet was a fiasco. It was long after dark when it finally got underway, and although there was a vast amount of food, it was badly cooked, badly served and close to inedible. (One wonders if the French had expected anything else of English food.) Edward had ordered tapestries bearing the royal arms, three leopards, and the arms of Piers Gaveston, six eaglets, to adorn the walls of the hall – a very visual sign of the significant position his friend held in his life.[31] Even by Edward's standards, pinning up Gaveston's arms on the walls in place of the royal arms of France, for his wife, was astonishingly tactless. He made matters worse by sitting next to Gaveston and ignoring everyone else, including Isabella, talking and laughing with his friend. Isabella's two uncles the counts of Valois and Evreux were grievously offended, although it is doubtful that they walked out of the banquet, as has sometimes been stated – which would have been a gross and unforgivable insult to Edward – while one of the English earls had to be restrained from physically assaulting Gaveston. Although it is understandable that a man in his twenties would prefer to talk to a friend he had known for many years than to a twelve-year-old he barely knew, there is no doubt that Edward's behaviour was extremely insulting to his wife, the French and the French king. Whether he intended to be rude, or just didn't care, is not certain, but offending his powerful father-in-law was incredibly foolish behaviour. Many illustrious guests visited the coronation and banquet, and thus witnessed Edward's discourteous conduct. Edward's sister Margaret and his brother-in-law John II, duke and duchess of Brabant, Isabella's uncles Charles of Valois and Louis of Evreux, and her brother, the future King Charles IV, attended. The king's cousin Arthur, duke of Brittany – like Edward, a grandson of Henry III – was there, with his brother-in-law, Guy, count of St Pol. Arthur had succeeded his father as duke of Brittany in 1305, when the unfortunate John II was killed in possibly the most extraordinary freak accident of the era: a wall collapsed on him as he led Pope Clement V's horse around Avignon. Edward's sister Mary the nun, their young half-brothers Thomas and Edmund, Count Amadeus V of Savoy, Count Gaston I of Foix and Henry of Luxembourg, future Holy Roman Emperor, brought up the rear of distinguished guests.[32]

After the banquet, the counts of Valois and Evreux returned to France and complained to Philip IV that Edward 'frequented Piers' couch more than the queen's'.[33] According to the much later chronicler Thomas Walsingham, Isabella herself wrote to her father declaring that her husband was 'an entire stranger to my bed', called herself 'the most wretched of wives', and accused Gaveston of being the cause of all her troubles, by alienating Edward's affection from her and leading him into improper company.[34] Isabella's letters from this period do not survive, however, and the story cannot be corroborated; Walsingham, writing many decades later, had no access to the queen of England's private correspondence to her father in 1308. The *Annales Paulini* reported the widespread rumour that Edward 'loved an evil male sorcerer more than he did his wife, a most handsome lady and a very beautiful woman', and the *Vita* said that 'Piers was accounted a sorcerer', as Edward was 'incapable of moderate favour, and on account of Piers was said to forget himself'.[35] Edward's lack of attention towards Isabella – who at twelve was hardly a woman yet – is unlikely to have stemmed from callousness, or a desire to be cruel to her. As she was too young to be his wife in anything more than name or to be of any use to him politically, he seems barely to have thought of her at all. It is difficult, however, to condemn Edward for shunning the bed of a girl of only twelve. Even in the fourteenth century, it was extremely rare for girls to become pregnant at a very young age.[36] Edward's three de Clare nieces all married at thirteen, but didn't bear their first children until they were sixteen or seventeen. His sister Margaret married at fifteen, was still living apart from her husband three years later and bore her only child when she was twenty-five, and other sisters, Eleanor and Joan, didn't marry until they were twenty-four and eighteen respectively. Edward's grandmother Eleanor of Provence married Henry III in early 1236 when she was twelve or thirteen, and bore her first child three and a half years later. Still, Edward could have treated Isabella with far more respect and consideration than he did. Despite her youth, she was his wife and his queen.

Parliament opened at Westminster three days after the coronation. Edward's antics had strengthened the already strong opposition to his favourite, and 'almost all of the earls and barons of England rose against Piers Gaveston, binding themselves by a mutual oath never to cease from what they had begun until Piers had left the land of England'.[37] Edward's only allies at this parliament were Thomas, earl of Lancaster, his cousin and Isabella's uncle, and Hugh Despenser the Elder. Despenser was the brother-in-law of the earl of Warwick, and is known as 'the Elder' to distinguish him from his son of the same name, who would become Edward II's great favourite in the late 1310s. Despenser the Elder was twenty-three years older than Edward but a close friend, and the only nobleman to remain completely loyal to Edward from the beginning to the end of his reign. Almost all the other earls and magnates demanded Gaveston's exile; he had 'aroused the hatred of nearly all the great lords of England, because the new king loved him excessively and irrationally, and supported him totally'.[38] The situation deteriorated rapidly. Edward was almost friendless, but determined to keep Gaveston at his side, and determined also to challenge the right of his nobles to impose conditions on him against his will. This was typical of Edward, who loved going out into the fields and digging ditches or building walls, chatting with craftsmen and villeins, yet the next minute stood on all his royal rights and dignity.

Edward spent Easter preparing for war. Afraid that his magnates might seize Gaveston, he fortified Windsor Castle as a stronghold where the favourite could remain in safety, and as a further precaution ordered the nearby bridges at Staines and Kingston to be dismantled, which must have annoyed the locals. At the end of April 1308, Edward returned to parliament, where he faced fresh demands to exile Gaveston. Emotionally reliant on his friend to a very great extent and unable to imagine life without him, Edward continued to refuse. Within a few months of his accession, he had brought his country to the brink of civil war over his emotional reliance on the arrogant Gaveston, who 'lorded it over them [the barons] like a second king, to whom all were subject and none equal'.[39] Edward's behaviour became the talk of the kingdom, and his popularity plummeted, according to *Lanercost*: 'The murmurs increased from day to day, and engrossed the lips and ears of all men, nor was there one who had a good word either for the king or for Piers.'[40] The *Vita* stated that 'the seditious quarrel between the lord king and the barons spread far and wide through England, and the whole land was much desolated by such a tumult ... it was held for certain that the quarrel once begun could not be settled without great destruction'. A letter written at this time agreed: 'Very evil are the times in England now; and there are many who fear that worse times are still in store for us.'[41] The writer was correct, and the pattern of impending civil war would repeat itself over and over for the next few years, as Edward lurched from one crisis to the next, crises almost entirely of his own making.

The barons had a useful ally on their side: the king of France. A newsletter of 14 May claimed that unless Piers Gaveston left England, Philip IV 'will pursue as his mortal enemies all who support the said Piers'.[42] *Lanercost* says that Philip 'cordially detested' Gaveston, 'because, as was commonly said, the king of England, having married his daughter, loved her indifferently because of the aforesaid Piers', and the *Polychronicon* also says that Edward neglected Isabella for Gaveston.[43] Both these chronicles, however, were written with many years' hindsight, after Edward's later favourite Hugh Despenser (the Younger) had succeeded in driving Isabella from her husband's presence in the 1320s, and it may be that the authors confused Gaveston with Despenser. Edward's supposed and frequently exaggerated neglect of Isabella was probably not the main reason for Philip's hostility; Gaveston's father Arnaud had escaped from Philip's custody when the French king was (legitimately) holding him as a hostage, and Gaveston himself had fought against Philip's forces in Flanders in 1297.[44] Whatever the reason for Philip's animosity to Gaveston, it was shared by his half-sister Marguerite, Edward's stepmother, and the French royals were said to have sent £40,000 to the English earls to fund their opposition to the royal favourite.[45] Even if this means *livres tournois*, the equivalent of £10,000 sterling, it still seems a ludicrous exaggeration. Whatever the correct amount of money, Edward retaliated by taking Marguerite's castles of Marlborough and Devizes into his own hands.[46] For the remaining ten years that she was alive, Marguerite played little if any role in Edward's life, and seems mostly to have stayed away from court, her relations with her stepson perhaps soured by her actions and Edward's anger with her.

Perhaps not entirely coincidentally, Edward granted his county of Ponthieu, which yielded revenues of about £1,300 a year, to his young wife on 14 May, the day the newsletter was written.[47] It is probably significant, and a sign of Edward's good faith towards Isabella and her father, that he granted her Ponthieu, as in 1306 he had intended to give the county to Piers Gaveston. His friend spent his brief exile there in 1307 at Edward's order, rather than in Gascony, as originally commanded by Edward I.[48] Isabella's role as leader of the opposition to Piers Gaveston is often overstated. At twelve, she was hardly in a position to play a significant role in politics, and the poor girl was thrust into a tense and difficult situation a grown woman might have struggled with. Her aunt the dowager queen, who could have helped her, withdrew from court, leaving her alone and vulnerable in a foreign country with a husband who made it clear that Piers Gaveston was his main priority, even above herself. However, although Edward and Isabella's marriage began and ended badly, for most of their relationship, there was genuine affection between the couple. Few of their personal letters survive, but one in which Edward called Isabella his 'dear heart' is still extant, as is one of Isabella's, in which she addressed Edward as 'my very sweet heart' five times.[49] Although often depicted as a neglectful husband, Edward frequently demonstrated great concern for Isabella's well-being, and for many years she supported him with notable loyalty.

At parliament in late April and early May 1308, Henry de Lacy, earl of Lincoln and leader of the formidable coalition opposed to Edward and Gaveston, demanded once again the favourite's exile. Only a handful of barons and knights remained loyal to Edward at this time. One was his cousin the earl of Lancaster, who seems, however, not to have offered Edward any practical help, and another was John of Brittany, earl of

Richmond, who was rather insignificant politically. Richmond was in his early forties and a first cousin of Edward II and Lancaster, his mother Beatrice being the sister of Edward I, and was the brother of the duke of Brittany. Other loyal allies were Guy Ferre, son of Edward's former tutor of the same name, and John Cromwell, Roger Mortimer and Hugh Despenser the Elder.[50]

On 18 May, having held out for many weeks, and faced with civil war, Edward finally gave in and agreed to exile his friend.[51] As a sop, and at Edward's insistence, Gaveston was allowed to keep his title of earl of Cornwall, but all his lands reverted to the Crown. In compensation, Edward granted him £2,000 worth of lands in his homeland of Gascony, including the city of Bayonne and the island of Oléron, and lands worth another £2,000 in England jointly to Gaveston and his wife Margaret, so he suffered no loss of income.[52] Robert Winchelsey, archbishop of Canterbury, threatened to excommunicate Gaveston if he didn't leave the country by 25 June. Anyone who impeded his departure or aided his return, except the king and queen, would face the same penalty.[53] Gaveston's fourteen-year-old wife was not included in her husband's exile, and was to be granted £2,000 a year from the revenues of Cornwall for her sustenance if she remained in England. However, Margaret accompanied Gaveston to Ireland, either on her husband's orders or her uncle's.[54]

On 16 June 1308, Edward hit on the idea of making Gaveston lord lieutenant of Ireland, a position he had granted to the earl of Ulster only the day before, thus ensuring that Gaveston left the country in triumph, not in disgrace.[55] Edward went to Bristol with his niece and nephew-in-law to see them off, and gave them a staggeringly generous gift of £1,180.[56] The Gavestons sailed on 28 June, three days after the deadline imposed by the archbishop of Canterbury. A distraught and furious Edward travelled to Windsor to be reunited with his queen.

Within a year of his accession, Edward managed to annoy his barons beyond bearing, offend the king of France, face civil war, act as though another person were his co-ruler, and give his barons little option but to force his beloved friend out of the country for the second time. His infatuation with Gaveston was almost entirely to blame. Edward was incapable of moderation, as his contemporaries remarked; if he had been more even-handed with his favour, his relationship with his friend would not have been such an issue. However, in his great love for Gaveston, he elevated him almost to the status of joint king. It is impossible to say how Edward felt about the hatred and resentment that his relationship with Gaveston and his friend's consequent domination of his favour engendered, whether he was even aware of it, or merely indifferent. His love for his friend blinded him to reality and to the foolishness of his actions.

There was no chance that Edward would tolerate Piers Gaveston's absence for long, and everyone must have realised it. Over the following year, Edward made strenuous and adroit efforts to get his friend back. Nine days before Gaveston even left England, Edward wrote to Pope Clement V and King Philip IV, giving a rather questionable version of the whole affair. He claimed that the earldom of Cornwall had been granted to Gaveston without Gaveston's prior knowledge, and at the urging of the barons.[57] This second point, at least, was not true. Edward also wrote that his magnates 'rose up against us in grave fashion, that they had no qualms to present themselves to us many times as enemies and complainers; and from this, one truly fears scandals and even graver dangers could arise in the kingdom and these lands'.[58] On the same day he wrote this, Edward granted the castle and town of Blanquefort in Gascony to the pope's nephew and namesake, Bertrand de Got.[59] Candidly, Edward explained that he hoped the grant would inspire the pope to regard his affairs more favourably, and asked him to lift the conditional sentence of excommunication on Gaveston.

Meanwhile, Edward's infatuation with his friend and subsequent lack of interest in Scotland were greatly aiding Robert Bruce in his campaign to make himself king in more than name only. In the spring of 1308, Bruce inflicted a heavy defeat on his greatest enemy John Comyn, earl of Buchan, a relative of John 'the Red Comyn' whom Bruce had killed in 1306. Buchan fled to England, where Edward welcomed him, though he died before 27 November 1308.[60] The remnant of the Comyn faction, which had dominated Scottish politics for decades, also removed themselves to England, including the young children of the Red Comyn. Edward lost the support in 1308 of another Scottish earl, William of Ross, who had previously been so anti-Bruce that he captured Bruce's womenfolk in September 1306 and sent them to Edward I to be imprisoned. Geographically isolated by Buchan's defeat, pressed hard by Bruce and his army, Ross sent pleas to Edward to assist him, writing, 'May help come from you, our lord, if it please you, for in you, Sire, is all our hope and trust.'[61] Placing all one's military hope and trust in Edward II was a bad idea, and Edward did nothing to help. Ross had little choice but to submit to Bruce and remained totally loyal to him for the rest of his life, a reminder of Edward's failure to retain a useful ally. The earl of Dunbar and lord of Argyll, who stayed in Scotland, were loyal to Edward, and so were other Scottish lords, including the eighteen-year-old earl of Fife Duncan MacDuff, now Edward's nephew-in-law as the husband of Mary Monthermer, one of Joan of Acre's daughters. The earls of Atholl, Angus and Strathearn lived in England by choice, and the young earl of Mar, Robert Bruce's nephew Donald, remained in prison at Bristol Castle. However, Bruce's campaign to make himself true king and ruler of Scotland was gaining rapid momentum. More and more men flocked to his banner.

In June 1308, Edward ordered a muster of his army at Carlisle for 22 August, to march into Scotland.[62] But he cancelled the campaign and signed a truce, after Philip IV sent his brother the count of Evreux and the bishop of Soissons to negotiate peace between the countries.[63] War in Scotland was part of Edward II's inheritance from his father, an unwinnable war which gobbled up his treasury and which he had no choice but to continue, willingly or not. Edward was far more interested in trying to bring Gaveston back to England than campaigning in Scotland. Over the next few months, he used a policy of 'divide and conquer' among his barons; he 'tried to break up their confederacy and draw over the more powerful to his side'. Edward also used his powers of patronage to reconcile them, granting them lands, favours and positions, with the aim of persuading them to agree to Gaveston's return; he 'bent one after another to his will, with gifts, promises and blandishments', which eventually had the desired result.[64] The natural loyalty of the magnates to the king helped him here. With Gaveston gone, there was little reason for most of them to continue opposing him.

In September 1308, the king spent some time at Byfleet in Surrey, one of Piers Gaveston's manors, where Edward had accommodation, and entertained the earls of Lancaster and Surrey.[65] At the end of the month, he attended a double wedding at Waltham Abbey in Essex: his seventeen-year-old nephew Gilbert de Clare, earl of Gloucester, married Maud de Burgh, and Gloucester's sister Elizabeth, just two weeks past her thirteenth birthday, married Maud's brother John de Burgh, eldest son and heir of the earl of Ulster. Many of the magnates had planned to hold a Round Table jousting tournament at the wedding, 'but some of them were afraid of being beset, and dreaded treachery, so that the plans came to nought'.[66] Edward himself attempted to hold a 'King of the Greenwood' tournament at Kennington, which also came to nothing when the barons refused to attend.[67]

While Edward was manipulating his earls to return to his side, his cousin Lancaster bucked the trend and left court, in November 1308. Until then, he had been in more or less continuous attendance on Edward, and what happened at this time is uncertain, but Lancaster gradually moved into the position of opposition to Edward that he would maintain for the remainder of his life, and the two men came to loathe each other. It is unlikely that Piers Gaveston was the cause of the breakdown in the cousins' relationship, as he was in Ireland, and Lancaster had always supported the pair, if in a rather lukewarm manner. There seems to have been no sudden, violent rift between the men, and possibly, Lancaster's departure arose from a trivial matter, and he was too stubborn or too proud to return to Edward afterwards.[68] Edward and Lancaster were very alike in some ways, both of them unable to set aside their own personal likes and dislikes in the interests of policy. The men had been close before

Edward's accession: a letter written by Edward in 1305, in response to one sent by Lancaster apologising that he could not attend Edward owing to illness, stated that he would come to visit Lancaster instead, 'to see and to comfort you'.[69] Lancaster was about five or six years older than his cousin, son of the dowager queen Blanche of Navarre, grandson of Henry III, uncle of the queen of England, brother-in-law of the king of France. He was already the proud owner of three earldoms, Lancaster, Leicester and Derby, and in due course would inherit his father-in-law the earl of Lincoln's two as well. His vast wealth and landholdings made him enormously influential, and the loss of his support was a severe blow to the king.

On 20 December 1308, Edward founded and generously endowed the Dominican priory at Langley in Hertfordshire where he would bury Piers Gaveston a few years later, 'in fulfilment of a vow made by the king in peril', whenever that might have been – probably on one of his sea crossings or on campaign in Scotland.[70] Edward, like his mother Eleanor of Castile, was a patron of the Dominicans, the Friars Preacher or Black Friars, and all his confessors were Dominican; the mutual affection of the king and the Dominicans lasted for many years.[71] Edward spent Christmas and New Year at Windsor with Queen Isabella, though he stayed at his favourite residence of Langley, where he often retired at times of stress and where he had spent much time with Gaveston, for most of December and the first few months of 1309. He might have seen the total eclipse of the sun on 1 February, which the Sempringham annalist claims, implausibly, to have lasted from midday until five in the afternoon, and presumably met the archbishop of Nazareth when he visited England in late January.[72] In February 1309, a whale supposedly eighty feet long was caught in the Thames, to the excitement of the St Paul's and London annalists.[73]

Edward began to treat his young wife with increasing respect, and in March and April 1309 gave her a cash grant of £1,122 and lands in Cheshire and North Wales, with the revenues backdated to the previous September.[74] On 4 March, Edward wrote to Philip IV, telling him that Isabella was in good health and 'will, God willing, be fruitful'.[75] Over time, Isabella became one of the great landowners of the realm, although the lands normally granted to the queen were still held by her aunt, the dowager queen Marguerite. In 1309, Edward continued to work on his earls, consumed with the need to bring Gaveston back from his Irish exile, where he was excelling in his role as lord lieutenant.[76] By June, he could count, more or less, on the support of a majority of his earls. In March 1309, Edward sent the bishops of Worcester and Norwich, and the earls of Pembroke and Richmond, to Avignon to speak to the pope on Gaveston's behalf.[77]

In late March or early April 1309, many of Edward's earls and barons met at a jousting tournament at Dunstable, apparently as a cover to discuss their complaints against the king.[78] Help soon came from another quarter, however: Pope Clement V gave Edward a pleasant twenty-fifth birthday present on 25 April 1309, when he agreed to nullify Winchelsey's threat to excommunicate Piers Gaveston.[79] Clement granted the absolution because Edward had finally been able to convince him, rather stretching the truth, that the dispute between the magnates and himself was settled. Parliament opened at Westminster two days later, although Edward didn't deign to appear until the beginning of May. Perhaps he knew that his barons intended to present a list of eleven grievances against his rule, which they worked out while supposedly jousting at Dunstable.[80] The grievances concerned escheators, purveyance, writs, petitions and the like, and included the statement that Edward had lost Scotland. Although this was somewhat inaccurate, as Scotland had never exactly been 'won', Edward's father had been acknowledged as overlord of the country in the early 1290s, while his own chances of imposing any kind of dominance over Scotland and Robert Bruce were receding ever further into the distance.

Edward, always willing to compromise himself in Piers Gaveston's interests, tried to turn baronial dissatisfaction to his own advantage, and promised that he would address the complaints in the next parliament if his barons consented to Gaveston's return. Despite his best efforts, most of the earls refused. However, Clement V's bull nullifying Gaveston's excommunication soon arrived, and on 11 June 1309, a triumphant Edward read it out. Three days later, levels of tension high, Edward ordered another ban on jousting tournaments, naming the earls of Lancaster, Gloucester, Surrey, Arundel and Warwick, but not Hereford, Lincoln, Richmond or Pembroke.[81] The abrupt changes in relations between Edward and his earls can be dizzying, and precisely why he feared the intentions of his nephew Gloucester and nephew-in-law Surrey at this time is not clear, as they had supported him for most of the previous year.

With the threat of excommunication gone, Edward boldly recalled Piers Gaveston without baronial consent. On 27 June, a year almost to the day since he had left, the favourite returned to England, jubilant at his accomplishments in Ireland and at his return. Edward travelled to Chester to meet him, delighted at the success of his strategy and to be reunited with his beloved. 'Very thankfully receiving him with honour as his brother', Edward greeted him as 'one returning from a long pilgrimage, [and] passed pleasant days with him'.[82]

Parliament opened again on 27 July 1309 at Stamford in Lincolnshire, Edward appearing with Gaveston at his side, to the dismay of many. On 5 August, Gaveston was restored to the lands of his earldom of Cornwall.[83] Two chroniclers say that the magnates grudgingly agreed to Gaveston's restoration on condition that he behave well towards them in the future.[84] On the other hand, the *Vita* says that 'none of the barons now dared to raise a finger against him [Gaveston] or to lay any complaint about his return. Their ranks wavered, and their party, divided against itself, broke up. So he who had twice been condemned to exile returned exulting and in state.'[85] The king now had to keep his promise to address the baronial grievances, codified as the Statute of Stamford, but, Edward being Edward, he thought he could wriggle out of it. Promises he made under duress, or while he was trying to recall his male favourites on the many occasions when they were banished from England, meant little to him.

Edward had done it. The previous year had shown him capable of great energy, persistence, diplomacy, and adeptness at playing off his barons, binding them to him by giving them lands and favours, and breaking up their formidable alliance. It was a shame for his realm that he didn't use his undoubted abilities more often, and actually govern his country, but he usually acted only when his friends and therefore his personal feelings were involved. The rest of the time, he hardly bothered, which his subjects must have found intensely frustrating.

Piers Gaveston was back from exile. Neither he nor Edward II had learned a thing from the experience, and they spent the next couple of years proving that they had no political sense whatsoever.

4

Another Exile

If it were possible, Piers Gaveston became even more objectionable to the barons after his 1309 return from exile than he had been before it. Secure in the knowledge that Edward had exerted himself for many months on his behalf and adored him as much as ever, he became still more arrogant: 'Scornfully rolling his upraised eyes in pride and in abuse, he looked down upon all with pompous and supercilious countenance ... indeed the superciliousness which he affected would have been unbearable enough in a king's son.'[1] The *Scalacronica* agrees that the 'great affection' which Edward bestowed on Gaveston made him 'haughty and supercilious' – although the author also calls him 'very magnificent, liberal and well-bred' – and *Lanercost* says that Gaveston 'had now grown so insolent as to despise all the nobles of the land'.[2] King and favourite continued much as they had before the exile, and a great deal of the support Edward had built up over the previous year began to evaporate, especially when Gaveston decided that giving the English earls insulting nicknames would be hilarious. Edward, utterly blind to the damage he and Gaveston were causing, tolerated his friend in this, or perhaps actively encouraged him. The only certainly contemporary nickname is the one Gaveston gave to the earl of Warwick, 'the Dog' or 'the Black Hound of Arden'. The others were not recorded until the reign of Edward's son or even later: 'Burst-Belly' for the (presumably very stout) earl of Lincoln; 'the Churl' or 'the Fiddler' for Lancaster; and 'Joseph the Jew' for Pembroke. Warwick retorted, 'If he calls me a dog, be sure that I will bite him so soon as I shall perceive my opportunity,' a warning Edward and Gaveston fatally chose to ignore.[3] The most puzzling of Gaveston's nicknames is *filz a puteyne*, 'whoreson', generally assumed to have been aimed at the earl of Gloucester in a malicious reference to his mother Joan of Acre's secret marriage to the squire Ralph Monthermer in 1297. It is more likely that it referred to Monthermer himself, as he was apparently illegitimate.[4] It seems improbable that

Gaveston would insult Edward II's late sister, his own wife's mother, in such a public fashion.

Piers Gaveston's offending men not known for their sense of humour was foolish, and both men failed to appreciate the danger he was courting by antagonising the powerful magnates. However, Gaveston did turn his fabled charm on to some of the earls, at least: his brother-in-law Gloucester – whose association with Gaveston argues against the notion that the king's favourite had called his mother a whore – Lincoln and Richmond. Henry de Lacy, earl of Lincoln, who had been a close friend and ally of the old king, seems to have grown uncomfortable with his opposition to the new one, while Richmond's chaplain, as well as claiming that Gaveston loved Richmond 'beyond measure', stated that the two men called each other father and son in their correspondence.[5] In addition, John de Warenne, earl of Surrey, very hostile to Gaveston since the tournament at Wallingford in December 1307, now became his 'inseparable friend and faithful helper'.[6] The author of the *Vita* had a point when he complained, 'See how often and abruptly great men change their sides ... the love of magnates is as a game of dice.'[7] The other earls, however, stayed away from Gaveston. Neither this, nor the knowledge that his friend's 'name was reviled far and wide' and that he was thought to be 'wicked, impious and criminal' bothered Edward; the more he heard that almost everyone in the country hated Gaveston, the more he loved him.[8] According to *Lanercost*, he cared neither for his own unpopularity nor for Gaveston's.[9]

Another man who must have been less than thrilled to hear of Piers Gaveston's return to England was Philip IV; on 13 April, Edward had asked his father-in-law to 'suspend his anger' with the Gascon.[10] Probably motivated by the cool relations between himself and the king of France, and casting about for allies, Edward sent a letter to his 'dearest cousin' King Fernando IV of Castile, great-grandson of Edward's grandfather Fernando III, asking him to continue his alliance and friendship with England.[11] Unfortunately, although Edward enjoyed amicable relations with Castile, the country was too far away to be of much use to him politically, and the alliance did not help him during the many crises of his reign. In December 1306, a papal nuncio named Pedro, Castilian by birth and cardinal-bishop of Santa Sabina, had visited England. According to a contemporary newsletter, Pedro had entered into an indenture with the magnates of Castile that Edward, as the son of King Fernando III's daughter Eleanor, would succeed as king of Castile should Fernando IV die without a male heir.[12] Fernando finally fathered a son in 1311 after ten years of marriage and thus spared Castile the trauma of Edward's governance (assuming the story is true). Edward I remarked to Cardinal Pedro that 'he should have a special affection for our dear son Edward, as he is of Spanish descent'; with Mary Tudor, daughter of Katherine of

Aragon, Edward is one of only two English monarchs in history with a Spanish parent. Edward added two castles, the symbol of Castile, to his great seal in honour of his mother and his Castilian ancestry, and the author of the *Vita* deemed his kinship with the kings of Castile to be one of his greatest assets.[13] Edward's uncle Enrique, one of Queen Eleanor's many brothers, had proposed Fernando IV's sister Isabel as a bride for Edward in 1303, but Edward I was forced to reject the offer, as his son's betrothal to Isabella of France could not be broken without England losing Gascony.[14]

On 30 July 1309, Edward summoned the earl of Gloucester and 174 others to muster at Newcastle 'to proceed with the king's army against the Scots'.[15] The campaign was later cancelled, as in 1308.[16] Edward still had no interest in fighting in Scotland, either because he had no stomach for war, or because he was distracted with Gaveston, or for some other reason – and this despite the fact that Clement V had absolved him from future 'homicides committed in time of war', thus giving Edward carte blanche to kill as many Scotsmen as he liked with the Church's blessing.[17] Philip IV sent envoys to attend Robert Bruce's first parliament in 1309, and even acknowledged Bruce as king of Scotland. Edward only called him 'earl of Carrick', his title before his accession, or, considerably less courteously, 'traitor and rebel'.[18] On 3 August, Edward wrote to complain to Philip IV about letters shown to him, in which Philip called Bruce 'king of Scotland' in the letter addressed to Bruce himself, but only 'earl of Carrick' in the letter to Edward. Edward's annoyance is very apparent, especially as Philip's envoy Sir Mahen de Varennes had hidden the letter acknowledging Bruce as king in the breeches of the messenger he sent to Scotland. (One wonders how Edward's men who found the letter happened to come across it.) Edward's letters to Philip usually begin 'To the very excellent and very noble prince, our very dear and beloved father, greetings and very dear affection', whereas this one opens abruptly with 'To the king of France, greetings'. Edward goes on to say brusquely, 'Kindly have regard for your own honour and ours,' and that he finds Philip's motives and Varennes' behaviour suspicious. The letter ends equally abruptly with no closing line at all.[19] Addressing Philip in rather less than courteous terms was as far as Edward dared go against the powerful king of France, though he was less reluctant to take out his anger on others on occasion; the later chronicle *Polychronicon* says – although no other source confirms it – that he 'smite men that were about him for little trespass'.[20] Edward had a vile temper, which he had inherited from his father: not only did Edward I pull out handfuls of his son's hair during their 1305 quarrel, he tore the coronet from his daughter Elizabeth's head and threw it on the fire in 1297, and had to pay compensation to a servant whom he hit with a rod and injured at his daughter Margaret's wedding in 1290.[21] For all Edward II's displeasure with his father-in-law, however, he himself was not averse to offering to recognise Bruce as rightful king when it served Piers Gaveston's interests, as he would demonstrate some years later.

Edward spent much of August and September 1309 at Langley, the place where he always felt most comfortable, with Isabella, Gaveston and, perhaps, Margaret, Gaveston's wife and Edward's niece. In early August, Edward wrote to King Haakon V of Norway, to whose niece Margaret the 'Maid of Norway' he had been betrothed as a child, informing him that he would be happy to renew the ancient bonds of friendship between the two countries, again making an effort to reach out to fellow kings in a bid for allies.[22] Edward summoned parliament at York, in October 1309 and again in February 1310, but most of his earls refused to attend, because 'as long as their chief enemy [Gaveston], who had set the baronage and the realm in an uproar, was lurking in the king's chamber, their approach would be unsafe'.[23] Little had changed since Gaveston's return from exile, and most of the magnates hated the favourite as much as ever. Edward continued to grant him lands and favours, although Queen Isabella and the loyal earl of Surrey were also the recipients of his generosity.[24] Edward, though, remained wilfully blind to political realities. An example of his indulgence towards Gaveston occurs in February 1310, when he pardoned his friend for the 'trespasses committed by him in hunting in the king's forests and parks and fishing in his ponds', then immediately granted him a 'licence to hunt in the king's forests and parks and to fish in his ponds'.[25]

The king spent a few days in November 1309 at Burstwick, a royal manor near Hull. Robert Bruce's wife Elizabeth de Burgh had been taken there in September 1306, after she and other members of Bruce's family were captured in Tain by the earl of Ross and sent to Edward I. Fortunately for Elizabeth, she was the daughter of Edward I's ally the earl of Ulster, and was sentenced to a far less harsh fate than Bruce's sister Mary and Isabel MacDuff, who crowned Bruce king and was claimed by some English chroniclers to be his mistress: they were incarcerated in cages at Berwick-on-Tweed and Roxburgh castles.[26] At an unknown date, Queen Elizabeth sent Edward II a letter asking him to grant her more money, as she didn't have sufficient clothes, headdresses or bed linen for herself or her attendants. She signed herself 'Elizabeth Bruce', not 'Queen Elizabeth', having told her husband at their crowning at Scone that he might be a summer king, but would never be a winter one – for which humiliation Bruce supposedly tried to kill her with his sword, but bystanders prevented him.[27] Edward improved her living conditions, granting her a household of two damsels, two squires and two valets, and gave her two pounds a week for their expenses.[28]

Edward and Piers Gaveston spent Christmas 1309 at Langley, probably glad to escape from the seething cauldron of tension they themselves were mostly responsible for, and passed the time 'making up for former absence by their long wished-for sessions of daily and intimate conversation'.[29] It would have been more sensible for Edward and Gaveston to discuss how they could stop offending the great magnates, as the new year of 1310 saw no improvement in relations between Edward and his barons. On 19 January, the king banned a jousting tournament, as he frequently did when he felt threatened.[30] The earls of Lancaster, Warwick, Pembroke, Hereford and Arundel came to parliament in February 1310 armed, and Edward was forced to send Gaveston away 'to a very safe place'.[31] Once again, relations between Edward and his earls see-sawed, and he now viewed his brother-in-law Hereford as a threat. Edward's cousin Aymer de Valence, earl of Pembroke, was usually one of his most reliable and loyal allies, and why he came to parliament armed at this time is unclear.

At parliament, the barons presented to Edward a petition that was a harsh indictment of his rule, and expanded on the grievances presented to him the previous year.[32] They claimed that Edward was misled by evil counsel and had wasted the treasury. He could not maintain his own household, and his officials extorted goods from poor people. He had lost Scotland, which they claimed had been left to him 'in good peace' by his father. His lands in England and Ireland were seriously dismembered, the people sorely grieved, and Edward had brought great shame on his country. The petition ended with a plea that Edward might redress these grievances.[33]

Therefore, in March 1310, Edward was forced to consent to the formation of a group who came to be known as the Lords Ordainer, to reform his household. Edward claimed that he consented to the reforms of his own free will, a face-saving measure, when in fact he was deeply humiliated and furious, and the magnates told him that if he refused, 'they would not have him for king, nor keep the fealty that they had sworn to him'.[34] This was the first time, though certainly not the last, that the barons held the possibility of deposition over Edward. At this time, however, the threat was almost certainly an empty one. Edward's heir was Thomas of Brotherton, the elder of his half-brothers, a child of only nine. Edward's disastrous reign had not yet reached the point where the Ordainers were willing to replace the king with a young boy. Still, Edward could not ignore the potent threat.

Of the eleven earls, eight – Pembroke, Lincoln, Lancaster, Hereford, Warwick, Arundel, Richmond, and Gloucester – were elected as Ordainers in the Painted Chamber at Westminster. The three absentees were Cornwall (Gaveston), Oxford, a political nonentity, and Surrey. The archbishop of Canterbury, six bishops and six barons completed the group.[35] Edward did everything he could to obstruct the Ordainers, and his behaviour at this time shows how exasperating he could be. Robert Winchelsey, archbishop of Canterbury, arranged a meeting with Edward, to discuss a letter the pope had sent, at Westminster at the end of February 1310. Edward announced that he needed more time to think about it, and postponed the meeting until 15 March. Although he was also at Westminster, he failed to summon Winchelsey to him for the meeting, and the archbishop, forced to wait on the king's pleasure, pressed him for an answer. The king sent his confessor to say that he was still unable to give one. Finally, at the end of March, he told Winchelsey that he would write to the pope directly and had no need to meet him after all. He had kept the archbishop waiting around fruitlessly for an entire month.[36]

In the summer of 1310, Edward finally decided to campaign in Scotland, after an absence of three years. His main aim was to avoid the Ordainers, who would remain in the south, working on their reforms of his government and household. Another important reason was that defeating Robert Bruce would strengthen his position enormously, and put an end to the claims that he had lost Scotland. Of the English earls, only three accompanied the king: Gaveston, Edward's nephew Gloucester, and his nephew-in-law Surrey. Edward pardoned Gaveston and six of his retainers for the death of one Thomas de Walkyngham of Yorkshire in early September 1310, though for what reason Gaveston had killed him – an accident, an unprovoked attack, self-defence – is obscure. Gaveston was also pardoned for 'all other felonies and trespasses with which he has been charged'.[37]

Edward travelled north throughout August 1310, accompanied by Queen Isabella. His wardrobe account records a payment of a pound to a woman he drank with on the way – a large sum, at least a few months' wages for her.[38] It is interesting to speculate on what they talked about as they drank together, and on where they drank, and why. Edward, described by fourteenth-century chroniclers as 'prodigal in giving' and 'liberal in giving', enjoyed being generous, and frequently handed out large sums of money to people who pleased him.[39] He once paid his painter Jack of St Albans, who 'made him laugh very greatly' by dancing on a table, two and a half pounds or about a year's wages by his own hands 'in aid of Jack, his wife and his children'. On one occasion when Edward was stag-hunting in Walmer, he gave a pound to his cook Morys, who 'rode before the king and fell often from his horse, at which the king laughed greatly', and the same year gave another pound to a servant named Will Muleward, who spent time with him at a wedding and also made him laugh hard.[40] Whatever Edward's faults, he didn't lack a sense of humour or the ability to laugh.

The campaign in Scotland, unsurprisingly, proved futile.[41] In late November 1310, Edward decided to spend the winter in Scotland, still trying to avoid the Ordainers, and he and Isabella spent the next few months at Berwick-on-Tweed, then on the Scottish side of the border. Isabella, clearly a fan of healthy eating, paid a total of fourteen pounds and seven shillings for 5,000 pieces of fruit on 16 November, 1,000 pears and 300 apples in early December, and 7,500 apples and 2,300 pears in the early months of 1311, while Edward spent over forty-six pounds on fish and 'lard and grease' during Lent.[42] The king's removal of the Exchequer and King's Bench from London to York 'much disturbed and outraged' the Ordainers, and 'many fear evil', according to an anonymous letter-writer.[43] The Ordainers realised the difficulty of curbing a king, especially one like Edward, who did exactly what he wanted, promised much and delivered little, and stood on his regal rights while elevating another man almost to the status of his co-ruler.

Edward sent Gaveston and the earl of Gloucester to parley with Bruce just before Christmas 1310.[44] Of Edward's personal courage in battle there is no doubt, but he was no general, and preferred negotiation to combat wherever possible. Contemporaries must have expected Edward, son of the man who conquered North Wales and grandson of the remarkable Castilian king who played an enormous and vital role in the Spanish Reconquista, to be a great warrior. Fernando III's most notable achievement was the conquest of Seville in 1248 after almost five and a half centuries of Muslim rule, and he made a triumphal procession into the city on 22 December that year; it is likely that Edward's mother Eleanor, then aged seven, was present, and possible that Edward heard about his grandfather's achievements from her or his older sisters. (Fernando is now the patron saint of Seville.) Unfortunately, what Edward's subjects got what was a man who closely resembled his other grandfather, Henry III, whose fifty-six-year-reign was a long history of baronial insurrections, failed military expeditions and lavish expenditure on foreign relatives and favourites. That Edward preferred hedging, ditching and digging to jousting and fighting did not endear him to his contemporaries, either: 'If only he had given to arms the labour that he expended on rustic pursuits, he would have raised England aloft; his name would have resounded through the land', laments the *Vita*.[45]

Meanwhile, in the south, the Ordainers prepared their reforms of government and Edward's household. One of the Ordainers, the earl of Lincoln, died at the age of sixty in early February 1311. Lincoln had been regent of England in Edward's absence, and the king sent his nephew Gloucester south to replace him, a great responsibility for the young man, not yet twenty.[46] The earl's death was a blow for Edward on two counts: firstly, Lincoln was a moderate and a royalist, despite his actions against Gaveston in 1308 and his role as an Ordainer, and secondly, Earl Thomas of Lancaster inherited his lands by right of his wife, Lincoln's daughter and heir Alice. Thomas of Lancaster now held five earldoms, Lancaster, Leicester, Derby, Lincoln and Salisbury, and had a gross annual income of £11,000, which made him by far the richest and most influential man in the country. Edward had even greater cause to rue the loss of his former ally. Lancaster had to pay homage to Edward for his new lands, but refused to cross the Tweed into Scotland to do so. Edward refused to return to England to accept the homage. Lancaster threatened to take a hundred knights to forcibly enter his lands, and once again, civil war loomed.[47] Eventually Edward caved in and agreed to meet his turbulent cousin at Haggerston, on the English side of the river, perhaps to save any future legal difficulties because Lancaster hadn't paid homage to him in England. The two men 'saluted each other amicably and exchanged frequent kisses', each concealing his antipathy for the other, and Edward hiding his annoyance that he had been forced to travel to meet Lancaster when etiquette demanded that his subjects should come to him. Supposedly Piers Gaveston accompanied Edward, but Lancaster 'would neither kiss him, nor even salute him, whereat Piers was offended beyond measure'.[48] Gaveston was not well at this time: an anonymous letter written at Berwick on 4 April announced that 'a secret illness troubles him much, compelling him to take short journeys', but that when he visited Edward and Isabella at Berwick, he found them both well.[49] Edward may have attended the funeral of his friend Bishop Anthony Bek at Durham Cathedral on 3 May 1311. He took over Bek's stud of 240 horses and bought his gold plate from his executors at a cost of £1,383.[50] The king was probably encouraged by the disunity among the Ordainers; relations between the earls of Lancaster and Gloucester were so bad that an anonymous letter-writer said that he feared a riot when the two men arrived in London.[51] On the other hand, a feud between the richest men of the kingdom increased the already sky-high tension in England, and London was already suffering unrest. Despite the efforts of the mayor, Richer de Refham, the city annalist writes of the 'rifflers and ruffians' terrorising the streets.[52]

Edward spent almost a year in the north and achieved nothing except infuriating his magnates still further, and failed even to engage Robert Bruce in battle, let alone defeat him. He finally bowed to the inevitable and summoned parliament, to begin in London on 8 August 1311, but didn't arrive until 13 August. He stayed at the house of the Dominicans, and paid Janin the Bagpiper two pounds for performing for him there.[53] The *Vita* says that Edward went on pilgrimage to Canterbury as a way of putting off the moment of reckoning at parliament, though looking at his itinerary it is hard to see when.[54] Piers Gaveston remained in the north, at the stronghold of Bamburgh, but kept in close contact with Edward.[55] Around this time Edward heard the sad news that his five-year-old half-sister Eleanor had died at Amesbury Priory, and he paid £113 for her funeral at Beaulieu Abbey in Hampshire.[56]

To Edward's horror, the forty-one Ordinances or reforms of his household presented to him at parliament limited his royal powers severely, and he protested that 'some things were disadvantageous to him, some fabricated out of spite, and he argued and pleaded that he was not bound to give his consent to these'.[57] But the Ordinance that caused him greatest consternation was the twentieth: 'Piers Gaveston, as a public enemy of the king and of the kingdom, shall be utterly cast out and exiled … forever and without return.' Edward was so desperate to save Gaveston that he finally agreed to accept all the Ordinances if the lords would only revoke the twentieth. He said, 'Whatever has been ordained or decided upon, however much they may redound to my private disadvantage, shall be established at your request and remain in force for ever. But you shall stop persecuting my brother Piers, and allow him to have the earldom of Cornwall.' This, however, the Ordainers refused to do. Edward refused to accept his friend's banishment, and, anguished at the thought of his being forced into exile yet again, gave vent to his emotions. He alternated between shouting insults and threats at the Ordainers and trying to cajole them with flattery and promises of favours, but to no avail. They warned him that if he did not consent to Gaveston's banishment, he 'might through imprudence be deprived of his throne and his kingdom'.

Faced with the possibility of losing his throne – the second time this threat was used – Edward had little choice but to accept the Ordinances, and they were published on 27 September 1311.[58] It had taken him six weeks to agree. This was a common feature of Edward's reign; he stubbornly dug in his heels and refused to do what his magnates wanted, yet inevitably was forced to bow to pressure in the end. In the four years since his accession, Edward had brought his kingdom to the brink of civil war numerous times, and for the remaining years of his reign, this terrible cycle would continue. Edward would not, or could not, be the king his subjects needed him to be. He persisted in his unconventional ways, flaunted his affection for Piers Gaveston, and utterly refused to modify his behaviour and attitudes.

On 8 October, Edward granted Piers Gaveston a safe-conduct to come to London.[59] The following day, he wrote to his kinsman Fernando IV of Castile, who had asked him to donate money for a crusade, informing him that 'he has been so engaged with the war in Scotland and other matters that he is unable to accede to this request'.[60] He also wrote to his sister and brother-in-law the duke and duchess of Brabant asking them to receive Piers Gaveston, and informed his father-in-law Philip IV that he was anxious to have a personal interview with him, presumably to ask him to help or protect Gaveston.[61] Unsurprisingly, this letter opened with flowery declarations of Philip's high and mightiness and Edward's enormous affection for his beloved 'father'. Queen Isabella also sent letters to Philip in November 1311, although the content of them is unfortunately unknown.[62] Gaveston himself, meanwhile, sent an Italian merchant named Blasius of Siena to Brabant and elsewhere to make financial arrangements on his behalf in early October.[63]

Gaveston was now exiled from England for the third time, probably an all-time record, and was ordered to 'leave and utterly depart from the realm of England and every lordship of the king' by 1 November 1311, from Dover, and nowhere else. If he did not leave, he would 'thereafter be treated as an enemy of the kingdom, the king, and the people'.[64] The Ordinances also mandated the removal of other people from Edward's court, most notably his French cousins Henry Beaumont and Beaumont's sister Isabella, Lady Vescy. Beaumont and Lady Vescy, like Edward, were great-grandchildren of Queen Berenguela of Castile and King Alfonso IX of Leon. In 1304, Edward I had appointed Lady Vescy as lifetime custodian of Bamburgh Castle, a rare honour for a woman, and Edward II, very fond of his mother's relatives, confirmed the appointment at the beginning of his reign.[65]

Gaveston departed into exile later than ordered, on 3 or 4 November, and not from Dover as instructed but from London or somewhere along the Thames.[66] It is not clear whether Edward was there to see him off, though it seems not, as his court, household and privy seal were at Windsor, 30 miles away, where government business continued.[67] If he did not go to say farewell to Gaveston, this is probably because he couldn't bear yet another parting from his beloved friend. He must have been distraught, though whether he realised that he himself was mostly to blame is hard to say. Had he learned his lesson from Gaveston's previous exile and behaved with circumspection, Gaveston might not have been banished yet again. Gaveston may have expected his exile to be permanent, or at least for some years, as on 22 October he was given letters of protection for five years, and appointed four attorneys for the same length of time.[68] His wife Margaret did not accompany him abroad this time, for the simple reason that she was six or seven months pregnant. Gaveston's earldom of Cornwall was revoked, but financial arrangements were made for Margaret, and she was allowed to keep Wallingford Castle.

Edward found time on 24 October 1311 to remember the Dominican priory at Langley he had founded three years earlier, and granted the house fifty pounds a year on top of the hundred pounds annually he had already given them.[69] In late October and early November, he gave Queen Isabella the palace of Eltham and lands in Kent and Lincolnshire; Isabella set off for Eltham immediately, accompanied by her husband's niece Eleanor Despenser (née de Clare), and wrote to Edward on 28 and 29 October.[70] Perhaps Edward was expressing his gratitude for her support of Gaveston: on 29 October, Isabella sent a letter to the receiver of Ponthieu 'concerning the affairs of the earl of Cornwall'.[71] Apparently she had agreed to help Gaveston in his exile, at least financially; perhaps in the naming of him as 'earl of Cornwall', which title had been stripped from him, we may see some sympathy on Isabella's part to her husband's favourite. Other than the period soon after her wedding, when the queen may have complained to her father about Gaveston and his relationship with her husband, there is little indication that she hated him, or resented his presence.

Piers Gaveston seems to have gone to Flanders.[72] There were rumours by late November 1311, however, that he had already returned to England, or perhaps had never left, and on 30 November two Ordainers were despatched to search for him in the West Country, where he was thought to be 'wandering from place to place'.[73] There were also rumours that Gaveston had returned to his castle at Wallingford, or to Tintagel in Cornwall, or was 'lurking now in the king's apartments'.[74] Edward fumed. And grieved. And, almost certainly, plotted to bring Gaveston back. It is likely that around this time, he wrote to the abbot of Glastonbury – and probably other churchmen, though the letters have not survived – asking him to search through his chronicles for information about people exiled from England during the reigns of his ancestors 'and for what reasons and at what time, and by whom, and how, they had been recalled'. Evidently, he was searching for a precedent by which he could bring Gaveston back from his banishment. The abbot of Glastonbury received Edward's letter on 2 January and replied two days later, enclosing a few extracts from his chronicles, which dated from 1210 to 1289. One of the precedents he found concerned William de Valence, half-brother of Henry III and father of the earl of Pembroke of Edward's reign, exiled from England in 1258 and allowed to return in 1261.[75]

Although Gaveston was gone from England, the tension had not: on 11 and 16 November, the king banned a jousting tournament at Northampton, and on the 28th he forbade the earls of Gloucester, Lancaster, Hereford, Pembroke, Warwick and Arundel from coming to parliament armed.[76] The earl of Surrey is the only notable absentee from the list, and remained very loyal to Edward at this time. Edward was, however, attempting to maintain amicable relations with his powerful kinsman Lancaster, who was seriously ill or had injured himself. The king wrote to Lancaster's adherent Sir Robert Holland on 20 November that 'we are very joyous and pleased about the good news we have heard concerning the improvement in our dear cousin and faithful subject Thomas, earl of Lancaster, and that he will soon be able to ride in comfort'.[77]

Further Ordinances were issued in late November, removing many of Gaveston's adherents from Edward's household, 'lest they should stir up the king to recall Piers once more'. Edward fumed again, declaring that the Ordainers were treating him like an idiot, and that he could not believe that 'the ordering of his whole house should depend upon the will of another'.[78] The king spent the festive season of 1311 at Westminster, probably playing dice on Christmas night, a tradition of his, when he spent up to five pounds.[79] Queen Isabella accompanied him.

The author of the *Vita* makes one of his rare mistakes when he says that Gaveston spent Christmas with Edward, but wherever Gaveston was, he was not with the king, as on 23 December, Edward gave Gaveston's messenger a pound for carrying letters between them.[80] What happened next is rather murky and confused, and the only certain thing is that Piers Gaveston returned to England in early 1312. Why he returned, when he had previously made arrangements for a long exile, is not known. Perhaps he only intended to slip into England for a little while and see his wife and the birth of his child, or perhaps Edward, in a fit of pique and hatred of the Ordainers, had ordered him back. According to the *Vita*, Edward, swore on God's soul – his favourite oath – that 'he would freely use his own judgement', and recalled Gaveston.[81] Unfortunately, Edward II had no judgement whatsoever, and his recall of Gaveston led to inevitable tragedy.

5

Death, Birth and Reconciliation

Edward left Westminster for Windsor on 27 December 1311, leaving Queen Isabella behind, although she sent him unspecified 'precious objects' for his New Year gift.[1] Sometime in early January, Edward collected his niece Margaret Gaveston from her castle of Wallingford, and headed to Yorkshire with her.[2] The 200-mile journey must have been dreadfully uncomfortable for Margaret, whose pregnancy was nearing full term, but she arrived safely in York and gave birth there to Gaveston's daughter Joan, named after her mother and Edward's sister Joan of Acre, on or around 12 January.[3] The king seems to have met Gaveston at Knaresborough on 13 January, and the two men rushed the 17 miles to York that same day, probably so that Gaveston could see his wife and newborn child.[4] It is possible that Gaveston intended to leave England once he had seen his family and knew they were well, but Edward took the decision out of his hands: on 18 January 1312, the king revoked his friend's exile and declared him 'good and loyal'.[5] Edward had his sheriffs proclaim the news, and two days later, ordered the restoration of the lands of Gaveston's earldom to him. A memorandum was added: 'These writs were made in the king's presence by his order under threat of grievous forfeiture.' By restoring Gaveston, Edward proved that he adored his friend beyond reason, and could not bear to be without him, and that he was prepared to face civil war for him. The writ revoking Gaveston's exile was written in French, not the usual Latin, which probably means that Edward himself drafted it; he could not have managed it in Latin. In 1317, he asked the archbishop of Canterbury to translate a papal letter from Latin into French for him, a fact which, with his taking his coronation oath in French, caused historians of the early twentieth century to condemn him unfairly as uneducated and illiterate.[6] Papal texts were, however, written in a Latin difficult and convoluted even for scholars to follow, and rather than criticise Edward for his lack of education or intelligence, we should perhaps acknowledge the common sense that drove him to ensure that he understood the letter by reading it in his mother tongue, rather than in a language he had learned in childhood but had had little occasion to use since.

The Ordainers, furious, ordered that Edward 'should not receive from his exchequer so much as a half-penny or farthing', with the result that he and Gaveston 'plundered the town and country, because they had not the wherewithal to pay their expenses'.[7] Desperate to protect Piers Gaveston, at any cost, Edward even tried to negotiate with Robert Bruce to take care of his friend, and, amazingly, offered to recognise Bruce as king of Scots if he took Gaveston under his protection. Robert Bruce refused, exclaiming, 'How shall the king of England keep faith with me, since he does not observe the sworn promises made to his liege men? ... No trust can be put in such a fickle man; his promises will not deceive me.'[8] This offer was simply incredible – Edward was prepared to throw away his claim to overlordship to Scotland, for the sake of Piers Gaveston.

Edward exchanged letters with his cousin and enemy, the earl of Lancaster, in late January. The content of these letters is unknown, but they are unlikely to have been amicable. Probably Lancaster had demanded Gaveston's surrender or immediate return to exile, which, of course, Edward refused.[9] He gave a pound each to three minstrels for their performance on 29 January, and sent Queen Isabella the expenses for her journey north in early February.[10] Around the same time, the Ordainers gathered at St Paul's in London to discuss their next moves. Despite their anger with the king, they were reluctant to wage war on him, a thing not lightly done.[11] Five of the earls, Lancaster, Warwick, Hereford, Pembroke and Arundel, bound themselves by oath to capture Piers.[12] In York on 20 February, after Margaret's churching – the purification ceremony forty days after childbirth – Edward and the proud parents the Gavestons celebrated the birth of Joan, Edward's great-niece. Edward paid the huge sum of forty marks to celebrate Margaret's purification, and the guests were entertained by his minstrel 'King Robert'.[13] A few days earlier, Edward had given Robert a pound to buy himself a 'targe' or shield, to use in a dance involving swords and shields, and paid two pounds to a minstrel sent to him by Queen Isabella's eldest brother Louis, king of Navarre, who performed for him.[14] Edward took minstrels with him everywhere he went and paid them handsomely, giving his singer Master William Milly two shillings a day, as much as a knight earned.[15] He had in 1305/06 spent the wildly excessive amount of £1,268 on minstrels and buying palfrey horses, a sum of money which reveals much of Edward's extravagance.[16] Meanwhile, Isabella made her way north, remaining in frequent contact with Edward via her messenger John Moigne and sending him a basket of lampreys. Her 200-mile journey took almost three weeks, which indicates how painfully slow medieval travel could be.[17]

Shortly after Isabella's arrival in York, she and Edward conceived their first child, the future Edward III, who was born on Monday 13 November 1312. Counting back thirty-eight weeks, roughly the length of a full-term pregnancy from the time of conception, brings us to 21 February (1312 was a leap year). On this date, Isabella's Household Book shows her to have been at Bishopthorpe, just south of York, and she probably arrived in the city later that day, or early the following day.[18] There is no doubt whatsoever that Edward was the father of Edward III, and we may assume that the boy was conceived within a few days of Isabella's arrival in York. The king and queen remained together in the city until early April, so even if Edward III arrived prematurely, there is no reason to think that Edward was not his biological father. Easter Sunday fell on 26 March in 1312, so Edward and Isabella, now twenty-seven and sixteen respectively, must have conceived their son during Lent, when intercourse was forbidden. This hardly lends credence to the notion that Edward slept with his wife unwillingly; Lent gave him the perfect excuse not to have sex with Isabella, if he didn't want to.

No record of the fourteenth century gives even the slightest hint that anyone believed Isabella had taken a lover and that Edward was not his son's real father. It is impossible that the sixteen-year-old queen of England could have conducted an affair and kept it secret. Although Isabella did have a relationship with Roger Mortimer many years later, this occurred when she was in France and beyond Edward's influence, after their marriage had broken down and long after she had borne her four children by Edward. This cannot be taken to mean that Mortimer, or anyone else, had been her lover years before. It is impossible for Mortimer to have fathered Edward III, as he was in Ireland in 1312. He was also in Ireland when Edward and Isabella conceived their next two children in 1315 and 1317, and away from court in 1320 when their youngest was conceived.[19] It was only in the late twentieth century that speculations about Edward III's paternity arose, because Edward II has become widely seen as a gay icon and it is therefore sometimes assumed that he must have been incapable of sexual relations with women. However, the existence of Edward's illegitimate son Adam demonstrates that he wasn't repelled by intercourse with women, and he may have enjoyed it enormously, for all we know. No one in the fourteenth century doubted that he fathered Isabella's children, and there is no reason at all for us to doubt it.

Sometime in March 1312, the archbishop of Canterbury 'seized his sword and struck Piers with anathema'; that is, he excommunicated Gaveston.[20] By mid-March, the anathematised Gascon had left York and gone to Scarborough, and Edward gave Gaveston's messenger the remarkable sum of fifty pounds, the equivalent of many years' salary, for bringing him 'good news' of his friend, whatever that might have been – perhaps that Gaveston had decided to stay in England.[21] At Easter, Edward continued a pleasant tradition of his father's: if the king was caught in bed on Easter Monday, his 'captors' had the right to drag him out, and he had to pay them a large ransom to free himself. Catching Edward still asleep was a far from difficult task, as he was a late riser, and in 1311 he had paid twenty pounds to three of his household knights who dragged him out of bed.[22] Some kind of ceremony was performed at night-time: later in his reign Edward gave gifts of one pound and two pounds respectively to the chamber valets Jack Coppehouse and Jack Pyk for 'what he did when the king went to bed', and five pounds to Sir Giles Beauchamp and ten marks (six pounds sixty-six pence) to Sir Richard Lovel 'for what he did in the king's chamber when he went to bed'.[23] At Easter 1312, Edward paid Isabella's ladies and damsels forty marks as their ransom for the pleasant custom of 'capturing' him in bed. One of the damsels was Alice Leygrave, Edward's former wet nurse, called 'the king's mother, who suckled him in his youth'.[24]

By the end of March 1312, Gaveston was back at York, and on 1 April, Edward told his father-in-law Philip IV that he had to hasten to Berwick-on-Tweed, as Robert Bruce was besieging the town.[25] However, he had no intention of going there. Piers Gaveston was far more important to Edward than his enemy seizing such a vital port, and besides, his own men were holding the Scottish border against him to prevent him sending Gaveston to Robert Bruce for protection. On 5 April, the two men left for Newcastle, perhaps because it was much further north and they felt safer there. Queen Isabella had joined them by 22 April, but soon moved on the nine miles to Tynemouth Priory, probably because Gaveston was ill: two men were paid ten marks each for looking after him.[26] Edward celebrated his twenty-eighth birthday on 25 April, and borrowed forty pounds from the Genoese merchant Antonio di Pessagno to buy 'large, white pearls' for Isabella, probably his response to the news of her pregnancy.[27] That the king felt himself to be in danger in his own realm is demonstrated by his grant to Gaveston of the custody of Scarborough Castle in early April: he ordered Gaveston to deliver the castle to no one but himself, except 'if it shall happen that the king is brought there a prisoner'.[28]

On the day he departed for Newcastle, Edward (unrealistically) ordered his vassals the counts of Foix and Armagnac and the lord of Albret – the three greatest territorial lords in the south of France – and another 120 Gascon viscounts and barons to bring themselves and armed men and horses to him, to aid him in the conflict against his barons, which he knew was inevitable. Three days later, he excused himself from a council of French peers in Paris, which he was eligible to attend as duke of Aquitaine and count of Ponthieu.[29] Meanwhile, the earl of Lancaster was slowly making his way north with the intention of capturing Gaveston, holding jousting tournaments on the way as an excuse to assemble armed men. On 3 May, Edward and Gaveston learned of his imminent arrival at Newcastle, which took them completely by surprise. They fled the few miles to Tynemouth to join Isabella, escaping Lancaster by only a few hours, leaving most of Edward's household behind.[30] On 5 May they left by sea, to the secure and fortified castle of Scarborough. Knowing that he and Gaveston would have to spend a few days in a small boat bobbing about on the North Sea, a rough and bleak prospect even in May, Edward sent Isabella by land instead, and they arranged to meet again at York. Isabella was in the first trimester of pregnancy, when the risk of miscarriage is high, and either she or the king decided that travelling by land would be a safer option for her.

The *Trokelowe* chronicle, written at St Albans (270 miles from Tynemouth) sometime after 1330, claims that Isabella begged Edward in tears not to leave her, but he callously abandoned her anyway despite her pregnancy, concerned only with Gaveston.[31] This is extremely improbable and no other source mentions the story. It is highly likely that *Trokelowe* confused this event with another occasion when the queen was at Tynemouth and this time truly in danger, ten years later.[32] It took Edward and Gaveston a full five days to sail down the coast from Tynemouth to Scarborough, a long and dreadfully uncomfortable journey, especially for a pregnant woman.[33]

King and favourite arrived at Scarborough on 10 May. Edward left Gaveston there and set out for Knaresborough, where he spent several days at Gaveston's castle and where some of his household joined him after travelling to the town by land. The king then went on to York, where he met Isabella on the 14th, only nine days after he had supposedly abandoned her at Tynemouth.[34] Clearly their meeting there was a prior arrangement, and Edward paid the queen's controller twenty pounds for the expenses of her journey on 16 May.[35] Isabella was so anxious to be reunited with her husband that she left most of her belongings behind at South Shields, and ignored a letter sent to her by her uncle the earl of Lancaster, promising that he would rid her of Gaveston's presence.[36] Nothing indicates that Isabella thought her husband had abandoned her or that she was angry with him for doing so, or that she wanted to stay away from him, or that she had any interest in acting against him, or that she disliked him, or even that she particularly desired Piers Gaveston's removal from her life. Records of Isabella's pregnancy in 1312 with the future King Edward III of England are sadly missing, though entries from Edward II's accounts of 1316 when she was pregnant with their second child show that he bought cushions for her carriage so that she could travel in greater comfort, and he is hardly likely to have been less concerned with her welfare in 1312 during a more important pregnancy. Given that Edward had bought his wife expensive pearls in late April, it would be very odd if he carelessly abandoned her to danger only a few days later.

The earl of Lancaster seized the baggage train of Edward and Gaveston, which they had been forced to leave behind at Tynemouth, and which included a gold ring with an enormous ruby called 'the Cherry' and a gold cup studded with jewels bequeathed to the king by Queen Eleanor, either his mother Eleanor of Castile or grandmother Eleanor of Provence. Lancaster took possession of sixty-three horses, including a bay and a black rouncy with stars on their foreheads, an iron-grey war-horse and a black horse from Edward's stud at Woodstock.[37] Edward seethed over the loss of his many valuable possessions, and pointed out a few months later that 'if any lesser man had done it, he could be found guilty of theft and rightly condemned by a verdict of robbery with violence'.[38]

By leaving Gaveston at Scarborough, Edward made a bad mistake: although the castle was well-fortified, it was not provisioned for a siege. Four men arrived to besiege Gaveston in the castle. One was John de Warenne, earl of Surrey, the only earl loyal to Edward the previous year, but recently persuaded by the archbishop of Canterbury to join the pursuit of the hated favourite. Another was Henry Percy, whose descendants became earls of Northumberland later in the fourteenth century. The third was Edward's cousin Aymer de Valence, earl of Pembroke, and the fourth Robert, Lord Clifford. Edward desperately tried to raise an army in York, with a conspicuous lack of success, but, just in case, the earl of Lancaster sat with his army between Scarborough and York to prevent the king relieving the siege.[39] Gaveston's sister was in the castle with him when the siege began on 10 May, the day Edward left him there.[40] A week later, the king ineffectually ordered Surrey, Pembroke, Percy and Clifford 'to desist from besieging Scarborough Castle', although he managed to keep in touch with Gaveston via letters.[41] On 19 May, however, with little other choice, Gaveston surrendered. He had few provisions, the castle was under constant assault by siege engines, and he must have known how little support he had and how futile his resistance was.[42] Certainly, he also knew that Edward would not be able to come to his rescue, and came out of the castle to negotiate terms. They were surprisingly lenient, so much so that the hostile author of the *Flores* assumed Edward must have bribed Pembroke.[43] Another source described the arrangement as the barons submitting to Gaveston, not vice versa.[44]

Gaveston would be held under house arrest at his own castle of Wallingford until he appeared before parliament to account for his actions, and was to be kept safely at all times. If he or the king disputed the terms of the truce, he would be free to return to Scarborough Castle. The deadline given for parliament to decide his fate was 1 August, and if this date passed with no decision, Gaveston would again be free to return to Scarborough.[45] Edward himself played a large role in this agreement, and the *Vita* states that 'the matter had been put forward by his own counsel'.[46] He surely hoped to come to some arrangement by that date, and free Gaveston. It was even said that he was prepared to grant the king of France custody of Gascony, if he and the pope would help Edward to protect Gaveston.[47] For Edward even to consider this, and to acknowledge Bruce as king of Scotland is proof of his deep love for Piers Gaveston, and his willingness to do just about anything to keep his friend safe. One wonders why he didn't just hand over the keys of his kingdom to the barons while he was at it. From around 26 to 28 May 1312, the earls of Pembroke and Surrey, and Henry Percy, met Edward at St Mary's Abbey. Whether Piers Gaveston was with them is not certain, as he is not mentioned. It is also not clear if he and Edward saw each other at this time; it is possible that Gaveston was under guard, and kept away from the king.[48] If they did not see each other, then 10 May 1312, the day Edward left Gaveston at Scarborough, was the last time the two men ever met.

Gaveston was placed in the custody of the earl of Pembroke, who took him south, to Wallingford. Edward and Gaveston kept in touch via messengers until 9 June, the day Gaveston and Pembroke reached the village of Deddington in Oxfordshire, about 30 miles short of Wallingford.[49] Edward gave a pound to one William de la Paneterie for lending him a bow and arrows on or shortly before 4 June, and sent a letter to his father-in-law Philip IV on the 11th pettishly declaring that he was 'grievously annoyed' with his subjects.[50] Probably not half as grievously annoyed as his subjects were with him, however – and not nearly as grievously annoyed as he would have been, had he known what was going on in Deddington. In his worst nightmares, he could hardly have guessed what would happen next.

On the night of 9 June, the earl of Pembroke decided to visit his wife Beatrice, and left Gaveston behind at the priory of Deddington under guard. The earl of Warwick, who loathed Piers Gaveston for his presumption and his insulting nicknames, seized an opportunity for revenge. Guy Beauchamp, about forty in 1312, was one of the few English earls not closely related to Edward II by blood or marriage. His character consisted of an odd mix of brutality, piety and cultured intelligence.[51] Early on the morning of Saturday 10 June, Piers Gaveston woke to the sound of chaos outside, horses' hooves clattering on the ground and men shouting. The earl of Warwick and a large armed force had surrounded the priory, and Gaveston heard the earl call out, 'Arise, traitor, you are taken!'[52] He must have known what terrible danger he was in, although even then his courage didn't fail him. He looked out of the window and, catching sight of the earl, laughed and shouted down that the 'black dog of Arden' had arrived. Beauchamp, shaking with fury that he could not curb Gaveston's tongue even when he had the Gascon surrounded by armed men, his rage failing to lend him eloquence, hurled back the not terribly witty retort that he was no dog, but the earl of Warwick.[53]

Warwick's men overpowered the guards left by the earl of Pembroke, dragged Gaveston out of the priory barefoot and bare-headed, and tore his belt of knighthood from him.[54] Surrounded by armed men, Gaveston was forced to walk through the streets of Deddington, a large crowd appearing to taunt him as soon as news spread. He was then given a mangy horse to speed his 30-mile journey to Warwick Castle. All the way, 'blaring trumpets followed Piers and the horrid cry of the populace'.[55] At Warwick, the earl cast Gaveston into the dungeon, in chains, and waited for the earls of Lancaster, Hereford and Arundel to arrive.

Warwick, Lancaster and the others had every intention of killing Gaveston. Lancaster, whom Gaveston had derided as the Churl and the Fiddler, declared, 'While he lives there will be no safe place in the realm of England.' Probably, they could see no alternative to killing him; if they exiled him for the fourth time, Edward would only recall him yet again, civil war would break out, and thus they decided that he should die.[56] According to the Bridlington chronicler, they called in the royal justices William Inge and Henry Spigurnel to pronounce judgement on Gaveston, though given the trust Edward placed in both men in later years, this seems unlikely.[57] On 19 June, the earl of Warwick sent a messenger to his prisoner, who insolently told Gaveston, 'Look to yourself, my lord, for today you shall die the death.'[58] The royal favourite was taken two miles along the road to Kenilworth until they reached Blacklow Hill, which lay on Lancaster's lands. The earl of Warwick lost his nerve and remained in his castle, while Lancaster took responsibility for the bloody act. As Gaveston was the brother-in-law of the earl of Gloucester, Lancaster and the others agreed to grant him the nobleman's death: decapitation, a privilege of rank, as beheading was much quicker than hanging, the method of execution reserved for common criminals. And so 'they put to death a great earl whom the king had adopted as brother, whom the king cherished as a son, whom the king regarded as friend and ally'.[59] The *Vita* has Gaveston sighing and groaning, and making an implausibly long and pious speech which sounds far more like something the author thinks he should have said, rather than anything the courageous and bitingly witty Gascon really would say. While Lancaster, Hereford and Arundel stood some distance away, one of Lancaster's Welsh men-at-arms ran Gaveston through with a sword, and as he lay dying on the ground, another cut off his head.[60]

The earls demonstrated their contempt for Gaveston by leaving his mutilated body lying on the dusty road, and returned post-haste to the safety of Warwick Castle. A group of cobblers found the body, laid it on a ladder and took it to the castle, where the earl of Warwick refused to have anything to do with it.[61] Ignorant of the etiquette governing this particular situation, and doubtless unwilling to incur the unpredictable king's wrath by carting his friend's body around the country, they not unreasonably took it back where they had found it. A group of Dominicans – Edward's favourite order – from Oxford were the next to come across Gaveston's body, either by accident or design, and took it to their house, where they embalmed it and sewed the head back on. An enormous ruby set in gold, worth £1,000 and a gift from Edward, was found on Gaveston's body, as were an emerald, a diamond 'of great value' and three more large rubies set in gold.[62] However, the Dominicans could not bury him, as he had died excommunicate.

And so passed Piers Gaveston, the charismatic and notorious favourite of a king. He was perhaps thirty or so when he died, the father of a five-month-old daughter and an illegitimate daughter, age unknown. So many centuries later, it is hard to see precisely what he did that was so objectionable. His arrogance, his presumption and his ostentation, and supposedly his love of fine clothes, irritated his contemporaries beyond bearing, but hardly merited death.[63] Whatever his relationship with Edward might have been, Gaveston did not die merely because the barons believed he was the king's lover, and it is inaccurate to portray him – as has sometimes been the case – solely as a martyr to his (and Edward's) sexuality. If Edward had been more even-handed with his favour, if he had defeated Robert Bruce, if he had not been so incapable of ruling his country, it is doubtful that his magnates would have much cared about his private relationship with Gaveston. The favourite was a scapegoat for Edward's failures, killed by men deeply dissatisfied with their king.

On the day of Piers Gaveston's death, Edward was at Burstwick with Isabella, now about four months pregnant. The king probably heard the news on or just before 26 June, after he and Isabella had returned to York. His primary reaction was utter rage.[64] His grief at the loss of his beloved friend must have been shattering. He had loved Gaveston for at least twelve years, nearly half his life, and been emotionally reliant on him to an extraordinary degree. Losing him must have been like losing part of himself, and his recalling Gaveston from exile three times despite the political consequences indicates that he felt he could not live without him. But however much Edward raged and howled in private, he managed to control his emotions in public for once, and said only,

By God's soul, he acted as a fool. If he had taken my advice he would never have fallen into the hands of the earls. This is what I always told him not to do. For I guessed that what has now happened would occur. What was he doing with the earl of Warwick, who was known never to have liked him? I knew for certain that if the earl caught him, Piers would never escape from his hands.

The writer of the *Vita* goes on to say, with notable compassion for a man with a low opinion of Edward, 'When this light utterance of the king became public it moved many to derision. But I am certain the king grieved for Piers as a father grieves for his son. For the greater the love, the greater the sorrow.'[65]

It is doubtful that Edward was telling the truth about guessing beforehand what Warwick would do. His reaction is probably that of a man in profound shock and disbelief, and, perhaps, he felt guilt that he had left Gaveston at Scarborough, or hadn't made enough efforts to release him from Warwick's custody, though in reality there was little he could have done. Besides, Edward must have known that Gaveston had not gone with Warwick willingly. The king managed to keep a hold on himself in public while he grieved in private and plotted revenge.[66] The earl of Lancaster, Edward's cousin and former ally, had done the one thing he knew the king would and could never forgive him for, and the dire relations between these two powerful men dominated the next decade. The *Scalacronica* comments on the 'mortal hatred, which endured forever' between Edward and Lancaster on account of Gaveston's murder.[67] Edward's later actions speak volumes about his genuine grief for Gaveston. That he adored him is beyond question, and until the end of his reign, he remained devoted to his memory.

Many people in the country rejoiced at Piers Gaveston's death. One contemporary Latin poem exults, 'Glory be to the earls who have made Piers die!' and another says, 'Blessed be the man who ordered the execution!' According to the *Vita*, 'The land rejoices, its inhabitants rejoice that they have found peace in Piers' death.'[68] Some people, however, were horrified at the earls' brutal and illegal act, and a groundswell of sympathy for the king swept the country. Gaveston's death strengthened Edward's position, especially as the earls of Surrey and Pembroke came back to his side, appalled by Gaveston's murder. The reaction of Gaveston's widow Margaret is not recorded, but she and Edward paid for two clerks to watch over his embalmed body, which the Dominicans dressed in cloth of gold.[69] Edward would later demonstrate enormous concern and care for Gaveston's earthly remains, and paid for Masses to be said for Gaveston twice a year, on 18 July – perhaps his birthday – and on the anniversary of his death, all over England. He asked the Dominicans to pray daily for Gaveston's soul, and gave them the large sum of eighty pence a day for the purpose.[70]

Edward gave lands worth 2,000 marks a year to Margaret for her sustenance.[71] He also took care of Gaveston's household, and his daughter Joan, the king's great-niece, was sent to Amesbury Priory with her cousin Eleanor de Bohun, daughter of the earl of Hereford and Edward's sister Elizabeth. The king granted them the generous sum of 100 marks a year. Sending girls to grow up at Amesbury was entirely normal, not Edward shoving his favourite's child out of the way. Several of Joan's relatives lived at Amesbury, which had been fashionable among royal ladies since Edward's grandmother retired there in the 1280s: Edward's sister Mary, his niece Joan Monthermer, and Isabel of Lancaster, daughter of the earl of Lancaster's brother Henry, were all nuns there.

Probably many of Edward's subjects sighed with relief that the 'evil male sorcerer' who had enslaved him was dead, and looked forward to a future where the king did not fawn over a man and show him excessive favour. However, Edward did not change. Although he did not take another male favourite until years later, emotional reliance on men was an important part of his make-up, and all the barons had achieved was, firstly, to arouse terrible anger and the desire for revenge within Edward, and secondly, to open the door to men who were far worse. Killing Gaveston was the worst hurt anyone could have inflicted on Edward, and he was the kind of man who could nurse a grudge for many years, as Lancaster would find out.

Edward left York on 28 June and travelled south through Lincolnshire towards London, leaving Isabella behind, to keep his pregnant wife out of the way of any danger. She sent him a letter the day after his departure.[72] Probably in an attempt to take his mind off Gaveston's death, the king gave a pound to Graciosus the Taborer (drummer) who played for him on 30 June, a pound to Janin the Conjuror for performing tricks in the king's private chamber at Swineshead Priory on 7 July, and three shillings to a group of acrobats for 'making their vaults' before him on 8 July.[73] He met the earls of Surrey and Pembroke, Hugh Despenser the Elder and Henry Beaumont in London, and at the house of the Dominicans made an impassioned speech addressed to the 'good people' of his capital, remarking on the marvellous situation wherein some of his magnates conducted themselves towards him as they should not, and asking the Londoners to defend the city against Gaveston's killers. The earls of Lancaster, Warwick and Hereford met at Worcester to discuss their next moves, then brought their army to Hertfordshire.[74] The Londoners supported Edward for once, and closed the gates of the city. On the other hand, the king summoned the earls of Lancaster, Warwick and Hereford to appear before him at Westminster or London, playing a double game, as he often did; Edward had an aptitude for political intrigue, if little else.[75] Rumours swirled: that Edward intended to seize Lancaster as soon as he entered London; that Lancaster would, with the help of a group of Londoners, capture Edward in the city.[76]

Some of Edward's adherents tried to persuade him to raise an army and make war on the earls, declaring that what they had done was treason.[77] Cooler heads advised caution, pointing out the dangers of fighting the powerful Lancaster, and that Edward would place himself at risk of being captured. Edward, understandably, strongly favoured war.[78] He was especially keen, at this juncture, to avenge himself on Warwick, and intended either to have his head or banish him from the country.[79] Probably he considered Warwick, as the abductor of Gaveston, as the prime mover in the affair. Later, however, he put all the blame on Lancaster, perhaps having heard that his cousin had taken most of the responsibility for the death on himself. The earls entered London armed, although Edward had expressly forbidden them to do so.[80] They knew that Edward 'would, if he could, proceed to take vengeance as though for a wrong done to himself', as the *Vita* perceptively points out.[81]

Edward's nephew the earl of Gloucester offered to mediate between the two sides. He told the king that the earls who had killed Gaveston were not, as Edward believed, his enemies, but rather his friends, and that everything they did was for Edward's own benefit. Edward, not surprisingly, was having none of it. He told his nephew,

> I protest that they are not my friends who strive to attack my property and my rights. If I may use my royal prerogative as other kings do, may I not recall to my peace by the royal power a man exiled for any reason whatsoever? Of this right they deprived me by their own authority, for the man to whom I had granted peace, they cruelly put to death ... Since they have seized my goods and killed my men, it is very likely that they do not wish to have any consideration for me, but to seize the crown and set up for themselves another king.[82]

Gloucester took himself off to Lancaster, Warwick and Hereford, who listened to Edward's complaints and announced that they had merely 'ordered to be killed a certain exiled traitor who lurked in the land'.[83] This was not an argument calculated to appeal to Edward. War did not break out, partly because Edward couldn't afford to fight one, but mainly because, revenge notwithstanding, he didn't need to, as his position had been strengthened by the earls' violent act. Tortuous negotiations between the king and Gaveston's killers dragged on for many months. Although eventually willing to come to terms with the earls – in public, at least – Edward dug his heels in again and said, 'Let the barons seek whatever they think may justly be sought; I will bow to their judgement in all things, but I will by no means charge Piers with treason.'[84]

Finally, shortly before Christmas 1312, Edward and the earls of Lancaster, Warwick and Hereford signed a peace treaty. The earls were to make obeisance to Edward in the great hall of Westminster Palace 'with great humility, on their knees', and would 'humbly beg him to release them from his resentment and rancour, and receive them into his good will'. The goods Lancaster had seized at Tynemouth were to be restored to the king on 13 January.[85] For some reason, Edmund Fitzalan, earl of Arundel, is not named in the treaty, although he was certainly present at Gaveston's death. Neither is he mentioned in the numerous pardons granted the following year. Why Edward didn't feel the need to pardon Arundel for his role in Gaveston's death is not clear, but perhaps because Arundel tried to help Gaveston, or spoke out for him – or at least, persuaded Edward that he did. Arundel's subsequent career trajectory is surprising: he became one of Edward's most loyal allies.

At the end of July 1312, Edward sent an escort to Yorkshire for Queen Isabella, judging that the situation was calm enough for her to return south. He spent the first three weeks of August in Dover and Canterbury, where he gave three shillings to John of Lombardy for 'making his minstrelsy with snakes before the king', and met Isabella, who had travelled south very slowly because of her pregnancy, on 9 September.[86] The king and queen were reunited for the first time since the end of June, and in the middle of September retired to Windsor Castle, where they would remain together for most of the following eight months. The dowager queen Marguerite, Edward's stepmother and Isabella's aunt, joined them there, with her brother Louis, count of Evreux.

Edward spent a few days in the park of Windsor on several occasions, perhaps digging a ditch or building a wall, using hard physical exercise as a way of soothing his grief, and gave two pounds to the earl of Pembroke's Welsh minstrel Coghin, who entertained him – and presumably the heavily pregnant queen – on 12 October.[87] On 20 October, he granted Isabella authority to make her will; married women needed their husbands' permission for this, and it was a common thing to do while in an age when pregnancy and childbirth were so risky.[88] While at Windsor, Edward probably received the news that his brother-in-law Duke John II of Brabant had died in Brussels on 27 October, at the age of only thirty-seven, and that Edward's twelve-year-old nephew had succeeded as John III.

On the feast day of St Brice, Monday 13 November 1312, Queen Isabella, who was now seventeen or almost, gave birth to a healthy son, the future King Edward III. Edward's joy at the birth of his heir went some way to assuaging his terrible grief over Piers Gaveston, and he gave his son his title of earl of Chester within days of his birth, and showered him with gifts and lands.[89] In December, Edward granted the enormous sum of eighty pounds annually to Isabella's steward John Launge and his wife Joan for bringing him news of the birth (though he was also at Windsor at the time), which gave them a higher income than some knights.[90] By the time he was a few weeks old, Edward of Windsor had his own household of many dozens of people, and Edward and Isabella visited him occasionally. The *Vita* expressed a wish that the boy would grow up to 'remind us of the physical strength and comeliness of his father'; evidently, Edward II's good looks and impressive physique were the only positive attributes the author could think of to describe him.[91]

The baby had seven godfathers, one of whom was his father's friend Hugh Despenser the Elder. Less than fourteen years later, little Edward would see this godfather hanged in his armour and his body fed to dogs, at his mother's instigation. To Edward II, the birth of a son and heir represented an enormous public relations coup, as it meant that God was favouring him and not his baronial enemies.[92] A healthy son and heir was seen as a blessing from God, bestowed on the king and his kingdom. Edward's subjects, especially in London, celebrated the news of the birth with immense joy and enthusiasm, dancing in the streets and drinking huge amounts of free wine for an entire week.[93]

Edward spent almost £1,250 on cloth for himself, his wife and son and their retainers in order for the royal family to look as splendid as possible during the festive season at Windsor.[94] On 19 December, he sent a palfrey horse worth six pounds and a saddle 'with a lion of pearls, and covered with purple cloth' worth five pounds to Nichola, wife of Piers Lubaud, the Gascon sheriff of Edinburgh and constable of Linlithgow.[95] Why Nichola was singled out for this honour is not clear, although it is probable that Lubaud was a cousin of Piers Gaveston.[96] The king, queen and their son travelled to Westminster in late January 1313 to enjoy pageants and other celebrations put on for them, most notably by the Fishmongers' Guild, then Edward returned to Windsor while Isabella went on pilgrimage to Canterbury to give thanks for the safe birth of her son.[97] She joined her husband at the beginning of March, and she and Edward spent most of March and April together at Windsor. On 27 April 1313, Edward finally ordered the release of Isabel MacDuff, countess of Buchan, from her prison at Berwick-on-Tweed.[98] Some years earlier he had freed Robert Bruce's sister Mary from the cage where his father Edward I had had her imprisoned at Roxburgh Castle; records are missing for Isabel, and one can only hope that the unfortunate lady hadn't spent six whole years incarcerated in inhuman conditions.

Edward finally received his and Gaveston's possessions, which Lancaster had seized at Tynemouth the previous May, on 23 February 1313, six weeks late. They included presents from his sisters; a gold crown encrusted with jewels, worth 100 marks; a crystal goblet; silver plates for fruit; a belt decorated with ivory, notched with a purse hanging down from it, 'with a Saracen face'; a gold buckle with emeralds, rubies, sapphires and pearls, a gift to Edward from the queen of Germany; a silver ship with four gold oars, enamelled on the sides; a gold dragon with enamelled wings; silver forks for eating pears; and many hundreds of other splendid and costly things.[99]

The king and queen spent almost two months in France between May and July 1313, to attend the simultaneous knighting of Isabella's three brothers, and for Edward to engage in the usual endless discussions with Philip IV regarding his duchy of Gascony. Two days before his departure,

Edward sent letters to four men: his correspondent of 1307, Oljeitu of the Ilkhanate; Davit VIII, king of Georgia; Alexios II, emperor of the Trebizond – a successor state of the Byzantine Empire, on the shores of the Black Sea in modern-day Turkey – and Renzong, emperor of Cathay (China). He asked them to give all possible aid to a Franciscan named Guillerinus de Villanova, travelling to preach the word of Christ to the infidels, as Edward named them.[100] Edward's information was somewhat out of date; King Davit had died two years earlier and been succeeded by his son, Giorgi. Whether Edward's messengers managed to reach these far-flung places, and to return to England safely, is not recorded. Edward also told the constable of Dover Castle that he was sending six 'Saracens' to him, and ordered Kendale to pay them sixpence a day each until his return from overseas.[101] Mysteriously, a Gascon called Richard de Neueby, 'who says he is the king's brother', received a large payment of thirteen pounds from Edward at the same time.[102] Perhaps Neueby – an odd name for a Gascon – was an illegitimate son of Edward I, though he is never heard of again. The *Vita* remarks at this time, 'Our King Edward has now reigned six full years and has till now achieved nothing praiseworthy or memorable,' a nicely laconic way of summing up the endless crises of Edward's reign.

Edward, Isabella and their large retinues departed from Dover at sunrise on 23 May 1313, having left his nephew Gloucester as regent.[103] Edward was keen to present himself well in France, and spent the astonishing sum of £1,000 on his clothes and jewels. The king and queen passed through Amiens on 28 May, when Edward gave seven pounds and three shillings to his minstrel Jakeminus de Mokenon for his performance, and entered Paris five days later, where 'the whole city rose up and went forth to meet them'.[104] The knighting of Isabella's brothers took place on 3 June, and Edward belted his eldest brother-in-law Louis, king of Navarre with the belt of knighthood. The two men and Philip IV then knighted about 200 others, including Isabella's two other brothers Philip and Charles and their cousin Philip de Valois: all of them future kings of France. At noon on Tuesday 5 June, Edward hosted a splendid banquet at St-Germain-des-Prés, which was held in tents open to public view and hung with rich cloths. Torches, candles and lamps burned even in the middle of the day, attendants on horseback served the guests, and Louis of Navarre's armourer created a 'castle of love' as the main attraction.[105] Edward suffered the embarrassment of missing a meeting with Philip IV two days later, as he and Isabella had overslept. The amused commentator Geoffrey or Godefroy of Paris gave their night-time dalliance as the reason, adding that it was hardly a wonder if Edward desired his wife, as Isabella was 'the fairest of the fair' and 'splendid of body'.[106] Edward's appearance as described by numerous fourteenth-century chroniclers – tall, handsome, elegant and enormously strong – makes it seem plausible that the queen also felt physical desire for him. The king stirred himself sufficiently that day to watch a large crowd of Parisians parade from the Île Notre-Dame to the Louvre, from the windows of Philip's apartments. He and Isabella, surrounded by a throng of ladies and damsels, saw the procession again later from a tower in their lodgings at St-Germain.[107] Geoffrey of Paris in his rhyming chronicle spelt Edward's name as Oudouart and Isabella's as Ysabiau and Ysabelot, which sound like affectionate nicknames for her, perhaps used by her family and her husband.

On the first anniversary of Piers Gaveston's death, 19 June 1313, Edward was at Pontoise, where Bernard the Fool and no fewer than fifty-four naked dancers performed for him; one hopes that all the nude flesh on display went some way to consoling him. He gave the dancers two pounds.[108] At Pontoise sometime after 11 June, a fire broke out in Edward and Isabella's pavilion during the night, and he gathered up the queen in his arms and rushed outside with her, even though they were 'completely naked' (*toute nue*). In doing so, he probably saved her life, although her arm was badly burnt and the couple lost many of their possessions. This was at least the second time that Edward had escaped from a fire: in April 1306, he gave ten shillings each to the watchmen who roused him from his bed and evacuated his household as flames swept through Windsor Castle.[109] Geoffrey of Paris, an eyewitness to Edward and Isabella's visit to France, says that Edward was keen to save his queen above all else 'because he loved her with fine love'.[110] Geoffrey evidently did not see Isabella as the victim of an uncaring, neglectful husband, and his testimony demonstrates that the couple were on close and intimate terms during the visit. Although we have little evidence of the state of their relationship at other times (as no one recorded it), there is no reason to suppose that the obvious pleasure they took in each other's company at this time was unusual.

The king had the pleasure of meeting Guillerinus de Villanova, the friar travelling east to convert 'infidels' on whose behalf Edward had sent letters a few weeks before, and gave him 'handsome presents', also giving twenty-four florins to various friars of Paris and a pound as an offering at the shrine of the Crown of Thorns at Sainte-Chapelle. On his departure, Philip IV presented him with a gift of four horses and armour.[111] The king and queen passed through the town of Hesdin on their way back to Boulogne and visited Mahaut, countess of Artois, whose daughters Joan and Blanche were married to Isabella's brothers Philip and Charles.[112] Edward and Isabella arrived back at Dover on 15 July at vespers, or sunset, and spent most of August and September 1313 at Windsor. It is possible that Isabella conceived a child while they were there and suffered a miscarriage in November, as the chance survival of an apothecary's account records two purchases of pennyroyal for her.[113] The traditional medicinal use of pennyroyal is to increase uterine contractions and menstrual flow, and it was used after miscarriages to clear the womb of any infection.

In the autumn of 1313, Edward finally came to terms with the earls of Lancaster, Hereford and Warwick, who continued stubbornly to maintain that they had merely acted against 'a public enemy of the land' and that Edward should be grateful to them for killing his beloved Gaveston.[114] On 16 October, the king officially pardoned the men and more than 350 of their adherents.[115] Gaveston's embalmed body still lay unburied with the Dominicans at Oxford; Edward could not bear to put him under the ground. Edward told the earls of Lancaster, Warwick and Hereford to 'lay aside all suspicion, and...to come to his presence, and freely obtain the goodwill that they had so often sought'.[116] Whatever he was feeling, he again kept control of his emotions as he watched them kneel to him, raised them and kissed them one by one, and absolved them.[117] The Sempringham annalist says that the earl of Arundel, whom Edward had not felt the need to pardon for his role in Gaveston's death, joined Lancaster, Hereford and Warwick in 'profess[ing] obedience and humiliation to King Edward in the great hall of Westminster.'[118] To mark their reconciliation, Edward invited the earls to a banquet, and the following day, they reciprocated.[119]

Edward had finally learned to conceal his passionate emotions in public, and behaved with all the appearance of friendliness and forgiveness. But later events were to show that Edward had not forgiven. If Lancaster and the others believed that they had done their country a favour by putting the charismatic and aggravating royal favourite to death, they could not have been more wrong. All they had done was ensure that the rift between Edward II and many of his magnates would never be healed, and that Edward's all-consuming need to avenge his friend's death would lead, a few years later, to an explosion of political violence and bloodshed unprecedented in English history.

6

Military Disaster and Famine

The few months after Edward's public reconciliation with the earls saw England more or less at peace, or at least, as peaceful as it possibly could be in Edward II's reign. Robert Winchelsey, archbishop of Canterbury and one of Edward's most recalcitrant enemies, had died on 11 May 1313, and on 1 October, Pope Clement V appointed Edward's friend and ally Walter Reynolds to the position, thanks in large part to Edward's bribes.[1] Reynolds did not impress his contemporaries: *Lanercost* calls him 'unworthy of any degree of dignity' because of his lack of learning and 'his mode of life,' the *Flores* says he was practically illiterate and indulged in 'immoderate filthiness of lust', and the *Vita* describes him as 'a mere clerk and was scarcely literate, but he excelled in theatrical presentations, and through this obtained the king's favour'.[2] Edward loved plays and enjoyed the company of actors, then considered respectively the work of the devil and the lowest of the low, though whether even he would have had Reynolds promoted solely on the grounds of his theatrical skills is debatable. More importantly, Reynolds had been a friend of Piers Gaveston, and in 1309, Edward described him to the pope as 'not only useful, but indispensable' and said that Reynolds 'has come to enjoy our confidence ahead of others'.[3] The king and queen attended Reynolds' enthronement at Canterbury on 17 February 1314 and remained in the city for a week, enjoying a splendid feast with the new archbishop. They then crossed the Thames Estuary to spend a few days at the royal residence of Hadleigh Castle near Southend.[4]

In late February Edward and Isabella separated, and the queen made her way to Sandwich, from where she sailed to France. Edward had asked her to present petitions concerning Gascony to Philip IV, who was far more likely to grant them to his daughter than to his son-in-law, and ordered his Italian money-lender Antonio di Pessagno to give Isabella nearly £5,000 for her expenses.[5] She departed for her homeland on the last day of February with a retinue of over seventy people, including her damsel Alice Leygrave, Edward's childhood nurse. Isabella was richer than she had been a few months earlier: probably in gratitude for bearing him a son, Edward gave her lands, manors and castles in Kent, Oxfordshire, Derbyshire and Northamptonshire in 1313 and 1314.[6]

On 15 March 1314, the night before Isabella arrived in Paris, her father had Jacques de Molay, grand master of the Knights Templar, burned alive on an island in the Seine. He is said, probably apocryphally, to have screamed out a curse from his pyre, challenging Philip and Pope Clement V, who had helped the French king suppress the Templars, to meet him before God's tribunal within a year. Both of them were dead before the end of 1314. It is possible that while she was in France, Isabella discovered that Marguerite and Blanche of Burgundy, respectively the wives of her brothers Louis and Charles, had been conducting extramarital affairs with the d'Aulnay brothers, Philip and Gautier, and informed her father.[7] If Isabella did break this scandal, as a few fourteenth-century chroniclers claim she did, her motives were almost certainly not vindictive. She was the daughter of two sovereigns and had been raised with a sacred sense of royalty, and therefore, would have been profoundly disturbed at the notion that her sisters-in-law might foist a child not of the royal bloodline on to the French throne. Her actions here also prove the ludicrousness of the suggestion that she would have taken a lover in 1312 and presented his child as Edward's.

Edward II, meanwhile, spent the end of March and beginning of April 1314 at St Albans Abbey, which was close to his childhood residence of Langley and must have been a place he knew well. He made an offering of a gold cross decorated with precious stones and containing relics of St Alban, and the St Albans chronicler comments approvingly on his munificence to the abbey; earlier that year, he had given them a gift of £100 and a loan of £300, and in 1325 pardoned all their debts to him.[8] On learning that his father had intended to rebuild the choir, Edward gave the monks a hundred marks and quantities of timber for the purpose, ordering that no expense should be spared in honouring God and St Alban, the first British martyr, who had died almost exactly a millennium earlier. Edward moved on the 70 miles to Ely near Cambridge, where he celebrated Easter Sunday, 7 April, at the cathedral. St Albans Abbey possessed the remains of St Alban, but Ely Cathedral owned a reliquary which they also described as 'St Alban's'. A curious Edward ordered the monks to open the reliquary, telling John Ketton, bishop of Ely, 'You know that my brothers of St Albans believe that they possess the body of the martyr, while the monks in this place claim to have the same body. By God's soul, I wish to see in which place I should chiefly pay reverence to the holy remains of the saint' ('by God's soul' was Edward's favourite oath). Edward raised the lid of the reliquary himself, and discovered that it was full of rough cloth, spattered with blood that appeared fresh, as if spilt only the day before. All the spectators fell to their knees at this miracle, including Edward, presumably, although he alone had the nerve to close the lid. He gave the monks of Ely many gifts and went away happy that the famous saint was venerated in two places, telling them, 'Rejoice in the gift of God, rejoice in the sanctity and merits of so great a martyr; for if, as you say, God does many miracles here by reason of his garment, you may believe that at St Albans he does more, by reason of the most holy body that rests there.'[9]

Pope Clement V died on 20 April 1314, five weeks after Jacques de Molay cursed him from the flames; perhaps Philip IV quaked in his boots at the news. More than two years would pass before the cardinals elected Clement's successor, and Edward wrote to them in December 1314, asking them to lose no time in choosing a new pope.[10] Five days after Clement's death, Edward spent his thirtieth birthday travelling from Torksey, north-west of Lincoln, to Hull. Isabella arrived back at Dover a few days later, where she received a gift of a porcupine, and immediately set off north to join Edward.[11]

Not entirely unexpectedly, Edward's long-suffering subjects did not have much longer to enjoy the fragile peace currently reigning in England, and the Scottish question soon raised its ugly head again. Although Robert Bruce had failed to capture Berwick-on-Tweed in 1312 while Edward was preoccupied with Piers Gaveston, he enjoyed numerous successes elsewhere. In 1313 and 1314, he and his lieutenants conducted a series of increasingly daring raids on Scottish castles still in English hands, including Perth, Edinburgh and Dumfries, and razed them to the ground.[12] Roxburgh fell to James Douglas in February 1314, despite the brave efforts of the Gascon custodian Guillemin de Fenes, who died during the attack.[13] The *Scalacronica* says that Edinburgh fell because of the treachery of the custodian Piers Lubaud, also a Gascon and apparently a cousin of Piers Gaveston, who subsequently joined Bruce's service. The *Vita* calls Lubaud 'perjurer and traitor'.[14]

The news that so many vital Scottish castles were lost distressed Edward, who 'could scarcely restrain his tears'.[15] He could hardly have been surprised, however, given that he had done nothing to defend the castles or made any effort whatsoever to exert dominance over Bruce, except for the feeble campaign of 1310/11, either because he didn't know how or because he simply didn't care. Although he refused to accept the fact, any chance he might have had to take up his claim to overlordship of Scotland had by now disappeared, and the *Scalacronica* says, 'The king of England undertook scarcely anything against Scotland, and thus lost as much by indolence as his father had conquered.'[16] And Edward had far more than the loss of Scottish castles to worry about: beginning in the late summer of 1311, as soon as Edward departed from Berwick after his unsuccessful campaign, Bruce and his adherents made frequent incursions into the north of England, where they burnt and plundered towns and villages and carried off goods, crops and livestock, unless the inhabitants agreed to pay them tribute to protect themselves. Bruce raised a great deal of money in this way, as much as £20,000.[17] These border raids would continue for much of Edward's reign. This was not entirely Edward's fault; he did make some attempts to strengthen the defence of the north.[18] However, his inability to protect his subjects from Scottish raids hardly helped to revise their low opinion of him.

In June 1313, however, came a challenge that even Edward could not ignore. Edward Bruce was besieging Stirling Castle, the most vital stronghold of them all: the castle controlled the crossing over the River Forth and thus access to the northern Lowlands and Highlands. Stirling was virtually impregnable, and the only hope Bruce had of capturing the stronghold was to starve it into submission. This would take a very long time, which didn't impress Bruce much. Neither, however, did it impress the castle's constable Philip Mowbray, Scottish but loyal to Edward II, who was staring months of discomfort and hunger in the face. Mowbray suggested a compromise, and proposed that if Bruce called off the siege, the constable would surrender the castle to him – on condition that an English army did not appear within three miles of Stirling to relieve the fortress within a year and a day.[19]

And so Edward II marched into Scotland in June 1314, to relieve Stirling – or Strivelyn, as it was then called – and, he hoped, to face Robert Bruce in battle and finally defeat him. He took probably the greatest army that had ever been seen in England, consisting of English knights and footmen, Irish soldiers, Welsh archers, Bruce's Scottish enemies, and knights from all over Europe, comprising 15,000 to 20,000 men. Edward took with him a vast baggage train of 216 carts, with jewellery, napery, costly plate, and ecclesiastical vestments for celebrating the victory. His nobles followed his example, and took along luxurious pavilions, silver eating vessels and selections of fine wines; the personal possessions of the earl of Hereford alone required an entire ship.[20] *Lanercost* says that Edward marched with great pomp and elaborate state, purveying goods from monasteries as he passed, and that he 'did and said things to the prejudice and injury of the saints', whatever that means.[21] Edward passed the time hunting, gambling and listening to music, having taken a trumpeter, fiddlers, bagpipers and other musicians with him.[22] He also took a travelling wine cellar.[23] Queen Isabella, who accompanied him as far north as Berwick, took a wooden altar which could be packed up and carried by a sumpter-horse.[24] Before Edward left England, he ordered the mayor of London to issue a proclamation forbidding 'rumpuses with large footballs' in public fields, an early reference to the enormously popular sport of later centuries. An entry in Edward's wardrobe account of 1299/1300 shows that he played a game called 'creog', perhaps an early reference to another sport, cricket.[25] On his way to Bannockburn, the king patched up his quarrel with Richard Kellaw, bishop of Durham, whom he held as his enemy because the bishop had not supported himself and Gaveston in 1308, after Kellaw gave him gifts of 1,000 marks and a magnificent war horse.[26]

Despite Edward's lack of military ability and experience, he seems to have believed that all he needed to do was show up, and he would win. This was, to put it mildly, a huge miscalculation, and the subsequent Battle of Bannockburn has gone down in history as arguably the greatest English military defeat of all time. Overconfidence was the biggest problem, both for Edward and the men around him, and the later chronicler Geoffrey le Baker points out that never before had a noble army been swollen with such arrogance.[27] A Latin song written shortly after the battle describes the English knights as 'too showy and pompous'.[28]

Only three of Edward's earls accompanied him to Scotland. One was his brother-in-law Humphrey de Bohun, earl of Hereford, who had drawn closer to Edward since Gaveston's death; the second, his nephew Gilbert de Clare, earl of Gloucester; and the third his cousin Aymer de Valence, earl of Pembroke. The earls who did not attend said that, because Edward had not received the consent of parliament to lead an army to Scotland, they would not accompany him, 'lest it should happen that they infringed the Ordinances'.[29] Many Scotsmen fought for the English king, including young John Comyn, who had good reason to hate the man who had stabbed his father the Red Comyn to death in the Greyfriars church in 1306. David de Strathbogie, earl of Atholl, whose father John had been hanged by Edward I in November 1306 but who was loyal to Edward II, did not participate in the battle but attacked the Scottish stores at Cambuskenneth, and the earl of Angus and his brother fought for Edward.

Edward did not fight on the first day of the battle, Sunday 23 June 1314, a series of skirmishes which went the way of the Scots. The earls of Gloucester and Hereford, respectively constable of the army and constable of England, quarrelled over who should command the vanguard, which tellingly demonstrates Edward's lack of leadership skills and control of his own army.[30] Gloucester was humiliatingly unhorsed during a clash, Hereford's nephew Henry de Bohun was killed by Robert Bruce himself, who cleaved Bohun's head in with his battleaxe, and the advance party of Edward's army, led by Robert Clifford and Henry Beaumont, sustained heavy losses against the schiltrons of Thomas Randolph. Schiltrons were formations consisting of a few hundred men in concentric rings, kneeling by pikes facing outwards. The pikes were about fourteen–eighteen feet long, made of ash with a sharpened steel point, and positioned at the height of a horse's neck or chest. Schiltrons can be visualised as a forest of pikes sticking out in every direction, a kind of enormous and deadly hedgehog, and were extremely effective against knights charging at them on horseback.

Edward awoke early in his silken pavilion on the morning of 24 June, and his squires dressed him in hose (leggings), a shirt, a gambeson or aketon – a thickly padded jacket – and his chainmail. A wrought-iron great helm protected his head, and he carried a sword, a mace, perhaps a dagger, and a lance, couched under his arm. Sir Roger Northburgh acted as his shield-bearer. Edward mounted his war-horse, which had armour and padding to protect its face and chest, and was dressed in trappings – material embroidered with the royal arms of England, which covered most of the horse except its eyes, chest and lower legs. Riding in the last battalion of cavalry, the royal banner of three leopards flying above his head, Edward went out to face the Scots. The evening before, Edward had had a heated row with his nephew Gloucester, unjustly and unreasonably accusing him of treachery and deceit for his suggestion that they take a day's rest and allow the army to recuperate. Desperate to prove himself, crying out 'Today, it will be clear that I am neither a traitor nor a liar', and also keen to take precedence over the earl of Hereford, twenty-three-year-old Gloucester galloped full tilt towards the Scots without waiting for an order from Edward to advance, his retainers riding close behind him. They expected the Scots to break ranks and flee on seeing hundreds of heavily armed men and horses thundering towards them. They didn't, and Gloucester and his men hit one of the Scottish schiltrons full on. The young earl came off his horse and 'was pierced by many wounds and shamefully killed', having made the horrible mistake of forgetting to put on the surcoat which identified him as a great magnate; had the Scottish soldiers known who he was, they would have captured him to raise an enormous ransom.[31] Many of his men died too, as the rest of the vanguard, following closely behind, couldn't pull up in time, and crashed into Gloucester's men, pushing them onto the pikes. Robert, Lord Clifford was probably also killed during this first assault. The schiltrons advanced, and the English cavalry advanced towards them, but were unable to make headway against the deadly forest of stakes. Horses reared in fright and screamed in pain, throwing their riders onto the ground or the pikes, and the battlefield became a nightmare scene: the cavalry continued to press forward, those behind unable to see what was happening at the front, pushing the men in front into range of the lethal pikes. Dead bodies, of men and horses, began to pile up before the schiltrons; riderless horses ran around, adding to the terrible confusion. Within minutes, the battle had slipped beyond Edward's control.

Edward, showing great courage and foolhardiness, was right in the thick of the mêlée, attacking ferociously 'like a lioness deprived of her cubs'.[32] At one point, his horse was killed beneath him, and Scottish soldiers rushed forward to capture him. His shield-bearer Roger

Northburgh was captured, but the king managed to mount another horse. Again, Scottish soldiers pressed forward to try to capture him, grabbing hold of his horse's trappings. Edward 'struck out so vigorously behind him with his mace there was none whom he touched that he did not fell to the ground'.[33] After perhaps no more than an hour or two of dreadful fighting, with countless men and horses lying dead underfoot and the ground wet and slippery with blood and gore, the earl of Pembroke realised the battle was lost. He grabbed the reins of Edward's horse and dragged the king, protesting, off the field. Five hundred knights surrounded Edward, their only thought to protect him at all costs. The *Lanercost* chronicler, a monk and armchair general, says unfairly, 'To their perpetual shame they fled like miserable wretches,' but given that the battle was lost, there was nothing else they could do but ensure the king's safety.[34]

James Douglas pursued Edward and his large bodyguard a full 60 miles to Dunbar on the south-east coast. After a long, desperate gallop, with Douglas and his men picking off stragglers and so close behind it was said Edward and his knights had no time to stop and pass water, the king finally reached Dunbar Castle safely. His ally Patrick, earl of Dunbar, opened up the drawbridge for him.[35] Edward later granted one William Franceis an income of fifty marks annually in gratitude for the unspecified 'kind service he lately performed for the king in his presence at Dunbar'.[36] Earl Patrick commandeered a fishing boat, and Edward sailed down the coast, with a handful of attendants, to Berwick.[37] He was incredibly lucky to escape capture by Douglas, and vowed to found a Carmelite friary at Oxford to give thanks for his deliverance.[38]

Queen Isabella and several noblewomen, including Edward's sister Elizabeth, waited at Berwick for the glorious army to return, proclaiming its glorious victory. Instead, the king arrived not at the head of a victorious army, but in flight, forced to travel by fishing boat. His shock and humiliation must have been profound. If Isabella felt any shame over her husband's awful defeat, however, she kept it to herself, and lent him her own seal to replace his, so that government business could continue. She tended her husband's wounds herself, and even cleaned his armour.[39] Edward spent forty marks on new clothes for a small group of knights from Germany who had fought for him at Bannockburn and arrived at Berwick dressed, or disguised, as paupers.[40]

The terrible toll soon became clear. Over 500 knights and noblemen had been killed or captured, including the young Scotsman John Comyn, who had been so keen to avenge his father's murder at Bruce's hands, and thousands of common soldiers. Other men lying dead on the battlefield were Edward's steward Edmund Mauley, his former steward Miles Stapleton, and Giles Argentein, said to be the third-greatest knight in Christendom after the Holy Roman Emperor and Robert Bruce himself.[41]

Argentein had been captured and held prisoner on Rhodes in 1311 on his way to the Holy Land, and in October 1313 Edward sent letters to eleven people, including the Byzantine emperor Andronikus Palaeologus and Edward's cousin the Empress Eirene, asking them to procure Argentein's release, a major diplomatic effort which had the desired result.[42] Argentein, once he had made sure that Edward was safe, returned to the battlefield and was killed. His reckless courage earned him the approval of contemporaries: 'Those who fall in battle for their country are known to live in everlasting glory,' comments the *Vita*.[43] Edward's brother-in-law the earl of Hereford was captured after Bannockburn, as were the Scottish earl of Angus and Lord Berkeley. Roger Mortimer was also captured, though Bruce released him without ransom and sent him home with Edward's captured shield and great seal, for which he courteously demanded no payment.[44] Edward's vast baggage train, said, probably with great exaggeration, to have been worth £200,000, fell into Scottish hands – a great and welcome windfall.[45]

As well as losing his dignity and his numerous valuable possessions, Edward was now deprived of the influence of his nephew Gilbert de Clare, earl of Gloucester, loyal to him and also respected by the barons as the scion of an ancient noble family and grandson of the old king. Gloucester's death meant that his vast lands and wealth would ultimately pass to ambitious and unscrupulous men. Robert Bruce treated Gloucester's body with considerable honour and respect: he personally kept an overnight vigil over the body, and the following day sent it back to England with full military honours, at his own expense. The men were second cousins – Bruce's grandmother was a de Clare – and were married to sisters, Elizabeth and Maud de Burgh. The body of Robert Clifford, the next highest-ranking Englishman to die in the battle, was also sent back to England with no payment demanded.[46]

Edward II has been condemned for military incompetence since 1314, and also for cowardice because he left the field. Yet remaining behind would not have won the battle and would only have resulted in his being captured, which would have been catastrophic. The ransom demanded by Bruce would have been massive, and Edward's giving up all claims to English overlordship of Scotland a basic requirement of release. His death would have brought his nineteen-month-old son to the throne, which meant a regency of many years standing until the boy was old enough to rule in his own right – and as later events were to prove, the people who replaced Edward in power were not one whit more competent than he was. Nor is it fair to condemn Edward for physical cowardice, as some writers have; he was no general, but he fought bravely, even recklessly, with disregard for the danger to his life.[47]

As disastrous as Edward's defeat at Bannockburn was, his capture or death would have been far worse. However, for the king of England, galloping away in ignominious flight from a battle he had fully expected to win, the realisation that he had at least spared his kingdom a crippling ransom or the perils of a long regency was no consolation whatsoever. And the humiliation was not yet over. In August 1314, Edward Bruce and James Douglas 'devastated almost all Northumberland with fire', plundering as far south as Swaledale in Yorkshire, burning Cumberland towns on their return, and carrying off livestock and crops.[48] Edward announced in late September that he had received a letter from Robert Bruce, in which the king of Scots declared that 'the one thing in the world he [Bruce] desires most is to have complete accord and friendship with us', and on 6 October he commissioned five men to negotiate a truce with Bruce.[49] He had little other choice.

Edward arrived in York on 17 July, and parliament opened there on 9 September. The king left the city on 7 September and rode the 17 miles to the village of Oulston, empowering three men to open parliament in his absence. He claimed that he was 'unable to be present on account of some important and special business' concerning himself, though what urgently required his attention in a small village is unclear, and this was perhaps an attempt on Edward's part to avoid facing his enemies.[50] If so, he evidently realised he could hardly avoid them for long, as he returned to York on 10 September. The earls of Lancaster and Warwick, who had refused to fight for Edward in Scotland, gloated over his failure, choosing to see the king's defeat as a consequence of his failure to abide by the Ordinances. Lancaster had raised an army at his stronghold of Pontefract in case Edward returned triumphant from Scotland and used the chance to avenge Piers Gaveston's death. Now, however, the army was used against Edward himself, as a threat to force the king to accept Lancaster as de facto ruler of England. For the next few years, Edward would be little more than a puppet-king. In no position to defend himself, he sat at parliament, forced to hear how his expenses would be reduced drastically to a mere ten pounds a day, and that his household would be purged and replaced by men sympathetic to Lancaster.[51] Queen Isabella, faithfully supporting her husband, attended parliament at his side. She had helped her husband to the best of her ability since Gaveston's death, and even her own uncle Lancaster came to regard her as an enemy. He ordered her income to be reduced, although Edward did his best to help her with grants from his own limited resources.[52]

Lancaster and Warwick were not the only ones to interpret the defeat at Bannockburn as evidence that God was showing his disfavour with Edward. A few weeks after the battle, a member of Edward's own household was arrested for speaking 'irreverent and indecent words' against the king: a messenger called Robert de Newington commented that nobody could expect the king to win a battle when he spent all his time idling, digging and ditching when he should have been hearing

Mass.[53] (How listening to Mass would have helped Edward win the battle was not explained.) Edward's reaction is unrecorded, and he was, in fact, sincerely and genuinely pious. Other men expressed their displeasure with Edward: in January 1315 a London goldsmith was accused of saying 'certain evil and shameful things about the king', and in December that year a clerk of Oxford said in public that Edward was not his father's son – perhaps only meaning that he was very different from Edward I, which was true.[54]

To please his sister Elizabeth, Edward arranged for the release of all his Scottish prisoners in exchange for his brother-in-law Hereford. The Scottish prisoners in England included Robert Bruce's wife Elizabeth de Burgh, his sisters Mary and Christina, his daughter Marjorie, and the bishops of Glasgow and St Andrews.[55] Another Scot in England was Bruce's young nephew Donald, earl of Mar, imprisoned as a child at Bristol Castle in 1306 but a member of Edward's household since around 1309, who received fifteen pence a day in wages for serving his uncle's enemy.[56] Mar set off to return to Scotland, the homeland he hadn't seen for eight years, got as far north as Newcastle, changed his mind, and went back to Edward.[57] For many years, Mar was to be a close friend and supporter of the king.

In December 1314, Edward assigned dower to the earl of Gloucester's widow Maud, the customary third of his nephew's lands.[58] Maud was claiming to be pregnant, which must have delighted Edward, as the enormous de Clare revenues would pour annually into his own coffers until the child turned twenty-one. People considerably less delighted at Maud's pregnancy were Gloucester's three sisters – Eleanor, Margaret and Elizabeth – and Eleanor's husband Hugh Despenser, as if Gloucester had died childless, the sisters would have divided his lands between them. It would later become apparent, however, that the pregnancy was not all it would seem.

Philip IV of France died in a hunting accident on 29 November 1314. Edward had heard of his father-in-law's death by 15 December, when he ordered the archbishops of Canterbury and York, all the bishops and twenty-eight abbots to 'celebrate exequies' for him.[59] Philip was only forty-six in 1314, and had three sons aged between twenty and twenty-five. No one could have guessed that within fourteen years all of them would be dead with no male heirs, and that the great Capetian dynasty would come to an end and the throne of France pass to Philip IV's nephew Philip de Valois. Queen Isabella's eldest brother the king of Navarre, known as *le Hutin*, the Stubborn or Quarrelsome, succeeded as Louis X, which meant that Edward owed homage to the new king for his French lands. As Louis reigned for little more than eighteen months, though, he managed to avoid the unpleasant duty of kneeling to his brother-in-law.

Edward and Isabella were at Langley on 6 December 1314, the feast day of St Nicholas, and the king gave two pounds to Robert Tyeis, who officiated as boy-bishop in his chapel. The royal couple spent the festive season at Windsor, where Edward played at 'tables' on Christmas Eve with members of his entourage.[60] He was a great fan of 'cross and pile', the fourteenth-century equivalent of heads and tails, and frequently borrowed money from his servants to play it, returning five shillings to his barber Henry on one occasion and eight pence to his usher Peter Bernard 'which he lent to the lord king and which he lost at cross and pile' on another.[61] Edward was at a low ebb, personally and politically, in late 1314, and his thoughts turned to his lost love, Piers Gaveston. On 27 December, he gave the chancellor and scholars of Oxford University twenty pounds to pray for Gaveston's soul, and a week later finally buried his friend, two and a half years after his death, at the Dominican priory he had founded at Langley in 1308.[62] Since June 1312, Edward had paid two custodians to watch over the body, and they lived very well at his expense; for a mere twenty-eight days in December 1314, he paid them fifteen pounds.[63] Edward had already demonstrated his concern for Gaveston's remains, spending, for example, £144 and fifteen shillings between 8 July 1312 and 7 July 1313, the sixth year of his reign. This included payment for 5,000 lbs of wax for candles to burn around the embalmed body.[64]

Gaveston's excommunication must have been lifted in order for him to be buried in consecrated ground, though when that occurred is uncertain; perhaps the visit of his elder brother Arnaud-Guilhem de Marsan to Avignon in the autumn of 1312 marks the occasion.[65] This means that Edward had, rather morbidly, kept Gaveston's body above ground for over two years when he could have had it buried, perhaps because he couldn't bear the thought of this final farewell to his friend, or because he had sworn 'first to avenge Piers, and then consign his body to the grave'.[66] Edward's weak position in late 1314 and early 1315, however, persuaded him to postpone his revenge for a time. He had not forgotten. It would just have to wait for a while. The funeral was a deeply emotional occasion for Edward, and he spent the vast sum of £300 on three cloths of gold to dress Gaveston's body, also paying £15 for food and £64 for twenty-three tuns of wine, around 22,000 litres.[67] Edward was deeply concerned with the well-being of Gaveston's soul and bodily remains: at the time of the funeral, he ordered a hundred Dominican friars to say Masses for Gaveston and his ancestors; between October 1315 and October 1316 he ordered every Augustinian house in England and Ireland to celebrate a daily mass for Gaveston's soul; in 1319 he paid for a Turkish cloth to be placed over the tomb, which was replaced later by gold cloth; in 1324 he sent his confessor to Langley to mark the anniversary of Gaveston's death, and in 1325 he sent a man there with 100 shillings to give to each friar, so they would remember Piers Gaveston. In 1326, the last year of his reign, he made provision for numerous clerks at numerous houses to pray for the soul of his lost love.[68] Edward did not forget those he loved. Sadly, Gaveston's tomb was lost at the Dissolution, though the tomb of Edward's grandson Edmund, duke of York, buried in the same priory in 1402, still survives. The earl of Hereford attended Gaveston's funeral, rather bravely considering he had been one of the men who condemned him to death, and so did Queen Isabella, the earl of Pembroke, Hugh Despenser the Elder and his son Hugh Despenser, Henry Beaumont, Bartholomew Badlesmere, the mayor of London, the archbishop of Canterbury, four bishops, fourteen abbots, fifty knights, large numbers of Dominican friars, and William Inge, the royal justice alleged, somewhat improbably, to have passed judgement on Gaveston.[69] Another attendee was Edward's fourteen-year-old half-brother Thomas of Brotherton, displaced as heir to the throne by Edward of Windsor, but created earl of Norfolk a month after his nephew's birth.[70]

As though the burial of Piers Gaveston had drawn a line under his past, another man, Roger Damory, came to Edward's attention. Damory, a knight of Oxfordshire, had previously been a member of the earl of Gloucester's retinue, and fought bravely at Bannockburn, which was perhaps the first time Edward noticed him. The *Vita* calls Damory a 'poor and needy knight', which seems accurate; he was a younger son with little chance of inheriting his father's lands.[71] In early 1315, Edward ordered Damory to stay at court with him, though it would take some time for the knight to really work his way into the king's affections.[72]

On 20 April 1315, Edward invited the archbishop of Canterbury and most of the nobility to a great banquet at Westminster Hall, which was damaged by a fire shortly afterwards.[73] This would be the last great feast anyone would enjoy for quite some time. Northern Europe suffered bizarre weather in the mid-1310s, and it rained heavily and constantly for much of the period from 1314 to 1316. In the flooding caused by this torrential rain, crops rotted away and livestock drowned in the waterlogged fields, and the tragic result was the Great Famine, which is estimated to have killed at least five per cent, and perhaps more, of the population of England. The rest of northern Europe suffered a similar death toll. The *Vita*, unaware that it was a pan-European disaster, knew exactly where to apportion blame: on the English themselves, who 'excel other nations in three qualities, in pride, in craft, and in perjury ... All this comes from the wickedness of the inhabitants'. He also blamed the fact that Saturn had been in the ascendant for three years, but now that Jupiter was about to succeed, the rain would cease and the fields be filled with abundance.[74]

In March and April 1315, Edward did his best to mitigate his subjects' misery by ordering the price of basic foodstuffs to be regulated. According to the *Anonimalle*, Edward passed these regulations with the advice of his privy council and without the consent of the magnates, and the chronicler rather unreasonably calls Edward's council 'feeble' and the regulations 'foolish', claiming that the king and his advisors were trying to 'deceive the common people'.[75] Among the foodstuffs regulated were: 'fat sheep', which should cost no more than twenty pence if unshorn and fourteen pence if shorn; a maximum of sixteen shillings for an ox not fed with corn, or twenty-four shillings if fed with corn and fattened; twelve shillings for a live fat cow; one and a half pence for a fat chicken; one pence for twenty-four eggs. The price regulations could not, however, be maintained for long; Edward's attempts to improve the situation resulted only in traders refusing to sell what few goods they had at an artificially low price.[76] *Anonimalle* and *Lanercost* state that a quarter of wheat cost forty shillings or more, six or eight times the normal price, and *Anonimalle* that 'two little onions' cost a penny, a few hours' wages for most people.[77] Such bread as was available could not satisfy hunger, as the grain was soaked from the endless rain and had to be dried in ovens before it was cooked, and contained minimal nutrients.[78]

When Edward stayed at St Albans Abbey from 10 to 12 August 1315, even he had difficulties buying bread for himself and his household.[79] Still, the king was in a far better position than the majority of his subjects: in Northumbria, already weakened and despoiled by Scottish raids, 'dogs and horses and other unclean things were eaten', and *Trokelowe* says that horse meat was precious and that 'fat dogs' were stolen.[80] And for others, imminent starvation drove them to far worse horrors than eating pets. Rumours of cannibalism were rife, and *Trokelowe* even claims, one hopes with great exaggeration, that some people resorted to eating children.[81] After the famine came a 'severe pestilence' which claimed many more victims. Dead bodies were so numerous they could hardly be buried.[82]

Although most people were too concerned with their own suffering to pay much notice, more bad news reached England. Robert Bruce's brother Edward invaded Ireland in late May 1315, and in May 1316 was crowned high king of Ireland at Dundalk, having taken control of almost the entire country except Dublin and a few castles.[83] The kings of England had been lords of Ireland for a century and a half: a papal bull issued in 1155 by Adrian IV, the only English pope in history, had authorised Edward's great-great-grandfather Henry II to take possession of the country, and granted him and his descendants the right to the title 'lord of Ireland'. In 1185, Henry II sent his teenage son, Edward's great-grandfather John, to govern the parts of the country under English control. Fortunately for Edward II in 1315, Roger Mortimer had returned to Ireland, where he spent much of his career, after the debacle of Bannockburn, and the king therefore had an ally in the country he could trust. Unfortunately, even Roger Mortimer's undoubted military ability was not sufficient to avoid a catastrophic defeat at the hands of Edward Bruce at the Battle of Kells in December 1315, and almost his entire army was annihilated.[84] Practically the only bright spot in the wet, hungry, desperate summer of 1315 was one of Robert Bruce's rare failures: he laid siege to the town of Carlisle for ten days, but failed to take it, thanks to the stout defence of Andrew Harclay, sheriff of Cumberland. The Scots 'marched off in confusion to their own country' on 1 August.[85] And in January 1316, Bruce failed in his second attempt to seize the important port of Berwick-on-Tweed. He and a large force launched a simultaneous attack by land and sea at night, by moonlight, but failed to capture the port, and James Douglas, Edward's pursuer after Bannockburn, barely escaped capture.[86]

In the summer of 1315, Maud de Clare, dowager countess of Gloucester, was still claiming to be pregnant, despite the length of time that had passed since her husband fell at Bannockburn. Hugh Despenser (the Younger), understandably, did not believe in the pregnancy. As the husband of the earl of Gloucester's eldest sister Eleanor, Despenser was in line for a big handout of lands, and he wanted them badly. The young man – he was about twenty-seven – gave warning of his hot-headed and impetuous behaviour when he seized Tonbridge Castle in Kent, which had belonged to the earl of Gloucester, in May 1315. Precisely what he was hoping to achieve by this is not clear, but he had to give it back, though he avoided a fine over the strange episode.[87] Five years in the future, Edward would become utterly infatuated with Hugh Despenser and fall over himself to give him any lands he wanted, once again bringing his country to civil war over his passion for a favourite. Although *Lanercost* claims that Despenser became 'the king of England's right eye' soon after the death of Piers Gaveston, Edward's behaviour here, by refusing to partition the de Clare lands, proves conclusively that Despenser was not yet in his favour.

Hugh Despenser's maternal uncle Guy Beauchamp, earl of Warwick, died on 12 August 1315 at the age of about forty-three, leaving his eighteen-month-old son, named Thomas after the earl of Lancaster, as his heir. Many decades later, the chronicler Thomas Walsingham reported a rumour that friends of Edward II poisoned Warwick in revenge for Piers Gaveston's death.[88] This is most unlikely to be true, though doubtless Edward didn't mourn much for him. Warwick's death left the earl of Lancaster politically isolated, and it became ever clearer to all that he had no more aptitude than Edward at ruling the country. In fact, the situation was becoming dire. Lancaster and Edward found it extremely difficult to work together, but Lancaster had no means of deposing the king, and Edward was not yet strong enough to overthrow his cousin. They and their respective households spitefully did their best to thwart each other, and their rivalry left England, in effect, ungoverned at a time when natural disaster called out for strong leadership.[89]

Edward spent most of 1315 with Queen Isabella, and from 10 to 12

June, they went to Canterbury on pilgrimage; both of them revered St Thomas Becket. On the 14th, Edward gave a pound to sailors named Thomas Springet, William Kempe and Edmund of Greenwich 'for their labour in taking a whale, lately caught near London Bridge'.[90] The *Scalacronica* says that Edward 'tarried in the south, where he amused himself with ships, among mariners, and in other irregular occupation unworthy of his station'.[91] That August, Edward proclaimed that the magnates of the realm should limit the number of courses served at their tables, on account of the 'excessive and abundant portions of food' they ate while many of their countrymen starved. The proclamation also limited the number of minstrels permitted to go to the houses of great lords to three or four a day, and they were not to go to the houses of 'smaller people' at all – 'unless requested to do so', it added helpfully.[92] Edward's enormous household of a few hundred people necessitated lavish expenditure on food, and the accounts for his ninth regnal year, 8 July 1315 to 7 July 1316, show that he spent £887 on food and £1,160 on wine.[93]

In the autumn of 1315, Edward went on holiday to the Fens with 'a great concourse of common people', despite the awful weather that year (it rained from May until October).[94] Centuries ahead of his time in recognising the pleasures of taking holidays by water, he spent a congenial month from mid-September to mid-October rowing and swimming at King's Lynn in Norfolk and at Fen Ditton and Impington near Cambridge, though he fell into the water and nearly drowned 'while rowing about on various lakes' one day, and his companions had to haul him out. Perhaps this was cosmic revenge for the occasion in February 1303 when eighteen-year-old Edward had to pay his fool Robert Bussard four shillings' compensation for playing a trick on him while they were swimming in the Thames at Windsor, and hurting him.[95] Edward was a great fan of water: Archbishop Walter Reynolds once returned to him a belt he had lost in the Thames, which probably means he was again swimming in the river.[96] While in the Fens, on 6 October 1315, Edward made a quick trip to Walsingham without his household to visit the shrine of Our Lady there.[97]

The author of the *Flores*, Edward's most vicious critic, sneered at the king's holiday, saying sarcastically that Edward went to the Fens to 'refresh his soul with many waters', a perfectly normal thing to do in later centuries but very strange to the fourteenth-century mind. No less a person than the pope condemned the king's amusements as 'childish frivolities' a few months later, and most of Edward's contemporaries must have found the concept of the king of England willingly spending time with a group of lowborn people profoundly shocking, a violation of the natural order.[98] In its haste to ridicule Edward, the *Flores* got the date of his holiday wrong and placed it at Christmas and New Year, but it is evident from Edward's itinerary that he was in the Fens in autumn, not December and January.[99] Winters of the era were often harsh: the *French Chronicle of London* says that in 1308/09 people walked across the frozen Thames from London to Southwark, and the city annalist vividly describes the Great Frost of the following year: 'There was such cold and such masses and piles of ice on the Thames and everywhere else that the poor were overcome by excessive cold,' adding that the river froze so solidly bonfires could be lit on it.[100] According to the *Flores*, the summer of 1305 saw burning heat, drought and a subsequent epidemic of smallpox, which afflicted young and old, rich and poor. This unusually hot summer was followed by an extremely cold winter, with snow and ice lying on the ground from 15 December 1305 to 27 January 1306 and again from 13 February to 13 April, and the winters of 1312/13, 1313/14, 1316/17 and 1321/22 were also bitterly cold, with much snow and frost.[101]

After his holiday, Edward spent most of the next few months at the royal hunting lodge at Clipstone in Nottinghamshire with Queen Isabella, and probably sometime in November they conceived their second son John of Eltham, who was born on 15 August 1316. As with their elder son Edward of Windsor, there is no doubt that they were together at the right time to conceive John, and no reason at all to think that anyone other than Edward II was John's father. While at Clipstone, Edward paid twenty marks to the London goldsmith Roger Frowyk for making a gold crown for him, with forty marks still owing, and gave thirty-five shillings to seventy Dominicans for 'performing divine service at the anniversary of the lady the queen, mother of the present lord the king'.[102] 28 November 1315 marked the twenty-fifth anniversary of the death of Eleanor of Castile, the mother Edward had barely known. Edward's parents were much on his mind in the early winter of 1315: he gave five pounds to a Nicholas Percy for compiling a book about the life and times of his father Edward I for him.[103] While at Clipstone, Edward sent his friend Sir William Montacute, with three other knights and thirty-six squires, to Barnard Castle in County Durham to rescue Maud, widow of Robert Clifford killed at Bannockburn. The unfortunate lady had been abducted by John le Ireys ('the Irishman'), and shortly afterwards married Sir Robert Welle, one of her rescuers.[104]

It was probably in late 1315 that Roger Damory, the impecunious knight who fought bravely at Bannockburn, began to gain a firmer hold on the king's affections. A series of grants to Damory, beginning in early December 1315 and continuing until 1317, track Edward's growing feelings for him.[105] It is possible to exaggerate the significance of this; the grants were by no means excessive, and in this part of his reign, Edward was for once using his powers of patronage sensibly and fairly. However, it would become clear a little later that Damory, a mere household knight, had gained far greater influence over the king than his rank and position warranted, and that once more, Edward was allowing his personal feelings to dictate his policy. And two other men grew close to Edward around this time, or perhaps the following year. One was Hugh Audley, who had joined Edward as a household knight at the time that Piers Gaveston went into his third exile, and who was a close relative of Roger Mortimer. The other was William Montacute, from an old noble family, whose father Simon had been an associate of Edward I. Whether these three men were Edward's friends or something more cannot be known, but whatever the nature of their relationships with the king, the men described by the *Flores* as 'worse than Piers' had begun their rise to power and influence, and would in time do their best to wreck any chances of peace between the king and the earl of Lancaster and to disrupt the fragile stability of the middle years of Edward II's reign.[106]

7

Conflicts, Marriages and an Abduction

Parliament opened at Lincoln on 27 January 1316, and Edward announced through his spokesman William Inge that he wished proceedings to pass as speedily as possible, to ease the burden placed on the city by the presence of so many people demanding food. Unfortunately, his cousin the earl of Lancaster thwarted his wish, arriving in Lincoln on 10 February and finally deigning to attend parliament on the 12th, more than two weeks late. To Edward's great annoyance, Lancaster was appointed his chief counsellor, finally gaining an official position despite having dominated the government for well over a year.[1] However, he thereafter took little part in government, preferring to stay at his favourite residence of Pontefract, where Edward and his council were forced to communicate and negotiate with him as though he were an independent potentate, or another king.[2]

During the parliament, the king's nephew-in-law Hugh Despenser gave more proof of his recklessness and his potential for violence by attacking a baron named John Ros in Lincoln Cathedral. Angry that Ros had tried to arrest Ingelram Berenger, one of his father's knights, Despenser repeatedly punched him in the face until he drew blood, and 'inflicted other outrages on him', forcing Ros to draw his sword in self-defence. Despenser claimed, with amusing implausibility, that he had merely stretched out his hand to defend himself and accidentally hit Ros in the face with his fist, after Ros 'heap[ed] outrageous insults on the same Hugh [and] taunted him with insolent words', and rushed at him with a knife. Despenser was fined the massive sum of £10,000, which he never paid, and Edward pardoned him for the assault four years later.[3]

Despenser, desperate for his wife Eleanor's share of her brother the earl of Gloucester's inheritance, once more raised the subject of the dowager countess's supposed pregnancy. He had been claiming for a few months – correctly, of course – that it was impossible for Maud de Clare to be pregnant by her husband, who had died at Bannockburn in June

1314. Two royal justices told Despenser that the Countess Maud 'at the due time according to the course of nature, felt a living boy ... and that although the time for the birth of that child, which nature allows to be delayed and obstructed for various reasons, is still delayed, this ought not to prejudice the aforesaid pregnancy'. The justices reprimanded Despenser and Eleanor for failing to apply to Chancery for a writ to have the countess's belly inspected, and as they had not observed due process, their negligence would redound to their own shame and prejudice. This took place a full twenty months after Gloucester's death; the legal system at its finest.

The king must have been delighted to learn that Queen Isabella was expecting another child, and on 22 February asked the dean and chapter of the church of St Mary in Lincoln to 'celebrate divine service daily for the good estate of the king and Queen Isabella and Edward their first-born son'.[4] The reference to 'their first-born son' probably indicates that Edward knew of Isabella's pregnancy by then. On 27 March, he gave twenty pounds to John Fleg, horse dealer of London, for a bay horse 'to carry the litter of the lady the queen' during her pregnancy.[5] He also paid the Lucca banking firm the Ballardi almost four pounds for pieces of silk and gold tissue, and flame-coloured silk, to make cushions for Isabella's carriage so that she and her ladies could travel in greater comfort.[6] The news of their child was a glimmer of happiness in an otherwise depressing world. The terrible famine still gripped England, and even in a hand-to-mouth economy where food shortages were common, nothing as bad as this had ever been seen before: 'Such a mortality of men in England and Scotland through famine and pestilence as had not been heard of in our time,' says *Lanercost*.[7] The unsuccessful regulations concerning the price of foodstuffs were abolished at Lincoln.

And more bad news came from South Wales. The earl of Gloucester had been lord of Glamorgan, and after his death, royal administrators ruled the lordship on Edward's behalf. One of them, Payn Turberville, was hated for his arrogance and tyranny. The famine raged as hard in South Wales as anywhere else, and the inhabitants, starving, beaten and extorted of money by Turberville, suffered terribly. Llywelyn Bren, lord of Senghenydd and Meisgyn, decided he had had enough. The earl of Gloucester had thought highly of Llywelyn and granted him high office, but Payn Turberville removed his authority and treated him with contempt, which led a furious Llywelyn to tell a room full of his supporters that 'the day will come when I will put an end to the insolence of Payn and give him as good as he gives me'. Turberville promptly denounced him to Edward for sedition, and the king summoned Llywelyn to court to explain himself. Llywelyn went cautiously, not sure of the reception he would get from the unpredictable Edward, intending to gloss over his insults to Turberville if he possibly could and, more importantly, to inform the king of his Welsh subjects' suffering. His worst fears came true: Edward refused to meet him, and promised that if Bren had truly uttered such things against a royal official, he would be hanged. He ordered Bren to appear at the Lincoln parliament to defend his actions.[8]

Bren had no intention of going to Lincoln when it would probably result in his swinging at the end of a rope. He took the only other option open to him and prepared for war, and on 26 January 1316 attacked the great stronghold of Caerphilly, which had been built by the earl of Gloucester's father in the 1270s. The news took a few days to travel the more than 200 miles from Caerphilly to Lincoln, and when Edward finally heard on 7 February, he immediately sent men to capture Bren and nip his rebellion in the bud, exclaiming, 'Go quickly, and pursue this traitor, lest from delay worse befall us and all Wales rise against us.'[9]

Bren was quickly overcome by the force sent by the king and submitted to the earl of Hereford, who sent him to Edward. Hereford, impressed with Bren's bearing and courage, asked the king to show him leniency, and Edward, perhaps regretting his earlier outburst, sent Bren, his wife, his five sons, his adopted son, and five others 'under safe custody at the king's expense' to the Tower. They were granted three pence a day for their maintenance (Bren and his wife) or two pence (the others).[10] By June 1317, only Bren and two of his sons are mentioned as prisoners in the Tower, the others presumably having been released.[11] The campaign against Llywelyn Bren was of short duration, but expensive; William Montacute alone took 150 men-at-arms and 2,000 footmen, at Edward's expense, and the royal treasury was still in a parlous state.[12] Trouble also broke out in North Wales, where Edward's chamberlain John Charlton and his wife Hawise Gadarn had a long-running feud with her uncle Gruffydd de la Pole over the lordship of Powys. In March 1316, Edward told Chancery, 'If this riot be not hastily quenched much greater evil may come in other parts of Wales,' and sent his steward John Cromwell to settle the row.[13] The last thing he wanted was a widespread uprising in the land of his birth, which, fortunately, never happened. On 24 April, the day before his thirty-second birthday, Edward asked the Dominicans of Toulouse to pray for him, perhaps in the belief that he and his realm needed all the intervention he could get.[14] It was fairly common for Edward to request the prayers of Dominicans in other countries for himself and his family: a year later, he asked the chapter of Pamplona to say prayers 'for the good estate' of himself, Queen Isabella and their children, and in later years, made the same request of the Dominicans of Marseilles, Paris, Rouen, Citeaux, Florence, Venice, Barcelona and Vienna.[15] Edward also gave twenty pounds to the Dominicans of Pamplona to pay for three days' entertainment, one day for himself, one for Isabella, and one for their son Edward.[16] The conflict with Scotland dragged on in the summer of 1316; the Scots invaded England as far south as Richmond in Yorkshire and the Furness peninsula in Lancashire, which they burnt and plundered.[17]

That spring, Edward received the sad news that his thirty-three-year-old sister Elizabeth, countess of Hereford, had died in childbirth on 5 May, and that her daughter Isabel, her tenth child, had also died. Elizabeth was only twenty months Edward's senior, and they had been close in childhood.[18] Edward got on well with his sisters, as he had with his stepmother Marguerite before she opposed Piers Gaveston, and there is no reason to think that he did not like women or enjoy their company. In 1305, when his father banished him from his presence, drastically reduced his income and took away most of his household, Edward's sisters came to his rescue. Joan of Acre – mother of the de Clare siblings, and twelve years Edward's senior – invited him to stay with her and lent him her seal so that he could continue to order goods, and Mary also invited him to stay. Elizabeth had previously been married to Count John I of Holland, but he died childless in November 1299, at the age of only fifteen. Edward spent most of the rest of Elizabeth's life chasing up the dower to which she was entitled, including the town of Dordrecht, from John's cousin and successor John II and John II's son William III, counts of Hainault and Holland.[19]

Of Edward's eleven or more sisters, only two, Margaret and Mary, remained alive. Margaret, the widowed duchess of Brabant, was nine years older than Edward and forty-one in 1316. She is the most obscure of his sisters who survived into adulthood, and seems never to have visited England after 1308, when she attended her brother's coronation. The other sister, Mary, five years Edward's senior, was a nun with no vocation. She had a private room, a luxurious bed, servants and hunting dogs at Amesbury Priory, Edward paid her gambling debts and sent her expensive gifts, and she often visited his court. Sometime in 1316, he spent over twenty-six pounds on fifteen pieces of tapestry for Mary to take back to Amesbury after one of her many visits to him, and the two were clearly deeply fond of each other.[20] Edward's only other remaining siblings were his two young half-brothers. The elder, Thomas, earl of Norfolk, was fifteen in early 1316, and would grow up to be a man whose achievements fell some way short of modest. Edmund was only fourteen months younger than his brother, but more than seventeen years younger than Edward. He still had no title, but Edward granted him lands, castles and manors for his sustenance.[21]

On 17 May 1316, Edward asked his brother-in-law Louis X of France and Navarre to strive to continue their friendly relationship. He sent another letter in the same vein to Louis's wife Clemence of Hungary, whom his clerk wrongly addressed as 'Queen Elizabeth'.[22] Louis died less than three weeks later on 5 June at the age of only twenty-six, supposedly from drinking chilled wine after a vigorous game of *jeu de paume*, an early form of tennis. He had married Clemence on 19 August 1315, five days after the death, in decidedly suspicious circumstances, of his adulterous first wife Marguerite of Burgundy. Louis left Clemence pregnant, and she gave birth on 15 November 1316 to a son who became king of France as soon as he took his first breath: John I, the Posthumous. The baby king died only five days later, and Queen Isabella's second brother the count of Poitiers succeeded as Philip V. Philip and Edward seem to have been on reasonably good terms, on a personal level at least, if not as kings: in 1316, the French king sent his brother-in-law bunches of new grapes, and a year later, a box of rose sugar.[23] Edward gave a generous gift of twenty marks on 7 August 1316 to the messenger who brought him the news that Philip's wife Joan of Burgundy had borne a son, Louis, on 24 June.[24] The boy lived for little more than six months, and Philip was, like his brothers, destined to die with no surviving son.

Edward spent most of June and July 1316 at Westminster, and on 23 July, he and a very pregnant Isabella travelled to Eltham Palace in Kent, which he had granted her in 1311. Three days later, he left her there and headed north, for a campaign against the Scots which he later cancelled. On his way from Kent to York, Edward touched and blessed 135 people suffering from scrofula, or the 'king's evil', and in the period between mid-August and the end of November performed the same service for another seventy-nine.[25] Edward blessed fewer people with scrofula than his father had; Edward I touched almost 1,000 sick in 1299/1300, for example.[26] Edward II did, however, once give eighty pence to a Maud of Newark, who had come to court seeking a cure from him.[27] He arrived in York on 16 August, accompanied by his niece Margaret Gaveston, and stayed in the convent of the Franciscans (Greyfriars, or Friars Minor) near the River Ouse. He stayed there for five weeks and gave the Franciscans ten pounds for the expenses of himself and his household, a sum which only covered a fraction of them.[28] Sometime in August he met his cousin the earl of Lancaster in York, and the two men had a furious row, probably because of Edward's ongoing and ever-increasing reluctance to accept the Ordinances of 1311, to which Lancaster was dedicated.[29]

On 7 August 1316, the cardinals at Avignon finally chose a new pope, after a delay of more than two years: Jacques Duèse, cardinal-bishop of Porto and a Gascon as Clement V had also been, who chose the name John XXII. Edward sent John gifts worth £1,604, including a cope 'embroidered and studded with large white pearls', several golden ewers, thirteen golden salt cellars, numerous golden dishes and bowls, a golden basin and a golden chalice. He also paid £300 for an incense boat, a ewer and a 'gold buckle set with diverse pearls and other precious stones' to be sent in Queen Isabella's name, and 100 marks for another cope embroidered by Roesia, wife of London merchant John de Bureford, also sent in the queen's name.[30] The gifts were intended, at least in part, as a bribe to encourage the new pope to treat Edward favourably in his disputes with Scotland. Around this time, Edward demonstrated his great generosity by giving a gift of £500 to Isabella's former nurse Theophania de Saint Pierre, lady of Brignancourt.[31]

Isabella, now twenty or twenty-one, gave birth to their second son on 15 August 1316, thus ensuring that Edward now had the proverbial heir and spare. It was fairly conventional at the time for a second son to be named after his maternal grandfather, Philip in this case, but the name John was chosen, probably in honour of John XXII.[32] Edward gave £100 to Isabella's steward who rode the 230 miles from Eltham to York to bring him the happy news, and *Trokelowe* comments on his joy at the birth of his son.[33] He had heard the news by 24 August, on which date he asked the Dominicans of York to say prayers for himself, Isabella, their son Edward of Windsor, 'and John of Eltham our youngest son, especially on account of John'.[34] Edward had a piece of Turkey cloth and a piece of cloth of gold delivered to Eltham to cover the font in the chapel during John's baptism, and ordered Isabella's tailor to make her a robe from five pieces of white velvet for her churching ceremony.

At the end of July, Isabella sent her messenger Godyn Hautayn with letters to the bishop of Norwich and her uncle the earl of Lancaster, asking them to stand sponsor to her soon-to-be-born child, but Lancaster failed to show up for the ceremony, a gross insult.[35] This is probably because the already tense relationship between Edward and Lancaster had deteriorated still further, and the *Flores* claims that Edward armed himself against his cousin.[36] Whether that is true or not, Edward was concerned enough about Lancaster's hostility to summon Isabella to him in York with all speed, fearing for her safety. The queen travelled very fast: on 22 September she was at Buntingford in Hertfordshire, 175 miles from York, and must have been reunited with Edward soon after the 27th, as on that date, the king paid her messenger a pound for informing him of the queen's imminent arrival.[37] It is possible that Edward took a malicious pleasure in the fact that he now had two healthy sons, while his overweening cousin Lancaster, in his late thirties, had no legitimate children and was not likely to have any. He and his wife Alice de Lacy detested each other and lived apart, while Lancaster 'defouled a great multitude of women and of noble wenches' and fathered at least two illegitimate sons.[38]

The king and queen spent most of October and November 1316 in and around York, and the king's minstrel 'King' Robert came to him for help, evidently because he was ill: Edward gave him a gift of seventy shillings, and another one of forty shillings a few months later, to cover his expenses.[39] On 1 November, the king gave five pounds to a violist named Robert Daverouns, sent to him by his second cousin Philip, king of Albania, prince of Achaea and Taranto, despot of

Epirus and titular emperor of Constantinople.[40] Edward also made some significant appointments: his friend William Montacute became steward of his household, replacing John Cromwell.[41] Roger Mortimer became lieutenant of Ireland, the position formerly held by Piers Gaveston, while his uncle Roger Mortimer of Chirk was reappointed justiciar of North Wales.[42] And the earl of Arundel, who had drawn closer to Edward since Gaveston's death – although he hadn't fought at Bannockburn – became captain of the king's forces between the River Trent and the Scottish town of Roxburgh.[43] Edmund Fitzalan, earl of Arundel, was almost exactly a year younger than the king, and half-Italian through his mother Alesia, daughter of Tomasso I, marquis of Saluzzo. His great-grandmother Beatrice of Savoy had been queen of Sicily, and his uncle Filippo was governor of Sardinia. He had married Alice, sister of John de Warenne, earl of Surrey, in 1306, having initially rejected her two years before.[44]

John Langton, bishop of Chichester, finally excommunicated the earl of Surrey in 1316 for abandoning his wife and keeping a mistress, which the bishop of Norwich had tried to do in 1313 before Edward II stepped in to prevent him. Grateful to Surrey for his support, Edward asked the bishop to defer the sentence, though he added piously, 'The king hopes that the earl will obey the orders of the Church.'[45] Surrey, now thirty, had several children with his mistress Maud Nerford, and decided to try to annul his unhappy marriage to Edward's niece Joan of Bar in order to marry Maud instead and make their children his heirs. Maud began legal action against Joan, who was cited while in Queen Isabella's presence in the lower chapel of Westminster Palace.[46] Edward did his best to steer the difficult course between loyalty to his niece and loyalty to a steadfast, politically useful ally. In August 1316, he allowed Surrey to surrender his lands to him, and granted them back with reversion to John and Thomas, two of his sons with Maud – meaning that he accepted Surrey's illegitimate children as the earl's heirs.[47] On the other hand, Edward paid all Joan's legal costs, and appointed his clerk Aymon de Juvenzano 'to prosecute in the Arches at London, and elsewhere in England' on his niece's behalf from July to November 1316. In November Joan left to go abroad, probably to stay with her brother Edouard, count of Bar in eastern France, and Edward gave her more than £166 to pay for the trip, having also paid her living expenses at the Tower of London for some years.[48]

In late December 1316, Edward sent an embassy to Pope John XXII, including Aymer de Valence, earl of Pembroke. In Pembroke's absence, Edward offered personally to act as his attorney, a very unusual act and proof of his great affection for and trust in his cousin – although, given the king's general ineptitude, probably something of a mixed blessing for the earl.[49] Edward excused himself shortly before Christmas from attending his brother-in-law Philip V's coronation, to be held on 9 January 1317, in an attempt to avoid having to pay homage for his French lands in

Gascony and Ponthieu.[50] This was to no avail: on 12 January, Philip invited Edward to present himself at Amiens for the purpose, though Edward managed to put off this annoying duty for several more years.[51] He spent Christmas Day 1316 at Nottingham with Queen Isabella, though whether their sons Edward and John were with them is uncertain. Edward of Windsor, the four-year-old earl of Chester, lived at the centre of a great household at Wallingford Castle – which, significantly, had formerly belonged to Piers Gaveston – while little John was cared for by his nurse Matilda Pyrie, in his brother's household.[52]

The court spent New Year 1317 at Clipstone, and a knight named William de la Beche played 'King of the Bean' – the person lucky enough to find the bean the cooks had added to the food, which gave him the right to preside over the seasonal festivities. Edward gave Beche 'a silver-gilt chased basin, with ewer to match', worth seven pounds, thirteen shillings and ten pence, on the Feast of the Circumcision, 1 January 1317.[53] He also gave six shillings and eight pence to John, son of Alan of Scrooby, who officiated as boy-bishop in his chapel on St Nicholas's Day, 6 December, and ten shillings to the unnamed child who acted as boy-bishop in his presence at St Mary's Church in Nottingham on 28 December, the Feast of the Holy Innocents.[54]

On 1 January 1317, Pope John XXII confirmed a two-year truce between Edward and Robert Bruce, calling Edward 'our dearest son in Christ, Edward, illustrious king of England', and Bruce 'our beloved son, the noble man, Robert de Bruce, holding himself king of Scotland'. On 17 March, John exhorted Edward to make peace with Bruce, and appointed two cardinals to travel to England and negotiate between the two kings.[55] However, the pope soon changed his tune, possibly because the embassy led by the earl of Pembroke had talked him round to Edward's point of view: eleven days later, he excommunicated Robert and Edward Bruce, and all those who were hostile to Edward II or invaded his kingdom. This time, John addressed Robert Bruce by his former title of earl of Carrick, and said he was 'unjustly pretending to occupy the throne of Scotland'.[56] In January, Edward appointed his cousin James of Spain as one of the Chamberlains of the Exchequer of the Receipt.[57] James was said to be illegitimate and was the nephew of Eleanor of Castile, presumably the son of one of her many brothers, although which one is uncertain.[58] Edward's Castilian uncles included Sancho, elected archbishop of Toledo at the age of eighteen; Felipe, who became archbishop of Seville also at eighteen and who gave up his ecclesiastical career to marry the Norwegian woman betrothed to one of his brothers; and the colourful Enrique, who was at various times a mercenary in North Africa, a senator of Rome and the regent of Castile, who spent thirty years in a Naples gaol and four in England at Henry III's expense after he rebelled against his brother Alfonso X and was exiled from Castile. Alfonso X himself was known as *el Sabio* or the Wise, and was a well-known writer, musician, lawmaker and astrologer; the Alphonsus crater of the moon is named after him. Alfonso knighted Edward II's father the future Edward I in 1254, when Edward was fifteen, just before he married Alfonso's half-sister Leonor.

Edward II spent the whole of February and March and part of April 1317 at his palace of Clarendon near Salisbury in Wiltshire, where he presided over a meeting of his great council. Possibly, the Clarendon meeting was the location where Edward and some of his courtiers planned to abduct Alice de Lacy, as her husband Thomas of Lancaster would later claim. Alice, when staying at her manor of Canford in Dorset in early May 1317, was snatched by Richard Martin, a household knight of the earl of Surrey, who took her to Surrey's castle of Reigate in Sussex.[59] Presumably Surrey, who was otherwise engaged with Maud Nerford, had no romantic inclinations towards the countess, although precisely what his motives were in abducting Alice remain unknown. It is possible that the powerful Lancaster had been instrumental in Surrey's failure to annul his marriage and in persuading the bishop of Chichester to excommunicate him, and that Surrey, whom the *Flores* calls 'one of the worst sycophants', saw a chance for revenge. If so, antagonising the powerful Lancaster was foolish in the extreme. The *Flores* writes that the abduction came about as the result of 'the violent boiling anger of the king', and that Edward convened a malicious assembly to cook up a deceitful plot against Lancaster, jealous of his great wisdom and integrity.[60] The *Vita*, better informed and considerably less hysterical than the *Flores*, reports without comment Lancaster's belief that Edward's friends plotted the abduction.[61]

In April 1317, Edward turned his attention to the vital question of his sons' future marriages, and received permission from John XXII to marry his children, now aged four and a half and eight months, to relatives in the fourth degree of consanguinity – that is, people with whom they shared a set of great-great-grandparents. The licence also applied to any future children he might have.[62] That month Edward finally bowed to the inevitable, stopped pretending that the dowager countess of Gloucester was pregnant nearly three years after her husband's death, and ordered the partition of the earl of Gloucester's lands among his three sisters.[63] The two widowed sisters, Margaret and Elizabeth, would become great landowners, and it was important for Edward to marry them to men he trusted, as their husbands would wield an enormous amount of influence. He saw a chance to promote his friends Roger Damory and Hugh Audley even further. Damory was now the supreme influence at the English court, rich and powerful thanks to Edward's favour.[64] The grants to him which had begun in late 1315 continued unabated throughout 1317, and his influence over Edward is obvious in the grants and favours issued at his request. Edward gave Damory many splendid presents, including a silver-gilt chalice 'with the cross engraved in the foot and six enamelled knots in the centre', an altar 'of black stone ornamented in the circumference with silver and gilded', an ivory image of the Virgin and Child, and a magnificent cross of ivory and cedar 'painted with four images standing on each side ... and round the base six images of ivory, painted, standing in tabernacles'.[65] Hugh Audley was also in favour, though not nearly to the same extent as Damory. In June 1315, Edward ordered the chancellor to complete some of Audley's business as soon as possible, so that Audley 'can return to us as quickly as we have instructed him to do'.[66] Audley swore an oath sometime in 1317 that he would 'aid him [Edward] in all things throughout his whole life, and in no wise depart from him come what might, on pain of forfeiture of all his lands', an oath he broke in 1321 after he and Damory became the king's enemies.[67] Audley owned war horses called Grisel le Kyng and Ferant de Roma; Grisel's name implies that the horse had been a gift to Audley from Edward.[68] And finally, William Montacute was also a significant man at court by 1317: as Edward's steward, he held an important position close to the king, and commanded the royal cavalry.[69]

Edward's niece, Joan of Acre's third daughter Elizabeth de Burgh (née de Clare), gave birth to her daughter Isabella Verdon, probably named after the queen, at Amesbury Priory on or shortly before 21 March 1317. This was eight months after the death of Elizabeth's second husband Theobald Verdon, who had abducted her from Bristol Castle in early 1316 and forcibly married her. Edward sent a silver-gilt cup with stand and cover worth a pound and ten shillings as a christening gift for his latest great-niece.[70] He was determined to marry Roger Damory to Elizabeth and bring him into the royal family, as he had done with Piers Gaveston, and sent his chamberlain John Charlton to Elizabeth with a letter to this effect even before Theobald Verdon's funeral in September 1316. Using flattery in a transparent attempt to persuade her to do his bidding, he described her as his favourite niece, which was a lie; he rarely showed her any kindness or support, in stark contrast to her older sisters Eleanor and Margaret and their cousin Joan of Bar.[71] In February or March 1317, when Elizabeth was heavily pregnant, Edward travelled the 10 miles from Clarendon to Amesbury, taking Damory with him, to put more pressure on her to marry his friend.[72] Damory was far beneath Elizabeth by birth and status; she was a king's granddaughter and would have become countess of Ulster if her first husband John de Burgh had lived longer, while he was merely the younger son of an obscure knight. However, she agreed to marry him. Realistically, she had little choice.

Edward also arranged the marriage of another niece to another friend, and on 28 April 1317 at Windsor Castle, attended the wedding of Piers Gaveston's widow Margaret to Hugh Audley. On the same day, William Montacute's eldest son John married Joan Verdon, stepdaughter of

Margaret's sister Elizabeth de Burgh and one of the four co-heiresses of her father Theobald; another advantageous marriage arranged by the king for one of his friends. Audley and Margaret's wedding was a lavish affair, and Edward gave three pounds in coins to be thrown over the heads of the bride and groom – generous though this was, it was less than half the amount he had provided for the same purpose at Margaret's wedding to Piers Gaveston. He also gave half a mark (eight shillings and six pence) in oblations, distributed in his presence in the chapel in Windsor park.[73] Roger Damory married Elizabeth around the same time; Edward stayed at Windsor from 23 April to 16 May 1317, and presumably attended the wedding there. The date is not recorded but the couple had married by 3 May.[74] Edward took the homage of Hugh Despenser, Hugh Audley and Roger Damory for the lands they would now control in right of their wives, although it would take another six months before the lands were partitioned.[75] While at Windsor, Edward paid half a mark to his goldsmith Walter de Spalding 'for making a silver image, weighing ten marks, for the use of the lord king'.[76]

Perhaps to postpone married life with Damory, Elizabeth – who continued to use her first husband's name, de Burgh, throughout both her subsequent marriages – went on pilgrimage to Canterbury with her aunt Mary the nun and their young cousin Isabella, one of the six daughters of the earl of Lancaster's brother Henry and also a nun at Amesbury Priory. Edward paid all their expenses.[77] William Montacute's newly married son John died that summer, still in his teens, and his widow Joan Verdon married again in February 1318 – a wife for the second time at fourteen and a half.[78] John Montacute was buried in the cathedral church at Lincoln on 14 August 1317, his funeral conducted with unusual ceremony: Edward paid forty clerks to pray for his soul, and thirteen widows to watch over his body. He arrived at Lincoln three days after the funeral, and gave generous alms at the Masses celebrated in the cathedral for the repose of John's soul.[79] Perhaps he felt sorrow that John had died while still a teenager and just married, or perhaps this is proof of his affection for John's father William. John's younger brother, also William, later became the closest friend and confidant of Edward's son Edward III, who made him earl of Salisbury.

It was probably Hugh Audley and Roger Damory's marriages to the most eligible women in England that prompted one of Edward's household knights to stage a theatrical protest against the king's promotion of new favourites in May 1317. As Edward dined at Westminster Hall at Pentecost, a woman entered, dressed as a stage-player – which must have pleased Edward, who loved actors – and riding a magnificently caparisoned horse. She rode around the hall, then turned to Edward on the dais, placed a letter in front of him, and rode out. Edward, amused, began to read the letter, but soon stopped, horrified; it was an indictment of the favouritism he showed his friends.[80] Although Edward released the woman and, impressed with the integrity of his household knight who had written the letter, gave him 'abundant gifts', he failed to take the sage advice. In 1317 and 1318, the pernicious influence of Edward's favourites grew ever stronger, and unknown to anyone, the worst of them all, the man who would one day bring about the king's downfall, waited in the wings for his opportunity.

8

Robbery, Holy Oil and an Impostor

The year 1317 saw a further deterioration in the already dreadful relations between Edward II and the earl of Lancaster, and the king foolishly allowed his friends Roger Damory, Hugh Audley and William Montacute to encourage him in his hatred and distrust of his cousin. At a council meeting at Clarendon in early 1317, they openly attacked him, calling him a traitor.[1] Lancaster sent messengers to the king, claiming that 'he fears [their] deadly stratagems' and complaining that 'they have already carried off the earl's wife to his disgrace and shame'.[2] Lancaster asked Edward to expel the earl of Surrey, Damory, Audley and Montacute from court, and demanded 'such satisfaction as he can get for the wrong done to him'.[3] He wrote to Edward to complain that his companions were 'not suitable to stay beside you or in your service ... but you have held them dearer than they ever were before ... every day you give them of your substance, so that little or nothing remains to you'.[4] Pope John XXII was also concerned about his extravagance and ability to pick the wrong friends, and wrote to the king frequently in 1317 and 1318 suggesting that he reduce his household expenses, hear divine offices with attention and reverence, and 'remove those friends whose youth and imprudence injure the affairs of the realm'.[5] Edward, as usual, ignored this sound advice, and responded to Lancaster, abruptly and impatiently, 'I will avenge the despite done to the earl when I can; I refuse to expel my household; for the abduction of his wife let him seek a remedy in law only.'[6]

Damory, Audley and Montacute had no intention of allowing Lancaster to diminish their vast influence over Edward, and selfishly counselled the king to remain hostile to his cousin. The *Flores* calls them 'men who stir up discord and many problems for the kingdom ... supporting his [Edward's] arrogance and lawless designs'.[7] The three men may have had more sinister motives for their plots and schemes against Lancaster: if they managed to engineer his downfall on the grounds of treason, his lands would be forfeit to the Crown, and it is possible that they hoped to persuade Edward to share them out among themselves.[8] Lancaster therefore had good reason to fear the royal favourites and to distrust the king, and in the summer and autumn of 1317, civil war threatened to break out.[9]

Edward asked his household and friends for advice about his hated cousin: 'You see how the earl of Lancaster has not come to parliament. You see how he scorns to obey our commands. How does it seem to you?' Some, no doubt Damory, Audley and Montacute among them, replied, 'Let the king pursue and take his despiser, and when he is taken put him in prison or exile him.' Other, wiser heads disagreed.[10] Edward, who had not forgotten his vow to avenge Gaveston's death on Lancaster, was inclined to agree with those who urged him to pursue the earl. Still, in the interests of trying to preserve the fragile peace, he summoned a council meeting to Westminster for 15 April 1317, inviting Lancaster and his confidant, Robert Holland. However, the two men failed to turn up, and Edward himself arrived three days late. He did send envoys to Lancaster, but to no avail.[11]

Edward or his advisers made another attempt to meet and come to terms with Lancaster, and he and members of Edward's council were summoned to a meeting to begin at Nottingham in July 1317. Roger Damory, Hugh Audley and William Montacute were not invited, but attended anyway. Edward arrived at Nottingham on 16 July and stayed there for three weeks, but once again, Lancaster failed to turn up. Edward sent him a letter remonstrating with him for holding private assemblies and for employing an unusual number of armed retainers, 'whence the people are considerably frightened'.[12] Lancaster refused to meet Edward unless Damory, Audley, Montacute and the earl of Surrey left court, and Edward refused once again to send them away. It seemed that the two men would never be reconciled. Lancaster spent most of his time at his favourite residence of Pontefract and was by now almost completely isolated politically, but far too powerful for Edward to ignore, thanks to his vast wealth and his five earldoms; 'By the size of his patrimony you may assess his influence,' comments the *Vita*.[13] Most of the magnates were, in 1317 and 1318, co-operating loyally with Edward, and Lancaster was very much a political outsider, followed only by some of the northern barons. For all Edward's faults and excessive favour to his friends, he had proved himself skilled over the previous years at attracting, and maintaining, the support of a vast majority of his magnates.

Edward spent late April, including his thirty-third birthday, and the first half of May 1317 at Windsor, then returned to Westminster, where he stayed for a month. During his stay there, he gave twenty ells of striped cloth to William de Horsham and three others for 'singing before the king in his chamber', and two pounds to his violist Richard to help support his wife and children. He also paid Peter de Foresta two pounds for making him 'a crown of wax of various colours and of various devices' for the feast of the Nativity of St John the Baptist on 24 June.[14] It was now exactly three years since his humiliating defeat at Bannockburn, but Edward had still not given up hope of defeating Robert Bruce; on 12 June, he ordered 1,400 barrels of wine, given to him by the inhabitants of Bordeaux and Saint Macaire for his use in the Scottish wars, to be sent to England.[15] And Piers Gaveston was still on Edward's mind. On 29 June, five years and ten days after his friend's death, he ordered the abbot and convent of Thame to take on six additional monks to celebrate divine service daily for Gaveston's soul and the souls of the king's ancestors.[16] Edward's demands for prayers for Gaveston's soul could be onerous. In the spring of 1317, the king asked Tupholme Abbey in Lincolnshire to take in a retired servant of his, but they replied, 'Although they would gladly obey him in all things, their very small income is already heavily burdened with the charge of finding a chaplain to say Mass for the soul of Sir Piers Gaveston, late earl of Cornwall.'[17]

Pope John XXII was concerned about the state of affairs in England, telling Edward that the land and its inhabitants 'are oppressed by wars, the Church is persecuted, and God's judgements are ready to fall', in contrast to the past, when England was 'a terror to barbarians'.[18] The cardinals he sent to negotiate between Edward and Robert Bruce arrived in Canterbury on 24 June 1317. They were Gaucelin D'Eauze or Duèse, a relative of the pope, and Luca Fieschi, an Italian nobleman by birth and a distant cousin of the king. Edward was at Woodstock when the cardinals arrived, attending the wedding of his squire Oliver de Bordeaux to Maud Trussell; he gave two pounds and ten shillings to be thrown over the heads of the couple at the chapel door, distributed nineteen pence in oblations during the nuptial mass, and gave Oliver and Maud rings worth thirty shillings each.[19]

On 7 July 1317, Edward founded the King's Hall (*Aula Regis*) at Cambridge University, which maintained thirty-two scholars from 1319.[20] It was the second college founded at the university, after Peterhouse in 1284. In 1546, Edward's descendant Henry VIII incorporated King's Hall and Michaelhouse – founded in 1324 by the chief justice Hervey Staunton, a staunch ally of Edward – into his new foundation of Trinity College. Edward and his almoner Adam Brome also established Oriel College at Oxford in 1326, and Edward was the first king of England to found colleges at Oxford and Cambridge, as well as one of two people throughout history to establish colleges at both universities, which he called 'the twin jewels in our crown'.[21] Fulfilling his vow after Bannockburn to found a friary in Oxford, Edward granted the Carmelites his palace of Beaumont in February 1318, and the Carmelites promised in return to celebrate divine service daily for Edward, Isabella and their children, and for the souls of Edward's ancestors.[22] Edward II is especially important in the history of Cambridge: in March 1317, he asked the pope to recognise its official status as a university, and John XXII duly granted a bull to this effect on 9 June 1318.[23] The king also asked John to 'extend and perpetuate the privileges' of the university in March 1318.[24]

Edward II liked books: he owned an illuminated biography of Edward the Confessor in French which cost fifty-eight shillings, a French romance (any kind of fiction, not necessarily a love story) which had belonged to his grandmother Eleanor of Provence and was delivered to him in 1298, a Latin history of the kings of England, a Latin prayer book, a book called *De Regimine Regum* (On the Ruling of Kings), and gave a romance of Tristan and Isolde to his favourite Hugh Despenser in 1326.[25] Unlike his father Edward I and son Edward III, however, he showed little interest in the exploits of King Arthur. Edward borrowed books – the lives of St Thomas Becket and St Anselm – from the library at Canterbury Cathedral, which he failed to return.[26] An inventory carried out at the Exchequer in 1323 revealed a booklet written 'in a language unknown to the English', which was in fact Welsh, and a book bound in green leather containing the chronicle of Rodrigo Jimenez de Rada, one of the predecessors of Edward's uncle Sancho as archbishop of Toledo.[27] Edward also loved drama, and in May 1306 spent five shillings and five pence on silk and other material 'for tunics made in the Gascon fashion, for the prince [of Wales]'s plays'.[28]

Although Edward's taste in books and decoration usually ran to the religious, he did enjoy more secular themes too, and ordered his painter Jack of St Albans to paint scenes from the life of Edward I in the lesser hall at Westminster, while a picture of four knights on their way to a tournament adorned his hall at Langley.[29] In February 1326, various items including colours, Arabic gum and white lead were bought for Jack to illustrate a book he was making for the king.[30] Edward bought a painting of St John the Baptist from John the Painter of Lincoln, which he kept in his chamber, and in 1322, ordered his tent on a Scottish expedition to be decorated with a picture of the evangelists.[31] Shortly before he turned seventeen in April 1301, he ordered a painter named William of Northampton to make 'a picture of blessed Thomas the martyr with the four knights who slew him' at Chester Castle.[32] This means Thomas Becket, the archbishop of Canterbury murdered in 1170 at the instigation of Edward's great-great-grandfather Henry II. Like his father, Edward venerated Becket: he was taken on pilgrimage to Canterbury for the first time at the age of fifteen months in July 1285, visited Becket's shrine sixteen times in the nineteen and a half years of his reign, and made offerings on Becket's feast day every year.[33] He inherited from his father, and passed on to his son, a large number of holy relics, including a thorn from the Crown of Thorns 'in a gold box ornamented with diverse precious stones', a fragment of the True Cross 'in a precious gold cross', the blood and a bone of St George, the blood and hair of St Stephen, a tooth of St Edward the Confessor, and sundry relics from other saints including John the Baptist, Mary Magdalene, Agatha, Agnes, Jerome, James the Less and the 11,000 virgins.[34]

The Sempringham annalist says, oddly, that in 1317 'there issued from the earth water-mice with long tails, larger than rats, with which the fields and meadows were filled in the summer and in August'.[35] Edward passed through Shelford in Nottinghamshire on 8 August 1317, where he attended Masses and distributed five shillings and sixpence in oblations at the church for the soul of his nephew the earl of Gloucester, 'whose heart lies there inhumed', although the rest of the young man's body was buried at Tewkesbury Abbey, Gloucestershire.[36] At Lincoln, the king and queen stayed at the Gilbertine priory of St Catherine's, where the body of Edward's mother Queen Eleanor had rested in November 1290 before her funeral cortège wound its way south to Westminster Abbey. Whether Edward stopped to admire the Eleanor Cross at Lincoln and to remember his mother is not known, but his journey to York itself is interesting: he stayed as far to the east of Pontefract, the earl of Lancaster's stronghold, as possible. The most direct route would have taken him right through the town, but Lancaster had blocked his way by placing armed guards on the roads and bridges south of York.[37] Edward was furious that one of his subjects would dare to impede his progress through his own kingdom, and later brought it up as one of the charges against Lancaster at his trial. Civil war between Edward and Lancaster, the two most powerful men of the kingdom, loomed once more, and the Scottish situation – despite the peace treaty arranged by the pope a few months earlier – did not improve. The Scots invaded the north of England in early July 1317, and Edward summoned an army at Newcastle in mid-September to go against them, though, as frequently happened, he later postponed and then cancelled the campaign.[38]

The king and queen arrived in York in early September, and sometime that month must have conceived their third child, Eleanor of Woodstock, born in June 1318. Before Edward's arrival in York, he sent envoys to Pontefract to negotiate with the earl of Lancaster, to try to make peace so that the Scottish campaign could proceed.[39] The envoys' aim was to persuade the king and the earl to meet face-to-face and resolve their difficulties; 'a love-day without the clash of arms,' as the *Vita* puts it. Unfortunately, Lancaster claimed to have heard a rumour that if he came to Edward's presence, the king would 'either have his head or consign him to prison', and, whether that was true or not, refused to meet Edward.[40] At the instigation of the two cardinals who had recently arrived in the country – they were with Edward at York in September – a date was finally set for a meeting, although it was eventually postponed until October 1318.[41] For now, at least, Edward agreed to take no hostile action against Lancaster and his adherents, and Lancaster agreed to attend the next parliament, due to be held at Lincoln in January 1318. Finally, Edward dismissed most of his soldiers, and Lancaster removed his guards from the roads and bridges south of York.

At the beginning of October 1317, Edward left York to return to London. The road through Pontefract was now clear, but instead of doing the sensible thing and ignoring Lancaster, Edward unwisely took it into his head, despite his promise a few days earlier not to take action against his cousin, to command his men to take up arms and attack him. One of Edward's friends – most likely Roger Damory – had persuaded him, in his own selfish interests, that the earl posed a threat to Edward and that he should attack him first. Fortunately for the stability of his kingdom, Edward, who was incapable of distinguishing between good and bad advice and who tended to believe and act on whatever the last person had told him, informed the earl of Pembroke beforehand what he was intending to do. He said, 'I have been told that the earl of Lancaster is lying in ambush, and is diligently preparing to catch us all by surprise.'[42] The astute Pembroke, who fortunately still retained some influence over the wayward king, managed to convince Edward that this was not the case, and the party returned to London safely – despite the fact that Lancaster did his utmost to make matters worse by leading his men out to the top of the castle ditch and jeering at Edward as he and his retinue travelled past.[43] Edward was understandably incensed at this appalling rudeness and *lèse-majesté*, and he was not a man to forgive and forget an insult; it would be another of the charges against Lancaster at his trial. On his journey to London, Edward's spirits might have been raised somewhat by Dulcia Withstaff, mother of his fool 'King' Robert, who came to visit him and received ten shillings.[44]

In the meantime a shocking event had taken place near Rushyford, between Darlington and Durham. On 1 September, Sir Gilbert Middleton attacked the new bishop of Durham, Edward's cousin Louis Beaumont, Louis's brother Henry, and the cardinals Gaucelin D'Eauze and Luca Fieschi, while the party was on its way to Durham for Beaumont's consecration. Middleton robbed the four men and imprisoned the Beaumonts at Mitford Castle until mid-October 1317, though the cardinals were soon freed, and the sheriff of Yorkshire gave them twelve horses to continue their way to Durham.[45] It is possible that the earl of Lancaster was involved in the attack, and it was believed at the time that the Scots were involved too, though this was never proved. Although the cardinals had come to mediate between Edward and Robert Bruce, their sympathy and support, like the pope's, were entirely in Edward's favour, and Bruce had already declared that he would refuse to meet them unless they acknowledged him as king.[46] John XXII, rightly or wrongly, blamed the Scots, telling Edward that he knew Robert Bruce had perpetrated outrages on the cardinals and 'laid violent hands' on the bishop of Carlisle as well.[47] The furious Gaucelin D'Eauze and Luca Fieschi excommunicated Middleton and his adherents, and Thomas of Lancaster, mortified, escorted the cardinals to Boroughbridge, twenty miles north-west of York, where the earls of Pembroke and Hereford met them and took them to Edward.[48] On 20 September, Edward, also furious and embarrassed that two high-ranking and well-connected churchmen, one of them his own relative, had been attacked in his kingdom, declared that he would 'punish the sons of iniquity' who had perpetrated the outrage.[49] He was as good as his word: three of his squires captured Middleton and his brother John at Mitford Castle in January 1318 and sent them to Edward, and the king ordered fourteen other squires to deliver them to the Tower of London.[50] On 24 January 1318, royal justices sentenced Gilbert Middleton to execution, and he suffered a terrible death by hanging, drawing and quartering.[51] Thomas of Lancaster escaped punishment over the episode.

And the powerful earl's lawlessness had not yet run its course. In early October 1317, he seized Knaresborough Castle in Yorkshire, which his retainer John Lilburn didn't surrender to the king until January 1318, and by the beginning of November had also forcibly gained possession of Alton Castle in Staffordshire.[52] Knaresborough had formerly belonged to Piers Gaveston, Alton to Theobald Verdon, but far more importantly as far as Lancaster was concerned, Roger Damory was the custodian of both.[53] Clearly, Lancaster saw Damory as his chief enemy at court, and determined to attack him. Edward ineffectually sent out orders to various sheriffs to retake the castles, and commanded Lancaster to 'desist completely from these proceedings'.[54] Not only did Lancaster fail to obey, he took numerous armed men to besiege and capture castles in Yorkshire which belonged to John de Warenne, earl of Surrey: Sandal, Conisborough and Wakefield. Lancaster also ejected Maud Nerford, Surrey's mistress, from her property in Wakefield, and by the beginning of 1318 had taken firm control over Surrey's Yorkshire lands.[55] Edward's chief priority, as ever, was the safety and well-being of his 'favourites', and he took Damory's lands in Yorkshire, Herefordshire and Lincolnshire into his own hands on 18 October 1317 in an attempt to protect Damory from his cousin's aggression, also ordering a clerk to remove Damory's stud-farm from Knaresborough to Burstwick. He restored Damory's lands to him on 2 December, assuming the danger from Lancaster was past.[56]

Lancaster must have been dismayed on 15 November 1317 when the English, Welsh and Irish lands of the late earl of Gloucester were finally partitioned, nearly three and a half years after his death at Bannockburn, among his three sisters and their husbands. Hugh and Eleanor Despenser, who had fought so hard for their inheritance, now held lands worth £1,415 a year, Hugh and Margaret Audley lands worth £1,292, and Roger and Elizabeth Damory £1,287.[57] Although they were nowhere near the same league as Lancaster, who had a gross annual income of £11,000, this wealth catapulted all three men to the forefront of the nobility. Hugh Despenser had still not reached the lofty position he would later occupy as Edward's favourite – Edward seems barely to have noticed him before 1318 – but as co-owner of the de Clare inheritance and the new lord of Glamorgan, he had become far more significant than previously. Lancaster's nemesis Damory, now the king's nephew-in-law, rich in his own right and not merely dependent on Edward's favour, with vast influence over the king, had become a much more powerful enemy. Lancaster's fear and hatred of him knew no bounds: the following July, he accused Damory of trying to murder him, and also claimed that he had intercepted letters at Pontefract, written by Edward and sent to Scotland, inviting the Scots to help kill the earl.[58]

The earl of Lancaster was not the only man to fear the malign influence of the men who surrounded Edward. By late November 1317, a group of barons and prelates, sick of the dreadful relations between Edward and Lancaster and the constant political instability it engendered, had formed themselves into a loose coalition known to early twentieth-century historians as the 'Middle Party'. The nucleus of the 'party' – an anachronistic term for the early fourteenth century – was the earl of Pembroke and Bartholomew Badlesmere, and also included the earl of Hereford, the archbishops of Canterbury and Dublin, and the bishops of Norwich and Winchester. The group was loyal to the king and determined to improve the relations between himself and Lancaster. In order to achieve this, they needed to limit the harmful and self-serving influence his friends, especially Roger Damory, held over him. To this end, the earl of Pembroke and Bartholomew Badlesmere signed an indenture with Damory on 24 November 1317, wherein the favourite promised that he would do his best to prevent Edward from taking action prejudicial to himself or his kingdom – a telling comment which demonstrates what little faith Pembroke and Badlesmere had in Edward – and if he were unable to dissuade him, would inform Pembroke and Badlesmere as soon as possible so that the three of them together could talk Edward out of whatever foolishness he might be planning. This was a sensible idea; the *Flores*, fairly, criticises Edward for making decisions 'in secret in his chamber, with his intimates', and complains that he broke his word, 'forgetting in the morning what he had said in the evening'.[59] This indenture may be unique, or it may be one of a series which Pembroke and Badlesmere signed around this time with Edward's friends, and the only one which happens to survive.[60]

On 3 November 1317, Edward appointed another friend and ally as the new steward of Gascony: his rather extraordinary choice was Antonio di Pessagno, a merchant of Genoa.[61] Pessagno, whose enormous wealth enabled him to make frequent loans to Edward, enjoyed a great deal of influence at the English court. In 1313, Biagio Aldobrandini of the banking firm the Frescobaldi wrote to his colleagues that Pessagno's influence equalled Piers Gaveston's: 'He is now in such a condition that he fears nobody, and what he wants is made in the court ... and the court is led according to his judgement.'[62] A grateful Pessagno gave the king a gift of two camels.[63] Edward had owned a camel as a child, which he kept in the stables at Langley, and his father brought a lion and a lynx back to England in 1289, when he was five.[64] In the early 1300s, Edward took a lion with him on his travels around the country, with its own cart, a collar, a silver chain and a keeper called Adam of Lichfield.[65] He kept a lion and a leopard in the Tower of London throughout his reign, allowing each animal six pence a day for sustenance, while Peter Fabre of Montpellier, 'keeper of the king's lion and leopard', received only one and a half pence a day in wages.[66] Both the lion and the leopard ate a quarter of mutton daily, even during the Great Famine, while six pence a day was more than most people in the country earned. Edward loved animals: he kept and bred greyhounds, bought the stud-farm of the late earl of Surrey in 1304, and frequently sent men to Spain to purchase horses for him. In the first year of his reign alone, he spent almost £1,200 buying horses.[67]

Edward and Queen Isabella spent Christmas 1317 at Westminster, where Edward spent one pound, thirteen shillings and six pence on a 'great wooden table' to be placed in the palace hall, and also paid thirty pounds to Thomas de Hebenhith, mercer of London, for 'a great hanging of wool, woven with figures of the king and earls on it'. By New Year, someone had realised that constantly taking the hanging up and down was damaging it, so Edward paid Thomas de Verlay six shillings and three pence to make and sew a border of green cloth around it.[68] The court spent New Year at Windsor, where Edward gave silver-gilt goblets worth seven pounds each to twenty-five knights, including Robert Umfraville, earl of Angus, who had been captured after Bannockburn.[69] This year, it was the turn of Thomas de Weston, a squire of Edward's household, to act as King of the Bean, and he received 'a silver-gilt basin with stand and cover, and a silver-gilt pitcher to match' from the king.[70] Edward gave rings to his nieces Margaret and Elizabeth and his sons Edward and John, although the latter was only sixteen months old. His five-year-old great-niece Joan Gaveston, Piers' daughter, received a gold ring with two emeralds and three pearls, worth thirty-two shillings, and another gold ring with six emeralds, worth twenty marks, went to his sister Mary, the nun. Queen Isabella's gift from her husband was an enamelled silver-gilt bowl, with foot and cover, worth seventeen pounds.[71] Edward received a New Year gift of a sort from Pope John XXII, who on 29 December once more excommunicated 'all those who invade the realm of England or disturb its peace'.[72]

By New Year 1318, Isabella had probably passed the first trimester of pregnancy, and it is likely that the king knew she was expecting their third child. Now twenty-two, Isabella had so far played little discernible role in English politics, although she had by the mid-1320s gained a reputation as a mediator between the king and his barons. Isabella's attitude towards Roger Damory and her husband's other male favourites is a matter for conjecture, although at some point she gave Damory a number of splendid gifts for his chapel, including a chasuble of red cloth 'sprinkled with diverse flowers of Indian colour', and there is no evidence of any hostility towards them on her part.[73] In July 1317, Edward gave his wife the county of Cornwall, formerly Piers Gaveston's, and in March 1318 granted her his county of Ponthieu for life.[74] And Isabella became even richer after 14 February 1318, when her aunt and Edward's stepmother Queen Marguerite died at her castle of Marlborough in Wiltshire, in her late thirties, and the dower lands she had held passed by right to Isabella.[75]

Edward's reaction to Marguerite's death is not recorded. He had been close to her before his accession, but possibly had never forgiven her for her opposition to Piers Gaveston in 1308. He appointed Marguerite's sons, his teenage half-brothers Thomas and Edmund, as the executors of her will.[76] On 8 March, Edward sent two pieces of Lucca cloth to lie over Marguerite's body at Marlborough, and sent six more pieces after it was moved to London shortly afterwards. He visited his stepmother's remains at St Mary's church in Southwark on 14 March, and attended her funeral at the Greyfriars church the following day, purchasing six pieces of Lucca cloth for himself and two pieces each for his sister Mary and Roger Damory.[77] After Marguerite's funeral, Edward travelled via Bow, Thundersley and Cressing to Clare Castle in Suffolk, where he spent 23–27 March 1318 with Roger Damory and his wife, Edward's niece Elizabeth, who was about seven months pregnant. Shortly before 18 May, she gave birth to a daughter, also Elizabeth, who would be Damory's only legitimate child and therefore his heir. Edward gave Damory's valet the huge sum of twenty pounds for bringing him news of the birth, an enormous increase on the price of the silver cup he had sent to little Elizabeth's half-sister Isabella Verdon the year before, although both girls were his great-nieces – probably evidence of his strong feelings for Roger Damory.[78] The Damorys had a household of at least fifty people, and their extant accounts of 1319 provide a fascinating insight into what they ate and drank in a day: forty gallons of ale and eight of wine, a hundred and fifty eggs, two ducks, six hens, thirteen pullets, half a carcass of salt beef, half a pig, a quantity of mutton, forty herrings, two salt stockfish, two ling, salmon, whiting and eels.[79]

On 18 March 1318, Edward sent more envoys, led by his good friend and ally William Melton, archbishop of York, to Scotland to arrange a peace treaty with Robert Bruce. A year later, he belatedly remembered to obtain the pope's permission to negotiate with an excommunicate.[80] Unfortunately for him, Robert Bruce finally managed to take the vital port of Berwick-on-Tweed on 2 April, after several unsuccessful attempts, although the castle, under the command of Sir Roger Horsley, held out until July.[81] The treachery of the Englishman Peter Spalding, who was responsible for a section of the town wall and whom the Scots 'bribed by a great sum of money ... and the promise of land', contributed in large part to James Douglas's success.[82] Edward, declaring himself 'justly incensed' at the 'carelessness' of the burgesses of Berwick, ordered their goods and chattels to be seized.[83] It was vital for Edward to retake Berwick, and on 10 June he summoned the earl of Lancaster and many others to muster against the Scots.[84] However, because of the endless conflict with Lancaster, the expedition did not take place until the following year, allowing Robert Bruce ample time to strengthen the town fortifications and make it much harder for Edward to retake. In May 1318, Scottish forces invaded Yorkshire, drove off many cattle, and 'made men and women captives, making the poor folks drive the cattle, carrying them off to Scotland without any opposition'.[85] The year 1318 was not, however, an unqualified success for the Bruces: the pope excommunicated Robert again on 28 June, and Robert's brother Edward, high king of Ireland, was killed at the battle of Faughart in October.[86] The *Vita Edwardi Secundi* in 1318 recalls the story of the biblical king Nebuchadnezzar, who 'began to flourish and the nations and kingdoms to bow down to him' only in the twelfth year of his reign, and goes on to say that 'neither has our King Edward who has reigned eleven years and more, done anything that ought to be preached in the market place or upon the house-tops'.[87]

In late April, Edward turned his attention to Langley Priory, which he had founded in 1308 and where he had buried Piers Gaveston, and wrote to the pope asking his permission to found a house of Dominican nuns there.[88] He probably intended to make his foundation independent of his own grants of money from the Exchequer, and as the Dominicans were not allowed to own property, he planned for the nuns to hold lands in trust for them.[89] Although Edward wrote again to John XXII in October 1318 and January 1319 asking him to appropriate the church of Kingsclere for the sisters and to expedite the process, and wrote to the master of the Dominicans asking him to have seven sisters ready to send, his plans foundered.[90] In 1349, his son Edward III finally established the sisters' house. Edward II took a great interest in Langley Priory: he gave them his garden next to the parish church, two plots of land, his dwelling called 'Little London' until the priory was ready for habitation, 700 marks for the costs of building the priory, and increased its annual grants to 500 marks a year in September 1312.[91]

On 18 June 1318, Queen Isabella gave birth to a daughter, Eleanor, at Woodstock Palace in Oxfordshire. Edward had been on pilgrimage in Canterbury, but managed to arrive at Woodstock on the day of his daughter's birth. The king and queen followed contemporary convention by naming their first daughter after her paternal grandmother, Eleanor of Castile, although the spelling 'Eleanor' didn't appear until much later, and in the fourteenth century was spelt Alianor, Alianore or Alienora. Edward's wardrobe accounts record a payment of 500 marks to Isabella for the 'feast of her purification'.[92] Shortly after her birth, Eleanor of Woodstock joined the household of her brothers Edward and John, under the care of a nurse named Joan du Bois.[93]

In July, Edward summoned a meeting of his great council at Northampton, and he and Queen Isabella left Woodstock on 27 June, only nine days after she had borne Eleanor. The council meeting at Northampton is best known for a 'certain unknown and ignoble individual' named John of Powderham, who came before Edward, claiming to be the rightful king of England. John said that he 'was the true heir of the realm, as the son of the illustrious King Edward [I]', and declared that 'my lord Edward [II] … was not of the blood royal, nor had any right to the realm'. Edward, who never lacked an ironic sense of humour, greeted John with the words 'Welcome, my brother'. John answered, 'Thou art no brother of mine, but falsely thou claimest the kingdom for thyself.'[94] John claimed to be the real son of Edward I and to have been switched in the cradle for a peasant baby.[95] In fact he was the son of a tanner from Exeter, and Edward summoned his parents to Northampton to have them questioned and examined.[96] John's claims became the gossip of the kingdom and 'annoyed the queen unspeakably', though it is extremely doubtful that Isabella believed them.[97] The *Anonimalle* claims that Edward decided not to execute John, but to employ him as a court fool. However, several magnates, not named, ordered him to be hanged and drawn.[98] There was no truth at all to the story, but the impostor was given widespread credence; most people found it hard to accept the fact that their king preferred hedging, ditching and swimming to governing, fighting and jousting, and believed John 'all the more readily because the said lord Edward resembled the elder lord Edward [I] in none of his virtues', according to *Lanercost*.[99] John of Powderham suffered death by drawing and hanging sometime between 20 and 24 July, and his body remained on public display until long afterwards.[100] It is unclear whether Edward witnessed the execution.

The appearance of the impostor might have encouraged Edward to pursue a topic he had been thinking about for some time, and he wrote to the pope asking for permission to be re-anointed with the holy oil of

St Thomas Becket. His sister and brother-in-law the duke and duchess of Brabant had brought the oil to his coronation in 1308, but Edward decided not to use it.[101] Dwelling now on the many misfortunes that had befallen himself and his realm since his accession and preferring not to accept his own culpability, he decided that his failure to be anointed with the oil, which was connected with a miraculous vision that the fifth king after the time of St Thomas Becket – Edward – would be a good man and a champion of the Church, was to blame. A friar named Nicholas de Wisbech, formerly the confessor of Edward's sister Duchess Margaret, persuaded the king to take up the matter with the pope, so that the miraculous properties of the oil might end his political troubles. The pope cautiously agreed, declaring that it would be 'no superstition or sin' for Edward to have himself re-anointed, but refused to send a cardinal and advised him to conduct the ceremony privately to avoid scandal.[102] Edward eventually came to his senses and sent an astonishingly candid letter to John XXII condemning his own weakness and 'dove-like simplicity' in believing the friar's blandishments.[103]

Since April 1318, a group of barons and prelates had been negotiating with the earl of Lancaster, and trying to persuade Edward and his unruly cousin to overcome their hostility to each other. In June, they came to a preliminary agreement: Edward would uphold the hated Ordinances, govern by the counsel of his magnates, and conciliate Lancaster, who was threatened with sanctions if he continued to hold armed assemblies. The Bridlington chronicler wondered at this agreement, declaring that bits were fastened on the king's teeth and that those who merited execution were given absolution instead, which, he thought, fostered hatred.[104] Lancaster's violence and lawlessness were thus condoned, as he was too powerful for the king to ignore and his co-operation with Edward was essential if England was ever to find peace. Lancaster eventually consented to meet the king on 7 August 1318, and the two men exchanged the kiss of peace. Edward gave his cousin a fine palfrey horse 'in recognition of his great love' of Lancaster.[105] A formal agreement, the Treaty of Leake, was signed in the town of Leake near Loughborough two days later.[106] Part of the agreement was for Roger Damory, Hugh Audley and William Montacute to be sent away from court. Surprisingly, Edward agreed. He would never have consented to Piers Gaveston's removal from court, at least not without being threatened and digging his heels in for months on end, and his actions here suggest that he had grown tired of his friends and was not willing to fight for them. On 20 October, Bartholomew Badlesmere replaced William Montacute in the key role of Edward's household steward, while Montacute himself was appointed steward of Gascony a month later, replacing Antonio di Pessagno.[107] Although this was an honour, Montacute must have known that he was deliberately being sent far away from Edward to limit his influence over the king.

And although Roger Damory's friendship with Edward was certainly not over, without constant access to the king's presence, his influence over him would henceforth be severely limited. And more good news came in the autumn of 1318. On 14 October, Roger Mortimer's ally John de Bermingham defeated and killed Edward Bruce, high king of Ireland, at the Battle of Faughart (also called the Battle of Dundalk), one of the very few military successes of Edward's reign. Bermingham sent Bruce's head to Edward for inspection; one hopes that Edward's friend Donald of Mar, who was Bruce's nephew, didn't have to see it. In gratitude, the king granted the earldom of Louth to Bermingham.[108]

Hugh Despenser, the new lord of Glamorgan, committed a shocking act sometime in 1318: he removed Llywelyn Bren, the Welsh rebel, who in 1316 had attacked Caerphilly Castle (which now belonged to Despenser), from the Tower of London, and had him grotesquely executed in Cardiff. Despenser's murder of Bren – for such it was, as he had no authority to commit such a dreadful act – attracted little censure or condemnation at the time, but was used against him three years later, and came back to haunt him in 1326. Edward did not punish Despenser, which is perhaps explicable by the fact that Despenser had already begun his rise in the king's affections. The parliament of October 1318 confirmed him as Edward's chamberlain, and he thus became the man who controlled access to the king both in person and in writing, a very influential position which Despenser exploited to the hilt. About thirty in 1318, Despenser was very well connected. His elder half-sister Maud Chaworth married the earl of Lancaster's brother Henry, the earl of Norfolk who died in 1306 was his step-grandfather and the earl of Warwick who died in 1315 his uncle, and the earl of Ulster his mother's first cousin. Despenser married Edward II's thirteen-year-old niece Eleanor de Clare on 26 May 1306 in the presence of her grandfather Edward I, who paid Hugh Despenser the Elder £2,000 for his son's marriage and gave Eleanor £29 to buy herself jewels.[109] Although the Despensers were reasonably wealthy and owned close to seventy manors in the Midlands and south-east of England, Despenser would not inherit an earldom and was thus hardly a brilliant match for the king of England's eldest granddaughter. The marriage seems to have been successful on a personal level, however, and the couple had at least ten children together during their twenty-year marriage.

The later chronicler Geoffrey le Baker writes of Edward's intense indignation at Despenser's 1318 appointment as chamberlain, as he hated him.[110] Although this is surely an exaggeration, Edward had never shown Despenser any favour before 1318, except for granting him permission to hunt in 1312, two wardships and the lands of two Scotsmen shortly before Bannockburn, which Despenser never obtained thanks to Edward's failures in Scotland.[111] Edward ordered the seizure of Despenser's goods at the beginning of 1310 as he had gone overseas without permission to attend a jousting tournament in Mons, and Despenser seems to have allied himself in the early years of Edward's reign with his uncle Warwick rather than his royalist father, to the anger of Edward's followers: the Ordainers demanded in 1311 that the members of the king's household who had attacked Despenser be removed from court.[112] Despite being Edward's nephew by marriage (though only about three to five years his junior) and son of one of his closest allies, Despenser's political influence prior to 1317 was severely limited, and he owned no lands at all; his father had to grant him the revenues of six of his own manors to give Despenser at least some income.[113] It is even possible that one of Edward's motives in pretending to believe in the countess of Gloucester's pregnancy was reluctance to hand over a wealthy lordship to a man he disliked and distrusted, although in 1317, the king, presumably recognising that Despenser would become rich and influential and it might be a good idea to court him as an ally, granted him several castles and manors in South Wales in lieu of 600 marks he owed Despenser.[114] Despenser's wife Eleanor, born in 1292, was a lady-in-waiting of Queen Isabella, and Edward's favourite niece (rather than her sister Elizabeth, as he pretended in 1316); he even paid her expenses out of court, a sign of great favour.[115] Roger Damory's departure from court – which Despenser, as one of the negotiators of the Treaty of Leake, may well have had a hand in – gave him free rein to exercise his charms over the king.

Parliament confirmed Despenser as chamberlain 'at the request and counsel of the magnates', which suggests that the earl of Pembroke and his allies trusted him, and even the earl of Lancaster did not object to his appointment, even though he hated Despenser's father.[116] The magnates' trust of Despenser implies that he had kept his true nature – his boundless ambition, greed, ruthlessness, cruelty and potential for despotism – hidden; they would never have placed him so close to the king if they had had the slightest idea how he would behave in office, how dangerous he would prove to be, and how much cause they would have to regret his appointment.

9

Household and Homage

On 6 December 1318, the four leading members of Edward II's household – his steward, chamberlain, treasurer and controller of the wardrobe – formulated an ordinance for the king's household.[1] The earliest surviving English Household Ordinance dates from 1279, and the 1318 one is the second-oldest still extant. Edward's household was divided into two main sections: the chamber, led by the chamberlain, and the hall, managed by the steward, men always of noble or knightly rank. Edward had a household of around 450 to 550 people, yet this was not the largest in the country; Thomas of Lancaster's contained a staggering 700 members.[2] Queen Isabella had her own household, of close to 200 people, and Edward paid all the costs. As he travelled through the country, finding and paying for provisions for so many people could prove burdensome. During the Great Famine in 1315, a brave cleric told Edward's confessor that 'the inhabitants used to rejoice to see the face of the king when he came, but now, because the king's approach injures the people, his departure gives them much pleasure and as he goes off they pray that he may never return'.[3] Edward had in August 1312 declared himself unable, owing to the 'arduous business' which followed Gaveston's death, to pay for his household provisions in Kent, which included 1,000 sheep, 500 oxen, 300 swine, 1,000 quarters of wheat and 2,000 quarters of oats.[4]

There was an astonishing degree of hierarchy and specialisation: in the hall, for example, Edward had a knight chief usher, two sergeant ushers, two knights marshal and two sergeants marshal. He had a personal bodyguard of twenty-four archers on foot, thirty sergeants-at-arms 'who will daily ride armed before the king's person', and, to provide his personal service, squires, valets or grooms and pages of the chamber. One of Edward's chamber valets was William Warde, who received a regular sum of money from the exchequer for, mysteriously, 'keeping a certain secret of the king in the palace of Westminster'.[5] Other chamber valets were Simon Hod, Robin Dyer and Wat Cowherd, who were not, as a modern writer has imagined, lowborn men whom the king had brought to court and with whom he was 'being promiscuous'. The 'substantial payments' they received supposedly as 'hush money' were simply the men's wages, which the king's staff were paid twice monthly.[6]

The king's accounts of the 1320s reveal he had several dozen squires, more than thirty valets, about half a dozen pages, a steward, knights, clerks and an usher of the chamber. The valets in 1326 included two women named Anneis and Joan, wives of Roger de May and Robin Traghs who were also chamber valets, and the women received the same wages of three pence per day as the men, with presumably the same responsibilities. Edward seems to have been fond of Joan Traghs in particular: he once gave her five shillings to buy clothes and a gift of ten shillings after she gave birth to her daughter, most unusually hired her as a valet of his chamber (all great households of the Middle Ages consisted almost exclusively of men), and continued to pay her wages for forty-four days when she was away from court, ill.[7] The frequent use of nicknames in Edward's extant accounts hints at affection and camaraderie among the royal household staff. The name Thomas is often given as Thomelyn; Richard as Hick or Richardyn; Hugh as Huchon; Roger as Hogge; Robert as Robin or Hobbe; Gilbert as Gibbe or Gibon; Nicholas as Colle; Simon as Syme; Edmund (then spelt Edmon or Esmon) as Monde; Walter as Watte; William as Wille; John as Janin, Janekyn or Jack; Isabella as Sibille or Ibote; Joan as Jonete. One of Edward's chamber valets was called Grete Hobbe, or in modern English Big Rob, and he also had servants called Litel Colle and Litel Wille Fisher.

Edward had two personal cooks and five valets to help them, and also had a 'server and keeper of the foods for his mouth', a squire who carved his meat and another who served him from his cup. The king used splendid knives for eating, which had silver enamelled or ebony handles, cost about twelve shillings each and had to be frequently replaced.[8] His musical needs were taken care of: there would be performers to 'make their minstrelsy before the king at all times that will please him'. The largest department was the marshalsea or stables, and Edward had, among many other servants, a man who 'will lead to the king the horse which he will mount; and he will receive the king when he dismounts'. The Ordinance was keen to keep 'undesirables' away from court. Prostitutes, if caught there three times, would be imprisoned for forty days. Edward's marshals were ordered to search the court weekly to find any people who hadn't sworn an oath of loyalty to the king; such people were to be 'taken and punished'. Members of the household were given the king's permission to visit their homes on occasion – wives and families were not allowed to live at court or even to follow behind – and received sums of money between five and a hundred shillings, depending on rank, for their travel expenses.

Rank and status dominated everything, including what kind of material people wore and what they ate. All food and drink including a gallon of ale per day was provided for free, though nobody below the rank of squire was entitled to eat roast meat but had to make to do with the boiled kind. Higher-ranking servants also received candles or a torch for their chamber and a pitcher of wine. The servants received clothing or livery as part of their wages, usually given out twice a year at Christmas and Pentecost, and the lower ranks also received four shillings and eight pence annually for shoes. The livery was usually colour co-ordinated, and the overall effect must have been colourful and vibrant. From 8 July 1315 to 7 July 1316, Edward spent £627 on clothes for his household. He received two tunics for himself in April 1316, comprising six ells of scarlet (expensive woollen cloth) with two ells of yellow cloth for sewing leopards, his heraldic arms, on them, and more scarlet for making bags.[9] He also received sixteen ells of green medley (dyed in the wool cloth) to make two sleeved tunics and two tabards. Green cloth lined with miniver was also given to the queen, their son Edward of Windsor, the king's sister Elizabeth and his nieces Eleanor and Margaret.[10] In November 1322, Edward purchased twelve ells of black and vermilion medley, at sixteen pence per ell, to make doublets (*courtepies*) for the squires of his chamber.[11] He paid twenty-one pounds to the London draper Simon Swanland in December 1325 for medley cloth for his carpenters and forty marks for forty cloths to make elbow-length cloaks for his chamber valets. Two pages received blue cloth at a cost of six shillings in April 1326 for tunics 'in the style of Gascony'.[12] Thomas of Lancaster, at Christmas 1313, gave azure cloth to the knights of his household, medley to his clerks and *mi-parti* (cloth divided vertically in two colours) to his squires, and the following summer gave the knights yellow cloth, the clerks red medley and the squires striped cloth.[13]

The day after the Ordinance was issued, Edward turned his attention to the important business of his elder son's marriage, and wrote to Count William of Hainault to arrange a marriage between young Edward and the count's eldest daughter, Margaret – not her sister Philippa, who did marry Edward III in 1328, as has often been assumed.[14] Edward also asked the pope to issue a dispensation for Edward of Windsor and Margaret to marry, as they were second cousins, both great-grandchildren of Philip III of France, and in November 1319 once again raised the issue, this time naming William's daughter as Sibilla, which was either an error – his careless clerk addressed the count as Robert – or a reference to another daughter who died young.[15] Edward spent the entire period from 9 January to 21 July 1319 in York, except for a few days at nearby Kirkham Priory in early April. The *Flores* reports that Queen Isabella gave birth to a daughter, Joan, while at York this year; no other source mentions this, however, and it is unlikely that a royal child could be born and leave no traces in the historical record – no funerary arrangements, for example.[16]

It is probable that the author confused the date of birth of their daughter Joan of the Tower, who was born in 1321.

Parliament opened on 6 May 1319 at York. Hugh Audley and his wife Margaret audaciously claimed the earldom of Cornwall as Margaret's inheritance from her late husband Piers Gaveston, a claim parliament refused, on the grounds that the lands which Edward had granted to Gaveston had been revoked.[17] On 2 and 12 June, Edward sent letters to Haakon V of Norway regarding debts which the Norwegian king owed to eight English merchants, unaware that Haakon had died on 6 May.[18] The king appointed his barber Laurence Elmham custodian of the royal forest of Galtres in Yorkshire, also granting him permission to appoint a deputy, as he was unable personally to perform his duties owing to his attendance on the king. Elmham claimed in 1330 to have served as Edward's barber for twenty-six years, though in 1325/26 a man called Henry is named as such in the king's chamber account.[19]

In November 1318, Edward had summoned men to muster at Berwick-on-Tweed, to besiege the port and take it back into English hands from Robert Bruce, who had seized it the year before. The campaign should have begun on 10 June 1319, but on 22 May, it was postponed until 22 July.[20] Although on 20 July Edward asked the two archbishops and all the bishops of England to pray for him on his way to Scotland, he didn't arrive at Berwick until 7 September, spending the whole of August in and around Newcastle.[21] The necessity of retaking the vital port of Berwick meant that even the earl of Lancaster co-operated with Edward for once, and the earls of Pembroke, Surrey, Arundel, Hereford, Atholl and Angus also joined the king. The nineteen-year-old Thomas of Brotherton, earl of Norfolk, attended, and Edward knighted his half-brother on 15 July.[22]

Predictably, the siege was unsuccessful. Despite the importance of capturing the port, the *Vita* implies that Edward decided to attack only on the spur of the moment.[23] Given such a slapdash approach – no one had even thought to bring siege-engines – it is hardly surprising that the attack failed.[24] Edward ordered a simultaneous attack by land and sea, and although his force 'almost scaled the wall in the first assault delivered with great fury ... the inhabitants regained their courage and defended themselves with spirit'.[25] Edward kept himself amused during the siege, and paid his minstrel 'King' Robert and two musicians sent to him by his brother-in-law Philip V of France for playing before him, ordered hunting dogs sent from Wales, and had two of his falcons brought from London. The falcons were named Damory, after his friend, and Beaumont, after his French cousin Henry Beaumont, and had probably been gifts from these men.[26] His father had in 1305/06 owned falcons called Blanchepoune, Skardebek, d'Engayne, Durham and Parson.[27]

As a decoying tactic, James Douglas and Thomas Randolph, earl of Moray, led an army into England and reached as far south as

Boroughbridge, near York. According to a captured Scottish scout, there was a plan to seize Queen Isabella, who was staying at a small manor of the archbishop of York, either Brotherton or Bishopthorpe.[28] The queen hastened to York, from where she escaped by water to the safety of Nottingham. A mortified Edward later gave her jewels and other gifts in consolation.[29] The *Vita* points out that 'if the queen had at that time been captured, I believe that Scotland would have bought peace for herself', and accuses the earl of Lancaster, almost certainly falsely, of plotting with the Scots to capture his niece in exchange for £40,000.[30] Perhaps to divert attention from himself, Lancaster in turn accused Hugh Despenser, though Despenser hardly had any compelling motives for wishing the queen to be taken hostage either, and this may represent Lancaster's awareness that Despenser, placed close to the king by the barons a few months before, was not nearly as malleable or safe as he had thought.[31] The fact remained, though, that someone had betrayed the queen's whereabouts to the Scots, and the culprit was probably a knight named Edmund Darel.[32]

On 12 September, the Scottish force defeated an English army hastily cobbled together by Edward's friend William Melton, archbishop of York, near the village of Myton-on-Swale.[33] So many clerics died – *Lanercost* says 4,000, with another 1,000 who drowned in the Swale – that the battle became known as the Chapter of Myton.[34] The abbot of St Mary's in York later founded a chapel in the village, 'in honour of the Transubstantiation and the flesh and blood of Our Lord', to pray for the souls of the men who died.[35] News of this latest military disaster reached Berwick on 14 September 1319, and the earl of Lancaster left the port two days later, though whether to protect his lands, to cut off the Scots' retreat or out of disgust with Edward is not clear.[36] Hugh Despenser, an enthusiastic letter-writer, told the sheriff of Glamorgan that

> the Scots had entered his [Edward's] land of England with the prompting and assistance of the earl of Lancaster. The earl acted in such a way that the king took himself off with all his army, to the great shame and damage of us all. Wherefore we very much doubt if matters will end so happily for our side as is necessary.[37]

Once again, relations between the king and his powerful cousin deteriorated, thanks in part to the actions of Edward's favourites, and the Bridlington chronicler also claims that some people deliberately fostered dissent and conflict between Edward and Lancaster, falsely reporting Edward's words to the earl and vice versa.[38] Although relations between the two most powerful men in the kingdom were, prior to the siege, outwardly amicable, Edward proved what was really on his mind by ominously announcing, 'When this wretched business is over, we will turn our hands to other matters. For I have not forgotten the wrong that was done to my brother Piers.'[39] Edward had not forgiven Lancaster for Gaveston's death, and still had vengeance in mind. Gaveston remained in his thoughts, as always, and seven years after his friend's death, he paid for a turquoise cloth to cover his tomb.[40]

Trokelowe says that Edward lay in wait for the Scots at Newminster, a Cistercian priory near Morpeth in Northumberland, and Edward's itinerary does indeed place him there on 19 September, but they eluded him by returning to their homeland by the western route.[41] By this time, Hugh Despenser had become close to Edward; the king promised to make his chamberlain keeper of the castle once Berwick fell. He also promised with his 'usual foolishness' to make Roger Damory constable of the town, thus presumptuously handing out favours he hadn't yet won.[42] Although Edward had consented to send Damory away from him the previous year, the knight evidently still remained high in the king's affections, and the *Flores* calls Edward's friends – presumably referring to Damory and Despenser – 'despicable parasites'.[43]

Thomas Randolph and James Douglas invaded England again at the beginning of November 1319, laying waste to much of Westmorland and Cumberland and returning to Scotland with 'a very large spoil of men and cattle'.[44] Therefore, Edward granted powers on 1 December to several men including Hugh Despenser to make a truce with Robert Bruce.[45] On this day, according to the Sempringham annalist, 'there was a general earthquake in England, with great sound and much noise'.[46] Robert Bruce confirmed a truce on 22 December, to run until Christmas 1321; it may have been Edward's frequent truces, at least in part, which led the *Flores* to condemn his notorious infamy and cowardice and declare that the king was a slave to idleness.[47] On 8 January 1320, John XXII republished the bull of excommunication against Bruce for his murder of John 'the Red Comyn' and his uncle in 1306.[48]

Edward spent Christmas 1319 at York, having invited the warden and thirty-two scholars of King's Hall, his foundation at Cambridge, to join him. Most of them arrived late, on 28 December, and one joined in an assault by the prior of the Dominicans of Pontefract on a William Hardy and was left behind in disgrace when the scholars returned to Cambridge.[49] The king remained at York for New Year, and gave Queen Isabella expensive jewels and other gifts.[50] Parliament opened on 20 January 1320, and perhaps the attendees saw the 'wonderful eclipse of the moon of many various colours' on the morning of 26 January, as recorded by the Sempringham annalist.[51] Edward told his magnates that he had arranged to meet his brother-in-law Philip V at Amiens on 9 March, in order to perform homage for Gascony and Ponthieu, and 'because time was getting on and the way was long, he could not remain there to complete all the business concerning the said parliament, if he wished to speed on his way'.[52] His half-brother Edmund of Woodstock, now eighteen and a first cousin of Philip V and Queen Isabella through his mother Queen Marguerite, was sent to Paris to arrange a safe-conduct for the king, and on 19 February Edward informed Philip that he would meet him at Amiens, and sent out commissioners to find lodgings for him in the town.[53] After parliament, Edward set off for London. On his way through Pontefract, Lancaster's retainers once again jeered at him, and Isabella, from the safety of the castle.[54] This time, however, Edward sensibly ignored – though certainly didn't forgive – this discourteous behaviour. The king and queen arrived in London on 16 February 1320, where the mayor and other senior officials of the city met them at Kilburn.[55]

On 17 April 1320, the pope canonised Thomas Cantilupe, bishop of Hereford, who had died in August 1282. This was due in part to the efforts of Edward himself, who wrote to Clement V and John XXII half a dozen times between December 1307 and January 1319, asking them to canonise Cantilupe.[56] The two archbishops and all the bishops of England asked Edward to be present at the 'translation of the holy body' in Hereford Cathedral on 14 June 1321, and he responded, 'It pleases the king to be there.'[57] Edward was at Lambeth on the day of Cantilupe's canonisation, when, according to the Sempringham annalist – who had a fondness for recording the weather – 'about midnight, there were frightful thunders heard, with lightning, and immoderately high wind'.[58] Sometime in 1320, the king provided further proof of his eccentricity by taking possession of a cottage within the precincts of Westminster Abbey, which he called Borgoyne, Burgundy. According to the disapproving Westminster chronicler the *Flores*, he jokingly took to calling himself 'king of Burgundy' rather than 'king of England'. The *Flores* goes on to comment that Edward's occupation of the cottage, which had a large garden, ditches encircling it and its own keeper, was 'not without sacrilege'.[59] Later in his reign, Edward spent a few days there on occasion, shunning his more luxurious accommodation, while most of his household lodged in more conventional locations at Westminster or at the Tower. The king said farewell on 17 May to the archbishop of Vienne, a papal nuncio who had come to England to negotiate with the Scots at Bamburgh, and gave him a pair of silver dishes and a silver-gilt basin, 'chased and enamelled, with ewer', worth seven pounds and ten shillings.[60] The earl of Gloucester's widow Maud died sometime in 1320, taking her motives for faking a three-year pregnancy to the grave, and her dower lands were divided out among her late husband's sisters and their husbands, making Hugh Audley, Hugh Despenser and Roger Damory richer by about £900 each per year.

Edward finally sailed from Dover to France on 19 June 1320, with, among dozens of others, Queen Isabella, Donald of Mar, Hugh Despenser, Roger Damory, the teenaged William Montacute, son of Edward's dead friend of the same name, and John Hastings, nephew and co-heir of the childless earl of Pembroke. Pembroke's wife Beatrice of Clermont-Nesle, who died later that year, accompanied Queen Isabella, while Pembroke himself remained in London as keeper of the realm.[61] Roger Damory was still in Edward's favour, but as events later in the year would prove, he was losing his position to the king's ruthless young chamberlain, Despenser. At Amiens, Edward stayed in the house of one Peter du Garde, and later paid him ten marks in compensation for 'all damage to his dwelling' caused during his stay. The king's chapel was placed in the house of John le Mouner, his offices in the house of Sanxia, the storeroom for his kitchen in the house of Margaret, and the passage between his chamber and chapel in the house of William le Mouner. Edward paid Peter le Peyntour a shilling and sixpence to paint shields of the king's arms in the streets of Amiens, 'in order to make known where the king's liveries were', and four pounds to a master carpenter to repair 'damage done by carpenters and others in the state rooms' of the court.[62]

On 29 June, Edward met Philip V at Amiens and did liege homage before the high altar of the cathedral. In 1259, Edward's grandfather Henry III had signed the Treaty of Paris with Louis IX, which had finally ended the many decades of military conflicts between England and France over the English kings' lands in France, but which inadvertently created new tensions by including many clauses which were vague or could be interpreted in different ways.[63] Three or four days after the ceremony, during a meeting between the two kings and their councils, Philip's advisers decided that some of the concessions which Edward was prepared to make were inadequate, and demanded that he take an oath of personal fealty to the French king as well. A clerk of Edward's, an eyewitness, gave this account of what followed: 'And when some of the said prelates and nobles leaned towards our said lord [Edward] and began to instruct him, our said lord now turned towards the said king [Philip] without having been advised,' and announced,

> We well remember that the homage which we performed at Boulogne [in 1308] was done according to the form of the peace treaties made between our ancestors, after the manner in which they did it. Your father [Philip IV] agreed to it, for we have his letters confirming this, and we have performed it already in the same fashion; no one can reasonably ask us to do otherwise; and we certainly do not intend to do so. As to the fealty [oath] we are certain that we should not swear it; nor was it ever asked of us at that time.

The clerk continued, 'And then the king of France turned to the men of his council, and none of them could say anything to contradict the response of our said lord.'[64] Edward's fluent and angry defence, spoken spontaneously without the benefit of any advice, reduced them to stunned silence, and the question of fealty was quietly dropped. As his remarks here show, Edward was an articulate and persuasive speaker and could think on his feet, and the *Scalacronica* calls him 'amiable in conversation' – as well as, uniquely, 'wise' and 'gentle'.[65]

Edward held a banquet in Amiens on 8 July, in a tent or pavilion, and gave the large sum of twenty pounds to the minstrels who performed there.[66] He and his retinue left the following day, made their way along the River Somme, and visited Abbeville, the capital of his county of Ponthieu, which he had granted to Isabella. The royal couple sailed from Wissant on 22 July, and the mayor and citizens of London rode out to meet Edward in early August: 'Dressed in clothes appropriate to their office, they greeted him in fine style.'[67] Edward's twenty-year-old half-brother Thomas of Brotherton, earl of Norfolk, went to the king at Langley in mid-August to ask advice about his marriage.[68] King Jaime II of Aragon had proposed his daughter Maria, widow of Pedro of Castile, as Norfolk's bride, but in August 1321 reported that Maria had decided to become a nun and he did not think he would be able to change her mind.[69] Norfolk married instead, at an unknown date perhaps in 1321, Alice Hales, daughter of the coroner of Norfolk: a decidedly odd choice for a man who was son and brother of kings of England and nephew of a king of France. Edward wrote on 27 August 1320 to the king of Cyprus, his distant cousin Henri de Lusignan, asking him to protect three Dominican friars going to preach to the 'Saracens', and on 14 September ordered 'five pieces of silk, embroidered with birds' to be laid on the body of the recently deceased countess of Pembroke at the conventual church of Stratford, London.[70]

Parliament opened at Westminster on 6 October 1320, and it was probably around this time that Edward and Queen Isabella conceived their fourth child Joan, who was born on 5 July 1321. Edward's son Edward of Windsor, earl of Chester, was summoned to this parliament for the first time, although he was not yet eight years old. After his eloquent defence to the king of France, Edward proved once again that he was more capable than many commentators have given him credit for. The chronicler Nicholas Trevet wrote that Edward 'showed prudence in answering the petitions of the poor, and clemency as much as severity in judicial matters, to the amazement of many who were there'.[71] Of course, the 'amazement' makes clear how uninterested and uninvolved Edward usually was. The opening speech of parliament said that Edward had summoned it 'in his great desire and wish to do all the things which concern a good lord for the benefit of his realm and of his people'. Edward's behaviour and demeanour at the October 1320 parliament excited more comment. Thomas Cobham, bishop of Worcester, wrote approvingly, albeit condescendingly, in a letter to Pope John XXII,

Besides, which, Holy Father, your devoted son, our lord the king, in the parliament summoned to London bore himself splendidly, with prudence and discretion, contrary to his former habit rising early and presenting a nobler and pleasant countenance to prelates and lords. Present almost every day in person, he arranged what business was to be dealt with, discussed and determined. Where amendment was necessary he ingeniously supplied what was lacking, thus giving joy to his people, ensuring their security, and providing reliable hope of an improvement in behaviour.[72]

Cobham's letter demonstrates that Edward was, for once, showing an interest in his duties and in his realm, and also prove that he could be wise, patient, judicious, merciful where necessary, and eloquent. But then, his subjects already knew that he had ability; it was just that, usually, he chose not to bother, as Cobham's letters also amply demonstrate. Edward II's problem was not lack of ability. It was lack of interest. On rare occasions, he chose to exercise his talents. Most of the time, he didn't.

Edward had finally, thirteen years after his accession, learned how to be a king. But 1320 would prove to be the highest point of his reign. The day after parliament ended, he took the step which would lead inexorably to the outbreak of civil war the following spring and the exile of his friends the Despensers.

10

The Despenser War

In October 1320, Edward II abandoned the prudent and capable behaviour he had been demonstrating for much of that year, and the latest crisis of his reign reared its ugly head in South Wales. The partition of the de Clare lands among Hugh Despenser, Roger Damory and Hugh Audley in 1317 had, in addition to making all three men rich and influential, perhaps inevitably caused much rivalry, discontent and envy among them. *Lanercost* says that 'being a most avaricious man, he [Despenser] had contrived by different means and tricks that he alone should possess the lands and revenues, and for that reason had devised grave charges against those who had married the other two sisters'.[1] The *Vita* agrees, saying that Despenser 'set traps for his co-heirs; thus, if he could manage it, each would lose his share through false accusations and he alone would obtain the whole earldom [of Gloucester]'.[2]

Despenser now decided that his lands of Glamorgan and Gwynllwg were not enough, and set his heart on gaining possession of the Gower peninsula, where Swansea lies. Gower belonged to a baron named William Braose, who had no son and who had at various times offered to sell Gower to his son-in-law John Mowbray, Despenser himself, the earl of Hereford, Roger Mortimer and his uncle Roger Mortimer of Chirk. All these men claimed that Braose had sold the reversion of Gower to them.[3] By the autumn of 1320, Hugh Despenser stood high in the king's favour, and Edward was infatuated with him. Geoffrey le Baker wrote a few years later that many people considered Despenser to be 'another king, or more accurately ruler of the king...in the manner of Gaveston, so presumptuous that he frequently kept certain nobles from speaking to the king. Moreover, when the king, out of his magnanimity, was preoccupied with many people addressing him about their affairs, Despenser threw back answers, not those asked for but to the contrary, pretending them to be to the king's advantage'.[4] According to the *Annales Paulini*, Edward had also allowed Gaveston to make decisions on his behalf.[5] Despenser's abuse of his position as chamberlain became obvious, and the *Brut* says that he 'kept so the king's chamber, that no man might speak with the king ... the king himself would not be governed by no manner of man, but only by his father and by him'.[6] The *Anonimalle* says that 'no man could approach the king without the consent of the said Sir Hugh' and calls him haughty, arrogant, greedy, evil and 'more inclined to wrongdoing than any other man'.[7] The *Vita* says, 'Confident of the royal favour, he did everything at his own discretion, snatched at everything, did not bow to the authority of anyone whomsoever.'[8] Regarding Despenser's enormous influence over the king, the *Flores* says that he led Edward around as though he were 'teasing a cat with a piece of straw', *Lanercost* that he was the 'king of England's right eye', and Knighton that he led Edward around for his own aggrandisement.[9]

The men who had heaved a sigh of relief at the death of Piers Gaveston now realised, to their horror, that Edward had replaced him with a man who was far worse and far more dangerous. *Scalacronica* says, 'the great men had ill will against him [Edward] for his cruelty and the debauched life which he led, and on account of the said Hugh, whom at that time he loved and entirely trusted'.[10] What the writer meant by 'debauched' is unclear, and there is even less evidence than with Piers Gaveston to tell us what kind of relationship Edward had with Despenser. He never referred to him as his brother, as he did Gaveston, and we have none of Edward's letters where he describes his feelings for Despenser. The favourite was ruthlessly determined to get what he wanted, and prepared to use the king's infatuation with him as a means to this end. He was, at least, honest about his ambitions, and told John Inge, sheriff of Glamorgan, on 18 January 1321, 'We command you to watch our affairs that we may be rich and achieve our ends...'[11]

John Mowbray, who must have been well aware that Despenser was now the king's favourite, took possession of Gower in the autumn of 1320, even though his father-in-law William Braose was still alive (he died in 1326). A furious Despenser persuaded Edward that, as Mowbray had not received a royal licence to enter the lands, Gower should be forfeit to the king.[12] The Marcher lords, the men who owned the lordships in Wales and along the English-Welsh border, protested that in the March, they did not need a royal licence to enter their lands, which was correct; as the old saying ran 'The king's writ does not run in the March', where the lords dispensed their own justice, were not subject to the jurisdiction of the local sheriff, and enjoyed sovereign powers in their lordships. Their role, in exchange for these privileges, was to keep the turbulent Welsh-English border quiescent. Since Edward I's conquest of Wales in 1282, however, this was no longer necessary; the Marchers thus had wide-ranging privileges but few responsibilities to justify them.[13] Edward, 'who promoted Hugh's designs as far as he could', ordered Gower to be taken into his own hands on 26 October 1320, presumably intending to grant it to his favourite.[14] However, the sub-escheator of Gloucestershire, Richard Foxcote, was unable to take possession of it thanks to the 'large multitude of armed Welshmen' who detested Despenser's lordship, and who gathered at the chapel of St Thomas at Kilvey near Swansea and prevented Foxcote 'executing the mandate, so that he could do nothing therein without danger of death'.[15]

The Marchers were furious and concerned. This latest infatuation of Edward's threatened their privileges, and no doubt they knew that Hugh Despenser was a very different proposition from Piers Gaveston, who with hindsight was probably coming more and more to be seen as harmless. 'Deeply moved by such abuse, the barons departed full of indignation, and meeting in Wales, they unanimously decided that Hugh Despenser must be pursued, laid low and utterly destroyed.'[16] Most of the men who owned lands in the Marches turned against Edward and Hugh Despenser: Humphrey de Bohun, earl of Hereford; Roger Mortimer of Wigmore, formerly a close ally of the king and his lieutenant of Ireland, and his uncle Roger Mortimer of Chirk; Roger Damory; Hugh Audley; John Mowbray; Roger Clifford, son of the Robert Clifford killed at Bannockburn in 1314; Edward's former chamberlain John Charlton; the earl of Lancaster's brother Henry; and fifty-year-old Maurice Berkeley, who succeeded as Lord Berkeley in July 1321 when his elderly father finally died, with his son Thomas and son-in-law John Maltravers. Edward cared little for the formidable coalition that was building against him; once again, he was prepared to put the wishes of a favourite above all else. The *Polychronicon* points out that he was 'passionately attached to one person, whom he cherished above all, showered with gifts and always put first; he could not bear being separated from him and honoured him above all others'. The *Scalacronica* agrees, saying that Edward was too familiar with his friends, shy with strangers, and 'loved too exclusively a single individual'.[17]

While all this was going on, Edward was still working towards an alliance between himself and Hainault, and in November 1320 wrote again to the pope to ask for a dispensation for his son Edward of Windsor to marry Margaret, daughter of Count William III.[18] Evidently, however, William had grown lukewarm on the alliance, and Edward wrote a frustrated letter to him four months later, saying that he would go ahead with other marriage plans for his son if he did not hear from William by 8 July 1321.[19] He also wrote to the cardinals who had been abducted and robbed by Gilbert Middleton in 1317 informing them that he could not recover their stolen possessions, on the prosaic grounds that he did not know where the items were to be found.[20] In December 1320, Edward paid three shillings and four pence to William, bookbinder of London, 'for binding and newly repairing the book of Domesday, in which is contained the counties of Essex, Norfolk and Suffolk', a manuscript dating to 1086 which still exists in the National Archives in Kew and is now known as 'Little Domesday'.[21] He spent Christmas and New Year at Marlborough in Wiltshire, probably with the pregnant Queen Isabella, spending nearly sixty pounds on the festivities for Christmas and Epiphany.[22] The Marcher lords left court over Christmas. Hugh Despenser knew how angry they were with him, and told the sheriff of Glamorgan on 18 January 1321 that 'envy is growing, and especially among the magnates, against us, because the king treats us better than any other'.[23] Edward, also well aware of the Marchers' hostility towards his friend, ordered the earl of Hereford and twenty-eight others not to attend armed assemblies or to make treaties 'prejudicial to the king and crown'.[24] The Marchers found a willing ally in the earl of Lancaster. Lancaster himself had few interests in the Marches but was willing to support anyone against his detested cousin the king, although he took no direct action in the events of 1321, preferring, as always, to lurk at his Yorkshire castle of Pontefract; even so, he was seen as the Marchers' leader.[25] For Lancaster to associate with his former enemies Roger Damory and Hugh Audley must have been anathema, but his desire to coerce the king took priority. For obscure reasons, he loathed Hugh Despenser the Elder, and wanted the Marchers to 'not only rise against the son, but destroy the father along with him'.[26]

On 12 January, Edward ordered the arrest, for a third time, of Robert Lewer, a valet of his household and formerly keeper of Odiham Castle in Hampshire, for 'trespasses, contempts and disobediences'. He had sent sergeants-at-arms to seize Lewer the previous summer, but Lewer resisted arrest and threatened to kill and dismember the men, in Edward's presence if need be.[27] Lewer grew up at court and acted as the king's water-bearer, responsible for drying his clothes and preparing his bath, though he was also a highly capable soldier. He 'was always ready for plunder and killing', which included murdering the husband of his mistress.[28] Edward was severely out of patience with him by 1321, describing him as 'so vile a person'.[29] The nature of Lewer's crimes is unknown, but he might have been angry that he had been replaced as constable of Odiham Castle by Hugh Despenser in February 1320, and his later actions demonstrate that he detested the Despensers and their influence.[30] Despenser, for his part, abused his position as constable of Odiham by removing the keeper of the park from his job, because he had once raised the hue and cry against Despenser's mother Isabel Beauchamp for taking five deer from the park without a licence.[31] Isabel died in May 1306; evidently, Despenser had a long memory.

Edward had returned to Westminster by 17 January 1321, and spent the next three weeks there. He attended a mass on 8 February at the church of Stratford, London, in memory of the late countess of Pembroke.[32] That afternoon, he rode to Havering-atte-Bower in Essex, a royal manor, where the following day he attended the wedding of one of his great-nieces: Hugh Despenser's eldest daughter Isabel, who married Richard, son and heir of Edmund Fitzalan, earl of Arundel. Isabel was eight, Richard seven.[33] Edward paid for a piece of Lucca cloth to make a veil for spreading over the heads of the child-couple during their nuptial mass, and gave two pounds in pennies to be thrown over them at the chapel door.[34]

The king left Westminster on 1 March with Hugh Despenser, and travelled slowly towards Gloucester. While at Fulmer in Buckinghamshire, he asked the Dominicans of Florence to pray for the good estate of himself, his family and his realm.[35] He took his mind off his troubles by attending to marital business, and wrote to King Jaime II of Aragon regarding the marriage of his eight-year-old son Edward of Windsor.[36] Jaime – to whose elder brother Alfonso III Edward's sister Eleanor had been betrothed from 1282 until Alfonso's sudden death in 1291 – had proposed his youngest daughter Violante, who was ten or eleven in March 1321, as a bride for the future king of England.[37] Edward also wrote to the pope asking him to grant a dispensation for the marriage of his widowed cousin the earl of Pembroke to another of his cousins, Marie, daughter of the count of St Pol.[38] On 28 March, Edward ordered the Marchers to come to him at Gloucester, but they failed to attend, which marks their transition from truculence to open hostility and defiance.[39]

The *Vita* says that the Marchers asked Edward to send Despenser away from him and have him come to trial to answer their complaints against him, 'otherwise they would no longer have him as king, but would utterly renounce their homage and fealty and whatever oath they had sworn to him'.[40] They also asked Edward to commit Despenser to the custody of the earl of Lancaster, and declared that they would guarantee to bring him safely to parliament to answer their complaints against him. With the example of Piers Gaveston, whose safety had been guaranteed by the earls of Pembroke and Surrey yet was killed by the earls of Warwick and Lancaster, still in his mind, Edward declared himself 'not without great wonder' at this demand, and responded 'it would be unfitting and dishonest to remove Hugh from the king's company'.[41] Both Edward and Despenser drastically underestimated the Marchers' discontent and willingness to use force and violence. Despenser, suffering one of his usual bouts of over-confidence, told the sheriff of Glamorgan 'do not doubt that neither he [Hugh Audley] nor any of his allies have the power to hurt any of us'.[42] An overly optimistic Edward wrote on 10 April to his friend William Aune, constable of Tickhill Castle and formerly of Piers Gaveston's household, 'Know that all things go peaceably and well at our wish, God be thanked'.[43] The king left Gloucester on 16 April, spending Easter Sunday, 19 April, at Bristol and his thirty-seventh birthday at Queen Isabella's Wiltshire castle of Devizes, where he gave ten shillings each to two minstrels the earl of Arundel had sent to him for their performance in his chamber.[44] Edward arrived at Westminster on 7 May and was probably reunited here with Isabella, now seven months pregnant, though the *Vita* says that Edward 'returned to London with his own Hugh always at his side', which can hardly have pleased the queen.[45]

Edward's commands fell on deaf ears. The Despenser War began on 4 May, when the Marchers, wearing a special tunic of green with the right quarter in yellow with white bends, attacked Despenser's castle at Newport, which fell three days later.[46] On the day the attacks began, Edward, oblivious, informed William Aune that 'we have nothing but good news before us'.[47] He also responded to a letter from some of his officials in Gascony, authorising the sale of a house in Condom known as the 'Earl's Hall' (*aula comitis*) on the grounds that it had become a 'brothel of worthless women', and gave a pound to the earl of Richmond's violist Merlin for performing for him.[48] Meanwhile, the Marchers rode through Glamorgan and besieged Cardiff, Swansea, Caerphilly and Despenser's six other Welsh castles, which also fell within a few days, and his towns.[49] They and their men tried to burn down the castles, and he later claimed a loss of £14,000 on twenty-three manors.[50] Innocents suffered from the general theft and pillaging; the prior and convent of Brecon informed Edward that 'they are greatly impoverished by the trouble there has been in the region', and the poor people of Swansea also petitioned the king for help.[51] Their rage and greed not yet sated, the Marchers and their followers then went on a rampage through the English lands of Hugh Despenser the Elder, sixty-seven manors in seventeen counties. Despenser later claimed losses of £38,000.[52]

The author of the *Vita*, despite his strong dislike of the Despensers, thought the Marchers had gone too far: 'Why did they destroy their manors, for what reason did they extort ransoms from their retinues? Though formerly their cause had been just, they now turned right into wrong.'[53] The Marchers themselves might have felt that their cause was a noble one. Given their violent and destructive behaviour, it is hard to agree. Claiming to be acting in Edward II's best interest and within the law, they killed and plundered his subjects and caused them untold distress. The Despensers may well have deserved such treatment, but their tenants did not, and although Edward's imprudent behaviour pushed the Marchers into rebellion, they put themselves equally in the wrong by inflicting misery on innocents. The bishop of Worcester, Thomas Cobham, informed the pope that the Marchers were capturing castles and committing homicides, and admitted that he had no idea why. He even said that only one of the marauding barons knew the real reason for the attacks, though what he meant by this is uncertain.[54] The letter of Cobham, who as a bishop was better-informed than most, probably demonstrates that few people understood the Marchers' aims, and it is doubtful that many cared; the loss of their anachronistic privileges was of little interest to anyone besides the Marchers themselves.

The Marchers took the king's sergeant-at-arms Guy Almavini prisoner, and stole the treasure Edward had stored at Neath Castle.[55] Around the same time, they committed far more serious acts of lawlessness: they captured John Iweyn, Despenser's constable of Neath, with his servant Philip le Keu, beheaded them at Swansea, and stole their goods.[56] The Marchers also killed at least sixteen other men, and wounded and imprisoned many others.[57] Roger Mortimer went to Clun and took over the castle there, which belonged to the earl of Arundel, the king and Despenser's ally. An indignant Arundel sent a letter on 4 June 1321 to 'the good and wise men of Shrewsbury' regarding a sum of money which he had asked them to guard and which he, probably not unreasonably, suspected Mortimer of wanting to steal. He begged them that 'you should keep safely for our use the money which you have received in our lord's [Edward's] town, for we do not under any circumstances intend that our cousin of Mortimer, who is so close to us in blood, should do us such a great injury, which we have in no way merited'.[58] Arundel had a long-running feud with his kinsmen the Mortimers, and even before the outbreak of the Despenser War, they were assailing his lordships in North Wales.[59]

Edward was evidently debating sending Despenser abroad for his own safety, as between 30 May and 12 June 1321, he granted safe-conducts to Despenser to go overseas, supposedly 'on the king's business'.[60] The steward of Gascony, Amaury de Craon, sent two envoys to England sometime in May with questions he required Edward to answer, but although the envoys spent three weeks with Edward, they reported that neither he, Despenser nor the earl of Pembroke had time to talk to them.[61] Edward has been criticised for this, on the grounds that he cared about nothing but his favourite's lands, but this is hardly fair; thousands of men were committing horrific acts of violence and plunder over a large part of his kingdom, killing, wounding and robbing his subjects, and no doubt he judged that any questions the steward of Gascony might have would have to wait.[62] Edward did find time on 21 May to give ten pounds to the messenger who brought him news of the birth of his latest great-nephew, the future Count Henri IV of Bar, son of Edward's nephew Edouard and Marie of Burgundy. Three days later, he purchased six pairs of boots 'with tassels of silk and drops of silver-gilt', which cost five shillings a pair, from Robert le Fermor, bootmaker of Fleet Street, and spent over twenty pounds to celebrate Ascension on 28 May.[63] He was, however, unable to attend the translation of St Thomas Cantilupe at Hereford Cathedral on 14 June, as he had wished.

The *Brut* says, 'When the king saw that the barons would not cease of their cruelty, the king was sore afraid lest they would destroy him and his realm.'[64] This may not be a gross exaggeration; the Despenser War, although short in duration, was terrifically violent, and as reports came to Edward of yet another manor attacked in yet another county, it must have seemed that his kingdom was descending into total anarchy. The earl of Lancaster remained in the north while his allies marched towards London. The Marchers seized victuals from local inhabitants and pillaged the countryside – not only Despenser manors – all the way from Yorkshire to London. John, Lord Mowbray and the knights Stephen Baret, Jocelyn Deyville and Bogo de Bayouse, for example, stole livestock, goods and chattels from the townspeople of Laughton-en-le-Morthen in Yorkshire, and even robbed the church.[65] Adherents of Roger Mortimer destroyed the houses of John Bloxham in Oxfordshire, stole his goods and assaulted his servants, while the monastery of St Albans, according to its chroniclers, was only saved from the general pillaging because one of the Marcher leaders (unnamed) fell ill at Aylesbury.[66] The Marchers had little choice but to turn to pillage and theft to feed their men, as for the most part, the inhabitants of the places they passed through had no wish to help them.

Edward sent his steward Bartholomew Badlesmere to an assembly of the earl of Lancaster and the Marchers at Sherburn, presumably as a spy. Badlesmere switched sides and joined the Marchers.[67] This proved to be an astonishingly unwise move on his part as the earl of Lancaster loathed him, for unknown reasons. He may have gambled that as Lancaster was prepared to ally himself with Roger Damory, whom he had once accused of trying to kill him, he would forgive Badlesmere also for whatever wrongs he thought Badlesmere had done him. If so, he miscalculated. On 28 July 1321, Edward II created his half-brother Edmund of Woodstock earl of Kent, a few days before Edmund's twentieth birthday, and 'girt his said brother with a sword as earl of the said county'.[68] This was most likely designed to limit Badlesmere's influence in Kent, where he owned great estates; he had hoped to become earl of Kent himself.[69]

Edward authorised the foundation of several houses for teaching logic and theology at Cambridge University on 5 July, at the request of his clerk Roger Northburgh, shortly to become bishop of Coventry and Lichfield on the death of Walter Langton.[70] Queen Isabella gave birth on the same day to their youngest child, named Joan (Johane, as it was spelt at the time) after Isabella's mother Queen Joan I of Navarre and perhaps after Edward's late sister Joan of Acre. Robert Staunton was granted a respite of eighty pounds on a debt of £180 he owed to the Exchequer for the simple expedient of travelling a couple of miles across London to inform the king.[71] Edward arrived at the Tower on 8 July and stayed with Isabella and his daughter for six days, and little Joan of the Tower soon joined the household of her older siblings, under the care of Matilda Pyrie or Perie, formerly the nurse of her brother John of Eltham.[72] On 26 July, Edward asked the Dominicans of Pontefract to pray for himself, Isabella and their children.[73]

The Marchers arrived outside London on 29 July, two weeks late for parliament, and the citizens refused to admit them.[74] Edward also refused to meet them or even to listen to their demands that the Despensers be perpetually exiled from England, and they and their heirs disinherited 'as false and traitorous criminals and spies'. The barons therefore placed themselves and their armies outside the city walls, at strategic locations, to prevent the king leaving.[75] They sent two knights as envoys to Edward to tell him that they wished both Despensers to be exiled, but Edward refused to meet the envoys, offering the rather feeble excuse that they had no letters of credence.[76] The Marchers finally entered London on 1 August 1321. The *Annales Paulini* say that Hugh Despenser was sailing along the Thames off Gravesend at this time, visiting the king at night and urging him to delay any agreement with the Marchers. Apparently incapable of reacting to anything except with violence, the Marchers threatened to burn the city from Charing Cross to Westminster if Despenser didn't desist.[77]

The Marchers demanded that if Edward refused to consent to the Despensers' exile, he would be deposed. The events of almost exactly ten years before, when the Ordainers had threatened him with deposition if he did not consent to Piers Gaveston's exile, were repeating themselves. The royalist earl of Pembroke told him, 'Consider, lord king, the power of the barons ... Do not for any living soul lose thy kingdom,' and, quoting the Bible, 'He perishes on the rocks that loves another more than himself.' He went on to advise the king 'if you will listen to your barons you shall reign in power and glory; but if, on the other hand, you close your ears to their petitions, you may perchance lose the kingdom and all of us'.[78] Even these heartfelt words and the renewed threat of deposition did not move Edward. Anguished at the thought of his friends being sent into exile, he continued to refuse. He suggested that they go to Ireland until the anger of the Marchers had cooled, and declared that it was deplorable for noblemen to be judged in such a manner and that he knew they were not traitors.[79]

It fell to Queen Isabella to break the deadlock. She went down on her knees before her husband and begged him, for the good of his realm, to exile the Despensers.[80] Finally accepting that he had no choice, Edward entered the great hall of Westminster on 14 August, with his cousins Pembroke and Richmond on either side of him, and agreed to banish his friends.[81] Chroniclers Adam Murimuth and Geoffrey le Baker both make the point that Edward was afraid of civil war if he did not do so, but never consented inwardly to the barons' demands, while the Rochester chronicler says that he was compelled by force and fear.[82] In the presence of Edward, but not the Despensers themselves, judgement was given against the two men, and it was decreed that they would be disinherited and perpetually exiled from England.[83] Even the author of the *Vita*, who criticised the Despensers severely and condemned their greed and brutality, thought 'they had been banished out of malice'.[84] The date of their departure was set as the feast of the Beheading of St John the Baptist, 29 August 1321.[85] Between 20 August and late September, Edward was forced to grant a pardon to more than 400 men for the murders, abductions, thefts and vandalism they had committed in the Despensers' lands.[86] Not surprisingly, he later protested that he had done this unwillingly and that any pardon he had given under coercion was invalid.[87]

On the day the Despensers were ordered into exile, Edward retired to his chamber, 'anxious and sad'. The next morning at breakfast, he invited Hamo Hethe, bishop of Rochester, to his table, and whispered to him that the Despensers had been condemned unjustly. Hethe replied consolingly that Edward could 'amend the defeat'. Edward responded that he 'would within half a year make such an amend that the whole world would hear of it and tremble'.[88]

It took him a little more than half a year, but he was as good as his word.

11

The King's Revenge

When he heard the news of his and his son's perpetual banishment from their homeland, Hugh Despenser the Elder 'cursed the time that ever he begot Sir Hugh his son, and said that for him he had lost England'. He immediately departed from Dover, and took himself off abroad somewhere.[1] As for his son Hugh Despenser, Edward II placed his friend under the protection of the men of the Cinque Ports, and Despenser, never one to sit around when there was money to be made, became a pirate in the English Channel, where he was 'master of the seas, their merchandise and chattels, and no ship got through unharmed'. Despenser attacked two great Genoese ships off Sandwich, killed their crew, and took for himself the vast wealth he found, supposedly £40,000.[2] Edward II's son paid compensation in the 1330s.[3] In June 1325, Edward officially pardoned Despenser for his piracy, on the extremely dubious grounds that 'he through fear of death adhered to diverse malefactors at sea and on land, and stayed with them to save his life, while they perpetrated depredations and other crimes'.[4]

Parliament ended on 22 August 1321, and Edward left Westminster five days later and travelled to the island of Thanet in Kent. It seems as though he sent most of his household away while he stayed with Despenser, plotting revenge on their enemies, as the well-informed royal clerk and chronicler Adam Murimuth suggests.[5] In the meantime, the Marchers retired to Oxford to stay close at hand in case Edward attempted to recall the Despensers. As they surely knew, Edward had no intention of allowing his friends to remain in exile. Over the next few months, he proved himself energetic and extremely capable in bringing about their return, which must have caused some people to wonder why he didn't behave like that more often; only when his favourites were threatened and his personal feelings were involved did he stir himself to action. Edward had a very loyal ally in the autumn of 1321: Queen Isabella. Between 3 and 24 August, and again between 23 October and 5 November, he granted her custody of the great seal, demonstrating the enormous trust he placed in his wife.[6] Isabella hated the Despensers and must have been glad to see them go into exile, but she hated to see her husband's royal powers eroded even more.

The king arrived at Portchester on 4 October, and stayed for eight days. It is likely that Edward secretly met Hugh Despenser again there, to discuss their next moves; at his 1326 trial, Despenser was charged with returning to England illegally during his exile. Despenser's crimes of 1321 might have encompassed more than piracy: Robert Batail of Winchelsea, baron of the Cinque Ports, and his allies attacked Southampton on 30 September. A petition by the people of Southampton claims that Batail and his men burnt and stole their ships, chattels, merchandise and goods to a loss of £8,000 in conspiracy with Hugh Despenser, who accused the townspeople of supporting the earl of Lancaster against the king.[7] Given that Edward placed Despenser under the care of the men of the Cinque Ports, and that the king arrived at Portchester four days after the attack on Southampton, the two men's involvement in this latest piece of lawlessness seems quite possible.

The plan which Edward and Despenser conceived centred around Bartholomew Badlesmere. Edward was furious with his former steward for switching sides and betraying him, and probably saw a kind of poetic justice in using Badlesmere as a dupe to strike at his other enemies. The king asked Isabella to set off for a pilgrimage to Canterbury, and on her way back to London, to ask for a night's accommodation at Leeds Castle, which belonged to Badlesmere. In fact, the usual route from Canterbury to London went through northern Kent and nowhere near Leeds. Badlesmere was with the Marchers at Oxford, having put his Kent castles in a state of defence in response to Edward's sending men into the county against him, but his wife was in residence at the castle. Edward hoped that she would refuse to allow Isabella entry, which would be a gross insult to the royal family and would give Edward an excuse to attack the castle.[8] Badlesmere owned many lands in Kent, which isolated him geographically from his allies in the Welsh Marches and the south-west of England. Roger Clifford was the nephew of Badlesmere's wife and Badlesmere's daughter was married to Roger Mortimer's son, so if Edward struck at Badlesmere, the Marchers would probably feel honour-bound to come to his aid and would thus be in armed rebellion against the king. Edward and Despenser knew that the earl of Lancaster detested Badlesmere, and gambled that the powerful magnate would not help him. In addition, although Lancaster and Isabella were not allies, she was his niece and the queen of England, and he could hardly be seen to defend a man who had insulted her. In this way, Edward could divide and conquer his enemies, and pick them off piecemeal.

The plan went off brilliantly. Isabella approached the castle with a military escort, and Lady Badlesmere refused to admit her, announcing that the queen must seek accommodation elsewhere.[9] Isabella ordered her escort to force an entry into the castle, and the garrison opened up a volley of arrows at them, killing six. Feigning outrage at the insult to his consort, when he must have been delighted that all had gone according to plan, Edward mustered men to attack Leeds. Badlesmere's wife had played right into his hands, and so did Badlesmere himself, informing Edward that he approved of his wife's conduct.[10] To 'punish the disobedience and contempt against the queen', Edward ordered the sheriffs of Kent, Surrey, Sussex, Hampshire and Essex to muster knights and footmen 'with horses and arms and as much power as possible' at Leeds on 23 October, and sent the earls of Pembroke and Richmond and the Scottish earl of Atholl as an advance guard. The city of London sent 500 men to the siege.[11] Edward arrived at Leeds on 26 October, and, apparently bored, ordered his hunting dogs sent to him.[12] His half-brothers Norfolk and Kent, now twenty and twenty-one, joined the siege, as did the earls of Surrey and Arundel.[13] With Pembroke and Richmond, this represented all the English earls alive in 1321 except Lancaster and Hereford, the shadowy Oxford who played no role whatsoever in Edward's reign, and Edward's son Edward of Windsor, earl of Chester, who was not yet nine.

Badlesmere begged the Marchers to take their armies and relieve the siege of Leeds. This put them in a very awkward position. Badlesmere was their ally, yet the men willing to fight against the Despensers were reluctant to take up arms against their king, and probably also reluctant to help a man who had so recently switched sides. Neither were they willing to be seen to acknowledge Badlesmere's insult of the queen, and indeed two chroniclers say they refused to go to the aid of the Leeds garrison out of respect for Isabella.[14] And the earl of Lancaster also played into Edward's hands, as Edward and Despenser had no doubt predicted he would: he sent the Marchers a letter, ordering them to not to aid the detested Badlesmere.[15] Leeds surrendered on 31 October, and thirteen members of the garrison were drawn and hanged shortly afterwards.[16] Although this was not unprecedented – King Stephen hanged nearly a hundred of the Shrewsbury Castle garrison for holding out against him in 1138 – men had never been executed for holding a castle against the king within living memory.[17] Edward's father and grandfather had not hanged the men who held Kenilworth Castle against them in the 1260s. Still, the author of the *Vita*, at least, approved of Edward's actions and described the executed men as 'robbers, homicides, and traitors', stating that 'just as no one can build castles in the land without the king's licence, so it is wrong to defend castles in the kingdom against the king'.[18]

By 12 November, Edward had heard that the earl of Lancaster was planning to hold an assembly at Doncaster, and forbade him, the earl of Hereford and more than 100 others from attending. Some of the men Edward ordered not to attend were in fact his allies, such as his half-brother Norfolk, his and Hugh Despenser's brother-in-law Ralph Monthermer, the earls of Arundel, Surrey, Atholl and Angus, and Ralph Camoys, another of Despenser's brothers-in-law.[19] Lancaster's attempts to win over men whose support he had no hope of gaining is a measure of the weakness of his position; he had hoped that the northern barons would help him, but they refused to go against the king.[20] Lancaster and his Marcher allies, despite Edward's prohibition, did meet on 29 November, probably at Pontefract rather than Doncaster.[21] They drew up a petition which accused Edward of supporting Hugh Despenser in his piracy and his attempts to persuade the king to attack the peers of the realm, and asked the king to respond by 20 December. Edward had no intention of doing so, and informed Lancaster, in a surprisingly mild letter, that imposing a deadline on him gave the impression that the king was the earl's subject, not vice versa.[22]

Edward ordered Walter Reynolds, archbishop of Canterbury, to summon the prelates to a provincial meeting at St Paul's on 1 December, and the day before, sent the earls of Pembroke and Richmond and Robert Baldock, lawyer, archdeacon of Middlesex and Despenser adherent, to present the Despensers' petition protesting their banishment.[23] Owing to the difficulty of winter travel and the short notice of the meeting, only four bishops attended the convocation.[24] Reynolds and the four bishops dutifully agreed to petition for the annulment of the judgement on the Despensers, while the earls of Arundel, Pembroke and Richmond claimed they had only consented to the exile through fear.[25]

After the meeting with Lancaster at Pontefract, the Marchers returned to the west of England and Wales with a great armed force.[26] By now, it was clear to everyone that Edward would go after the men who had had the nerve to attack his friends, kill, assault and rob his subjects, hold castles against him, and steal from him personally, 'because they had taken for their own use and wasted the goods of the exiles, which ought rather to have gone to the treasury'.[27] On 30 November 1321 he began to make preparations for a campaign against the Marchers, despite the season – in the interests of his friends, he was no longer 'paralysed by sloth', as the *Flores* describes him.[28] The alacrity with which he set off against the Marchers in the dead of winter stands in stark contrast to his frequent postponement and cancellation of Scottish campaigns. Queen Isabella, supporting her husband, allowed Edward to give custody of her castles at Devizes and Marlborough to Oliver Ingham and Robert Lewer (whom Edward had forgiven).[29] Edward issued a safe-conduct for Hugh Despenser to return to England on 8 December, and the same was issued to Hugh Despenser the Elder on Christmas Day.[30]

Edward spent the first few days of December 1321 at Westminster and Isleworth. He sent a letter on the 10th to the treasurer, Walter de

Norwich, asking him to 'provide sixteen pieces of cloth for the apparelling of ourselves and our dear companion [Isabella], also furs, against the next feast of Christmas', also ordering more cloth and linen for Isabella and her damsels and 'other things of which we stand in need, against the great feast'. He paid £115 for these items.[31] He then travelled to Cirencester, accompanied by the earls of Kent, Norfolk, Pembroke, Richmond, Surrey, Arundel, Atholl and Angus, and additionally, 'many powerful barons … promised to lend aid to the lord king'.[32] He spent Christmas 1321 at Cirencester, spending eighty-seven pounds on the festivities, while Queen Isabella probably remained at Langley.[33]

The king wrote on 4 January to ten of the bishops who had not attended Walter Reynolds' convocation in December, asking their opinion on the judgement that the Despensers' exile had been unlawful and should be revoked, demanding a response 'without delay'.[34] Thomas Cobham, bishop of Worcester, endorsed the verdict, but Walter Stapeldon, bishop of Exeter – who would be murdered in 1326 for his alliance with Edward and the Despensers – responded that although the judgement was unjust, only parliament could revoke it. An annoyed Edward rebuked Stapeldon for sending such a churlish reply and ordered the bishop to send a different answer and to come to him in person immediately. Stapeldon, a principled man, courageously risked the king's wrath and repeated his first answer.[35]

Before Edward's arrival in the west, the Marchers had seized Gloucester and thus controlled the bridge over the Severn. When they heard that the king was approaching Gloucestershire, they fled from him rather than engage him in battle, although their army was nearly four times bigger than his, burning and devastating the countryside as they went.[36] Too afraid to confront the king directly, they once more vented their anger and frustration on innocents.[37] The Marchers were desperately hoping for the earl of Lancaster's support, but he failed to come to their aid – although he had begun besieging the royal castle of Tickhill near Doncaster by 10 January, presumably because its constable William Aune was Edward's spy in the north.[38] On 5 January, Edward sent letters to the pope and his brother-in-law Philip V of France, unaware that Philip had died three days earlier, and on the 9th, renewed the safe-conduct for Hugh Despenser.[39]

The Marchers retreated up the western side of the Severn, burning the bridges as they went to prevent Edward and his army crossing, but still not daring to confront him directly. Roger Mortimer, his uncle Roger Mortimer of Chirk and the earl of Hereford arrived in Bridgnorth before Edward, and 'made a serious attack upon the king. They burned a great part of the town and killed very many of the king's servants'.[40] Edward ordered the constable of Bristol Castle to arrest those who had beaten, wounded and killed townspeople, stolen 'garments, jewels, beasts and other goods,' and imprisoned people 'until they made grievous ransoms'.[41] The *Vita* says bitterly that in 1322 the Marchers 'killed those who opposed them, [and] plundered those who offered no resistance, sparing no one'.[42] Edward sent men to attack the lands of his former chamberlain John Charlton, whose son and heir was married to one of Roger Mortimer's daughters, forcing Charlton to leave his allies to go to defend his lands.[43] Edward pardoned Charlton some months later, which in 1326 would prove to have been a bad mistake.[44]

Edward arrived at Shrewsbury on 14 January and finally gained the west bank of the Severn. He offered safe-conducts to those Marchers who were in the vicinity, the earl of Hereford and both Roger Mortimers, to come to him.[45] Edward pointedly excluded Bartholomew Badlesmere by name from the safe-conducts, which demonstrates his fury at Badlesmere's switching sides; Edward II was not a man to forgive and forget a betrayal. Hereford did not go to the king, but on 22 January the two Roger Mortimers 'deserted their allies, and threw themselves on the king's mercy'.[46] The *Vita* goes on to say that the other Marchers were astonished and tearful at this desertion, but in fact the Mortimers had little choice but to submit to Edward: Sir Gruffydd Llwyd, a staunch ally of the king, and the violent Robert Lewer had been attacking their lands, the Mortimers' men were deserting them, and they were running out of money. On 13 February, the two men were taken to be imprisoned in the Tower of London.[47] Given the numerous crimes they had committed and encouraged in the previous few months – homicide, assault, theft, plunder, vandalism, false imprisonment, extortion – this fate was hardly undeserved, and a petition to Edward from 'the community of Wales' later that year begged the king not to let them return there.[48]

Edward took to calling the baronial rebels the 'Contrariants' around this time.[49] Claiming that Adam Orleton, bishop of Hereford, was supporting them, Edward publicly upbraided him when he reached Hereford, and went hunting in Orleton's parks with his brother the earl of Kent, without Orleton's permission.[50] He spent thirty-five pounds to celebrate the feast of the Purification on 2 February at Hereford.[51] On 6 February, Lord Berkeley and Hugh Audley the Elder, father of Edward's former favourite, surrendered to Edward, who sent them to prison at Wallingford Castle. The following day he took Berkeley Castle into his own hands, unaware of the tragic role it would play in his life in 1327.[52] The remaining Contrariants fled towards Yorkshire to seek refuge with the earl of Lancaster, their last hope of defeating Edward. Lancaster, using the pseudonym 'King Arthur', wrote to Robert Bruce's adherent James Douglas to inform him that the earl of Hereford, Roger Damory, Hugh Audley and even the hated Bartholomew Badlesmere had come to him at Pontefract. The men were, treasonably, prepared to treat with the Scots, as long as the Scots did what had previously been discussed: 'to come to our aid, and to go with us in England and Wales' and 'live and die with us in our quarrel'.[53] Although Bruce remarked of Lancaster, 'How will a man who cannot keep faith with his own lord keep faith with me?' the Scots king was willing to take advantage of anything or anyone that might distract Edward from Scotland and sow discord in England.[54] Lancaster had been suspected for some years of conspiring with the Scots; it was noticed that when their forces raided the north of England, they left his lands alone, and although Lancaster had a great army at Pontefract, he did not attempt to pursue the Scottish raiders.

Edward pointed out in a letter to Lancaster that joining the Contrariants would render him guilty of treason.[55] His cousin responded untruthfully that he had drawn no rebels to himself, nor was he accustomed to nourish rebels, but if he knew where such were to be found, he would kill them or expel them from the country.[56] Precisely when Edward decided to attack Lancaster is not clear, but it is possible that he had had it in mind for a long time; the man who had stated at the siege of Berwick in September 1319, 'I have not forgotten the wrong that was done to my brother Piers' was hardly likely to miss the opportunity to go after Lancaster and finally take revenge for the death of Gaveston. Still working on the principle of dividing and conquering his enemies, he may well have gambled that Lancaster would not intervene and help the Marchers until it was too late, as indeed happened. Edward knew his cousin well; he knew of his lethargy and his desire to stay at his favourite castle of Pontefract and take little active role in events while he did his best to control them from a distance. He also understood his cousin's willingness to allow his personal feuds, the most obvious example being Bartholomew Badlesmere, to affect his political decisions; after all, he did exactly the same thing himself. Lancaster's siege of Tickhill Castle gave him the excuse he needed to mount a campaign against his overbearing cousin, and on 13 February, he announced his intention of going to raise the siege.[57] The king also issued another safe-conduct for the Despensers to return to England.[58] By 16 February he had heard that Charles IV, Queen Isabella's only surviving brother, had succeeded Philip V as king of France, and asked him to send men to help him fight Lancaster and the Contrariants. Given that Charles was Lancaster's nephew, this was a rather impertinent request.[59]

Edward left Gloucester on 18 February, captured the earl of Lancaster's great Warwickshire stronghold of Kenilworth on the 26th, and arrived at Coventry the following day. By 1 March, William Melton, archbishop of York, had discovered the treasonable correspondence between Lancaster and Scotland and sent it to Edward, who ordered him, the archbishop of Canterbury and all his sheriffs to make the letters public.[60] Edward wrote on the same day to the barons and men of Winchelsea that they should 'bear in mind how the king began what he has now done in part by their counsel lately given to the king on the water', and reminded them that they had promised to help him wherever he went.[61] When Edward met the sailors of Winchelsea at sea is uncertain; presumably it had something to do with Hugh Despenser's piracy or the attack on Southampton. The Despensers met Edward on 3 March, bringing a large number of armed men with them. Edward must have been overjoyed to be reunited with Hugh Despenser, though no doubt most people were considerably less thrilled that the avaricious favourite and his unpopular father had returned. On the day he met them, Edward asked the Dominicans of Vienna to pray for himself, Isabella and their children.[62] In a splendid piece of theatre, Hugh Despenser prostrated himself in the snow before the king, arms outstretched, and begged Edward not to unfurl his banners against the opposition, which would mean an outright declaration of war.[63]

Hearing of Edward's advance, the earls of Lancaster and Hereford and their allies left Pontefract on 1 March, broke the siege of Tickhill, and took up position at Burton-on-Trent near Tutbury Castle in Staffordshire, which belonged to Lancaster. Edward seized Lancaster's vast lands on 3 March.[64] The Contrariants held the bridge at Burton against the king, but after three days of skirmishing their army was outflanked and they fled back to Pontefract. Edward pronounced them traitors, and ordered all the sheriffs of England, the justice of Chester and the bishop of Durham to arrest Lancaster, Hereford, Damory, Audley, Badlesmere, and others. Edward's letter also mentions that he had been unable to cross the fords because of flooding, and the Sempringham annalist says that the earl of Lancaster lost many supplies 'through a great flood of water' when travelling from Pontefract to Tutbury on 1 March.[65] The Rochester chronicler says that snow lay on the ground for most of the first three months of 1322, and that the roads were hazardous, impeding Edward's progress; presumably a temporary thaw and a mass of melted snow caused the flooding.[66] Edward reached Tutbury on 11 March, where the rebels had left some of their goods behind at the priory, including a barrel of sturgeon worth three pounds. The prior presented it to Edward, who allowed him to keep it, although he ordered the prior to send the other goods, which included jewels, to John Sturmy and Giles of Spain, squires of his chamber.[67] The king also seized a vessel of gold and silver valued at over £140, which belonged to Roger Damory.[68]

When the Contrariants fled from Burton-on-Trent, they left Damory, who had been badly wounded while trying to prevent the royal army crossing the river, behind. He was condemned to the traitor's death, but the court informed him that because Edward had loved him well in the past, the king would respite the punishment – although the charge of treason stood, which meant that Damory's heir, his daughter Elizabeth, and her descendants were perpetually disinherited.[69] Damory died of his wounds at Tutbury Priory on 12 March, though *Lanercost* and the

French Chronicle of London give 'grief' as the cause of his death, and his widow Edward's niece Elizabeth claimed in 1326, rather disingenuously, that he was 'pursued and oppressed until he died'.[70] The less sympathetic *Vita* points out that Damory was an impoverished knight who rose to prominence through the king's favour, so that when he turned against Edward 'many marked him down as ungrateful'.[71] Edward was not present at his deathbed, having moved on to Derby; how he felt about the man he had once loved dying in rebellion against him is a matter for speculation.

Once back at Pontefract, some of the Contrariants decided to throw themselves on Edward's mercy. The earl of Lancaster, however, believed that this was unnecessary and that his close kinship to the king would save him.[72] After much debate, they decided to flee to Dunstanburgh, another of Lancaster's great castles on the Northumbrian coast. According to the very pro-Lancastrian *Brut*, Lancaster at first refused, protesting that they would be seen as treacherously fleeing towards the Scots, but Roger Clifford's waving his sword in his face soon changed his mind, and they set off for the north.[73] Queen Isabella wrote to Andrew Harclay, sheriff of Cumberland, and Simon Warde, sheriff of Yorkshire, ordering them to cut off the retreating rebels.[74] The Contrariants had only managed the thirty miles to Boroughbridge, where the Great North Road met the River Ure, when they found Harclay waiting for them, and were forced into battle on 16 March. Boroughbridge had, perhaps ironically, once belonged to Piers Gaveston.[75] The royalist army led by Harclay took up schiltron formations, used to such great effect against Edward at Bannockburn, and defeated the Contrariants, despite the greatly superior numbers of the Contrariants' army. The earl of Hereford died horribly, with a lance thrust up his back passage by a Welsh soldier hiding under the bridge; whether Edward felt sorrow, pity, triumph or something else for his brother-in-law's terrible death is unfortunately not recorded.[76] A document proving the Contrariants' traitorous alliance with Scotland was, perhaps rather conveniently, found on Hereford's body, and the possessions he had stored at Fountains Abbey were sent to Harclay, including a gold cup, a silver cup, forty dishes and two horses worth three pounds.[77]

Lancaster asked for an overnight truce, during which many of the Contrariants' soldiers deserted, and surrendered to Harclay the following day. The *Vita* gives an account of how the Contrariant knights and noblemen who had fought tried to escape:

Some left their horses and putting off their armour looked round for ancient worn-out garments, and took to the road as beggars. But their caution was of no avail, for not a single well-known man among them all escaped. O calamity! To see men lately dressed in purple and fine linen now attired in rags and imprisoned in chains!

The author, however, who disliked the rebels even more than he disliked the Despensers, immediately goes on to describe the royalist victory as 'a marvellous thing, and one indeed brought about by God's will and aid, that so scanty a company should in a moment overcome so many knights'.[78] As well as pretending to be beggars, some men tried to flee the country or to hide by donning religious habits.[79] Edward sent members of his household to round up the escaping Contrariants and seize their goods, and inhabitants of Yorkshire joined in the hunt. One knight gave himself up to the rector of Escrick and handed over to him his sword and the seven shillings he was carrying, and another surrendered to the abbot of Fountains and gave him his money, sword, silver cups, dishes, saucers and a horn. Two knights caught in Knaresborough were among those who had thrown away their fine possessions, and were 'taken bare'. Eleven men were captured thirty-five miles away at Selby the day after the battle, and their goods were sent to the king. They included a pair of silk garters adorned with silver and red enamel with a cross bar of silver, a 'great silver chain containing twelve links with a pipe at the end,' twelve buttons of green glass adorned with silver gilt, eight of silver wire and five of white silver, seven pearls the size of peas, a purse of silk worth a mark, a book worth ten shillings, eight horses, six silver dishes, two 'worn swords' and an old dagger. Three Contrariants captured at Ripon handed over seven horses, armour, a bed and nine ells of striped cloth, men of Edward's marshalsea seized a red doublet worth forty marks which belonged to John, Lord Giffard, and a John Ryther took possession of a 'coat of armour of great price, and a pack with robes and good furs' belonging to John, Lord Mowbray. Hundreds of horses were also seized.[80]

The earl of Lancaster was taken to Pontefract Castle, his own favourite residence, whose constable had surrendered to Edward without a fight. He was forced to put on garments of the striped cloth which the squires of his household wore, an intentional humiliation of a man of high birth and rank. On the way to York, a crowd of people threw snowballs at him, called him a traitor, and shouted, 'Now shall you have the reward that long time you have deserved!'[81] Edward waited for his cousin at Pontefract, where rumour had it that the earl had built a tower in which to hold the king captive for the rest of his life. Lancaster was imprisoned there instead.[82] A triumphant Hugh Despenser hurled 'malicious and contemptuous words' into Lancaster's face on his arrival.[83] Lancaster was put on trial in the great hall of his own castle, the justice Robert Malberthorpe, Edward, the Despensers, the earls of Kent, Pembroke, Richmond, Surrey, Arundel and the Scottish earls of Angus and Atholl sitting in judgement on him.[84] The result was a foregone conclusion, and Lancaster was not allowed to speak in his own defence as his crimes were deemed 'notorious', known to everybody. He exclaimed, 'This is a powerful court, and great in authority, where no answer is heard nor any excuse admitted,' but given that he had executed Piers Gaveston without a trial, he was hardly innocent on that score himself.[85] The list of charges comprised the many grievances Edward managed to dredge up against his cousin, going back to Lancaster's seizure of his possessions at Tynemouth in 1312.

Lancaster's judges sentenced him to death by hanging, drawing and quartering, though Edward commuted the sentence to mere beheading, respiting the hanging and drawing out of love for Queen Isabella according to the *Brut*, and out of respect for Lancaster's royal blood according to the *Vita* and the Sempringham annalist.[86] The parallels between the deaths of Gaveston and Lancaster did not unnoticed: he was 'beheaded in like manner as this same Earl Thomas had caused Piers Gaveston to be beheaded'.[87] The *Vita* agrees, saying, 'The earl of Lancaster once cut off Piers Gaveston's head, and now by the king's command the earl himself has lost his head. Thus, perhaps not unjustly, the earl received measure for measure'.[88] Edward arranged Lancaster's execution as a parody of Gaveston's death, and had him taken outside to a small hill, mirroring Gaveston's 1312 death on Blacklow Hill. Lancaster was forced to ride 'some worthless mule' and 'an old chaplet, rent and torn, that was not worth a half-penny' was set on his head. A crowd of spectators again threw snowballs at him.[89] *Scalacronica* also makes the connection between the deaths of Lancaster and Gaveston, and says that Lancaster was executed 'at the very place where he had once hooted, and made others hoot, at the king as he [Edward] was travelling to York'.[90] Edward had never forgiven Lancaster's jeering at him in 1317; it was one of the charges against his cousin.

It had taken him just under ten years to do it, but finally Edward had forced Thomas of Lancaster into a position where he could take revenge for the death of Piers Gaveston. Presumably at the king's order, Lancaster was forced to kneel facing towards Scotland, in a pointed reminder of his treasonous correspondence with Robert Bruce, and was 'beheaded like any thief or vilest rascal' with two or three strokes of the axe.[91] The sudden downfall and death of Lancaster, enormously wealthy and of royal blood, shocked the country; not counting Piers Gaveston, Lancaster was the first English earl to be executed since Waltheof in 1076. Miracles were being reported at the site of his execution within weeks, his numerous faults forgotten, people remembering only that he had opposed the king's tyranny.[92] A campaign to canonise Lancaster – surely one of the unlikeliest saints of all time – began in 1327, and his cult grew in popularity; as late as the Reformation, his hat and belt preserved at Pontefract were used as remedies in childbirth and for headaches.[93]

The day after Lancaster's execution, Edward sent men to pronounce judgement on the other Contrariants, and bearing in mind that they had made war on him and wrought great and needless destruction on his realm and subjects, he had some of them sentenced to death.[94] During their trials, they were forced to wear the green and yellow tunics they had adopted as their uniform in May 1321.[95] Twenty or twenty-two noblemen, including Lancaster and six of his knights, were executed in various towns in March and April 1322, including Roger, Lord Clifford, John, Lord Mowbray and Sir Jocelyn Deyville, whom *Lanercost* calls 'a knight notorious for his misdeeds', in York. Fourteenth-century chronicles were consistent in recording the names of the men executed, though the figures have been inflated in some modern books by the inclusion of knights killed at Boroughbridge, and the executions of men who had committed treason, theft, assault and other crimes are often emotively described nowadays as a 'bloodbath' or a 'reign of terror'.[96] The king's loyal Scottish friend Donald of Mar captured Bartholomew Badlesmere and took him to Canterbury. On 14 April, Badlesmere was dragged three miles to the crossroads at Blean, hanged and then beheaded, and his head set on a spike over the gate into Canterbury at Edward's own command as an example to those who would betray the king. Badlesmere is the only Contrariant known to have been hanged, drawn and quartered, because he had fled and because he had been Edward's steward.[97]

Chroniclers give variously sixty-two, eighty-three and a hundred Contrariants imprisoned.[98] The total is difficult to ascertain, as dozens of men were released on payment of a fine between 1322 and 1325, such as Sir Thomas Gurney – a man who would play an essential role in Edward II's life some years later – who was released from the Tower and restored to his lands in exchange for £100. The fines varied wildly between £2 and £3,000.[99] Edward gave many men, including Gurney, permission to pay off their fines in instalments, a form of political blackmail also used by his father Edward I and great-grandfather King John.[100] The Contrariants in prison were granted three pence a day for their sustenance, the same amount as the Welsh lord Llywelyn Bren had received in 1316, though Roger Mortimer of Chirk received six pence.[101] The Contrariants probably deserved their treatment, but the nastiest aspect of Edward II's behaviour is the way he ordered the arrest and imprisonment of some of their wives or widows and children, at least for a few months. Badlesmere's widow Margaret, for example, was temporarily imprisoned but released from the Tower on 3 November 1322 and given a reasonably generous financial allowance, but Roger Mortimer's wife Joan was held in some form of captivity, with eight attendants, for the rest of Edward's reign. This was not unprecedented: Edward's father had incarcerated the women of Robert Bruce's family in 1306, and sent Bruce's ten- or twelve-year-old daughter Marjorie to the Tower of London and his nephew Donald of Mar, the same age or younger, to Bristol Castle.

Edward did show mercy on occasion when he considered his sheriffs to have been excessively zealous in arresting and imprisoning Contrariant adherents. Between March and May 1322, he ordered the release of a number of men on the grounds that proof of their adherence to the Contrariants was insufficient, and pardoned well over a hundred of Lancaster's adherents within weeks of the earl's execution.[102] The Lancastrian knight Thomas le Blount became Edward's steward, and another, Richard Talbot, captured after Boroughbridge, joined the Despensers' retinue. Yet these instances of clemency were all too rare, and Edward's often arbitrary vindictiveness ensured the existence of numerous disaffected, desperate men, deprived of their lands and income and, in some cases, their families. Some men managed to escape from England, and later caused conflict between Edward and his brother-in-law Charles IV when the French king allowed them at his court. Chroniclers were horrified at the way the king behaved towards the defeated rebels in 1322, though they had been considerably less concerned about Edward I's executions of numerous Scottish opponents (including the earl of Atholl) and his imprisonment of their families in 1305/07, behaviour which Edward II presumably took as an example. Edward I had also ordered Dafydd ap Gruffydd, brother of the last Welsh prince of Wales, to be hanged, drawn and quartered in 1283 and thereby set two precedents: that rebellion against the king could be considered treason, and that men of high rank could die for the crime.[103] *Anonimalle* calls Edward in 1322 'a man of great vengeance', while *Lanercost* cries, 'O the excessive cruelty of the king and his friends!' Edward's most vicious critic the Westminster chronicle *Flores Historiarum* goes over the top as usual by claiming that Edward 'hated the magnates with such mad fury that he plotted the complete and permanent overthrow of all the great men of the realm together with the whole English aristocracy'.[104]

On 14 July 1322, five men – the mayor of London, three justices of the court of Common Pleas and the chief baron of the exchequer – condemned Roger Mortimer and his uncle Mortimer of Chirk to death. Eight days later, Edward commuted their sentence to life imprisonment, which would prove to be one of the worst mistakes he ever made.[105] Edward's change of heart is sometimes assumed to have been the result of Queen Isabella's influence, which is unlikely and based solely on hindsight, given her later relationship with Mortimer. Why Edward changed his mind is unknown, but after Hugh Despenser's return from exile, Isabella's influence over her husband was limited, and it is debatable if she would have been able to convince him to spare the Mortimers. Perhaps Edward remembered that Mortimer had previously been his loyal ally and Piers Gaveston's, and had voluntarily surrendered to him. Whatever the reason for his decision, it is likely to have been made against the wishes of Hugh Despenser, who loathed the Mortimers.

Some people did benefit from the events of 1322: Andrew Harclay, for example, sheriff of Cumberland and the victor of Boroughbridge, became earl of Carlisle.[106] The men who benefited the most were, of course, Hugh Despenser father and son, who were granted numerous manors forfeited by Contrariants. Edward also granted five forfeited manors to his niece Eleanor Despenser, to pass after her death to her third son, Gilbert.[107] One person who did not benefit, though, was Queen Isabella – perhaps a sign that the royal marriage was starting to deteriorate. Isabella apparently joined her husband in the north before her uncle Lancaster's execution: Edward's squire Oliver de Bordeaux informed the earl of Richmond that the king and queen 'were well and hearty, thank God' on St Cuthbert's day, 20 March, which seems to mean that he saw them together.[108] The king reached Pontefract on 19 March, which would imply that Isabella was also in the castle when Lancaster was tried and executed on the 22nd.

Edward wrote to inform the pope of recent events on 25 March 1322; John XXII advised him to ascribe his victory to God. Far from showing sympathy to the men whom Edward had executed and imprisoned, John excommunicated 'those nobles and magnates who attack the king and his realm'.[109] Edward finally revoked the hated Ordinances of 1311, and annulled the judgement of exile and disinheritance on the Despensers. Hugh Despenser the Elder became earl of Winchester, an appointment which perhaps surprisingly attracted little criticism from contemporaries, though for some reason his son's claims to the earldom of Gloucester were not pressed. Although Despenser would one day inherit the earldom of Winchester from his father, it was a considerably less prestigious title. Either Edward had finally learned some sense, or more likely, Despenser was by now so powerful and wealthy that even the earldom of Gloucester hardly sufficed for him, though evidently it didn't occur even to him to award himself the grandiose earldom of March, or earl of all the English-Welsh borderlands, as the next royal favourite Roger Mortimer would do in 1328.

The spring of 1322 marked Edward II's triumph. But from now on, everything began to go wrong for him, and the remaining years of his reign were a downward spiral that ended in complete ignominy. He and Despenser ruled so capriciously, arbitrarily and repressively as to make countless more enemies and, with hindsight at least, to make their downfall seem inevitable. Solvent for the first time in his reign – the vast income from the Contrariants' forfeited lands and Despenser's despotic efficiency combined to make him 'the richest king that ever was in England after William Bastard of Normandy', as the *Brut* has it – and with his enemies dead, in prison or in exile, Edward had the chance to rescue his disastrous reign.[110] He failed to take it.

1. Edward's tomb and effigy in Gloucester Cathedral.

2. Edward's tomb and effigy, with his feet resting on a lion. (Photos by author, with permission of the Very Reverend Dean of Gloucester)

3. Kenilworth Castle, Warwickshire, where Edward was forced to abdicate in January 1327. (Courtesy of Steve Taylor under Creative Commons)

4. Warwick Castle, where Piers Gaveston was imprisoned in 1312. (Courtesy of Tony Hisgett under Creative Commons)

5. Tower of Gloucester Cathedral. (Photo by author)

6. An inscription outside Gloucester Cathedral, formerly King Edward's Gate. (Photo by author)

7. Caernarfon Castle, North Wales, Edward's birthplace in 1284 when it was a building site. (Courtesy of Peter Broster under Creative Commons)

8. Berkeley Castle, Gloucestershire, where Edward was held in captivity in 1327.

9. Inside Berkeley Castle; Edward was held in the keep, on the right. (Photos by author)

10. Edward's coronation, from a manuscript of the early fourteenth century. (Courtesy of the Master and Fellows of Corpus Christi College, Cambridge; MS 20, folio 68r)

11. Knaresborough, North Yorkshire, where Edward spent much time. (Photo by author)

12. Caernarfon Castle and town. (Courtesy of Reinoud Kaasschieter under Creative Commons)

13. Ludlow Castle, Shropshire, which belonged to Edward's most dangerous enemy Roger Mortimer. (Courtesy of Darren Musgrove under Creative Commons)

14. Knaresborough Castle, which Edward gave to Gaveston. (Courtesy of David Pacey under Creative Commons)

15. A cross erected near Leek Wootton, Warwickshire, in the nineteenth century to mark the spot where Piers Gaveston was killed in June 1312. (Courtesy of Andrew Donkin under Creative Commons)

16. Stirling Castle, Scotland, near the battlefield of Bannockburn. (Courtesy of Liz under Creative Commons)

17. Rievaulx Abbey, North Yorkshire, where Edward was almost captured by a Scottish force in October 1322. (Courtesy of Reinhold Behringer under Creative Commons)

18. Edward's effigy in Gloucester Cathedral. (Courtesy of BazzaDaRambler under Creative Commons)

19. Tomb of Edward's chamberlain and favourite Hugh Despenser the Younger in Tewkesbury Abbey. (Photo by author, with permission of the vicar and churchwardens)

20. Caerphilly Castle, South Wales, which belonged to Hugh Despenser and was where Edward and Despenser fled in October 1326. (Courtesy of deadmanjones under Creative Content)

21. Westminster Abbey, where Edward's parents Edward I and Eleanor of Castile are buried. (Courtesy of Elentari86 under Creative Commons)

22. Trinity College, Cambridge, *c.* 1865. Edward's 1317 foundation of King's Hall was incorporated into Trinity on its foundation in 1546. (Courtesy of Cornell University Library)

23. Seville Cathedral, southern Spain, where Edward's maternal grandfather San Fernando, king of Castile and patron saint of the city, is buried. Edward's uncle Felipe was archbishop of Seville. (Photo by author)

24. Letter of the archbishop of York in January 1330 saying that Edward is still alive, over two years after his funeral. (Courtesy of Warwickshire County Record Office; MS CR136/C2017)

25. Oriel College, Oxford, founded by Edward and his almoner in 1326. (Wikimedia commons)

26. The Great Mosque of Cordoba, southern Spain, captured by Edward's grandfather Fernando in 1236. (Photo by author)

27. Clifford's Tower, York. Three noblemen, including Roger Clifford, were executed here in March 1322 after rebelling against Edward. (Photo by author)

28 (*left*). Sutton Bank, North Yorkshire. Edward's forces were defeated at the battle of Byland here in October 1322. (Photo by author)

29 (*below*). Edward's great seal, with two castles of Castile for his mother's homeland. (From *The Pictorial History of England*, 1846, Vol. 1)

30. The Cistercian monastery of Las Huelgas, Burgos, northern Spain, where Edward's parents married in 1254. (Courtesy of Lumiago under Creative Commons)

31. Scarborough Castle, North Yorkshire, where Piers Gaveston was besieged in May 1312. (Courtesy of Kate Johnson via Creative Commons)

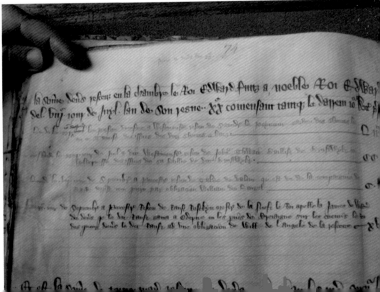

32. A page of Edward's chamber account of 1325/26, calling him 'King Edward son of the noble King Edward'. (Photo by author with permission of the Society of Antiquaries of London)

33. Edward, by artist Mark Satchwill. (Used with permission)

12

Tyranny, Miracles and an Escape

The year 1322 marked the beginning of Edward II's tyranny. The *Vita* comments, 'The harshness of the king has today increased so much that no one however great and wise dares to cross his will ... the nobles of the realm, terrified by threats and the penalties inflicted on others, let the king's will have free play ... whatever pleases the king, though lacking in reason, has the force of the law.'[1] The *Brut* says at the time of Boroughbridge, 'So much unkindness was never seen in England before,' and 'The land was without law, for Holy Church had no more reverence than it had been a brothel' – though in fact the author doesn't blame Edward for the lawlessness, and Sir Thomas Gray, author of the *Scalacronica*, considered that 'the commons of his [Edward's] time were wealthy and protected by strong laws'.[2] Whether the common people of England suffered under a higher crime rate in the 1320s than at any other time in the fourteenth century is doubtful; it was the land-owning class who were victims of the Despensers and their greed. Despenser treated the widows of Contrariants and other vulnerable women cruelly, imprisoning, for example, Elizabeth Comyn for a year until she handed over some of her lands to his father and himself. At his trial in November 1326, Despenser was even accused of torturing a 'Lady Baret' by breaking her limbs until she went insane – presumably a reference to Joan Gynes, widow of Stephen Baret, a Contrariant executed in 1322.[3] As Despenser was perfectly willing to force widows to grant him their lands but is not known to have been a sadist who had people tortured for fun, his motive must presumably have been to gain control of Joan's lands. In 1324, however, her three manors were in Edward's hands, not Despenser's.[4] The charge of torture against Despenser sounds too specific to have been completely invented, yet it is extremely odd that neither Joan nor any of her family later petitioned Edward III for restitution, and even stranger that none of the contemporary chroniclers noticed such a horrific act; the alleged torture is not mentioned anywhere. They might have ignored the torture of a lowborn woman, but never a highborn one. Whatever happened between Despenser and Joan, the story of her broken limbs and insanity is likely to be, at best, a gross exaggeration at a time when all the ills of the 1320s were being heaped on one man's head.

Edward granted the peninsula of Gower, ownership of which had begun the civil war in the first place, to Hugh Despenser, and Despenser subsequently forced his sister-in-law, Roger Damory's widow Elizabeth de Burgh, to give up her valuable lordship of Usk (worth £770 a year) in exchange for the peninsula (worth £300 a year), nastily ordering his men to 'strip Gower for our profit' before handing it over to her. Using quasi-legal methods, he deprived her of Gower as well in 1324.[5] Elizabeth did keep all her English and Irish lands, if only because Despenser, busily building himself an empire in South Wales, had no interest in them. According to Elizabeth's own testimony of May 1326, Edward arrested her counsellors and threatened that if she refused to submit to his will, he would allow her to hold none of her lands as long as he lived.[6] Edward made no attempt to protect his niece, and not only did he tolerate Despenser's appalling treatment of her, he actively colluded in it, behaviour which shows him in the worst possible light.

Despenser was restored to his position of royal chamberlain after his return from exile, which he would hold until his death in November 1326, and came to enjoy supreme power at court and over the king. *Scalacronica* comments on Despenser's vast influence over the king, and says that Edward 'after his example, did everything that wholly unfitted him for chivalry, delighting himself in avarice and in delights of the flesh'.[7] By 1326, Despenser enjoyed an annual income of over £7,000 – and this does not even include the value of his goods in Wales, by far the largest part of his landholdings – which made him by far the richest man in the country after Edward and even wealthier than his brother-in-law the earl of Gloucester had been.[8] Despenser's riches grew and grew over the next few years, and he was by far the most important English customer of the Italian banking firms the Bardi and Peruzzi, holding almost £6,000 with them in January 1324.[9] The king's infatuation with his favourite knew no bounds, and despite Despenser's wealth, Edward even paid for his household essentials, spending, for example, thirty shillings on wax for him, and giving five pounds to the keeper of Despenser's horses for taking good care of the animals.[10] When Edward paid £130 for a new royal ship, it was called, inevitably, *La Despenser*.[11] Despenser's father also came to wield great influence, and the hundreds of petitions which followed hard on their 1326 downfall reveal how they were able to extort, imprison and take anything they wanted. Hugh Despenser, untouchable, engaged in any act of lawlessness he felt like, all of which took place with Edward's full knowledge and acquiescence, and as the king he must be held accountable for the flagrant breaches of the law he permitted and in many cases encouraged and facilitated. The man who loved the company of the lowborn, who delighted in digging and thatching and being wildly generous, became a despot, willing to trample over the rights of many to please his beloved favourite.

One notable feature of the period in and after 1322 is the deterioration of Edward's relationship with Queen Isabella. For fourteen years, she had been his loyal and supportive ally and helpmate, but after the victory at Boroughbridge, Isabella appears so rarely in the records as to give the impression that she had retired to a convent.[12] It is impossible to know what happened, but the impression is one of a sudden crisis in the marriage. The couple had no more children after 1321, which may be a symptom of their declining relationship (or possibly also of the declining fertility of one or both of them). In later years, Isabella blamed Hugh Despenser for coming between her husband and herself and took to dressing in widow's weeds to mourn the death of her marriage, though whether this necessarily meant that Edward and Despenser had a sexual relationship is not certain. Despenser's relations with his wife Eleanor certainly continued: she bore more children in 1323 and 1325.[13] It is likely that Despenser, who as royal chamberlain strictly controlled access to Edward, managed to stop or curtail considerably Isabella's ability to communicate with her husband, though why Edward permitted Despenser to do this is an unanswerable question. Isabella's hatred of Despenser is painfully apparent, and he was the only one of her husband's favourites to arouse her ire to such an extent. Other than the period soon after her wedding, there is no evidence that she complained about Piers Gaveston, and if she disliked Roger Damory and Hugh Audley or objected to their relationship with her husband, there is likewise no evidence of it. Hugh Despenser was different: he had a definite agenda, to become as rich as possible and the most powerful man in the country. Isabella did not form part of his plans. After his return from exile, his position as royal favourite was unassailable; there is nothing to show that Edward was ever willing to give him up or send him away from court, as he had done with Damory and Audley, not even in 1326 when his throne depended on it. The later chronicler Jean Froissart wrote about Despenser, 'Without him nothing was done, and through him everything was done, and the king trusted him more than everybody else,' and the *Polychronicon* noted that as Despenser's power waxed, the queen's waned.[14] The deterioration of Edward and Isabella's relationship was to have tragic consequences for the king.

Edward summoned his army in March 1322 to go, yet again, against the Scots that July, 'to repel with God's help their obstinate malice'.[15] Robert Bruce invaded England in mid-June and burned and pillaged as far south as Preston in Lancashire, and *Lanercost* claims that he even plundered the monastery of Holm Coltran, although his father was buried there.[16] Edward had still not given up hope of defeating Bruce and becoming overlord of Scotland, though one wonders if even he had to admit to himself that he was at least fourteen years too late. He left York on 21 July, the day he sent Hugh Despenser's eldest son Hugh, who was probably only thirteen, to take 'fat venison' in the royal forests, parks and chases in twenty-three counties, also sending his huntsman William Twyt or Twici to Lancashire for the same purpose.[17] Twici wrote a French treatise called *Le Art de Venerie* around 1320; the earliest text on hunting written in England, it opens, 'Here begins the art of hunting, which Master William Twici, huntsman of the king of England, made in his time to instruct others.'[18] The records are sparse, but it appears that Edward enjoyed hunting; Queen Isabella certainly did, and in 1325 boarded her hunting dogs with the prior of Canterbury, who wrote to Hugh Despenser to complain that they were eating him out of house and home.[19]

Edward's illegitimate son Adam, in his mid-teens or thereabouts, accompanied him to Scotland, probably serving his father as page or squire. The king's wardrobe accounts record four payments totalling thirteen pounds and twenty-two pence to the boy between 6 June and 18 September to buy himself equipment and other necessities, given either to Adam directly or to his tutor (*magister*) Sir Hugh Chastilloun. He was openly acknowledged as 'the bastard son of the lord king'.[20] All the English earls alive in 1322, excepting nine-year-old Chester and the ever-obscure Oxford – that is, Surrey, Arundel, Winchester, Carlisle, Richmond, Pembroke, Kent and Norfolk, as well as the earls of Atholl, Angus and Louth – also went to Scotland with the king. It is hardly worth noting that the campaign, the last one Edward would ever lead, ended in failure and disaster. He left Scotland at the beginning of September and spent most of that month in Newcastle. On 2 October he summoned the sheriff of Yorkshire, the earl of Carlisle, the bishop of Durham, William Aune and others to bring horsemen and footmen to him at 'Blakhoumor' (Blackhow Moor) between Thirsk and Helmsley.[21] Presumably, he had been made aware that Robert Bruce and his army were ravaging around Carlisle, about 110 miles to the north-west. He could hardly have guessed what would come next: Bruce gathered his entire army and marched towards Yorkshire, and by 13 October had reached Northallerton, only fifteen miles from where Edward was staying at Rievaulx Abbey.[22] Hearing of their arrival, Edward scrambled a force to meet them, while he himself remained at the abbey. On 14 October, the king's cousin John of Brittany, earl of Richmond, met the Scottish army at Roulston Scar, about seven miles from Rievaulx. The much smaller English force was defeated, and Richmond himself was captured. Now fifty-six, he would spend two years as a prisoner in Scotland until Edward raised Bruce's ransom demand of 14,000 marks.[23] His sacrifice gave Edward enough time to flee before the Scots could capture him. Humiliatingly, the king was forced to hard to the abbey of Bridlington on the coast, fifty miles away, leaving all his plate, treasure, food and even his horse trappings and harness behind, 'to the great shame and ruin of the king and the realm'.[24] Even his privy seal was captured, though the Scots courteously returned it.[25] The Bridlington chronicler asks rhetorically, 'What worse fate could befall the English than to behold their king fleeing from place to place in the face of the Scots?'[26] *Flores* describes Edward as 'spurring on his horse, trembling and defenceless', and the *Lanercost* chronicler, the armchair general who unfairly condemned the men who left the field of Bannockburn as 'miserable wretches', says, 'Ever chicken-hearted and luckless in war and having already fled in fear from them in Scotland, he [Edward] now took to flight in England'.[27]

For the second time in eight years, the king was forced to flee from a Scottish force, and this occasion was far more humiliating than in 1314. Leaving the field after Bannockburn was really the only sensible thing Edward could have done, and he had at least fought courageously in the battle. In 1322, by contrast, he was over a hundred miles inside the borders of his own kingdom, and did not even face Bruce on the battlefield – though given that most of his army had been disbanded and he was attended by a small retinue, this was most probably not cowardice but pragmatism; he simply could not allow the numerically far superior Scottish force to capture him. Still, this flight was a deep humiliation, and the *French Chronicle of London* says that Edward 'returned to England in shame' and subsequently 'much oppressed his people with misery and hardship'.[28] *Scalacronica* says that after the debacle, Edward 'kept himself quiet, undertaking nothing of honour or prowess, but only acting on the advice of Hugh le Despenser so as to become rich'.[29] Having spent the first fifteen years of his reign short of money thanks to the enormous debts left to him by his father and his own extravagance, Edward showed himself from 1322 onwards to be almost pathologically obsessed with increasing and holding on to his wealth, and the *Flores* also comments on his 'insatiable avarice'.[30]

At the time of the battle, Queen Isabella was staying at Tynemouth, about ninety miles to the north of her husband's position. She later accused Hugh Despenser of 'falsely and treacherously counselling the king to leave my lady the queen in peril of her person' at Tynemouth.[31] Edward's concern for his wife is in fact apparent in the number of letters he rushed off at this time. Unable to ride all the way to Tynemouth and fetch her himself, he did the next best thing: he ordered men he trusted to help her. He commanded the constable of Norham Castle to take Isabella under his protection; should Scottish troops approach Tynemouth, he was to enlist the assistance of the constables of all the castles in the north-east.[32] Edward also ordered the earls of Richmond and Atholl and his steward Richard Damory (Roger's brother) to raise troops, who included some of Hugh Despenser's men, and go to her aid. Isabella, who loathed Despenser, refused to accept the presence of his soldiers, even though they would be commanded not by Despenser himself but by three men she had no reason to distrust, one of whom (Richmond) was her kinsman. Edward then sent Isabella's countryman Henri, lord of Sully and butler of France, visiting England, to Tynemouth with his troops to protect her. Unfortunately Sully was caught up in the chaos, and the Scots captured him at Byland – though Bruce treated him as a honoured guest.[33] With hindsight, Edward's decision to send Isabella to Tynemouth seems absurd, but she had safely accompanied him on campaign in 1310 and 1314, staying much farther north than Tynemouth, and it probably never occurred to him that she would be in danger.

According to a French chronicle which, with Isabella's accusation of Despenser, is the only source for the incident, the queen's squires fortified Tynemouth Priory against a possible Scottish raid and arranged a boat for her, and she sailed down the coast to safety. The chronicle also claims that two of Isabella's attendants died on the journey, one when she went into premature labour.[34] Had the Scots captured Isabella, they would have demanded an enormous ransom, and it would have unthinkable for Edward not to pay it. For Despenser, whose main interest in life was amassing vast amounts of money for himself and the king, this would have been anathema, and therefore it is hard to imagine that he would have wanted the Scots to capture the queen, as some commentators have suggested.[35] Besides, his own wife was attending the queen: Edward wrote to Eleanor Despenser at Tynemouth on 13 September, and after he reached York in mid-October sent twenty pieces of sturgeon to his wife and thirteen to Eleanor.[36] Pope John XXII commended Despenser in January 1324 for his 'good services, as related by Henry, lord of Sully', whom Edward had sent to Isabella's aid.[37] It is difficult to believe that Sully, who was in a good position to know what had really happened, would have recommended Despenser to the pope had he held him in any way responsible for Isabella's ordeal, and John XXII, who wrote frequently to both Edward and Isabella, never mentioned the incident.

Whoever was to blame, Isabella was incensed, and relations between king and queen worsened further. Edward gave a messenger ten shillings on 19 December for bringing him letters from his wife, but there is little evidence of contact between the couple for the next few months.[38] Four days later, the king informed sheriffs that Isabella was going on pilgrimage at 'diverse places within the realm' until the following autumn.[39] It is not certain that she ever went, and although perhaps she did, this may also have been Edward's putting a politic face on her angry departure from him, or that he had sent her away from him.

Edward lost two people in the autumn of 1322: the brutal Robert Lewer, whom he had once pardoned for threatening to dismember his servants and who subsequently played an important role in the campaign of 1321/22, was ordered to be arrested on 20 September.[40] Lewer stole goods belonging to Hugh Despenser the Elder, earl of Winchester, then went to manors which had belonged to the executed Contrariants Henry Tyes and Warin Lisle and ostentatiously handed them out as alms. Lewer seems here to have been acting against the Despensers, rather than Edward himself. Edward ordered all his sheriffs to pursue and take Lewer dead or alive.[41] Lewer's rebellion, if it may be dignified by the name, soon petered out, and Edward gave two pounds on 19 December to a messenger who brought him news of his capture.[42] Lewer was subjected to the terrible, but usual, punishment for those who refused to plead: *peine forte et dure*, lying on the floor in thin clothes pressed with a great weight of iron.[43] *Flores* says he died on 26 December 1322.[44]

And sadly for the king, his illegitimate son Adam died on the Scottish campaign, perhaps of the dysentery which decimated the English army. Edward's reaction to this loss is unfortunately unrecorded, though he had his son buried at Tynemouth Priory on 30 September, with a silk cloth with gold thread placed over his body.[45] The identity of Adam's mother or what became of her is also unknown, but we may surmise that as Edward acknowledged Adam as his son, he must have had a fairly serious relationship with her. Adam is very obscure and no reference to him before 1322 has yet been found, but a letter of that summer which is almost certainly talking about him says that 'all good qualities and honour are increasing in him'.[46]

After his flight from Rievaulx, Edward spent late October and early November in York, where he gave a pound to the earl of Louth's minstrel Sourelius for performing before him, and two pounds to a monk of Rievaulx to buy a habit.[47] The king probably saw the sky 'of a colour like blood' on 31 October from terce to vespers, or 9 a.m. to sunset, as recorded by the Sempringham annalist and the *Brut*.[48] On the way back to York, Edward stayed at Thorne near Doncaster, where he gave two shillings each to ten fishermen 'who fished in the king's presence and took great pike, great eels and a large quantity of other fish'. A John Waltham gave him two salmon.[49] It is hard to think of another medieval king of England who would willingly have stood by a river in damp chilly November to watch people fishing, and the king's chamber account sheds more light on Edward's enjoyment of 'low' pursuits and fondness for the company of the lowborn: for example, he went to the forge at Temple Hirst to chat to his blacksmith, John Cole.[50] The account also records a payment of two pounds to the Carmelite friar Walter Mordon, 'whose Mass the king often heard in the chapel' at Temple Hirst.[51] Edward decided to spend the winter in the north, and on 27 December, once more ordered a muster of his army at York on 2 February 1323, a campaign destined never to take place.[52]

Edward spent Christmas at York, and ate porpoise, sturgeon, swans, peacocks, herons, pigeons, venison and wild boar, among much else.[53] He paid two women for singing for him in the garden of the Franciscans on 26 December, presumably a mild day.[54] Whether Isabella was with her husband is not clear, though Edward's niece Elizabeth was present, and he threatened her that she would hold no lands from him if she refused to agree to Despenser's demands to exchange her rich lordship of Usk. It is difficult to reconcile the two images of the ever-contradictory king here: the amiable, easy-going man chatting with fishermen and blacksmiths, and the harsh, angry man hurling threats at his own niece.

The queen was in London by 12 January 1323, with Hugh Despenser's wife Eleanor, and spent the next few weeks in residence at the Tower. Isabella wrote a letter to the treasurer on 17 February, from the Tower, asking him to ensure that her 'dear and beloved cousin' Joan Mortimer, wife of Roger Mortimer and held under house arrest with eight attendants, received promptly the money allocated for her sustenance. This has sometimes been seen as evidence of the queen's collusion with Joan's husband Roger, with whom the queen began a relationship in about late 1325. Although it is possible that Mortimer smuggled a message from his cell to Isabella asking for her help, it is more likely that the queen was simply motivated by concern for a noblewoman who was her distant cousin. Eleanor Despenser also wrote a letter on Joan's behalf, on the same date and also from the Tower; it is safe to say that she was not colluding with Mortimer.[55]

Eleanor Despenser had grown very close to her uncle Edward, who in 1323 gave her a huge gift of one hundred pounds for her illness after childbirth and paid all her expenses during her stay at the royal manor of Cowick. The king owned a ship named *La Alianore la Despensere* after his niece.[56] Although Edward had always been extremely fond of Eleanor, in the last year or two of his reign there is abundant evidence that they had become extremely familiar: there are numerous entries in his chamber account relating to privy dining, visits and many gifts including caged larks and goldfinches, jewels, horses, clothes and large sums of money. So close were they, in fact, that a Hainault chronicle even stated that they were having an affair.[57] Michael Prestwich suggests that the chronicler may have heard the story from Isabella's entourage when the queen was in Hainault in 1326.[58] The *Flores* wrote of Edward's 'infamy and illicit bed, full of sin' and said that he was 'condemned by God and men' and had 'removed from his side his noble consort and her sweet conjugal embraces'.[59] Whether Edward's 'illicit bed' meant sexual relations with men, an incestuous affair with his niece, both, something else entirely, or was merely an invention of a man who detested the king in order to discredit him, is unclear. Edward lavished gifts on those he loved, most notably his male favourites and his son Edward of Windsor, and by that token he certainly loved Eleanor. No English chronicler even hinted at an incestuous relationship between the two, however, except perhaps the much later writer Henry Knighton, who made the rather cryptic comment that when Isabella was abroad in 1325/26, Eleanor was treated as though she were queen.[60]

There is no evidence for the twenty-first-century suggestion that Hugh Despenser had sex with Isabella or raped her, a theory based solely on Isabella's statement in 1326 that Despenser had 'dishonoured' her, which means his success in drastically limiting her influence over her husband and even her ability to communicate with him, his reduction of her income, and other issues she raised against him which distressed her.[61] If Isabella really had accused Despenser of such a serious and shocking crime, it is odd that no one mentioned it – neither chroniclers, the pope nor Isabella's brother the king of France ever hinted at a sexual assault, nor was it one of the charges against Despenser at his trial when Isabella accused him of many other things. Despenser harried widows and others in his overwhelming desire to possess ever more lands, certainly deeply unpleasant behaviour, but there are no grounds for accusing him of sexual violence, and no reason to suppose that he had any carnal interest in Isabella.

While the queen was at the Tower in early 1323, Edward remained in Yorkshire, where he gave two pounds to four clerks for playing interludes before himself and Hugh Despenser in the great hall at Cowick, and spent three shillings playing dice.[62] The royal favourite now controlled a huge area of South Wales, and after the earl of Pembroke's death in 1324 would gain even more. Edward received a 'private message' from Edmund of Woodstock, earl of Kent, on 13 January.[63] Edward seems to have been very fond of the younger of his half-brothers, whom he trusted and sent on various important missions abroad. By contrast, his other half-brother Thomas of Brotherton, earl of Norfolk, rarely appears in Edward's accounts, and the king showed him little favour.[64]

The end of 1322 was mostly peaceful, but inevitably, this was not to last. Andrew Harclay, earl of Carlisle, growing tired of Edward's endless failures in Scotland and his inability to protect the north of England, met Robert Bruce at Lochmaben on 3 January 1323.[65] They agreed that England would recognise Bruce as king, that Edward would be granted the marriage of Bruce's son and heir – Bruce in fact had no son until March 1324 – and that Bruce would pay England 40,000 marks of silver over ten years.[66] On 8 January, Edward declared that truces with the Scots must not be made without his consent and ordered Harclay to come to him immediately.[67] It is probable that Harclay's rival Sir Anthony Lucy had prior knowledge of the meeting and informed the king, as Edward gave Lucy's messenger a pound on 2 January for bringing his letters to him; for only five days to pass between the Lochmaben meeting and Edward's response to it, 3 to 8 January, otherwise seems impossibly fast.[68] Harclay failed to obey Edward's summons, and the king, 'exceedingly put out (and no wonder!)' ordered his arrest on 1 February.[69] *Lanercost* gives a colourful account: Anthony Lucy and a group of knights and men-at-arms hid their weapons under their clothes to disguise their hostile intent, and arrested Harclay while he was dictating letters in the great hall of Carlisle Castle.[70] Edward sent the earl of Kent, the chief justice of the King's Bench and others to 'degrade' Harclay. This involved tearing the golden spurs of knighthood from his boots and removing his belt of earldom, and, according to the *Brut*, breaking his sword over his head.[71] Lucy told him, 'Now art thou no knight, but a knave.'[72]

Harclay was condemned to the full horrors of the traitor's death by hanging, drawing and quartering, his head to be set on London Bridge and the four quarters of his body publicly displayed in Carlisle, Newcastle, Shrewsbury and York. On 3 March, Harclay died well and bravely at Carlisle: when he heard the sentence, he announced, 'You have divided my carcass according to your pleasure, and I commend myself to God,' and gazed towards the heavens, hands clasped and held aloft, as horses dragged him through the streets of the town he had defended so staunchly for many years.[73] Harclay's sister Sarah Leyburne finally received permission to bury his remains in August 1328.[74] *Lanercost* points out that he was 'a single individual, none of whose business it was to transact such affairs', and certainly he had considerably overstepped his authority, but it is easy to sympathise with his growing frustration with Edward.[75] The king, with his usual malice towards family members of people who angered him, ordered the treasurer and barons of the exchequer to remove Harclay's cousin Patrick Corewen from his position as sheriff of Westmorland, and appoint instead 'a successor of undoubted loyalty'.[76] Harclay had certainly committed treason, though unlike the earl of Lancaster did not do so for his own benefit, but to spare the inhabitants of northern England the endless suffering inflicted on them by Scottish raids. Although Edward had no choice but to punish Harclay, he thus destroyed a man who had always been loyal to him, who had staunchly defended Carlisle and Cumberland against Robert Bruce for years and who was one of the very few men of the reign to enjoy military success.

Still unwilling to take responsibility for his own failures in Scotland, Edward sent a bitterly sarcastic letter to his kinsman Louis Beaumont, bishop of Durham, on 10 February 1323, reminding Louis that his brother Henry had once told the king that if Louis were appointed to the bishopric, 'a defence like a stone wall would be provided for those parts', in contrast to the negligence of Louis's predecessor Richard Kellaw.

Edward fumed, 'The king knows actually that greater damage is done in the bishopric by the bishop's default, negligence and laziness than in the time of his predecessor.'[77] Given that Edward himself had few equals when it came to negligence and laziness, there is much of the pot calling the kettle black about this letter. On a happier note, he gave five shillings to a girl who had travelled the thirty miles from York to Pontefract to bring him ale as a gift from her mother Alice de Brunne, and amusingly, one of his clerks had to pay four pence to replace a key which opened a chest of money, 'which the king himself lost'.[78] Somewhat mysteriously, Edward gave twenty-two shillings to John Sturmy and other squires of his chamber, 'sent secretly on the king's business without other mention', in late January. In February at Pontefract, Edward accompanied his valet Edmund 'Monde' Fisher (father of his page Little Will Fisher) to buy fishing nets.[79]

But yet more problems beset the king in early 1323: Lord Berkeley and Hugh Audley the Elder almost escaped from Wallingford Castle when they overcame their guards and took over the castle. The *Vita* says that only the quick thinking of a boy in the gatehouse, who realised that something was amiss and raised the hue and cry, prevented their flight.[80] The Sempringham annalist has a completely different story, saying that the castle was taken by Lord Berkeley's wife Isabel, the much older half-sister of Eleanor Despenser.[81] Edward sent his steward Richard Damory and the sheriffs of Oxfordshire and Berkshire to besiege the castle, though the *Vita* gives the earls of Kent and Winchester as the men responsible.[82] This was, or at least Edward believed that it was, the first stage of a plan to seize Windsor Castle and the Tower of London, where many Contrariants were imprisoned.[83]

It was around this time that Edward suddenly took it into his head to try to claim a share of Provence in the south-east of France, and wrote several letters to this effect to the pope, asking for his help.[84] His claim came through his grandmother Queen Eleanor, second of the four daughters of Count Raymond-Berenger V of Provence, and also through the third daughter, Sanchia, who married Richard of Cornwall, brother of Edward's grandfather Henry III; Edward was also her heir. In fact Edward had no genuine claim to Provence, as Raymond-Berenger had left the entire county to his fourth daughter Beatrice in his will. Edward wrote to Beatrice's grandson Robert, king of Sicily and count of Provence, asking him to 'restore to the king amicably' the portions of the county that Edward said fell to him by inheritance.[85] Although Edward wrote again to John XXII and Robert in August 1323, nothing came of it, and he abandoned his efforts.[86] His envoys to Robert of Sicily were Rigaud d'Assier, the French bishop of Winchester, and John Stratford, archdeacon of Lincoln; d'Assier died on the trip, and John XXII appointed Stratford to his vacant bishopric.[87] Edward, who had written to the pope several times asking him to elect Hugh Despenser's ally Robert Baldock, was furious, and asked John XXII to revoke Stratford's appointment.[88] Subsequently Edward petulantly refused to grant a petition simply because it was supported by Stratford, with whom he declared himself 'exceedingly incensed' and described as 'faithless and ungrateful'.[89] In November 1323, Edward ordered the keepers of more than seventy ports and the sheriffs of twenty counties not to permit Stratford to leave the country.[90] He forced Stratford to acknowledge a huge debt of £10,000 to him in June 1324, and began proceedings against him before the King's Bench. Hugh Despenser extorted £1,000 from the unfortunate bishop, which he deposited with his Italian bankers, the Peruzzi.[91]

Late 1321 had seen the beginning of an extraordinary vendetta on the king's part against some of the English bishops, which he continued into 1323 and beyond. Edward wrote to the pope about Henry Burghersh, bishop of Lincoln, whose appointment he himself had actively promoted, complaining that Burghersh was insufficiently qualified and that he, Edward, had been deceived by him.[92] That Burghersh was the nephew of the executed Bartholomew Badlesmere was not, of course, a coincidence. The king asked John XXII to translate Burghersh and John Droxford of Bath and Wells to other offices outside England and replace Droxford as bishop with Edward's friend William, abbot of Langdon; Droxford had supported the Marchers in 1322, or at least Edward believed that he had.[93] John Hothum of Ely – who had acted as Piers Gaveston's attorney in 1311 – also fell from favour in 1322 for obscure reasons and William Airmyn of Norwich infuriated the king in 1326, though Edward reserved his most virulent hatred for Adam Orleton of Hereford, whom he persecuted.[94] Always prone to emotional outbursts, Edward told the pope that Burghersh, Droxford and Orleton were 'the worst poison' and 'descended from the race of traitors', and declared that they had brought notorious misfortunes to England and that he could no longer bear the scandal of having them in his kingdom.[95] John XXII refused to translate them from their bishoprics, and told John Stratford that 'God is offended' by the king's actions.[96] Even Edward's friend and ally Walter Reynolds, archbishop of Canterbury, was not immune from the king's wrath. On one occasion, Edward flew into such a screaming fury with Reynolds that the archbishop was forced to invent a hasty excuse in order to escape from the king's presence.[97] Edward's vile temper and unpredictable moods became ever worse as he grew older. Still, his rages were an exercise in restraint by the standards of his Castilian cousins Sancho IV and Alfonso XI, who on occasion beat their relatives and dissident nobles to death with their own hands.[98]

Edward spent the first half of March 1323 at Knaresborough Castle, which had once belonged to Piers Gaveston. He had not forgotten his earlier wish to found a house of Dominican nuns at Langley, and wrote to the master of the Dominican order asking him to find four devout women.[99] Presumably Hervey was unable to find any, as nothing came of it. Miracles were still being reported at the site of the earl of Lancaster's execution in 1323: 2,000 people, some from as far away as Kent, gathered to pray and make oblations at Lancaster's tomb in Pontefract.[100] The archbishop of York twice had to remind his archdeacon that Lancaster was not a canonised saint and order him to disperse the throng gathering at the earl's tomb, some of whom were crushed to death.[101] Edward sent his clerk Richard Moseley to investigate, the king's attitude to the situation apparent from his description of the crowd as 'malefactors and apostates' and his comment that they were praying 'not to God but rather to idols'. The crowd made their feelings clear, too: Moseley was assaulted, and two of his servants killed.[102] The *Brut* includes a bizarrely disgusting story in which Hugh Despenser, troubled and angered by the 'great heresy' of the alleged miracles, sent a messenger to Edward to inform him about them. As the messenger passed through Pontefract, he 'made his ordure' at the place where Lancaster had been beheaded – and later suffered punishment for this sacrilegious act when he 'shed all his bowels at his fundament'.[103] Miracles were also said to have taken place at the execution site of the Contrariants Henry Montfort and Henry Wilington: the mayor of Bristol told the king that Montfort's brother bribed a poor child with two shillings 'to pronounce to the people that he received healing of his sight'.[104]

Less than four months after Andrew Harclay's abortive negotiations with Robert Bruce, Edward finally bowed to the inevitable and signed a thirteen-year peace treaty with Scotland. He still refused to recognise Bruce as king of Scots, which has far less to do with his own stubbornness or stupidity than the fact that such a recognition would make him profoundly unpopular among his magnates; he had already been accused several times of 'losing' Scotland, and this would be one of the charges against him at his deposition. In 1328, Queen Isabella and her favourite Roger Mortimer, ruling the country in the name of the underage Edward III, signed the deeply unpopular Treaty of Northampton, or the 'Shameful Peace' as many people in England called it, which finally recognised Bruce as king and arranged the marriage of Edward II's daughter Joan of the Tower to Bruce's son and heir David. Thomas Randolph, earl of Moray, travelled to England to negotiate terms in May 1323, and Edward sent several hostages to Tweedmouth to assure Bruce of his safe return.[105] Edward signed the treaty on 30 May; Bruce ratified it a week later.[106]

Early June 1323 found Edward in communication with King Sancho of Majorca regarding a robbery committed by some Englishmen on Sancho's subjects, and with Queen Isabella's uncle Charles, count of Valois, who had proposed a marriage alliance between one of his many daughters and Edward's ten-year-old son Edward of Windsor.[107] Valois also sent envoys to England sometime before January 1324 to negotiate other marriages between his family and Edward's, this time involving the latter's two daughters Eleanor and Joan, one of whom was proposed as a bride for Valois's youngest son and the other for one of his grandsons.[108] The queen had joined Edward at Cowick by 10 June. The king spent the rest of the summer in Yorkshire, and Isabella probably remained with him, though once again her whereabouts are uncertain and it is possible that she resumed her pilgrimage. Edward gave two pounds to the minstrel of Hugues de Bouville, chamberlain of his brother-in-law Charles IV, who played before him and perhaps Isabella at Pickering, and on 15 August sent a gift of 'coursing dogs' to Charles.[109]

On 1 August 1323, the feast of St Peter in Chains, the king's most dangerous enemy Roger Mortimer escaped from the Tower of London, having fed his guards sedatives in their wine, and made his way to the Continent. Five days after the escape, Stephen Segrave, constable of the Tower, was still seriously ill from the sedatives.[110] Edward, at Kirkham in Yorkshire, heard the news on 6 August, and ordered all the sheriffs and keepers of the peace in England and the bailiffs of fifteen ports to pursue Mortimer with hue and cry and take him dead or alive.[111] Assuming that he had fled to Wales, Edward ordered the loyal Welshmen Rhys ap Gruffydd and Gruffydd Llwyd to search for him there, though an inquisition taken at Portsmouth as early as 10 August established that Mortimer had taken a ship to the Continent.[112] On 26 August, Edward told his brother the earl of Kent that he thought Mortimer was intending to travel to Ireland, and, afraid that Mortimer's escape was only the first of many Contrariants breaking prison, also told the constables of no fewer than eighty castles to guard their charges safely – which demonstrates what a large number of men were still in prison, despite the many who had been released on payment of a fine.[113] Edward's insecurity and paranoia are painfully apparent in 1323; eighteen months after his victory over the Contrariants, his reign was descending into a nightmare of fear and unrest. For this, he had no one to blame but himself.

Several chronicles claim that Edward had been intending to execute Mortimer, who was therefore compelled to escape before the sentence was carried out, while others do not mention an impending execution.[114] The *Flores'* account of the event owes far more to the story of St Peter's escape from Herod's prison than to reality, being almost a direct quotation from various verses of Acts of the Apostles.[115] Whether Edward really was about to put Mortimer to death, or if this was merely a rumour that found its way into several chronicles or an invention to explain his dramatic escape, is not clear; the *Brut*, implausibly, has Mortimer fleeing the day before his planned execution. Adam Murimuth, who came to know Mortimer well after 1326, says only that he escaped and fled to France and does not mention an impending execution.[116] Nor is there anything in any official record to confirm that Edward was planning his death.

Historians have wondered whether Queen Isabella had anything to do with Mortimer's escape, but the first people to suggest that she did – indeed, the first people to suggest that she had any kind of relationship with Mortimer before late 1325 – were the dramatists Christopher Marlowe and Michael Drayton in the 1590s.[117] Isabella was not in or near the Tower at the time that Mortimer escaped, as sometimes stated; she was probably with Edward in Yorkshire. There is no evidence that as early as 1323 Isabella had any interest in acting against her husband, nor that she had ever had any personal contact with Mortimer. Chronicler Geoffrey le Baker decades later invented a conspiracy whereby two bishops (Orleton of Hereford and Burghersh of Lincoln), Isabella, Roger Mortimer and Charles IV of France conceived a cunning plan to bring about Edward's downfall years before it in fact happened, Mortimer's escape being the first step in this deep conspiracy. Although this story has often been repeated as fact, it owes far more to Baker's overheated imagination and many years' hindsight than to anything resembling reality. Mortimer was an intelligent, resourceful and courageous man, and it is far more probable that he planned his escape himself, working on the sympathy of his guards, including Gerald Alspaye, who fled with him. Sympathetic Londoners – Edward II was extremely unpopular in his capital – procured the sedatives for him.[118] Mortimer later made his way to Charles IV's court. Although it has been postulated that Charles would never have welcomed Mortimer without Isabella's recommendation, this is not the case: Mortimer was a nobleman, an experienced and able soldier and administrator and still only thirty-six, and such men were welcome anywhere. Besides, Mortimer was not alone at the French court. Other English exiles, men who had fled after Boroughbridge, among them John Maltravers and William Trussell, accompanied him there. So if Isabella asked her brother to welcome Mortimer, presumably she must also have asked him to receive the other exiles, which seems improbable.

Edward was still ordering numerous bailiffs to search for Mortimer in September, and by 1 October, had finally learned where he was: in Picardy, with his kinsmen the Fiennes brothers.[119] As early as mid-November 1323, Mortimer incited 'aliens to enter the kingdom and to murder the king's counsellors', meaning the Despensers, Mortimer's detested cousin the earl of Arundel and Despenser's protégé Robert Baldock, whom Edward appointed chancellor of England in August 1323.[120] Although Mortimer was the most important Contrariant to break prison, he was not the only one: Hugh Audley escaped from Nottingham, Thomas Berkeley from the Tower of London, Robert Walkfare and two others from Corfe, Henry Leyburne from Devizes and Robert Holland from Northampton, all in the last year or so of Edward's reign.[121]

Edward made a renewed onslaught against Roger Mortimer's family and supporters in March and April 1324, and ordered a commission to find people who had adhered to him in 1322.[122] This was no doubt inspired at least in part by his frustration at being unable to recapture his enemy, though as Mortimer had sent assassins to kill Edward's friends, it is hardly surprising that the king would retaliate, and Mortimer fled the country in the full knowledge that he was leaving his family to Edward's not-so-tender mercies. His wife Joan and her servants were moved from Southampton to Skipton-in-Craven, and three of their eight daughters – Margaret Berkeley, Joan and Isabella – were sent to live at separate convents and granted the small amounts of fifteen pence (Margaret) or twelve pence (Joan and Isabella) per week for their sustenance.[123] Three of Mortimer's four sons remained under Edward's control, though Geoffrey was reunited with his father on the Continent.[124] Edward also began proceedings against Mortimer's ally Adam Orleton, bishop of Hereford, whom he had publicly reprimanded for aiding the Marchers in 1322. It is odd that he waited two years to prosecute Orleton for this if he genuinely believed the charge to be true, and it probably represents Edward's frustration and anger at Mortimer's escape rather than anything else. The vindictiveness with which Edward pursued Orleton is astonishing: he confiscated the bishop's lands, and even allowed his goods to be thrown into the street to be ransacked and looted by passers-by.[125] This, of course, ensured that Orleton would join the king's enemies in 1326, and was also one of the factors which gradually lost Edward the support of the archbishop of Canterbury, who had long been one of his most loyal allies. As for Orleton, he had lost favour with Roger Mortimer within months of Edward's deposition and was probably not nearly as committed to the Marcher as Edward believed, and the king would have been far more sensible to court the intelligent and able bishop as an ally. But then, common sense was hardly one of Edward's defining features. He also foolishly alienated his cousin Henry of Lancaster, who had taken no part in the 1322 rebellion of his brother Thomas, with whom he had a cool relationship.[126] Edward claimed that Henry had abetted Orleton, and, angered by Henry's adoption of his brother's coat of arms and a cross he had erected in Leicester in Thomas's memory, accused him of treason.[127] As with Orleton, this ensured that in 1326 Henry would also join the king's enemies, taking the enormous Lancastrian faction with him. Edward did allow Henry to assume the earldom of Leicester in April 1324, but retained most of the Lancastrian inheritance himself, including the great castle of Kenilworth.[128]

Edward visited Liverpool for the only time in his reign in late October 1323, paying a ferryman two shillings to take himself and part of his household across the Mersey, and in early November spent a night at Vale Royal, a Cistercian abbey in Cheshire his father had founded in 1270.[129]

That he was furious and deeply concerned about Roger Mortimer's escape is apparent from the strenuous efforts he made to capture him and his actions against Mortimer's supporters, but neither Edward nor anyone else could have predicted that it would set off a chain of events which would ultimately result in his deposition, and he soon had more pressing problems to deal with.

Not entirely surprisingly, these problems arose in his French duchy of Gascony. One of Edward's exasperated officials wrote in 1314 that 'the Gascon business is like a mighty sea, full of shipwrecks, and has no port of safety', and Edward I had gone to war with the French over the duchy in 1294.[130] The accession of Charles IV of France in January 1322 meant that Edward now owed homage for Gascony and Ponthieu to the last of Queen Isabella's short-lived brothers. Charles politely waited until Edward had destroyed the Contrariants and until England was quiet, and sent Edward amicable letters in July 1323 asking him to present himself at Amiens between Candlemas (2 February) and Easter (15 April) 1324. Edward, predictably, made excuses, claiming that England was still in a state of turmoil and he could not possibly leave.[131] Charles had probably expected this, but a particularly unfortunate piece of timing soon turned the situation dangerous, and a sergeant-at-arms, a wooden stake and the lord of Montpezat were about to inadvertently start a war between England and France.

The trouble began in the small Gascon village of St-Sardos. Philip V had in 1318 granted permission for a *bastide*, a fortified town, to be built there, and on 15 October 1323 a French sergeant-at-arms drove a stake bearing the royal arms of France into the ground, to claim the land. This was a direct provocation to Edward, who could hardly be expected to tolerate a French fortress in the middle of his duchy. Raymond-Bernard, lord of nearby Montpezat, took matters into his own hands and hanged the sergeant-at-arms from the stake he had just erected, and burned the village to the ground. News of this offence reached Charles IV on 1 November, but Edward himself did not learn of the event until three weeks later, just after his messengers had departed to proffer his excuses for delaying homage – most unfortunate timing. Ralph Basset, Edward's new steward of Gascony, and Raymond-Bernard made matters worse by refusing to appear before Charles IV at the Paris *parlement* of February 1324 to explain their actions.

Charles wrote to Edward acknowledging his brother-in-law's problems with Scotland and his other 'great business'. Addressing Edward as 'fair brother' and talking of 'the love which we have for you', he told him that he did not hold him responsible for the St-Sardos outrage and that he was willing to postpone the ceremony of homage until 1 July 1324.[132] Edward, however, was angry with Charles, believing that he had welcomed Roger Mortimer and other Contrariants at his court, and wrote to him in November asking him to banish them from France. Edward's envoys told him on 13 December 1323, 'As for Mortimer and the other rebels, forbidden to stay within the power of the king of France, they are received and favoured on the power of the count of Boulogne.'[133] Edward believed in October 1324 that the exiles had found refuge with Count William of Hainault, and asked him to arrest them and send them to him.[134] Relations between Edward and the count of Hainault had cooled considerably since their marriage negotiations of the late 1310s, and William followed a pro-French line, his wife Joan being the daughter of Charles IV's uncle Charles, count of Valois. In 1323 and 1324, men of Hainault attacked several English ships, and Edward ordered that all Hainault ships be seized in retaliation.[135] William wrote curtly to Edward in January 1324 to say that many of his own subjects had been robbed in England, and 'he has often written to the king for restitution, but the king has done nothing. If the king will act he will act'.[136]

Edward and Isabella spent Christmas 1323 at Kenilworth, where the king gave a pound each to two minstrels of the bishop of Ely who performed for them. He also gave half a mark each to three of his watchmen to buy themselves 'winter tunics for their night vigils'.[137] The couple travelled west and spent six days in mid-January 1324 as guests of Hugh Despenser at his Worcestershire castle of Hanley, where the king gave a bonus of two pounds to twelve carpenters for building a new perimeter wall, drawbridge and hall, described as the 'finest in the land'.[138] Edward made a quick visit to Despenser's nearby manor of Tewkesbury, where he placed a bright green and gold cloth on the tomb of his nephew the earl of Gloucester in the abbey.[139] He also spent a few days in the town of Gloucester, where, although he couldn't have known it, he would one day be buried.

During the February/March 1324 parliament at Westminster, a group of prelates – not the queen, as sometimes stated – petitioned Edward to allow the bodies of the Contrariants executed in 1322 decent burial, and he duly ordered the sheriffs of London, Middlesex, Kent, Gloucestershire, Yorkshire and Buckinghamshire to take the bodies down and bury them.[140] In the spring of 1324, Edward sent two envoys to France to try to settle the St-Sardos affair and to postpone his homage: his brother Edmund of Woodstock, earl of Kent, and Alexander Bicknor, archbishop of Dublin. These were hardly the wisest choices. Although Kent was Charles IV's first cousin and a staunch ally of Edward, he was still only twenty-two and inexperienced, while Archbishop Bicknor loathed Hugh Despenser and could, therefore, hardly have been expected to do his best on Edward's behalf. Edward sent more envoys to Charles IV in June, doing his utmost to make an awkward situation even worse by failing to travel to Amiens to pay homage and ordering the envoys 'to make excuses and defence' for his non-appearance.[141] They found Charles IV at Annet-sur-Marne on 5

July, four days after Edward should have paid homage, in the process of marrying his third wife Jeanne, fourteen-year-old daughter of Count Louis of Evreux and thus Charles's first cousin; her sister Marie was married to Edward's nephew John III, duke of Brabant.[142] Charles brusquely told the envoys that because he had 'found no man' for Gascony or Ponthieu on the appointed date, he had taken them into his hands before their arrival. Charles sent his uncle Valois into Gascony with an army in early August, and suddenly Edward II was at war with France.[143]

13

Catastrophe in Gascony

A bizarre plot to kill Edward II and the Despensers by necromancy was discovered in the spring of 1324, when John of Nottingham admitted that a group of people from Coventry had asked him to make wax figures of the three men. John and his assistants tested their method by driving a leather bodkin or a sharpened feather two inches into the figure of Richard de Sowe, who was supposedly discovered soon afterwards out of his mind and unable to recognise anyone. After they removed the bodkin from the figure's forehead and drove it instead into the heart, Sowe died within a few hours. Before they could try out the wax figures of Edward and the Despensers, John's lodger Robert gave the game away to the authorities.[1] Despenser wrote to the pope to complain about the 'magical and secret dealings' threatening him, and received an unsympathetic response.[2] Despenser, all-powerful at court and supremely rich, was living in a nightmare world of fear and paranoia; well aware of how much he and his father were hated, for good reason, his frantic, desperate pleas to Edward in 1325 not to leave him behind in England to travel to France were ultimately to bring about his and the king's downfall.

On the verge of war with France and in need of allies, Edward reached out to the Spanish kingdoms, and wrote to King Jaime II of Aragon regarding a marriage between Edward of Windsor and Jaime's daughter.[3] Edward also sent envoys to his kinsmen in Castile, asking the twelve-year-old King Alfonso XI and his regents to give credence to what the envoys told them. The regents included Edward's first cousin Juan Manuel, lord of Peñafiel and one of the greatest Spanish writers of the Middle Ages; Felipe, lord of Cabrera and Ribera; Juan el Tuerto ('the one-eyed'), lord of Biscay, and his mother Maria Diaz de Haro. Edward addressed Felipe and Juan el Tuerto as his nephews, though they were in fact his first cousins once removed.[4]

Edward spent Easter and his fortieth birthday, 25 April, at his favourite residence of Langley. A Household Ordinance issued in June 1323 stated that Edward should make an offering of five shillings before the Cross every Good Friday and that the coins should subsequently be made into 'cramp-rings', thought to be a cure against muscle cramps and epilepsy. He was also to make an offering of three shillings to the thorn of the Crown of Thorns, if he had the relic with him.[5] Piers Gaveston was still on Edward's mind, and in June 1324 he sent his confessor to Langley Priory to keep the twelfth anniversary of Gaveston's death. He also sent Brother Robert Asessour to Langley in January 1325 with the large sum of five pounds for each friar, so they would remember his friend in their prayers.[6]

In early June 1324, Edward sent the experienced diplomat the earl of Pembroke – the ambassador he should probably have sent in the first place – to Paris to negotiate the Gascony problems and the question of homage. Unfortunately, Pembroke died before he reached the city, on 23 June, when he collapsed suddenly after dining and died unshriven in his servants' arms.[7] The *Brut* has a scurrilous story of Pembroke being murdered while sitting on the privy, which the writer thought was God's vengeance, as Pembroke had been one of the men to condemn 'Saint Thomas of Lancaster' to death.[8] Edward had forced Pembroke to swear on the Gospels in June 1322 that he would always be obedient and faithful to him, because 'the king was aggrieved against him for certain reasons … and could not assure himself of the earl', most probably because Pembroke had persuaded Edward to consent to the Despensers' exile in August 1321.[9] The childless Pembroke left as his heirs his nephew John Hastings and his nieces Joan and Elizabeth Comyn, whose father was murdered by Robert Bruce in 1306 and whose brother John was killed at Bannockburn. Edward's undoubted affection for Pembroke, at least before 1322, did not prevent him allowing Hugh Despenser to harass the dowager countess and Pembroke's heirs over his debts, lands and goods.[10]

At war with France and with his French lands confiscated, Edward ordered all French subjects in England to be arrested and their goods seized. The French complained that this seizure would be worth more than the revenues of Gascony.[11] Charles of Valois took his army into the Agenais (the modern department of Lot-et-Garonne) in early August, and demanded the surrender of its capital, Agen, from the earl of Kent, now Edward's lieutenant in Gascony. Kent had already angered the residents by abducting a young girl and enforcing heavy levies of money.[12] Naively, he allowed himself to be boxed in at the castle of La Réole, and Valois, half-brother of the late Queen Marguerite and thus Kent's own uncle, besieged him there for five weeks. Valois had always followed an anti-English line, and played an important role in the plot of 1294 which deprived Edward I of Gascony for almost a decade; a chronicler wrote that 'he persecuted the English with an inveterate hatred', although this didn't prevent him desiring a marriage alliance between his children and

Edward II's.[13] Hugh Despenser told Kent that the only reason for the late arrival of ships carrying money for his aid was that 'a strong wind was against them, which we cannot turn by our own command', a statement clearly intended humorously but which also demonstrates Despenser's arrogance, with its implication that he controlled everything except the weather.[14] On 22 September 1324, Kent signed a six-month truce with Valois.[15]

Edward's response to his half-brother's truce six days later was once more to order the arrest of all French people in England, and also citizens of any Gascon towns which had surrendered to the French.[16] Although the constable of Bordeaux had written in a panic on 1 September that the whole of Gascony was on the verge of falling, it did not: the French won the Agenais and part of the Gironde, Agen fell on 15 August, but Bordeaux and Bayonne, the most important cities, remained in English hands, as did numerous other towns.[17] Edward wrote again to Jaime II of Aragon in September 1324 claiming untruthfully that he had not been summoned to pay homage to Charles IV, and grumbled about Charles's 'severity and malevolence'. He asked Jaime to send men to aid him against Charles, and sent the same letter to Alfonso XI of Castile and the regents Juan el Tuerto and his mother Maria Diaz de Haro.[18] The following day, Edward appointed four men, including the earl of Kent, to negotiate a marriage between his son Edward and one of Jaime II's daughters.[19] In February 1325, Jaime declared that the marriage alliance between his family and Edward's was 'not agreeable ... in the manner and form under which it was proposed'. Edward explained that he was eager to make 'an alliance of love' with Aragon, and sent two more envoys to negotiate any union 'as shall seem suitable and opportune'.[20] He was forced in October 1325 to apologise to Pedro Lopez de Luna, archbishop of Zaragoza, for his envoys' failure to present themselves or communicate their business to him, declaring himself annoyed by their error.[21]

Even before Jaime II rejected the marriage of Edward of Windsor, Edward began negotiating for his son to marry Alfonso XI of Castile's sister Leonor, who was probably born in 1307 and was thus a few years older than young Edward (born in 1312), and had been abandoned on her wedding day in 1319 by Jaime II's son.[22] Thirteen-year-old Alfonso XI himself was betrothed to Edward's elder daughter, six-year-old Eleanor of Woodstock, and Edward declared himself prepared to pay £15,000 as Eleanor's dowry.[23] Edward's long and eager letters to the regents about the marriages go beyond mere diplomatic courtesy, and suggest that he, half-Castilian himself, was delighted at the thought of two of his children marrying into Castile. Carried away with enthusiasm for his young cousin and future son-in-law Alfonso XI, Edward wrote that he 'rejoices greatly that providence has illuminated abundantly the boldness of Alfonsus's youth by gifts of virtues and natural and gracious good qualities, as widely diffused fame has made known and is as now spread to the ends of the world'.[24]

Jaime II did consent to a betrothal between Edward's younger daughter Joan of the Tower and his grandson the future Pedro IV, who was born in September 1319 and was two years Joan's senior.[25] Because Edward had heard that Jaime 'is old and decrepit and it is not certain that he is not dead' – in fact, Jaime lived until November 1327 – he corresponded instead with Jaime's son Alfonso, Pedro's father, though his letters to Aragon betray none of the 'rejoicing' of his letters to Castile. King Afonso IV of Portugal was also keen for a marriage alliance between his family and Edward's, and wrote to the king proposing his daughter Maria, born in February 1313, as a bride for Edward's son. Edward wrote to Afonso and Queen Beatriz, both of whom were his close relatives, explaining that his son was to be married elsewhere, but as he desired friendship between the countries, he was willing to arrange another marriage between their children.[26] In the end, because of Edward II's deposition, none of his planned marriage alliances went ahead.

Edward's diplomatic efforts in fact did him little good as regards his war with France. Jaime II and his parents had endured a long struggle with Charles of Valois and his great-uncle Charles of Anjou over control of Sicily, and Jaime had no desire to go to war with France on England's behalf, though he did declare himself willing to act as an intermediary between the two sides.[27] Castile proved more amenable to Edward's requests for military aid than Aragon, and Juan el Tuerto informed Edward in early 1325 that he was willing to raise 1,000 knights and 10,000 footmen and squires for a year, or longer if Edward required, if the king of England paid their expenses.[28] Hugh Despenser, keen for Edward not to leave England to lead an army into Gascony in the belief that his life would be in danger in the king's absence, was hoping that Castilian and Aragonese soldiers would fight a war on England's behalf.[29] Ralph Basset, steward of Gascony, advised Despenser to have the English treasury searched for ancient documents pertaining to Castile, because he had heard from 'some old people' that the kings of Castile had often claimed homage for the part of Gascony as far north as the River Dordogne. Alfonso X had incited a rebellion in Gascony in 1253 with a view to invading and taking over the duchy, though he renounced his claims to it the following year when his half-sister Leonor or Eleanor married the future Edward I. Presumably Basset was hoping that, seventy years after the wedding of Edward II's parents, Castile would decide to fight France for a share of the duchy, an unrealistic proposition to which Despenser did not even bother to respond in his next letter to Basset.[30] Charles IV of France, unhappy with Edward's search for allies in Spain, said that Edward was acting 'against the crown of France' and deemed it a 'crime of treason'.[31]

Walter Reynolds, archbishop of Canterbury, believed in autumn 1324 that Roger Mortimer and the other English exiles were ready to attempt an invasion of England with armed men from Hainault, France and Germany, while Hugh Despenser thought that the exiles would soon lead an invasion force into Norfolk and Suffolk, with the aid of the count of Hainault and the king of Bohemia.[32] This invasion never came about – the English exiles had no chance of striking at Edward as early as 1324 – but it may have been the threat of it which prompted Despenser to withdraw almost £2,500 from his Italian bankers between 31 October and 3 December, paid to him in 'florins of Florence'.[33] This suggests that Despenser was considering fleeing abroad, though when the invasion finally arrived, two years later, he stayed with Edward. The atmosphere of fevered suspicion in England at this time is nicely illustrated by two panicked letters to Despenser in September 1324, telling him that a fleet of foreign vessels with a hundred armed men aboard each ship had been seen in Falmouth and mysteriously disappeared in the middle of the night. This turned out to be a group of Genoese merchants making their annual trip to the Netherlands, with armed men to guard their valuable cargo.[34]

On 18 September 1324, Edward took Queen Isabella's county of Cornwall into his own hands, supposedly because it lay on the coast 'in the more remote parts of the realm' and might be invaded by the French. The king also seized all of Isabella's other lands and castles, though he failed to explain how inland counties such as Wiltshire and Oxfordshire might be vulnerable to a French invasion.[35] Edward assigned Isabella instead an income from the Exchequer, said by several fourteenth-century chroniclers to be merely a pound a day, a gross underestimate: in fact she was granted 3,920 marks, or £2,613, six shillings and eight pence, annually, a little over seven pounds a day, considerably lower than her pre-September 1324 income of £4,500 but hardly a 'fraction' of it, as sometimes stated.[36] Sophia Menache points out that it is doubtful if Isabella 'suffered a substantial economic setback' in 1324, though the queen was, understandably, outraged at the loss of her lands.[37] She and her household could certainly live on the amount: the earl of Lancaster had in 1314 reduced Edward's expenses to ten pounds a day for a household more than twice the size of the queen's, and Edward's father, during one of their quarrels in 1305, allowed him only £155 a month or just over five pounds a day for his household costs.[38] Edward had taken his stepmother Queen Marguerite's lands and castles into his own hands in late 1317, so the move was not unprecedented, yet Edward soon restored Marguerite's lands to her, and it is hard to escape the conclusion that his seizure of Isabella's estates was intended punitively.[39] Precisely what Edward's motives in punishing his wife were is uncertain, though the queen herself blamed Hugh Despenser and his ally Walter Stapeldon, bishop of Exeter and treasurer of England. Isabella's French attendants, excepting her chaplain, were not exempt from the arrest of Charles IV's subjects – although Edward did permit other French people to remain in England – and were either imprisoned or forced to return to their homeland.[40] Charles IV was justifiably furious at the treatment of his subjects.[41] Supposedly Isabella managed to smuggle a letter to her brother complaining that she held no higher position at court than that of a servant and that Edward was a 'gripple miser', i.e. mean to her but generous to another, although this was only recorded at the end of the fourteenth century by the chronicler Thomas Walsingham, who had no access to Isabella's correspondence.

At an indeterminate date before 6 February 1325, Edward set up a household for his and Isabella's daughters, six-year-old Eleanor and three-year-old Joan, under the care of Isabel Hastings and her husband Ralph Monthermer. This has often been misunderstood in the last few years to mean that Edward was further punishing his queen by cruelly removing her children from her. The girls remained in Isabel Hastings' care until 19 February 1326, and the following day Edward appointed Joan Jermy, sister of his half-brother the earl of Norfolk's wife Alice Hales, to be in charge of the girls' household.[42] Isabel Hastings was Hugh Despenser's sister, but evidently a trustworthy, maternal type: when Edward's niece Elizabeth attended his funeral years later, she left her two young daughters in Isabel's care, despite her understandable hatred of Isabel's brother, who had treated her appallingly.[43] Isabel's husband Ralph Monthermer was the widower of Edward's sister Joan of Acre, whom he had married in early 1297 when the future king was twelve, and thus had a claim to being the uncle of the royal daughters. Also at an uncertain date, Edward and Isabella's second son John of Eltham (born 1316) was placed in the care of Edward's niece Eleanor Despenser, though this is only known from an undated membrane of Eleanor's expenses for looking after him and an entry in Edward's chamber account of June 1326 stating that the two had travelled to Kenilworth together.[44] Eleanor's care of John might have lasted only a few weeks, and there is no evidence at all that it began in September 1324, as is almost inevitably stated nowadays.

When Isabella later accused Hugh Despenser of persuading Edward to reduce her income and of dishonouring her in numerous other ways, she said nothing about her children being 'removed' from her. Nor is there any evidence that she believed her husband had deprived her of her children, or that anyone else, including the pope and the king of France, thought that Edward had done anything out of the ordinary. No chronicler waxed indignant about the king's establishment of separate households for John, Eleanor and Joan either.[45] Yet it is often unfairly used nowadays, in a world with very different cultural and familial norms, as a stick to beat Edward for his supposed nastiness towards his wife. All the people Edward appointed to look after his children were members of his extended family: his niece, his niece's sister-in-law, his former brother-in-law, his half-brother's sister-in-law. It is hard to see how any of them were an inappropriate choice.

The establishment of separate households for the royal children certainly does not mean that the queen never saw her children again or that Edward intended this, and granting custody of young royals to noblewomen and setting up their own households was entirely normal. Edward I ordered in 1301 that his eldest grandchild, ten-year-old Gilbert de Clare, be sent to live with the boy's step-grandmother Queen Marguerite, even though Gilbert's mother Joan of Acre was alive. Eleanor de Bohun, another grandchild of Edward I, also lived in Marguerite's household and later at Amesbury Priory at her uncle Edward II's expense, though her mother Elizabeth lived until 1316 and her father the earl of Hereford until 1322.[46] In the summer of 1340, Edward III set up a household for his children Isabella, Joan, Lionel and John, aged eight, six, twenty months and four months, under the supervision of the lady de la Mote, and Joan had previously been in the care of the dowager countess of Pembroke. Edward II and Isabella's elder daughter Eleanor of Woodstock was in the custody of her sister-in-law Queen Philippa in 1331, not her mother.[47] Edward I set up a household for his younger sons Thomas and Edmund when they were still babies in 1301, and they did not live with their mother Queen Marguerite.[48] No one ever accuses Edward I or III of cruelty to their wives on this account, however; Edward II is judged differently for doing the same thing as other kings by some modern commentators determined to put a negative spin on everything he did.

Lanercost and *Flores* say that Edward and Despenser appointed Eleanor Despenser as a kind of guardian over Isabella in 1324, charged with spying on her, carrying her seal and monitoring her correspondence.[49] This may have some truth in it, though far from being foisted on the queen, as is sometimes claimed, Eleanor had been her lady-in-waiting since at least 1311 and probably since Isabella's arrival in England in 1308. In July 1311, Isabella paid for ale for Eleanor's breakfast when they were staying near Durham, and in October that year had to make alternative arrangements for transporting Eleanor's possessions, 'because the lord Hugh le Despenser her husband stole away from her her sumpter-horses and other carriage'.[50] Eleanor was with Isabella at Tynemouth in 1322 when Edward supposedly abandoned his queen to danger at Hugh Despenser's instigation, and with her in the Tower in early 1323 when they both wrote letters on behalf of Roger Mortimer's wife. There is nothing to indicate hostility between the two women in 1324/25, either because Eleanor had been given custody of Isabella's son John to punish the queen or because she had been appointed some kind of spy over her, and Isabella sent letters to the justice John Stonor on behalf of Eleanor's chaplain John Sadington in early 1326, after her refusal to return to England.[51]

Parliament opened on 20 October 1324 in London and Westminster, its aims to discuss the war in Gascony. Edward's opening address, delivered in French, is the only one of his parliamentary speeches to survive. He began,

> Lords, I have shown you certain things which concern the Crown which have come under debate, as one who is your chief and who has the sovereign keeping of it, and as one who is ready to maintain the Crown in all its rights, with your counsel and aid, and to defend it as far as a man can, by the power of all your might, on which matter I have always asked for your counsel, and have done nothing in the said business without counsel, in which I believe that I have done my part,

and asked for advice from every man present (and then, one hopes, took a breath after such a long sentence). Parliament decided that Edward must lead an army into Gascony in February or March 1325, on the grounds that the king of France had maliciously deprived him of his inheritance.[52]

Hugh Despenser's dominance of the English government is obvious from the many letters between England and Gascony during the St-Sardos war, which were mostly sent to and from him rather than Edward. His correspondents addressed him in fawning terms: 'To the very noble and wise man, his very dear and very honourable lord', 'To the very puissant, very noble, very honourable and wise lord, if it please him' and 'My very dear and very dread lord' are typical examples.[53] Even Despenser's social superiors were not immune from the desire to flatter him. In a letter of May 1325, the earl of Surrey carefully addressed him as 'very dear cousin' five times in five sentences. The earl of Kent, for his part, called Despenser 'very dear nephew' or 'beloved nephew' no fewer than seven times in four sentences in one letter, and in another, told Despenser that he had heard news of his good health, 'for which we devoutly thank God'.[54] Despenser's self-importance, arrogance and certainty of his hold over the king are evident from the many letters where he speaks for himself and Edward: 'It seems to the king and to us that...' and 'the king and ourselves think that...' appear frequently.[55] An interesting light is thrown on standards of literacy among the nobility of the early fourteenth century by Despenser's statement in letters to two men that he had read their previous correspondence out loud to the king in detail.[56]

In the end, Edward did not take an army to Gascony, and although he never visited his duchy, the *Scalacronica* thought it was 'the country and nation which he loved best'.[57] As it was the homeland of Edward's beloved Piers Gaveston, the chronicler's statement may be correct. Despenser informed Ralph Basset that Edward would go to Gascony with 'a great and noble array' and, interestingly, with Robert Bruce, if the 'business' between them went well. The draft of this letter reveals that Despenser at first named Bruce as 'king of Scotland' (*le roi Descoce*), then ordered his scribe to cross that part out.[58] Edward opened negotiations with Robert Bruce again in 1324, probably because he was worried that Bruce would join with France against him, and offered safe-conducts to Bruce's envoys.[59] They arrived in England in November, and presented Bruce's demands that 'Scotland should be forever free from every English exaction', that the Scottish king should be restored to the barony in Essex which he had forfeited to Edward I in 1306, and that England should return the Stone of Scone to Scotland (it remained in London until 1996, exactly 700 years after Edward I had removed it). Bruce also proposed that Edward's son Edward of Windsor marry one of his daughters. Edward responded, in a fascinating illustration of how he had been raised to think of Scotland as part of his inheritance and subject to England,

> How without prejudice to our Crown can we surrender the right we have in Scotland, which from the coming of the Britons to the coming of the Saxons and down to our own time, is known always to have been subject to our ancestors; which, although in rebellion it often spurned our authority, was, nevertheless, as no one doubts, reduced to its due state of servitude, though unwillingly?

Edward refused to restore Bruce to the Essex manor Edward I had confiscated, claiming, 'It is not fitting that the son should make void what his father decreed,' and said that he would be willing to return the Stone of Scone to the Scots 'if their other demands were not beyond all reason'. He also declared that Bruce's proposal that one of his daughters marry Edward's son 'is unsuitable for us'. However, both sides did agree to maintain the truce, and Robert Bruce did not join Charles IV.[60]

The king spent Christmas 1324 at Nottingham, though whether Isabella was with him is uncertain. If the couple were together, it would be the last Christmas they ever spent in each other's company. Edward moved on to Ravensdale in Derbyshire, where he gave an Epiphany gift of fifty shillings to his minstrels and two shillings to his piper Little Alein for his performance, and perhaps watched deer coursing, as Ravensdale had a course about a mile long and 80 feet wide enclosed by hedges.[61] The king must have heard the sad news that his great-niece Joan, Piers Gaveston's daughter, had died of an unspecified illness at Amesbury Priory on 13 January, probably the day after her thirteenth birthday.[62] Edward had in 1317 arranged a marriage for Joan with John Multon, eldest grandson of the earl of Ulster, but she died before the wedding took place. The eccentric Edward spent much time in 1325 at Burgundy, his cottage at Westminster, and was there on 12 February 1325 watching two squires of his chamber, Berduk de Till and Giles of Spain, perform some kind of act for his entertainment involving fire. Unfortunately it went badly wrong, and both of them burnt their arms and, in Berduk's case, his thighs too. Edward gave them the large sum of twenty pounds in compensation.[63] He spent a month from mid-February to mid-March at the Tower of London, and gave a pound to Thomelyn the psalterer for playing for him there.[64]

Two staunch allies of the king died in the early spring of 1325: Robert Umfraville, earl of Angus, and the king and Hugh Despenser's brother-in-law Ralph Monthermer, who left sons Thomas and Edward and daughters Joan, a nun at Amesbury, and Mary, countess of Fife. Monthermer had married Edward's widowed sister Joan of Acre in secret in early 1297, and Edward I, who had been negotiating for her to marry Count Amadeus V of Savoy, imprisoned Monthermer in fury. He married his second wife Isabel Hastings (*née* Despenser) in 1318 also without the king's permission, and Edward II temporarily seized their lands and fined the couple 1,000 marks, though he pardoned the debt in 1321.[65] Edward's daughters Eleanor and Joan remained in Isabel Hastings' custody, and he granted her 'the king's houses' within the walls of Marlborough Castle 'for the safer dwelling of herself and the king's daughters'.[66] The number of the king and Despenser's supporters was dwindling rapidly, though Edmund Fitzalan, earl of Arundel, was still close to them, and his daughter Alice married Edward's nephew John de Bohun in 1325.[67]

Edward's reign began to stagger towards its disastrous end in March 1325 when he sent Queen Isabella to France to negotiate a peace settlement with her brother Charles IV, a journey from which she would finally return eighteen months later with an invasion force. Given the ultimate result of Isabella's trip to France, who first conceived the idea that she should go has been the subject of much debate. The often-repeated notion that Charles IV of France conceived the idea with the aim of helping his sister, Roger Mortimer and other enemies of Edward's regime in some deep conspiracy to deprive Edward of his throne is implausible in the extreme.[68] The Lanercost chronicler and Geoffrey le Baker, with years of hindsight, turned the chaos of the end of Edward's reign into a coherent narrative and invented a preconceived pattern and plan which never existed: *Lanercost* thought that Isabella had 'astutely contrived' to leave England with her son – who remained in England for six months after her departure – and Baker invented a conspiracy whereby the bishops of Hereford and Lincoln worked on the queen in order to persuade her to bring down the Despensers. The much later chronicler Jean Froissart, who wasn't even born until about 1337 and is for the most part utterly unreliable for Edward II's reign, presented Isabella as a persecuted victim expelled from Edward's kingdom with her son at risk to their lives, escaping from Winchelsea to France after pretending to go on pilgrimage to Canterbury.[69] The Hainault chronicler thought that Edward had ordered the arrest of his wife and that she fled to Paris with the earl of Kent, while French chroniclers wrote that Isabella had been banished from Edward's kingdom and 'crowned the exiled queen, tortured by her cruel husband, with a martyr's halo'.[70]

These wildly inaccurate accounts have been followed rather too slavishly by some later writers, and it is still sometimes written today that Isabella fled to Paris because of Edward's mistreatment of her. It had been suggested as early as April 1324 that Isabella might intercede with her brother on Edward's behalf.[71] Charles IV's counsellors suggested at the beginning of 1325 that Isabella and her elder son Edward of Windsor, earl of Chester, should travel to France, the queen to negotiate for peace and the earl to pay homage for Gascony and Ponthieu on his father's behalf. Although happy enough for Isabella to travel to her homeland, Edward's own counsellors 'with one voice' refused to allow young Edward to go, understandably unwilling to send the twelve-year-old heir to the throne to an enemy country until peace had been established.[72] Geoffrey le Baker thought that the boy might fall prey to many misfortunes if he were exposed to 'French cunning and greed'.[73] The suggestion to send the young earl of Chester to France has sometimes imaginatively been seen as evidence that Charles IV was planning a trap for Edward at the instigation of Isabella and Roger Mortimer, who were hoping to get her son out of the country to use him as a hostage. Pope John XXII, who called Isabella an 'angel of peace', wrote to her several times between April 1324 and January 1325 begging her to use her influence with her husband and her brother to bring about their reconciliation and declared that the hope of peace would be 'greatly promoted' if she went to France, and is in fact by far the most likely person to have suggested her journey.[74] Edward wrote in May 1325 that he had sent Isabella at the pope's urging, and as this was six months before she refused to return to him, there is no reason to assume that he was not telling the truth.[75]

It is often assumed, and stated as fact, that Isabella's trip to France was the result of careful planning and manipulation, that she had behaved submissively to convince her husband and the Despensers that she was no political threat, while she secretly plotted with the English exiles and the bishops who had suffered at Edward's hands to bring down the Despensers and perhaps even her husband. Although it is beyond all doubt that Isabella hated the Despensers, when she first decided to act against them cannot be known. She may well have decided to use her absence to impose conditions on Edward for her return, but it seems extremely unlikely that she knew as early as March 1325 that she would ultimately return at the head of an army with his deposition in mind. The *Vita* ends abruptly in late 1325 and is the only chronicle not written with the benefit of hindsight. The author said nothing about conspiracies cooked up between conniving bishops, ruthless exiles and disgruntled queens, and evidently it didn't occur to him that Isabella might be plotting against her husband.[76]

Lanercost claimed in the 1340s that Hugh Despenser 'was exerting himself at the pope's court to procure divorce between the king of England and the queen' and to this end sent the Dominican friar Thomas Dunheved to the pope, and that this was the reason for Isabella's willingness to 'escape' to France. The *Annales Paulini* repeat the rumour that Edward was trying to annul his marriage to Isabella.[77] Although it is just possible that Edward was contemplating this course of action in 1326, when Isabella was holding their son hostage and planning an invasion of his country, it is unlikely in the extreme that he would have attempted to annul his marriage in 1324 or 1325, at a time when offending her brother the king of France would have been disastrous. No proof of the chroniclers' statement has ever been discovered in the Vatican archives, and Dunheved's mission to the pope in fact concerned, according to a letter of John XXII himself, Edward's grievances against the archbishop of Dublin.[78] As divorce in the modern sense was unknown, Edward could only have hoped to persuade the pope to grant an annulment, which would mean that their marriage had never been valid in the first place. Not only did Edward have no grounds for an annulment – the only possible reason would have been for consanguinity, for which they had received a dispensation – it would have made their children illegitimate, at a time when Edward was negotiating their marriages with the royal houses of Spain. Many rumours were flying around England in the final years of Edward's reign, most of them untrue, such as the statements in various chronicles that Edward had it publicly proclaimed in 1326 that 'the queen of England might not be called queen' and that his wife and his son were his enemies.[79] The royal clerk and chronicler Adam Murimuth, who visited the papal court in 1324 and was therefore in an excellent position to know what was happening, does not say anything about Edward trying to get an annulment as he surely would if there were any truth to the story, and when Thomas Dunheved wrote to Edward in 1325, he did not mention it.[80]

Ironically, given later developments, Edward was concerned that Roger Mortimer and the other English exiles on the Continent might hurt the queen in some way, and that 'perils and dishonours' might befall her.[81] A few days before Isabella's departure, Edward asked the Dominicans of Venice to pray for her, himself and their children.[82] The queen and her retinue sailed from Dover – not a secret escape from Winchelsea, as invented by Jean Froissart – on 9 March 1325, and arrived at Wissant the same day.[83] She travelled in great state: Edward gave her £1,000 for her immediate expenses and authority to withdraw more money from the Bardi in Paris as and when needed, and she received at least £3,674 from them.[84] The king did not accompany his wife to Dover, but remained at the Tower of London; he had no way of knowing that he would never see her again. In letters of December 1325, Edward wrote that Isabella and Hugh Despenser had always behaved amicably towards each other in his presence and especially before Isabella's departure, and talked of 'the great friendships that she held to him [Despenser] upon her going beyond sea'. Edward also claimed that he had seen no evidence of Isabella's dislike of Despenser, saying, 'When she departed, towards no one was she more agreeable, myself excepted,' which has sometimes been seen as proof of the queen's brilliant deception of her husband and his favourite, but is just as likely to represent Edward's capacity for self-deception.[85]

Isabella made her way to Paris, visiting relatives, including her brother Louis X's widow Clemence of Hungary, and holy sites. If she was in touch with her husband's enemies, or in love with Roger Mortimer and desperate to see him, there is not the slightest sign of it. She wrote to Edward on 31 March 1325, addressing him five times in the letter as 'my very sweet heart' (*mon tresdoutz coer*), informing him that she had met her brother Charles IV at Poissy and found him very difficult to deal with. Isabella ended by writing, 'My very sweet heart, may the Holy Spirit by his grace save and keep you always.'[86] Pope John XXII sent Charles IV a very strange letter a few weeks later, saying that Isabella had sent a messenger to him 'about a story of a monk and an abbot and his nephews, which the king is not to believe', which sounds more like the beginning of a joke than a papal letter.[87]

Edward spent most of April 1325, including his forty-first birthday, at Beaulieu Abbey in Hampshire, where his little half-sister Eleanor had been buried in 1311. He had, as late as 20 February, been intending to lead an army into Gascony on 17 March, but the campaign was cancelled.[88] An army finally departed at the beginning of April 1325 under the command of the earls of Surrey and Atholl, having once more been delayed by contrary winds, to Edward's anguish; the truce Kent had negotiated with Valois on 22 September 1324 only lasted for six months.[89] The *Vita* criticises Edward for not paying his foot soldiers, who were perforce compelled to pillage the Gascon countryside for food, though one wonders how much they found, given that the clerk Nicholas Hugate told Hugh Despenser in December 1324 that 'in this country, one will find nothing except wine'.[90]

Thomas le Blount, formerly an adherent of Edward's cousin Henry of Lancaster, replaced Richard Damory as steward of the royal household on 14 May, and the king appointed his loyal friend William Melton, archbishop of York, as treasurer of England on 3 July, replacing Walter Stapeldon, bishop of Exeter.[91] Edward wrote a brusque letter to Walter Reynolds, archbishop of Canterbury, saying he had heard that Reynolds, 'wishing to disturb the archbishop of York', had ordered his suffragans not to celebrate divine service in Melton's presence or even communicate with him.[92] The king seems now to have become profoundly irritated with Reynolds, formerly his close friend, and asked the pope once again on 28 May, unsuccessfully, to depose Adam Orleton from his bishopric of Hereford.[93] The king dined with a barge-master called Adam Cogg several times in June 1325 – evidently he was as fond of the company of the lowborn as ever – and gave two shillings to a fisherman called Cock atte Wyk who presented him with a 'great eel' and other fish, and ten shillings to his chamber valet Robin Traghs, whose wife Joan had borne him a daughter.[94] Edward opened parliament at Westminster on 27 June, departed for the Tower on 14 July, and spent the rest of that month and the first half of August in Essex, where he received letters from his niece Joan of Bar, countess of Surrey, in France with the queen.[95] It was perhaps when Edward was staying at Portchester Castle in the early summer of 1325 that Hugh Despenser and his allies Robert Baldock and Robert Holden, respectively chancellor of England and controller of Edward's wardrobe, imprisoned over thirty merchants at the castle for a week until they consented to buy a few dozen tuns of 'rotten and putrid' wine at many times its market value.[96] Despenser, supremely rich, was able to make loans of £100 each to the abbots of Hailes, Leicester and Waltham, £400 to his father, 100 marks to his sister Isabel Hastings and 200 marks to the earl of Richmond.[97] Edward gave Despenser a present of eighty-four mares in July 1325, sent to his South Wales castle of Chepstow.[98]

In France, Queen Isabella and her brother Charles IV drew up a draft peace treaty on 30 May and sent it to Edward. He ratified it on 13 June, ordering all his sheriffs to proclaim the news that England and France had made peace.[99] Its terms were catastrophic for Edward, which was not Isabella's fault, and it is unlikely that any other envoy could have thrashed out better ones. The date for performing homage was postponed until 29 August.[100] If Edward failed to travel to Beauvais and perform homage, this would mean that Gascony would be forfeit to Charles IV, Edward would lose the duchy's revenues and face enormous criticism; given his failures in Scotland and the accusations of losing that country, he simply could not afford to let Gascony go. Edward was reluctant to go to France, however, nervous at the thought of Roger Mortimer and the other exiles on the Continent and that they might kidnap or assassinate him. He was also afraid that he would be indicted in the French court for the death of Thomas of Lancaster, Charles IV's uncle.[101] And travelling to France presented Edward with another huge dilemma. He could not go with Hugh Despenser, as it was said that the favourite would be arrested and perhaps tortured if he set foot in France.[102] Yet he could not leave Despenser behind either, surely remembering what had happened to Piers Gaveston in 1312 when he left him at Scarborough. Edward had backed himself into a corner: he could not go to France with Despenser, he could not go to France without Despenser, and he could not avoid paying homage. His only other choice was to send his son in his place, making Edward of Windsor duke of Aquitaine and count of Ponthieu and allowing him to perform homage to Charles IV instead. This alternative also had serious drawbacks. Edward would lose control of the lands and their income, and far more dangerously, the king was well aware that his enemies could capture young Edward, not to mention the more general risks of sending his heir to a hostile country. The king's grandfather Henry III had in 1253 been equally reluctant to send his fourteen-year-old son, Edward II's father, to Castile, in case Alfonso X took him as a hostage.[103]

Edward's indecisiveness as to the correct course of action is painfully apparent. At first he resolved to go himself, without Despenser: the pope had heard by the end of June 1325 that Edward was ready to go to France, and he had started making preparations to depart by 20 July.[104] He told Robert Kendale, constable of Dover Castle, that he would go to France around the Assumption, 15 August, and ordered Kendale to provide as many ships as necessary for himself and the magnates accompanying him (the ship which would carry him personally was *La Jonete* of Winchelsea).[105] On 21 August, Edward began issuing letters of protection for his retinue, asking the Dominicans of Lincoln on the same day for their prayers on behalf of himself, Isabella and their children.[106] He received over £3,515 in French gold florins and silver plate worth £1,768 from his Italian bankers the Bardi, for his expenses and for gifts at the French court.[107] Edward changed his mind on 24 August and told Charles IV that he would not be able to travel to France as he had suddenly been taken ill, which was almost certainly feigned, given that Edward, healthy, strong and fit, rarely suffered a day's illness in his life.[108] Six days later, the day after he should have performed homage at Beauvais, Edward changed his mind again and appointed his son, who was still only twelve – he would turn thirteen on 13 November – regent of England during his absence overseas.[109] On 1 September, Edward informed the bishop of Durham that he was 'shortly going to France'.[110] The very next day, however, Edward changed his mind yet again and appointed his son count of Ponthieu prior to sending him to pay homage, though evidently he was still unsure as to whether he was doing the right thing and continued issuing letters of protection for his own retinue to accompany him to France on 3 and 4 September. He waited until 10 September before making his son duke of Aquitaine.[111] Charles IV wrote to Edward on 4 September declaring that sending Edward of Windsor instead would be acceptable to him, but as Edward had known that since the beginning of 1325, it is debatable whether the letter affected his decision, and besides, he had already made his son count of Ponthieu by the time he received the letter.[112]

The king spent the second half of August and early September hovering in Kent, staying at the archbishop of Canterbury's manor of Sturry, at Dover Castle and with his close friend William the abbot of Langdon, while he debated what he should do. According to Adam Murimuth, Edward and his councillors continued to discuss while at Langdon – the king was there from 24 August to 3 September, with, among many others, Murimuth himself – whether he should travel overseas.[113] Possibly they continued the discussions during the meal they ate in the abbey garden on 30 August, when Edward, the Despensers, the earl of Arundel, the chancellor Robert Baldock and others dined on large quantities of fish and seafood including sole, crabs, whiting, codling, sea bass, mullets, bream and salted herring. Edward did his best to relax: he spent two pence playing dice, gave twenty shillings to twenty-two local men who played a ball game for his entertainment, and paid twelve pence to 'three small children, brothers' who sang for him in his garden. He also gave twenty shillings in compensation to a Thames fisherman named Colle Herron, whose goods had been burned, presumably in an accident, 'when he was with the king the last time he was in Hadleigh' in Essex. The king still enjoyed spending time with his lowborn subjects, and gave seven shillings to four Thames fishermen who spent time with him and four shillings and sixpence to a group of carpenters who travelled with him from 16 to 21 August.[114]

With hindsight, Edward's decision to send his son to France, given that it resulted in Isabella's seizing control of the boy and invading England, seems the most incredible folly, and many writers have assumed that he stupidly fell into his wife's clever trap and that he was blind to the dangers. Edward's indecisive behaviour in the autumn of 1325 in fact demonstrates that he was completely aware of the risks. If he had been as oblivious to the consequences of his actions as many commentators have assumed, he would have blithely sent his son to France without a second thought. That Edward was also well aware of the dangers of sending his son to the Continent unmarried, in the knowledge that someone could arrange young Edward's marriage and use the girl's dowry to pay for ships and soldiers to invade England, is obvious from his injunctions to his son, both in September 1325 and in subsequent letters, not to marry 'without the king's consent and command'.[115] He made a very bad decision, but this does not mean that he made it blindly and unthinkingly, and if Edward had gone to France himself and been assassinated or captured by his enemies, historians would no doubt ask how he could have been so stupid as to travel abroad when he could have sent his son instead. Whichever decision Edward made in September 1325 is likely, in retrospect, to have been the wrong one. As for the alleged trap which Isabella and her supposed allies, the English exiles on the Continent, were planning for him, there is nothing at all to suggest that Isabella had ever been in contact with them or sympathised with them. It is more likely that in fact she was hoping for her husband to come to France so that she could talk to him without the constant irritation of Hugh Despenser's presence and persuade him to treat her with the respect and courtesy she deserved as his queen.

It was Despenser who finally persuaded Edward not to travel abroad, and the *Anonimalle* says that he 'lamented piteously to the king that if he passed beyond sea, he [Despenser] would be put to death in his absence', a story confirmed by Adam Murimuth and the *Vita*.[116] Edward, concerned about his friend's safety and his own, therefore made the decision which would lead inexorably to the loss of his throne, the decision for which he has unfairly been criticised as a fool ever since.

He sent his son to France.

14

The Queen Takes a Favourite

Edward of Windsor, earl of Chester and now duke of Aquitaine and count of Ponthieu, had joined his father in Kent by late August 1325, accompanied by his household and his nine-year-old brother John of Eltham. The young duke sailed from Dover on 12 September, his father's injunctions not to marry without his approval no doubt ringing in his ears.[1] The boy performed homage for Gascony and Ponthieu to his uncle Charles IV at Vincennes on the 24th, in the presence of his mother and others.[2]

Edward II, who happily had no way of knowing that he would never see his son again, travelled via Leeds Castle to the village of Maresfield in Sussex, where he spent ten days at the end of September. Maresfield, on the edge of Ashdown Forest, was a royal deer hunting reserve and presumably Edward hunted while here. Surprisingly, given his recent certainty that his life would be in danger without the king's presence, Hugh Despenser did not remain with Edward but went instead to Tonbridge in Kent, where Edward sent him letters.[3] The king travelled slowly through Surrey to Westminster, staying at Banstead, a manor he had given to Isabella in 1318, and Bletchingley, forfeited in 1321 by his former favourite Hugh Audley, where the living quarters and the chapel were hastily cleaned and refurbished before his arrival.[4] While at Bletchingley, Edward himself bought a 'red cow' from one Maud Croweprest, and at Maresfield gave a parker who had once served in his household ten shillings to buy himself a cow.[5] He arrived at Banstead late in the evening of 5 October, and at midnight sent out messengers ordering the array of his army on land and sea to be renewed because of 'some news which he had heard', also summoning the treasurer, his friend and close ally William Melton, and other members of his council to come to him at Banstead on the 7th, 'at the king's rising'.[6] On the day he returned to Westminster, 9 October, Edward gave ten shillings to Jack the Trumpeter of Dover, who had bought forty-seven caged goldfinches for Edward to give to his niece

Eleanor Despenser.[7] Edward stayed at his palace of Sheen from 12 to 18 October, with Eleanor, paying her expenses and ordering forty bundles of firewood for her chamber.[8] Hugh Despenser, for his part, set off for Wales: he was at Caerphilly on 9 October, and still away from court on 19 November, when Edward wrote to him.[9] On 16 October, Edward asked the pope to grant dispensations for his children Eleanor of Woodstock and Edward of Windsor to marry Alfonso XI and Leonor of Castile, and sent letters to Jaime II of Aragon's son Alfonso and the regents of Castile on the 18th, thanking them for their affection for him and 'the gracious and benevolent way' they had handled his affairs.[10] He left Sheen for Cippenham that day, and bought fish from five Thames fishermen as he travelled along the river; his clerk carefully noted that it was Edward himself, not one of his servants, who purchased the fish. Edward also gave a hundred shillings to the bailiff of Kingston to repair the bridge there, because, he said, the last time he passed that way, he had noticed defects in it. While at Cippenham, the king gave a pound to a woman who had brought him a gift of ale, bread and more fish, and twenty-five shillings to his valet Will Shene and his new wife Isode as a wedding present.[11] He gave the large sum of ten marks each on 20 November to three members of his household whom he had sent hastily to Wales to bring him news of Hugh Despenser's welfare, having heard from Jack Pyk, a valet of his chamber, that Despenser had been killed. They returned to reassure him that the chamberlain was, 'by God's mercy', perfectly well.[12]

In the meantime, Edward's half-brother Edmund of Woodstock, earl of Kent, perhaps unwilling to return to England and face the king and Despenser's wrath over his mishandling of the La Réole siege, had joined Edward's enemies. Kent received permission from John XXII on 6 October to marry a woman to whom he was related in the third or fourth degree, and married Margaret Wake sometime in December.[13] A woman from a minor baronial house was hardly a great match for a king's son, so this almost certainly represents an alliance with Roger Mortimer: Margaret was his first cousin. Kent loathed the royal favourite, resenting – understandably – the fact that Despenser had deprived him of his position at court and political influence with his half-brother. He continued, however, to write to Edward assuring him that his intentions were not treasonable and that he had done nothing against the king's wishes, and Kent's later actions demonstrate that in 1326 he sought the downfall of the Despensers, not necessarily Edward himself. Edward confiscated his lands in March 1326.[14]

Sometime in the late autumn or early winter of 1325, Queen Isabella made the momentous decision not to return to England and her husband. The news may have been brought to Edward by Walter Stapeldon, bishop of Exeter, whom Edward had sent to France with his son. Stapeldon, seen by many as a close associate of the Despensers, fled from Paris dressed as a common traveller, in the belief that some at the French court meant him harm. A furious Isabella sent him a sharply worded letter on 8 December accusing him of being more obedient to Hugh Despenser than to her, and of dishonouring herself, Charles IV and Edward.[15] Isabella declared,

> I feel that marriage is a joining together of man and woman, maintaining the undivided habit of life, and that someone has come between my husband and myself trying to break this bond; I protest that I will not return until this intruder is removed, but discarding my marriage garment, shall assume the robes of widowhood and mourning until I am avenged of this Pharisee.

The *French Chronicle of London* confirms that she took to wearing clothes 'as a lady in mourning who had lost her lord'.[16] Isabella's speech and wearing widow's weeds have usually been interpreted as defiance of her husband and an open declaration of rebellion against him, and not seen for what they really are: exactly what they seem to be, an expression of her genuine sorrow at the breakdown of her marriage and fury at the role played in it by the 'Pharisee' Hugh Despenser. Isabella expressed no hostility towards Edward himself either at this time or later, and explained that she was unable to return to him because she felt herself to be in physical danger from Despenser.[17] The real meaning of Isabella's speech has been overlooked because of the frequent and wrong assumption that the royal marriage was nothing but a tragic disaster and that she despised her husband. But Isabella hated Despenser, not Edward, because she thought Despenser had destroyed her marriage, which implies that she felt it had been a successful one before his intrusion into it. Her speech indicates that she hoped to bring Edward back to his senses, to shock him so that he would send Despenser away and she could resume her normal married life with him, and makes it seem unlikely that at this point she was in love with Roger Mortimer and had been plotting with him for years against her husband. Edward, emotionally or politically reliant on Hugh Despenser, refused.

Isabella's servants, whom she could no longer afford to pay, began arriving back in England in early December, and Edward reimbursed their costs and gave them cash gifts. Roger Querndon, his son's Dominican confessor, had also returned by early 1326, when Edward gave him two pounds by the hands of his own confessor, Robert Duffield.[18] Henry Beaumont, who had witnessed Edward of Windsor's homage to Charles IV on 24 September, must have returned to England, as the Sempringham annalist says that he was imprisoned in February 1326 'because he would not swear to the king and to Sir Hugh Despenser the son, to be of their part to live and die'. He was certainly in prison at Warwick Castle by early August 1326.[19] John Stratford, bishop of Winchester, also returned to England in late 1325, despite the appalling way Edward had treated him.[20]

The king stopped his wife's expenses in mid-November, and, short of funds, Isabella was forced to borrow 1,000 Paris *livres* from Charles IV on 31 December 1325.[21] This was less than a month's income for Isabella even on the reduced amount imposed on her in September 1324, and was a loan, not a gift – hardly a sign of her brother's great favour towards her, as it has sometimes been interpreted. Parliament, the last Edward would preside over, began on 18 November 1325 at Westminster, though the king stayed a dozen miles away at Isleworth throughout. No official record of this parliament survives, but it is reasonable to assume that the queen's refusal to return or to send Edward's son back to him dominated. According to the *Vita*, Edward reminded parliament that Isabella had gone to France to make peace and should have returned immediately once this was achieved,

and on her departure she did not seem to anyone to be offended. As she took her leave she saluted all and went away joyfully. But now someone has changed her attitude. Someone has primed her with inventions. For I know that she has not fabricated any affront out of her own head.

This 'someone' was most probably not Roger Mortimer, who had not returned to the French court at this point, and it is likely that Edward was referring to the earl of Richmond, his cousin and the queen's; Edward said in March 1326 that he had ordered Richmond many times to come to him but the earl was staying with Isabella and urging her not to return, and the king condemned Richmond's disobedience and ingratitude. Richmond wrote to Edward explaining his actions, 'which excuses the king deems wholly frivolous'.[22]

Edward's priority at this point was to defend Despenser before parliament, and he claimed that his chamberlain was 'much cast down' by Isabella's hostility to him. The king's obstinate refusal to see Isabella's point of view and his continuing to put Despenser's interests and feelings above hers must have hurt her even more. Edward repeated his conviction that Isabella 'has been led into this error at the suggestion of someone, and he is in truth wicked and hostile whoever he may be'. He asked all the English bishops to write to her, 'that she whom the teaching of evil men incites to guile, may be led back to the due path of unity'.[23] The bishops repeated obediently in their letter that Despenser had 'solemnly demonstrated his innocence before all' and produced the friendly letters the queen had sent him from France as evidence.[24] How Edward felt about Isabella's declaration that she felt like a widow is unknown – surely he too regretted that he had allowed their marriage to deteriorate to this point – but her refusal to return to him with their son was a public humiliation, not to mention a huge political danger.

Edward's utter refusal to send Despenser away from him, listen to his wife or take her seriously left Isabella with no choice but to stay in France and act on her threat to avenge herself on Despenser. To this end, in late 1325 she arranged a betrothal for their son Edward of Windsor, without Edward II's consent. William, count of Hainault, had long held grievances against Edward II for his failure to do justice to the count's men who had been robbed in England, and although Edward offered safe-conducts for the count's envoys to come and 'treat with the king or his deputies touching damages on both sides' in September and November 1325 and again in 1326, it was too late, and the count threw in his lot with Isabella.[25] William's wife Joan de Valois, Isabella's first cousin, was in France between 1 December 1325 and 19 January 1326 with her daughter Philippa to visit her father the count of Valois, who died on 16 December.[26] This was presumably the first time that Edward of Windsor met Philippa of Hainault, his second cousin and future wife. Edward II wrote to his kinswoman Maria Diaz de Haro, lady of Biscay, on 1 January 1326, vehemently assuring her that his son was not going to marry in France. Just two days later, his certainty was given the lie by his pleas to the pope not to grant a dispensation for his son's marriage to any member of the French royal family without his consent. John XXII respected Edward's wishes, and did not grant the dispensation until late August 1327, seven months after Edward's deposition.[27] Edward's greatest error was not just to send his son to France, but to send him unmarried. Without military support provided by the father of young Edward's fiancée, the exiles would not have been able to raise enough money, ships and troops for an invasion; if this had been possible, they would have struck against Edward II before 1326.

At some point after Isabella's refusal to return to England, Roger Mortimer came into her life. The first reliable evidence that they were allies or more comes from Edward II's proclamation of 8 February 1326, when he said that Isabella 'is adopting the counsel of the Mortimer, the king's notorious enemy and rebel'.[28] Edward also wrote to Charles IV and Edward of Windsor on 18 March to complain that his wife 'draws to her and retains in her company of her counsel the Mortimer, the king's traitor and mortal enemy'.[29] Isabella first saw Roger Mortimer when she was twelve. He attended her wedding at Boulogne in January 1308, and was one of the four bearers of the royal robes at her and Edward's coronation the following month. Whether they had had any personal contact before late 1325 is unknown, and Mortimer's feelings for the queen are difficult to determine. Given the enormous benefits which accrued to him from becoming the queen's favourite – he ruled England through Isabella and Edward III from early 1327 to October 1330, granted himself an earldom and became at least as wealthy as Despenser had been – it seems overly convenient that he just happened to fall in love with her, just as one would doubt that Hugh Despenser genuinely fell in love with Edward. Neither Mortimer nor Despenser was the kind of man to whom things just happened; both of them were ruthless and ambitious men who could wait years for their opportunity and then grab it with both hands. Without Isabella and her son, Mortimer had no chance of revenge against Edward and the Despensers or of seeing his home and family again.

Isabella and Mortimer, whose wife Joan was still incarcerated in 1326, may have had a sexual relationship: *Lanercost* reports a rumour that at the time of Mortimer's downfall in 1330 'there was a liaison suspected between him and the lady queen-mother, as according to public report', and Geoffrey le Baker's scurrilous and unreliable *Vita et Mors Edwardi Secundi* of the 1350s says that Isabella was 'in the illicit embraces' of Mortimer.[30] Adam Murimuth, a royal clerk, wrote that they had 'an excessive familiarity', a remark reminiscent of chroniclers' statements about Edward and Piers Gaveston.[31] Edward himself said in a letter of March 1326 that Isabella 'keeps his [Mortimer's] company within and without house', usually assumed to be a euphemistic reference to adultery, though the phrase occurs in the context of Edward's complaining about Isabella's retention of Mortimer as a member of her council.[32] One chronicle refers to Mortimer as Isabella's *amasius*, 'lover', though three chroniclers use the same word to describe Gaveston's relationship to Edward, and others describe Mortimer only as 'chief of her council' or even just as a member of Isabella's faction.[33] For a relationship inevitably said by modern writers to have been sexual, there is surprisingly little evidence that it certainly was. The reticence of the chroniclers and the fact that the many enemies Isabella and Mortimer made during their regency of 1327 to 1330 never used adultery or sexual impropriety as an accusation against them suggests that if they were indeed lovers, they were very discreet and no one was sure what was going on, contrary to the frequent statement in modern accounts that the two flaunted their affair or that Isabella openly took Mortimer as her lover. Their supposedly passionately sexual five-year affair produced no children; the unreliable Jean Froissart claimed a few decades later that Isabella was pregnant in the autumn of 1330, but no other source even hints at this.

It is very likely that, at least at the beginning, Isabella and Mortimer's relationship was a political alliance between two people who loathed Hugh Despenser and who needed each other to bring him down. When they decided that Edward II should also be brought down, or even if they agreed that he should be, is impossible to say. No one had ever deposed a king before in English history; no one could have known for sure if it was even possible or how they might achieve it, for all the empty threats of deposition aimed at Edward throughout his reign. Events of 1325 to

1327 have been interpreted with decades or centuries of hindsight and knowledge of Edward II's downfall, and it has always been assumed that Isabella and Mortimer must have plotted for months or years to destroy the king and planned it with the help of Charles IV and others. This is not necessarily the case, especially as Isabella's presumed desire to overthrow her husband is predicated on an assumption that the royal couple detested each other, which they certainly did not.

Edward wrote to Isabella on 1 December 1325, the last letter he would ever send his wife, defending Hugh Despenser and saying that the favourite had 'always procured her all the honour with the king that he could'. Given Despenser's efforts since 1322 to reduce Isabella's influence with her husband and even her ability to see him, and her statement that Edward and Despenser's behaviour made her feel like a widow, this was either a blatant untruth or proof of an astonishing capacity for self-deception on Edward's part. Edward reminded Isabella that her duty was to be in his company and to obey his commands, and ordered her to come to him with all speed, bringing their son, as 'the king has a great desire to see and talk with him'. Edward resisted for as long as possible the notion that Isabella would not return, renewing letters of protection for her retinue as late as 26 January 1326.[34]

This was not in fact a vain hope. In a letter to the archbishop of Canterbury of 5 February 1326, the queen declared that no one must think she had left her husband 'without very great and justifiable cause', writing that Hugh Despenser wished to 'dishonour us by all his power' and that she had hidden her hatred of him to escape danger, as he was in full control of the king and realm. Isabella wrote, 'We desire, above all else, after God and the salvation of our soul, to be in the company of our said lord [Edward] and to live and die there.' The queen referred to Edward in her letter as her 'very dear and very sweet lord and friend', which is very unconventional (conventional would be simply 'very dear lord') and indicates her strong feelings for him. Isabella certainly did not feel 'profound revulsion' for her husband as a modern writer has claimed; her letter and much of her behaviour in the 1320s imply genuine hurt and bafflement at Edward allowing Despenser to come between them and ruin a marriage in which she had been happy.[35] Later in 1326, the queen wavered and talked of returning to Edward. For her to rebel not only against her husband and lord but an anointed king, must have been enormously difficult for her, and it would be astonishing if she didn't have second thoughts on occasion.

Edward also wrote on 1 December to Charles IV and others, asking them to do all in their power to return Isabella and his son to him, as 'the king is very uneasy because he has such loss of her company' and greatly wished to see his son, also showing himself excessively anxious to defend Hugh Despenser against Isabella's hostility.[36] Edward, although highly emotional himself, was not good at reading other people's emotions, or capable of much insight. Because he loved Despenser, he could see no faults in him, and the tone of his letters implies that he was genuinely astonished that Isabella didn't think Despenser was as marvellous as he did. The king wrote a short letter to his son on 2 December, reminding him that he must remember what Edward had enjoined on him at Dover – not to marry – and to travel back to England, with his mother if possible but alone if she refused.[37] Edward was desperate to have his son back in England, well aware of the dangers of his heir slipping out of his control. That night, he travelled down the Thames from Westminster to Sheen to pay a quick visit to Eleanor Despenser, gave his niece a remarkably generous gift of a hundred marks, and went back to Westminster the same night. He took eight of his chamber valets to attend him during the visit, including Syme Lawe, Wat Cowherd and Jack Edriche, all of whom received four shillings in the boat 'in the king's presence' to buy themselves boots for the water. Eleanor Despenser must have been heavily pregnant at the time or had just given birth, as Edward made an offering of thirty shillings on 14 December to the Virgin Mary, in gratitude that God had granted Eleanor a 'prompt delivery of her child'. Edward also ordered his almoner John Denton to give sixpence each in alms to forty 'poor pregnant women'.[38]

The king spent a quiet Christmas, his last as a free man, at Bury St Edmunds in Suffolk, and gave a pound to the messenger who brought him letters from Eleanor Despenser.[39] Edward saw her in 1326 at Haughley near Stowmarket, and received a palfrey horse with saddle and all other necessary equipment from Eleanor as her New Year gift to him. He visited his half-brother Thomas of Brotherton, earl of Norfolk, for a few days in early January with a large retinue.[40] Norfolk, as annoyed with the king and Hugh Despenser as their brother the earl of Kent was, was probably in touch with Kent in France, and hastened to join Isabella and Mortimer on their arrival later in the year. Not only had Edward allowed Despenser to buy Norfolk's lordship of Chepstow for a ridiculously small amount, he also temporarily confiscated Norfolk's hereditary office of Earl Marshal, actions seemingly designed to alienate his brother from him, although Edward did try to make amends by giving Norfolk a gift of £200, making him commissioner of array in seven counties and putting his sister-in-law Joan Jermy in charge of the household of his daughters Eleanor and Joan in February.[41] Edward spent a week at South Elmham in Suffolk, giving Hugh Despenser's Carmelite confessor Richard Bliton two pounds 'for what he did in the park of South Elmham when the king ate', and arrived at Norwich on 18 January, where he paid thirty shillings for fourteen ells of Coggeshall cloth to make tunics (*cotes*) for the wives of five of his chamber valets. The cloth, however, was found to be too stiff for the purpose, and the king bought instead eighteen ells of 'bright blue

English cloth' to make *cotes hardies* (close-fitting, sleeved coats or gowns) with hoods for the women, at twenty pence an ell.[42]

While Edward was at Norwich, he heard the shocking news that Roger Belers, chief baron of the Exchequer, had been stabbed to death on 19 January at Rearsby in Leicestershire, by the la Zouche brothers, the Folville brothers and others. Roger Belers was pardoned for adherence to Thomas of Lancaster in 1318, though had switched sides to the Despensers by 1321, and Hugh Despenser appointed him as his attorney in July 1322.[43] Belers' murder can therefore perhaps be interpreted as hostility towards Despenser, though at the time of his death he was on his way to dine with Thomas of Lancaster's brother Henry, no friend of Despenser although the men were brothers-in-law.[44] Edward appointed several men, including the earl of Arundel, Donald of Mar, his steward Thomas le Blount, his former steward Richard Damory, and Henry of Lancaster himself to investigate the murder.[45] The Folville brothers fled abroad but returned with Roger Mortimer's invasion in the autumn, and subsequently became the most notorious of the criminal gangs who roamed England during Edward III's reign.[46]

Edward co-founded Oriel College at Oxford with his almoner Adam Brome on 21 January 1326, and the foundation charter says that love of the Blessed Virgin and a desire to increase her 'divine cult' motivated him to establish the college. The king declared his zeal for sound learning and religious knowledge, granted Brome, the first college provost, and the scholars permission to acquire sixty pounds' worth of lands and property, and specifically requested that five or six of the first ten scholars be students of canon law.[47] The foundation was originally named the Hall of the Blessed Mary; the name 'Oriel' comes from a house called La Oriole granted to the college after Edward's deposition. Walter Reynolds, archbishop of Canterbury, informed Edward at this time that a joint invasion by France and Hainault could be expected shortly, though Henry Eastry, prior of Canterbury, doubted the story and believed that Charles IV had no real intention of invading England. Edward himself evidently believed that Charles would indeed invade England on his sister Isabella's behalf, though whatever he may have thought, this was highly unlikely; the French king may well have wanted, out of fraternal affection, to protect Isabella, but this did not extend to invading a sovereign country on her behalf.[48] Edward told Count William of Hainault on 22 January that he was willing to satisfy all reasonable demands of the count's subjects who had been robbed and slain by Englishmen, a proposal that offered too little, and came too late.[49] William was committed to the thought of his daughter being queen of England. Edward was equally committed to a Castilian alliance, and again informed the king and queen of Portugal that his son was marrying the king of Castile's sister.[50]

Edward appointed Hugh Despenser's eldest sister Aline Burnell as constable of Conwy Castle in North Wales, presumably at Despenser's request, on 30 January.[51] It was a rare honour for a woman to be put in charge of such an important stronghold. The king dined with his sister-in-law Alice, countess of Norfolk, on the same day, at Burgh in Suffolk, and gave a pound each to the minstrels – Henry Newsom, harper, and Richardyn, citoler – who performed for them. He gave her sister Joan Jermy a silver cup worth seventy-five shillings, and remained in touch with Alice, paying her messenger a hundred shillings on 5 June for bringing him her letters.[52] Edward spent the first few days of February 1326 at Walsingham, and presumably visited the shrine of Our Lady there. He bought two pounds' worth of 'masts, cables and other equipment for ships' from a merchant of Lynn, which his clerk carefully recorded as being 'for the king's use', and several weeks later invited a group of shipwrights from London to visit him at Kenilworth.[53]

On 4 February, Edward ordered numerous sheriffs, mayors and bailiffs to search anyone leaving the country to make sure that they were not taking armour, horses, gold, silver or money with them without his permission. Five days later he issued a proclamation that no one except merchants, who were to be searched and made to swear an oath that they were not carrying weapons or letters prejudicial to Edward or his subjects, might leave the country without his special licence.[54] This proclamation had already been issued in December 1325, and would be repeated several more times in 1326.[55] Edward also ordered all his sheriffs and John Sturmy and Nicholas Kyriel, admirals of his fleet, to be prepared to set out against 'the aliens, strangers and enemies of the king who may attack the realm'. The recipients of the letter were ordered to receive Isabella and Edward of Windsor 'honourably and courteously' and to treat all the others as the king's enemies but 'to save the bodies of the queen and Edward'.[56]

The king ordered an inquisition a few days later into a whale cast ashore at Walton, and wrote to Jaime II of Aragon's son Pedro, count of Ribagorza, and to Eleanor Despenser.[57] A rather fascinating entry in Edward's chamber account of 7 February records a very large payment of twenty marks to his squire Oliver de Bordeaux 'when the king sat beside his bed a little before midnight' at Harpley in Norfolk.[58] Another indication of the familiarity between the king and his household staff and their families is a royal gift of twenty shillings to Edward Pymock, son of another of Edward II's squires: Pymock was said to be the king's *confrere*, brother or companion, and he is elsewhere called *le petit Pymock*, 'the little Pymock'. An odd nickname for one of Edward's chamber staff was *le petit Cotel le Roi*, 'the king's little Knife'. Edward gave a gift of twenty shillings later in 1326 to be shared among six of his (more than thirty) chamber valets who woke up at night whenever he himself awoke, in recognition of their hard work.[59] His Household Ordinance of December

1318 stated that he should choose four of his thirty sergeants-at-arms to sleep outside his chamber 'as near to it as they can', with the other twenty-six to remain in the hall 'to be nearby when the king needs them'.[60] In addition to the four sergeants outside his chamber door, and the six or more valets presumably inside, Edward had a sergeant porter 'who will guard the door of there where the king sleeps'.

Edward and Hugh Despenser were apart once again, and the king sent frequent letters to his chamberlain in London between 11 February and 31 March while he himself stayed in Leicestershire and Staffordshire and at the great Warwickshire stronghold of Kenilworth.[61] He gave a gift of forty shillings to a retired sailor he met while riding through Tamworth, who had become destitute and a beggar.[62] Sailors paid out of the king's accounts earned three pence a day, so this represented almost half a year's wages in the man's former job. A pleasant interlude took place on 11 March, when Edward gave, with his own hands, fifty shillings (two and a half pounds) to his painter Jack of St Albans for dancing before him on a table and making him laugh; he intended the money to support Jack's wife and children. Edward was evidently coping with the stress of Isabella and Mortimer's impending invasion better than Hugh Despenser, who was said to have 'made a small affray' in Northamptonshire in late February.[63]

Also in late February, Edward ordered all his keepers of the peace to be 'more active in dispersing unlawful assemblies and arresting malefactors, as the king is astonished to hear that these evils are now more frequent than before their appointment, which may be set down to their negligence and connivance'.[64] Knowing that an invasion was coming and that his enemies abroad had many supporters in England, Edward did all he could to avoid his fate; but in fact there was little he could do, nearly two decades of misrule ensuring that he was widely unpopular and that there were few men indeed who would fight to save him. Discontent had been rife in England since 1322, but there was no one in the country capable of organising and leading a revolt against the king and the Despensers. Queen Isabella and her son served as powerful figureheads for the rebels abroad, who had – and must have known that they had – considerable support in Edward's kingdom. There is little to indicate that Isabella enjoyed much popularity in England before 1326, although several chroniclers comment approvingly on her efforts to negotiate and make peace between her husband and his barons.[65] The Lanercost chronicler, apparently attempting the world record for the number of times he could write 'England' in one short sentence, says 'it was publicly rumoured in England that the queen of England was coming to England'. Not to be outdone in repetition, Edward ordered men in Portchester and Southampton to arrest everyone 'entering the realm to spy out the secrets of the realm in order to do certain things prejudicial to the king and his realm' on 10 March.[66] The Lanercost chronicler thought that Isabella wanted to avenge herself on the Despensers for the execution of her uncle the earl of Lancaster.[67] Even more damaging than the rumours of invasion, however, were the rumours that Edward had publicly declared his wife and son to be his enemies and exiled them from his realm, and intended to harm them. He wrote to the pope indignantly refuting this, and his surviving proclamations make clear that although he named Isabella's allies as 'the king's enemies', he specifically excluded Isabella herself, Edward of Windsor and the earl of Kent, even after the invasion.[68] According to the *Brut*, Edward was informed after his deposition that people suspected him of wanting to strangle his wife and son to death. He responded, 'God knows, I thought it never, and now I would that I were dead! So would God that I were! For then were all my sorrow passed.'[69] If Edward truly was informed that people believed him capable of murdering his own wife and son, it is hardly a wonder that he was deeply upset.

The king seized the lands of the men refusing to return to England with the queen in March 1326, and told the constable of Dover Castle to arrest anyone bringing in or taking out of the realm letters contrary to his proclamation of a few weeks earlier, as 'the king is astonished to hear that many enemies and rebels continue to do so and are not arrested'.[70] His only hope in averting an invasion lay in persuading his son to come home to him or persuading Charles IV to send the boy back, and he wrote to both of them on 18 March. Isabella had told Charles that she 'greatly wished to be with the king and in his company, as a good wife ought to be with her lord', but reiterated that she was afraid of Despenser. Edward once more devoted many lines to defending his 'dear and faithful nephew' Despenser to Charles, complained about Isabella retaining Mortimer in her council, and asked his brother-in-law not to have 'regard to the wilful pleasure of woman'. He promised that Isabella did not 'receive evil or villainy from the king or from anyone else, and the king would not suffer her to do so for anything'. Edward of Windsor had also written to his father, saying that he remembered the king's injunctions to him at Dover not to marry, and promised always to obey Edward's orders with all his power. He had supposedly claimed that he 'cannot come to the king so speedily as the king has ordered him, by reason of his mother, who is ... in great uneasiness of heart' and that it was his duty not to leave Isabella for long in her unhappiness, which sounds far more like something dictated by the queen herself than by an adolescent boy. Edward, in 'wrath and indignation', threatened his son with forfeiture of all that he had if he did not return to England.[71]

Isabella, in using her son as a weapon against her husband, forced Edward of Windsor to choose between his parents: young Edward could either betray his father, or abandon his mother. The *Vita* says that the boy hated Despenser the Elder, earl of Winchester, and he can hardly have felt any less hatred for Hugh Despenser, his father's favourite and perhaps his lover.[72] Almost certainly, he desired the Despensers' removal from his father's side as much as his mother did. If Edward of Windsor stayed with his mother and helped her and her allies destroy the Despensers, however, he would be committing treason, betraying and disobeying his father, and would ultimately invade his kingdom with an army. If he went back to his father, he would leave his mother with a choice of returning to England and her husband, perhaps to be imprisoned or sent to a convent, losing her income and her position, or remaining in France with her brother, where she would be dependent on Charles IV for income, reduced to the status of a petitioner. As for the boy himself, whichever parent he chose, he would lose the other. The emotional strain inflicted on a thirteen-year-old, faced with this dilemma, can only be imagined. Although Isabella told Edward that she would not prevent their son returning to him, this was untrue. The boy was little more than a prisoner.[73]

Edward II spent the whole of April 1326 at Kenilworth and most of May in Gloucestershire and Wiltshire, giving generous amounts of cash to those members of his wife and son's households still straggling back to England, supposedly for their expenses but presumably also for showing loyalty to him.[74] While at Kenilworth, he ordered his chamber valets to help a group of workmen dig and enclose a ditch and palisade in the castle park, and the valets received a gift of two barrels of ale from the mother of a local resident as they worked.[75] On 13 April, Edward told the archbishop and prior of Canterbury and the abbot of St Augustine's that 'an invasion of the realm by aliens is threatened', ordering them to prepare themselves to defend the realm, and told his admirals John Sturmy and Nicholas Kyriel two weeks later to prepare and equip as many ships as possible, as he wished 'to provide for the safety of his realm and to escape the machinations of the evil wishers who are scheming to aggrieve him and his realm by sudden attacks'. He also ordered Sturmy and Kyriel to 'cause the actions of those men beyond sea to be spied upon diligently and watchfully'.[76] Meanwhile, relatives of Contrariants executed in 1322 were doing their best to make trouble for the king in England: the castle of Tickhill, where Edward's friend, the none too scrupulous William Aune, was constable, was besieged that April by John Mowbray's fifteen-year-old son and Roger Clifford's brother, among others.[77] In many ways, however, Edward's life continued in much the same way as it always had: he gave five shillings to his page Little Will Fisher for 'what he did when the king mounted his horse' at Kenilworth, another five shillings to a man who gave him twelve chickens, and varying amounts of money to many others who brought him presents of fish and other food – all of which he handed over to his subjects with his own hands. Edward also bought himself many splendid jewels and clothes, including two gold crowns studded with rubies, pearls and emeralds which cost ninety pounds, a silver crown, a gold chaplet, a white velvet hat lined with miniver, and several hats of vermilion velvet, one decorated with bells and another 'powdered with diverse animals'.[78]

On 11 May 1326, Charles IV's young wife Jeanne of Evreux was crowned queen of France at Sainte Chapelle in Paris. Isabella was an honoured guest, and although Roger Mortimer had not been invited, perhaps out of respect to Edward II, he went anyway and carried Edward of Windsor's train.[79] Edward II was furious and sent a bitter complaint to his son on 19 June, although the boy had surely had little say in the matter. This letter was the last contact he ever had with his son. Edward's fury and anguish are apparent, especially as his son had told him untruthfully that Mortimer was not an adherent of himself or his mother, 'whereby the king considers himself very evilly paid'. Edward wrote that his son had not behaved as a good son should by obeying his father's commands, once more threatened him with forfeiture if he did not return, and ordered him again not to marry. He ended the letter by writing that if his son was 'contrary and disobedient hereafter to his will ... he will ordain in such wise that Edward [of Windsor] will feel it all the days of his life, and that all other sons shall take example thereby of disobeying their lords and fathers'.[80] As it turned out some months later, this was an empty threat, but it must have pained the young duke of Aquitaine to read such harsh words. The king distracted himself from his woes on 19 May by attending the wedding of Hugh Despenser's niece Margaret Hastings to Robert Wateville in Marlborough, where he must have seen his daughters Eleanor and Joan – as far as Edward knew, the future queens of Castile and Aragon – who were living there. He gave a pound to the servant Will Muleward, 'who was for some time with the king and made him laugh greatly'; despite the crisis he was facing, Edward's sense of humour remained intact. There are many references in his chamber journal of May and June 1326 to his playing cross and pile, and he celebrated the Nativity of John the Baptist on 24 June – exactly twelve years after his defeat at Bannockburn – by playing dice with Giles Beauchamp, a knight of his chamber. He also bought four cows to provide 'milk for the mouth of the king and Sir Hugh [Despenser]'.[81] Edward was in dire straits in 1326, but at least he was getting enough calcium.

Pope John XXII in Avignon was exerting himself to bring about a reconciliation between the king and queen and avert civil war, and sent envoys, the archbishop of Vienne and the bishop of Orange, to both Edward and Isabella 'to remove the dissension' between them. The envoys had full powers to 'remove any obstacles' which hindered the couple's reconciliation.[82] The main obstacle was Hugh Despenser, but Edward would not send him away, even at this desperate stage. The Rochester chronicler thought that the envoys' mission was to ensure the safe return of the queen, her son and the earl of Kent to England, while Henry Eastry believed that they had persuaded Isabella to return on condition that the Despensers retired from court and that the queen was fully restored to her estates.[83] Edward granted the envoys a safe-conduct to travel to England, and sent a letter to the constable of Dover Castle ordering him to treat them 'courteously and amiably'.[84] This contradicts the beliefs of several contemporary chroniclers: the *Annales Paulini* claim that the envoys were 'anxious and afraid' at the thought of meeting the king, and the *French Chronicle of London* says, ludicrously, that Edward had threatened them with death. This rumour reached the ears of John XXII, who informed Edward that he did not believe the king would mistreat them.[85]

The envoys stayed at the archbishop of Canterbury's castle of Saltwood in Kent. Edward arrived there at the end of May, and, keen as ever on the outdoors and physical exercise, went into the park with his steward Thomas le Blount, Hugh Despenser's nephew-in-law Robert Wateville and others to play a ball game.[86] He then met the envoys and did his best to allay their fears by spending a convivial few days in their company, and paid all their expenses. Hugh Despenser also met them and rebutted the accusations the queen had made against him (Despenser and Edward talked to the envoys in French, their words later translated into Latin for the pope). Although Isabella had sworn by God and all the saints that she would not return to England unless her enemies the Despensers were removed from her husband's side, she did inform Roger Mortimer in the spring or early summer of 1326 that she had decided to return to Edward.[87] A furious Mortimer 'caused her to believe if she came to him [Edward] he would have killed her with a knife or murdered her in another manner ... and by his other subtle scheming, he caused the said queen not to come to her said lord'. Mortimer's rage is understandable; if Isabella returned to England with her son, his plans and his daring escape from the Tower would count for nothing, and he would be forced to remain an impoverished exile on the Continent, with no chance of seeing his home and his family again. It is unclear whether the 'he' who would kill Isabella meant Mortimer or Edward, though Hugh Despenser thought Mortimer was referring to himself when he (Despenser) related the story to the bishop of Rochester soon afterwards. Whether she believed Mortimer's threats or not, Isabella changed her mind again and decided to go ahead with the plans for invasion.

John XXII wrote frequently to Hugh Despenser, telling him in February 1326 that

his participation in the king's government is given by the queen as a reason for her being unable, without personal danger, to return to the king. The pope suggests that Hugh should retire, and should devise methods by which the queen may no longer fear to return to her husband.

The pope, evidently irritated with Despenser, asked him in April 'to abstain from provoking enmities, and to study to promote friendships'. He had evidently recovered from his irritation two weeks later when he commended Despenser for his 'good offices' in promoting concord between Edward and Isabella, and urged him to continue.[88] John was doing his best to remain neutral, and wrote several times to Isabella urging her to reconcile with her husband, also saying that he 'supposes that the queen has not delayed ... to betake herself to the king's presence' on the advice of others.[89] As late as May 1327, more than three months after Edward's deposition, John XXII was urging Charles IV to use his influence to bring the couple back together, and there is no reason to suppose that the pope, despite his annoyance with the king over his mistreatment of some of the English bishops, favoured Isabella over Edward.[90]

Edward gave another generous gift of twenty marks to Eleanor Despenser in early June, sent pomegranates to two members of Hugh Despenser's household lying ill at Saltwood, and gave a pound to a fiddler for an especially pleasing performance.[91] On their way to London in mid-June, the king and Despenser met Hamo Hethe, bishop of Rochester, at Boxley Down in Kent; during the journey, Edward borrowed three shillings from his usher Peter Bernard to give to 'a poor man' he encountered.[92] Hethe had long been an ally of Edward, and almost uniquely was kindly disposed towards Despenser, and rode with the two men for a while. According to the Rochester chronicler William Dene, an associate of Hethe, Despenser informed the bishop that the papal envoys had sought guarantees for the safe return of Isabella, her son and Kent, and pointed out that no such guarantees were necessary as they could return to England in safety at any time. Despenser also told Hethe that Roger Mortimer had threatened to kill Isabella should she return to Edward. The king and Despenser spent the night of 15/16 June at Rochester with Hethe, and Edward asked the bishop if it were true that a queen of England who had defied her husband had been put down out of her royalty, perhaps an indication that he was by now considering an annulment of his marriage, though if he was, there is no confirmation of it in any other source. The following day, Hethe accompanied Edward and Despenser as far as Gravesend, and Edward told him ruefully, 'You have not asked me for anything. For you have done many things for me and the Lord Hugh, and I have not rewarded you. I have done much for those who are ungrateful, whom I promoted to high rank, and who are now my chief enemies.'[93]

In late June, Edward sent envoys to negotiate with Robert Bruce, yet again.[94] Bruce had signed a treaty with France in April, which provided for mutual military aid against Edward – clearly a breach of the 1323 truce – and some Scotsmen attempted to seize Carlisle Castle and four castles in Northumberland.[95] Edward could not, however, have known the astonishing fact that Isabella and Mortimer had come to an agreement with Bruce that they would recognise him as king of Scots, and Scotland as an independent kingdom, if he agreed not to invade England at the same time as their own invasion and thus prejudice their chances of success.[96]

Things went from bad to worse for Edward II in the summer of 1326: in addition to the growing tension with Scotland and the impending invasion of England, the situation with France deteriorated again. Edward set out his claims to be 'guardian and administrator of Gascony' in Edward of Windsor's name in late June, in an attempt to limit the damage caused by the loss of his son. Charles IV, claiming to be protecting his nephew's rights in the duchy, began reoccupying the areas of Gascony from which he had been in the process of withdrawing, and Edward would end his reign once more at war with France. He asked the citizens of Bayonne on 6 July to 'annoy and injure' all Charles IV's subjects, and, still fearing an invasion from that country, ordered all monks who were citizens of France and who lived near the coast to be moved inland.[97] Charles IV arrested all English people in France and seized their goods, and Edward retaliated in kind as soon as he heard the news.[98] Edward appointed Oliver Ingham as steward of Gascony in March 1326. Ingham raised an army of Gascon and Spanish mercenaries and regained Saintonge and the Agenais from the French, and on 7 July Edward gave twenty marks to two sailors of Bayonne who brought him letters from Ingham, informing him that two great cities which had been opposed to him had been taken back into his hands out of the power of the king of France.[99] Isabella, however, handed all these lands back to Charles IV in March 1327 when she signed a humiliatingly one-sided treaty with him, also agreeing – astonishingly – to give up the whole of Gascony with the exception of a narrow coastal strip to France and to pay her brother 50,000 marks in reparation.[100] Edward II gave ten marks on 9 June 1326 to his chamber squire Garsy Pomit 'for what he did in the king's chamber when he ate, in aid of the said Garsy because his son came with news from the parts of Gascony', though the news was unspecified.[101]

Edward, perhaps remembering happier times and never a man to forget someone he had loved deeply, asked the convent of Leeds in Kent on 28 June 1326 to pray for Piers Gaveston's soul, fourteen years and nine days after Gaveston's death.[102] He spent early July at Sheen, Byfleet and Henley-on-Thames, where he gave a pound to a Spanish minstrel who played the gittern and lute for him, and on 11 July dined with his niece Eleanor Despenser in the park at Windsor. The king gave his cook Will Balsham, formerly of the queen's retinue in France, two pounds to buy a hackney horse on which to follow the pair into the park; the money was given to Balsham 'by the king's own hands between two silver dishes'. Edward was at his Westminster cottage of Burgundy on the 15th, where twenty-eight men were hired to clean the ditches around it 'in the king's presence' – he paid for drinks for them – and visited Sir Robert Wateville, Hugh Despenser's nephew-in-law, at his London house on the 20th.[103] The king returned to his palace of Sheen where he spent two days with Eleanor Despenser, then travelled by water to Byfleet still in Eleanor's company; he also gave or lent her husband Hugh a manuscript of the doomed love story of Tristan and Isolde around this time. Edward, as he so often did, handed out generous gifts to fishermen and women, and bought roach and dace for Eleanor. A John of Walton, who 'sang before the king every time he passed through these parts by water' and presented the king with a bucket of fish, received two shillings for his efforts. Edward wrote to his daughters in Marlborough on 25 July and to Hugh Despenser in Wales at the same time, the king and his favourite being apart yet again.[104] The *Annales Paulini* say that there was a great drought in England in the summer of 1326. On 24 July, Edward met several of his subjects at or near Sheen: he gave six pence to Jack le Frenche, who brought him fresh well-water at his command (perhaps an indication of the heat); six pence to Robyn atte Hethe, 'who suffers from a great illness'; three pence to Wille de Pykingham, who retrieved a knife one of Edward's squires had dropped in the Thames; twelve pence to Jack Meryn, who brought him a gift of lampreys; and five pence to Edward le Parker, who brought the king two pike and needed the money 'to repair his house'.[105]

Roger Mortimer's uncle Roger Mortimer of Chirk died in the Tower of London on 3 August 1326, though as he was about seventy, well beyond average life expectancy for the era, and had outlived all his siblings by decades, there is no reason to suppose that his death was suspicious.[106] Maurice, Lord Berkeley and Hugh Audley the Elder, father of Edward's former favourite, also died in 1326, still in captivity. The king dined on or shortly before 8 August with Hugh Despenser's sister Isabel Hastings, formerly in charge of his daughters' household, who had been replaced in February by Joan Jermy. Edward gave Joan a gift of twenty marks, and forty shillings to her damsel Jonete.[107] On 22 August, at the royal palace of Clarendon in Wiltshire, Edward himself joined in when twenty-two men made hedges and a ditch in the park, and he borrowed twelve pence from his servant Elis Pek to give to a man named Gibbe working with him in the ditch, so that he could buy himself shoes.[108]

On 27 August, Edward's son was formally betrothed to Philippa, daughter of the count of Hainault and granddaughter of Charles of Valois. As King Charles IV still had no son, Valois's son Philip was heir to the French throne. There was a chance that Queen Isabella might try to claim the throne for her son, who was, apart from his younger brother John of Eltham, Philip IV's only grandson. The Valois family therefore had an interest in allying with Isabella so that she would renounce her son's claim to the French throne. Edward's reaction to his son's betrothal is not recorded, but he must have been furious and anxious. At some point before this date, Isabella had left France and gone to Hainault; whether she left France of her own accord or was expelled by her brother Charles IV is a matter of some debate. The *Brut* says that Hugh Despenser sent masses of silver to the French court as a bribe to send her back, but that his envoy was captured and Isabella herself seized the money.[109] The *Flores* claims that Charles IV and the entire nobility of France had promised to help Isabella's invasion of England, a ludicrous statement, although the dramatic story that Charles was about to arrest her and she fled to Hainault in the night after receiving a warning from her cousin Robert of Artois is also unlikely.[110] Charles did nothing to prevent Isabella's invasion, but there is nothing to indicate that he actively helped her, either.

Once more at war with France, Edward could use Charles as a useful scapegoat for all his problems, and wrote in May 1326 that Charles was detaining his son, 'whom the king, trusting to his affection, sent to him, against the king's will'.[111] Edward found it easier to pretend that Charles was detaining Isabella and his son than to admit that the queen did not want to return because of Hugh Despenser and that it had been his own error – however understandable when seen in its proper context – to send Edward of Windsor to France. Edward II asked for the prayers of the Dominicans of Paris, of all places, on 12 April and from the Dominicans of Oxford on 6 September, on behalf of himself and his realm; for the first time, Isabella and Edward of Windsor were not included in the prayers.[112] On or around 31 August, the king attacked Normandy with a force of about 140 ships, possibly in an attempt to seize his son, said in 1327 to have been 'in those parts' – though the king told the archbishops of Canterbury and York and the universities of Oxford and Cambridge that his intention was 'to restrain the malice of the men of the king of France in case they wish to enter the realm'. The force was repulsed with heavy losses, the last thing Edward needed with his wife's invasion imminent, though a French ship called *la Dorre* was captured and taken to Winchelsea.[113] Hugh Despenser, aware that the invasion could come at any moment, withdrew a massive £2000 from his Italian bankers the Peruzzi on 16 September.[114]

Edward was at the Tower of London on 27 September when he received the shocking news. The invasion force of Queen Isabella, Roger Mortimer and their allies had finally arrived.

15

Invasion, Abdication and Imprisonment

Isabella and Mortimer's invasion force left Dordrecht on 21 or 22 September 1326, ninety-five ships containing perhaps 700 mercenaries and the queen's allies including Edward of Windsor, the king's half-brother the earl of Kent, his former steward John Cromwell, and Contrariants who had fled the country in 1322. In total the force consisted of perhaps 1,000–1,500 men.[1] They landed on 24 September at Orwell in Suffolk, on or near the lands of Edward's other half-brother the earl of Norfolk, who immediately went to join them, despite having been appointed to defend the counties of Norfolk, Suffolk, Essex and Hertfordshire against the invaders. The bishops of Hereford, Lincoln, Ely and probably Norwich also joined the queen.[2] On the day the fleet arrived, Edward II, as yet unaware of the situation and as keen on buying himself fish as ever, went to the postern gate of the Tower of London and paid a passing fisherman three shillings for two salmon, while one of his servants paid nine pence for a pair of buckskin gloves for him. News of the landing reached him on 27 September.[3]

Edward could hardly, in his worst nightmares, have guessed how astonishingly quickly the force would progress through his realm and how little support he had; his and Hugh Despenser's ruthless rule and greed for the last few years ensured that most of his influential subjects, and even many of his own household, abandoned him. The destruction of his fleet in Normandy some weeks before and the alacrity with which the earl of Norfolk joined the rebels ensured that the small invading force, which could easily have been destroyed on arrival, progressed with little or no opposition. Isabella and her allies headed west in triumph and, perhaps, amazement at the lack of resistance or hostility; most of Edward's men either fled from them or joined them. Five days after the landing, they arrived at Bury St Edmunds, where Isabella helped herself to – or 'caused to be taken for his [her son's] affairs' as she euphemistically glossed the theft – £800 which Edward II's ally Hervey Staunton, chief justice of the court of Common Pleas, had stored at the abbey, to pay her soldiers. Staunton died a year later without recovering the money.[4] On 9 October Isabella placed a reward of £2,000 on the head of Hugh Despenser as a response to the king's declaring on 28 September that Roger Mortimer and others 'have brought with them alien strangers for the purpose of taking the royal power from the king', and offering a ransom of £1,000 on Mortimer's head.[5]

At Wallingford on 15 October, a proclamation was read out in the name of the queen, the duke of Aquitaine and the earl of Kent, in which Hugh Despenser was accused of damaging the realm and Church, sending great men to their deaths and much else. Edward II himself incurred no criticism and was never, at this time or later, said to be a tyrant, but presented instead as the victim of an evil counsellor, whom Isabella and her allies had come to destroy in order to end the oppressions suffered by the people of England.[6] Shortly afterwards, the bishop of Hereford, Adam Orleton, publicly accused Edward of being a sodomite, and preached a sermon from Genesis: 'I shall put enmity between you and the woman, and thy seed and hers, and she shall bruise your head'. Orleton was to claim in 1334 that he had been referring to Hugh Despenser, not Edward II.[7] Ian Mortimer points out that Edward had become 'the target of political lies and anti-royalist propaganda'.[8] Isabella, daughter of the master propagandist Philip IV, well knew the benefits of public relations, far better than Edward did. With Edward's son, the future king, in their party, few men were willing to fight against them, especially as they marched under the royal banner. The defection of his half-brother Norfolk must have been a bitter blow to Edward; an even worse one was soon to come when his cousin Henry of Lancaster declared for the rebels, joined Isabella at Dunstable, and seized money and goods belonging to Hugh Despenser the Elder, earl of Winchester.[9] Henry brought the northern lords with him, including his son-in-law Thomas Wake and Henry Percy, and with the loss of the influential Lancaster, Edward's cause was doomed. The earl of Arundel remained loyal, and apparently so did Arundel's brother-in-law the earl of Surrey, but the grand coalition of the queen, the Contrariants, Lancaster, at least three or four bishops, the northern lords and the king's half-brothers was unassailable. Edward heard the bad news of Henry of Lancaster's defection on 10 October and seized his lands, sending his teenage great-nephew, Hugh Despenser's eldest son Hugh (known as Huchon or Hughelyn), to take possession of them.[10]

As early as 28 September, the day after he learned of the force's arrival, Edward must have realised how little support he had, and offered all felons in prison a pardon, excepting the murderers of Roger Belers and any adherents of Roger Mortimer, if they would join him.[11] On this day, he ordered men in four counties to raise hundreds of footmen to 'repel the invaders' and take them alive or dead. The order was repeated to his Welsh allies Rhys ap Gruffydd and Gruffydd Llwyd, while Sir Robert Wateville was ordered to raise footmen in six counties and 'do what harm he can to [the rebels] except to the queen, the king's son and the earl of Kent'.[12] Edward surely remembered the Marchers trapping him in London in 1321 and realised the impossibility of holding a city hostile to him, and so he left his capital on 2 October, leaving his beloved niece Eleanor Despenser – the last time he or Hugh Despenser would see her – in charge of the Tower. His ten-year-old younger son John of Eltham also remained there. The king and the two Hugh Despensers travelled west, carrying at least £29,000 from the treasury with them, towards South Wales, where Despenser held the majority of his lands and where Edward was popular and hoped to be able to raise support. The king left some personal items with Simon Swanland, future mayor of London and a draper who provided cloth for the royal household, which included two 'good and beautiful' Bibles; a cloth-of-gold cloak edged with white pearls and silver; three velvet garments with green stripes and matching hat; a green coverlet with three matching tapestries; a cushion cover of vermilion sendal (a fine, light silk); and three 'gilded acorn branches'.[13] The king also left behind a silver ship for alms and a number of silver cups, plates, pots and saucers at the Tower.[14] Edward wrote from Acton on 3 October that he had heard his wife was writing to all the cities and commonalties of the realm, and ordered them not to open the letters but to arrest the bearer and send him to the king. No one was to favour 'the king's wife or his son Edward or anyone in their company so long as they behave as they do now', and all others in their company were to be treated as his enemies.[15] Even at this desperate stage, Edward refused to name Isabella, their son or his brother Kent as his enemies, though he pointedly referred to Isabella as 'the king's wife', not as queen (his chamber account of this period, however, continues to call her 'my lady the queen'). Isabella, meanwhile, was ransacking the manor of Baldock in Hertfordshire, apparently for no other reason than it belonged to the brother of the detested Robert Baldock, chancellor of England and ally of Despenser.[16]

London exploded into anarchy and chaos. The city tended to be politically volatile and anti-royalist, or rather anti-authority; Mortimer and Isabella would find out for themselves two years later that the affections of the Londoners were fickle, but for the moment, the city stood firmly on their side. The mayor Hamo de Chigwell had been one of the men who sentenced Roger Mortimer to death in 1322, so had every reason to feel trepidation at Mortimer's return, and indeed he was replaced as mayor by Mortimer's adherent Richard de Béthune soon afterwards and saved his life only by swearing to support Isabella.[17] Eleanor Despenser soon had little choice but to surrender the Tower to the mob, who appointed John of Eltham as nominal guardian of the city. An emergency convocation of the archbishop of Canterbury and the bishops of London, Rochester, Winchester, Exeter and Worcester held at Lambeth on 13 and 14 October decided to send two envoys to the queen. The following day, tragedy struck when Walter Stapeldon, bishop of Exeter, former treasurer of England, founder of Exeter College at Oxford in 1314 and ally of Edward II, was pursued by an angry crowd and beheaded with a bread knife in Cheapside while trying to reach sanctuary inside St Paul's.[18] Two of his squires were killed with him, and his head was sent to the queen, who had been so furious with him for 'dishonouring' her a few months previously. A merchant named John Marshal, a close ally of Hugh Despenser, was also dragged out of his house and beheaded, and Bernard or Arnold of Spain, a wine merchant, likewise, at a place called 'Nomanneslond'.[19] The bishop of London Stephen Gravesend was lucky to avoid the same fate, and Edward's remaining allies in London thought it prudent to leave the city: Geoffrey Scrope, chief justice of King's Bench, escaped across the Thames on a horse belonging to Archbishop Reynolds, Reynolds commandeered the horses of the bishop of Rochester Hamo Hethe, and Hethe himself was forced to flee on foot.[20]

Edward II and the Despensers travelled west, followed at some distance by the invaders. It is interesting to note that the annals of Newenham Abbey written shortly afterwards remarked that *rex et maritus eius*, 'the king and his husband', fled to Wales; evidently some contemporaries believed that Edward's relationship with his chamberlain was sexual or romantic.[21] Edward was aware of his wife's movements: he gave two shillings to a man who brought him news of Isabella when she was near Cambridge, and later gave a pound to a valet sent to Gloucester to spy on her arrival.[22] The king and his chamberlain spent 9–12 October in Gloucester, and by the middle of the month were at the great castle of Chepstow. Despenser the Elder, meanwhile, went to Bristol. Edward's bad temper and anxiety are apparent from an entry in his chamber account of 12 October, when four of his valets were refused their wages because 'the king has long had ill-will towards them'.[23] This was unfair and not the fault of his valets, who had done nothing wrong; twenty-four of them loyally remained with him until at least 31 October, the last day the chamber journal was kept.

In the face of such overwhelming opposition, few men were willing to fight for the king, not even the household knights who had served him so faithfully during the Marcher campaign of 1321/22. Even long-term Despenser adherents such as John Inge, Ingelram Berenger and Despenser's brothers-in-law Ralph Camoys and John St Amand are conspicuous by their absence in 1326. The fact that Edward II lost the support of all those who mattered most is beyond question, but he was not quite as friendless as is often assumed. Roger Mortimer and Isabella paid 158 men in three ships for pursuing the Gascon lord Arnaud Caillau along the coast of Devon and Cornwall between 8 and 20 December 1326.[24] Caillau served Edward faithfully and had long been in favour with the king, who made him a household knight in March 1313 and keeper of the island of Oléron, and raised him to other positions in Gascony. The timing of Caillau's pursuit strongly suggests that he had been with Edward until shortly before his capture in mid-November, and the fact that Mortimer and Isabella sent 158 men after him implies they were very keen to catch him. Edward's devoted friend Donald, earl of Mar, Robert Bruce's nephew, remained with the king until at least late October, when he returned to his homeland after an absence of twenty years and tried to persuade Bruce to invade England and help Edward. Nor was this the end of Mar's involvement in Edward's affairs: he spent much of 1327 attempting to free him and restore him to the throne, and joined the earl of Kent's conspiracy to free the supposedly long-dead Edward in 1330. On 12 October 1326, Edward II ordered Malcolm Musard to raise footmen in Worcestershire. Musard was a knight and notorious gang leader who supported Edward in 1321/22, but subsequently turned against the king: Edward ordered his arrest in December 1323 for adhering to the Contrariants, and he was imprisoned in the Tower by June 1324.[25] Musard acknowledged a debt of £100 to Isabella – not Edward – on 6 August 1326, six weeks before the invasion, 'to save his life and to have his lands again' and was pardoned the following day for his adherence of 1322.[26] Given that Edward had imprisoned him for over two years, it would hardly be surprising to find that Musard joined the queen. He didn't: Isabella seized his lands and goods in May 1327 on the grounds that he had supported Despenser the Elder against herself and her son, and Musard was in prison at Worcester by 8 November that year.[27] He also joined the earl of Kent's conspiracy to free Edward in 1330.[28]

John de Toucestre was a member of Edward's household whom the king sent to Reading Abbey in November 1325 to receive 'sustenance for life' on his retirement.[29] Evidently, however, he left his abbey to fight for Edward after the invasion, as he was ordered on 10 October 1326 'to select all men at arms wherever he goes and to lead them to the king'. Toucestre, like Musard and Mar, joined Kent's conspiracy in 1330. A John Beauchamp of Somerset claimed in 1327 that Toucestre and Richard Brown of Halford led men of Shepperton to Bristol to fight against Isabella and her son, supposedly against their will.[30] Another of the king and Despenser's supporters was Adam of Sodbury, abbot of Glastonbury, indicted before the sheriff of Somerset shortly before 1 December 1326 – within days of Hugh Despenser's execution – for concealing treasure belonging to Despenser and his ally Robert Baldock in his abbey.[31] Abbot Adam was accused in 1327 of committing crimes in the company of men known to be plotting to free Edward from captivity. John Giffard of Essex claimed that his manor had been attacked by Roger Wodeham and more than fifty armed men, who said that Giffard was an enemy of Edward and Despenser and belonged to the queen's faction, and stole some of Giffard's horses to ride against Isabella. Wodeham was a valet of Edward II's chamber and constable of Hadleigh Castle in Essex, and the petition says that he and his dozens of armed men went to South Wales with Edward and Despenser, and remained with them until they sailed from Chepstow on 20 October. Presumably after Edward's capture, they returned to Essex and, according to Giffard, tried to kill him and his men for their adherence to Isabella.[32] The speed and success of the invasion took the king's supporters by surprise, and most of his loyal Welsh allies failed to meet up with him in Wales. Edward II was popular there, but Despenser was hated for his tyranny and his 1318 execution of Llywelyn Bren. If Edward had sent Despenser away from him, he would no doubt have had far more success in attracting support; but then, if he had been willing to send Despenser away from him, he wouldn't have been in this position in the first place.

On 20 October at Chepstow, Edward replaced Hugh Despenser's sister Aline Burnell as custodian of Conwy Castle with Sir William Erkalewe, presumably because he felt he needed an experienced military man in charge of such an important stronghold. He sent men named Roger and Richard Flete 'to diverse parts of the realm on his affairs' the same day, to what end is unclear.[33] Also on that day, the king, Despenser, Despenser's confessor Richard Bliton and the chancellor of England Robert Baldock – and possibly the earl of Arundel – set sail from Chepstow, probably heading for Lundy Island (which had been in Despenser's possession since 1321) in the Bristol Channel and ultimately, probably Ireland, where Edward may have hoped to find allies and perhaps even raise an army to launch a counter-invasion.[34] The Lanercost chronicler expressed his alarm that if Edward had reached Ireland he might have sailed from there to Scotland and attacked England with the help of the Irish and Scots.[35] Despite Bliton praying to Saint Anne 'that she would send us a good wind', however, the boat went nowhere, and on 25 October they were forced to put in at Cardiff.[36] Jean Froissart, unreliable as ever, claims that the weight of their sins kept them at sea for eleven days.[37] The king's attempted flight by sea meant that his enemies could claim he had abandoned his kingdom, and so they appointed his son Edward of Windsor as regent in his place on 26 October.[38] The memorandum on the Close Roll names the bishops and magnates then at Bristol with the queen. As well as those mentioned above, they included the archbishop of Dublin; Henry Beaumont, whom Edward had imprisoned earlier that year; William la Zouche of Ashby, who had fought for the king at Boroughbridge in 1322; and perhaps most painfully for Edward, Robert Wateville, to whom he had shown considerable kindness and generosity in 1325/26.[39]

Shortly before he sailed from Chepstow, on 18 October, the king paid a messenger for bringing him letters from Hugh Despenser the Elder, earl of Winchester.[40] The earl had been left to defend Bristol, and the queen arrived there also on 18 October. The city fell on the 26th, and on the 27th Winchester was given a mock trial in front of William Trussell, a judge who had fled from England after Boroughbridge, in the presence of Roger Mortimer, the earls of Norfolk, Kent and Lancaster (as Henry of Lancaster, earl of Leicester, was now styled), Thomas Wake and the queen. Winchester, who was sixty-five – not ninety, as stated by Froissart – was given a mock trial deliberately arranged as a parody of Thomas of Lancaster's in 1322, for which the Despensers alone were blamed.[41] The earl of Kent, watching the trial, had also been one of the men who sentenced Lancaster to death, though the hypocrisy of this went unremarked. Because Lancaster had been executed in 1322 without the right to defend himself, Winchester was also denied the right to speak. Lancaster had been forbidden the right to speak because he had forbidden Piers Gaveston the right to speak in 1312. To no one's surprise, least of all Winchester's, no doubt, he was sentenced to death and hanged immediately on the public gallows in his armour, in front of a jeering crowd. His body was cut down and fed to dogs, and his head carried to the town of Winchester on a spear to be displayed in public there.[42] The Bridlington chronicler alone mourned his death, lamenting, 'O sorrow!' and describing Despenser as a great and powerful man.[43] Edward II at Neath in South Wales had heard the news by 5 November, and one assumes that he mourned sincerely for the nobleman who had remained loyal to him from the very beginning of his reign, and who had perhaps been a father figure to him.[44] A chronicle written at Bury St Edmunds Abbey – over 200 miles from Bristol – claims that Isabella pleaded for the earl's life to be spared but Roger Mortimer and Henry of Lancaster overruled her, which seems unlikely. The Flemish chronicler Jean le Bel, an eyewitness to Despenser's execution, does not mention that Isabella did this, and neither does any other source. Precisely how Isabella's social inferiors would have dared to overrule her wishes in public is not clear. She had sworn that she would destroy the Despensers, and her subsequent actions against Hugh Despenser the Younger's children hardly demonstrate that she was overflowing with forgiveness towards the family.

On the day of the earl of Winchester's death, Edward and Hugh Despenser arrived at the latter's stronghold of Caerphilly. They stayed there until 2 November then left, for reasons which are hard to explain, given that the castle could, and did, withstand a siege for many months. The numerous possessions Edward took with him, which must have required many carts to transport all the way from London, were later found and inventoried at Caerphilly. They included a red retiring-robe with saffron stripes and embroidered with bears; a black cap lined with red velvet and decorated with butterflies made of pearls; a white cap lined with green velvet and decorated with gold trefoils; eight cushions of purple velvet and red samite (a heavy silk); a counterpane and mattress of red sendal lined with green sendal; a canopy and curtains of red sendal to surround his bed; two silk curtains with gold stripes; and a sword, girdle and scabbard enamelled with the arms of Castile. Edward also took more practical items, including crossbows and numerous pieces of armour, and a great deal of plate, including three brass pots marked with the letter E, 279 silver saucers marked with a leopard, and other random items such as a chain for his greyhounds, a plectrum for a lyre, four small pennons embroidered with Edward's arms to decorate trumpets, and items for his chapel, including a bag of incense. £14,000 in cash was found in twenty-seven barrels.[45] Edward left Hugh Despenser's knight John Felton in charge of Caerphilly Castle and made him swear on the Gospels not to deliver it to Isabella or to his son, an oath Felton kept; he and the dozens of other men within, who included Despenser's teenage son Huchon, refused to surrender to the castle's besiegers until the following March when Mortimer and Isabella finally agreed not to execute Huchon.[46]

Edward's chamber journal was kept for the last time on 31 October, either because his clerks had abandoned him or because they had given up in despair.[47] The final entry records wages to five carpenters and twenty-four chamber valets, including two women, Joan Traghs and Anneis de May, for the twenty days since 12 October.[48] Some of the king's chamber staff were among the garrison of Caerphilly Castle pardoned on 20 March 1327 for holding it against the queen, which implies that they remained there when Edward left on 2 November, perhaps at his command.[49] Also on 31 October, Edward took the fealty of his nephew John de Bohun, eldest son of the earl of Hereford killed at Boroughbridge in 1322, and allowed him his lands, although John would not come of age (twenty-one) until 23 November 1327.[50] John's brother Edward, about fourteen, was also with the 'baffled king' as he 'wandered houseless around Wales', as *Lanercost* put it.[51] Desperately, Edward sent out orders for 400 footmen to be brought to Cardiff, ordered men to keep the ports along the South Wales coast safe against his enemies and even offered felons a pardon if they would come to Caerphilly Castle and defend it, but no one was listening anymore.[52]

Edward, Despenser and their remaining followers spent the period from 2 to 10 November at Margam Abbey and Neath. On the 10th, Edward appointed envoys to negotiate with Isabella: his nephew Edward de Bohun; the abbot of Neath; Rhys ap Gruffydd; and the royal squires Oliver de Bordeaux and John Harsik.[53] Isabella, who held the upper hand and had no reason to negotiate, showed no interest, and indeed it is not certain if the envoys ever went. What Edward was hoping to achieve by leaving Caerphilly for Neath is unclear; by now he probably had no plans at all and was merely, hopelessly waiting for the inevitable. He had with him his Great Seal, £6,000 and some of the chancery rolls, which were later found at Neath and Swansea by Henry of Lancaster and taken to Isabella.[54]

Edward's movements for the next few days are uncertain. He seems to have left Neath on 11 November and attempted to make his way back to the castle of Caerphilly, perhaps because he knew he was being pursued by a group of men sent by Isabella and Mortimer: Henry of Lancaster, William la Zouche, who would marry Despenser's widow Eleanor in 1329, and two sons of the Welsh nobleman Llywelyn Bren, hideously executed by Despenser in 1318.[55] On 16 November, the king and Despenser were captured near Llantrisant, in a place later known as the Vale of Treachery, with a small handful of followers. They were the chancellor Robert Baldock, the king's controller Robert Holden, a sergeant-at-arms called Simon of Reading, knights named Thomas Wyther and John Bek, a valet named John le Blount and a clerk named John Smale.[56] The *Annales Paulini*, dramatically, say they were captured in the middle of a terrific storm, and the author of the *Anonimalle* reveals his ignorance of Welsh geography by declaring that Edward was taken near Snowdon.[57]

Although Edward II remained king of England in name for another nine weeks, his influence ended at that moment. And so his reign staggered to an ignominious end with him wandering around Wales with a handful of followers. As the king, however, he was still treated with respect and deference, and his cousin Lancaster took him to his castle of Kenilworth (recently restored to him), via his castle at Monmouth. On 20 November, Edward was forced to give up his Great Seal to Adam Orleton, bishop of Hereford. The memorandum on the Close Roll claims, implausibly, that Edward deliberated for a while then announced that 'it pleased him to send his great seal to his consort and his son', and thus it was carried to the queen and the duke of Aquitaine, who had turned fourteen on 13 November.[58]

On 16 November, Edward II saw Hugh Despenser for the last time, both of them knowing that the powerful chamberlain was going to his death. How Edward felt is a matter for speculation. Did he regret his dependence on Despenser, which had brought him to this? Did he blame Isabella for what he saw as her faithless betrayal, and refuse to acknowledge his own culpability? Whether he was upset, or furious, or denying reality, or vowing revenge, is unknown, and in a sense, it hardly matters. Events were now out of his control. Although most of the men who remained with the king were released, Robert Baldock the chancellor, who as a cleric could not be executed, was sentenced to perpetual imprisonment. He was handed over to the not so tender mercies of Adam Orleton, who imprisoned him in his London house, which some months later was broken into by a mob. They dragged Baldock to the notorious Newgate prison, where the unfortunate man died soon afterwards in torment.[59] Simon of Reading was sentenced to death and hanged on a vague accusation of insulting the queen – not in fact a capital offence – and without a trial.[60] The reasons for this are mysterious; although Reading has been described in modern times as a close personal friend of Hugh Despenser, his knight or his marshal, he was merely a sergeant-at-arms in Edward II's household.[61]

In Hereford on the day after the king's capture, Edmund Fitzalan, earl of Arundel, was executed. Arundel, now forty-one and present at Piers Gaveston's death in 1312, had come over to the king and the Despensers' cause when they were strong. Now he must have realised that he had backed the wrong horse, but to his credit, he remained loyal, a rare example of a former enemy of Edward II who changed sides and stayed at the king's side. Arundel was captured by John Charlton, Edward's chamberlain until replaced by Hugh Despenser in 1318, whom Edward had pardoned for allegiance to the Contrariants in 1322. According to Adam Murimuth, Roger Mortimer hated his cousin – Arundel's grandmother was the elder sister of Mortimer's father – with a 'perfect hatred', and Arundel's death had far more to do with a private vendetta than with any kind of justice.[62] The two had been on opposing sides in 1321/22, were long-term rivals for land and influence in Wales, and of course Arundel had been a staunch adherent of the king and Despenser and married his son and heir to Despenser's daughter. These felonies sufficed to condemn him, and he was beheaded by a 'worthless wretch' who needed twenty-two strokes of the axe to sever the unfortunate earl's head, perhaps because a blunt blade had been ordered. *Lanercost* says he 'was condemned to death in secret, as it were', and there is no evidence that he had a trial.[63] Two other men, John Daniel and Robert de Micheldever, were beheaded with him, also without a trial.[64] Daniel was the keeper of two of Mortimer's manors and of one belonging to Mortimer's mother, and had been appointed in March 1326 to search for men who had supported Mortimer as a Contrariant. Micheldever was a squire of Edward II's chamber.[65] It is unclear what either man had done to merit execution, and not only were they not given a trial, they were not even accused of any crime. The goods Arundel had stored at the cathedral church of Chichester were delivered to Isabella and Edward of Windsor four days after his death, and included £524 in six canvas sacks, a silver salt cellar 'enamelled all over', a silver-gilt enamelled cup with matching basin, and seven partly broken cups.[66]

Hugh Despenser, Robert Baldock and Simon of Reading were taken from Llantrisant to Hereford and subjected to every indignity possible. Despenser was tied to a mean horse, in the same way as Thomas of Lancaster had been in 1322, his coat of arms was reversed, and a 'chaplet of sharp nettles' was set on his head. Through all the villages they passed, the populace came out to shriek their joy at the downfall of the hated royal favourite, to blow trumpets and bang drums, and to throw things at him. Biblical verses were written or carved onto Despenser's arms, shoulders and chest, including 'Why do you boast in evil?' from Psalm 52. Four years almost to the day later, the same verse would be read out to Roger Mortimer as he went to his own execution.[67] There was much discussion as to where Despenser would be put on trial and executed, Isabella favouring London. Despenser, however, refused all food and drink so that 'he was almost dead from fasting', and so it was decided to judge him in Hereford on 24 November so he would not die by his own will and cheat the queen of her revenge.

Before he died, Despenser was given a mock trial during which William Trussell, who had also presided over his father's trial, read out a long list of charges against him in French.[68] Some of them are true or partly true, some are perfectly ludicrous, and most of them pile all the blame for Edward II's failed reign on Despenser's head. The king's enemies did not yet dare blame Edward himself, at least not publicly, for his manifold failings, and Despenser was a useful scapegoat.[69] He was accused of sole responsibility, with his father, for Thomas of Lancaster's death, the earl of Kent's attendance at Lancaster's execution and at those of the Despensers still escaping the notice of chroniclers; murdering, executing and imprisoning many magnates; piracy (correctly); leaving the queen in peril at Tynemouth in 1322; destroying the privileges of Holy Church, robbing prelates and plundering the Church 'as a false Christian'; forcing the king to ride against the Contrariants in 1322; trying to bribe people at the French court to kill the queen; and most curiously of all, of breaking the limbs of one Lady Baret until she was 'forever more driven mad and lost'. Another charge was that he 'procured discord' between Edward and Isabella, more evidence of the queen's anger that Despenser had come between herself and her husband.

The verdict was never in doubt: Sir Hugh Despenser, lord of Glamorgan, then probably in his late thirties, was sentenced to be hanged, drawn and quartered. Trussell ended the sentence by declaring, 'Withdraw, you traitor, tyrant, renegade; go to take your own justice, traitor, evil man, criminal!' Despenser was tied to a hurdle and dragged by four horses through the streets to the castle, his own, where a gallows fifty feet high had been especially erected. A noose was thrown around his neck and he was hauled up and partially strangled, then lowered onto a ladder, where according to Froissart, his penis and testicles were cut off, 'because he was a heretic and a sodomite, even, it was said, with the king, and this was why the king had driven away the queen', though this was not part of his sentence. His heart and intestines were cut out and thrown onto a fire, 'because he was a false-hearted traitor'. Merciful death came at last when he was beheaded. Simon of Reading, the obscure sergeant-at-arms, was hanged below him. Despenser's head was taken to London and, to great jubilation, placed on London Bridge, and the four quarters of his body were sent to Carlisle, York, Bristol and Dover to be displayed in public.[70] Shortly after Roger Mortimer's own execution in November 1330, Edward III granted permission for 'the friends of Hugh' to gather and bury his remains wherever they wished, which they duly did at Tewkesbury Abbey, where his tomb still exists.[71]

The precious goods Despenser kept in the Tower of London, which included almost thirty gold cups with matching ewers, were transferred into Isabella's possession on 6 December.[72] On 1 January 1327, Isabella ordered Despenser's middle three daughters Joan, Eleanor and Margaret, aged roughly ten, seven and four, to be sent to three separate convents and forced to take the veil as nuns. Evidently the queen believed this matter to be extremely pressing, as the girls were to be 'admitted and veiled without delay'.[73] Despenser's eldest daughter Isabel, about fourteen, escaped the order as she was already married to the earl of Arundel's son, as did his youngest daughter Elizabeth, a baby or possibly still *in utero*. Edward II had sent three of Roger Mortimer's daughters to convents in 1324, but they were not forced to take binding, lifelong vows as nuns. It has been suggested that Isabella's motive was to prevent anyone claiming the Despenser lands through the girls via marriage, which is most unlikely, as the lands were forfeit to the Crown and the de Clare inheritance belonged to their mother. Besides, as the girls had four brothers, their chances of inheriting their parents' lands were remote.[74] More plausibly, the order is further evidence of Isabella's virulent hatred of Despenser and her fierce desire for revenge on him, which, his execution notwithstanding, still remained, and thus she lashed out at some of his children. The girls' mother, Despenser's widow Eleanor, was detained at the Tower of London – according to a Hainault chronicler, in case she might be pregnant by her uncle the king – and their eldest brother Hugh or Huchon was imprisoned until 1331.

Edward II's reaction to hearing of his beloved chamberlain's terrible death is not recorded, and indeed it is not even clear where he was on 24 November, as he had been given into the custody of Henry of Lancaster, and Lancaster attended Despenser's execution.[75] One hopes that Edward wasn't forced to watch it. Two months later, when a deputation from parliament visited Edward at Kenilworth, William Trussell was their main spokesperson and officially renounced the kingdom's allegiance to Edward. Perhaps the man who pronounced the death sentence on Despenser was sent deliberately in order to inflict maximum emotional pain on Edward, as surely there must have been other men who could have gone instead. If this was the plan, however, it backfired: Trussell 'knelt before our lord the king and cried him mercy, begging him to pardon his trespasses against him, and he [Edward] pardoned him and gave him the sign of peace in front of them all'.[76]

Edward reached Kenilworth Castle by 5 December, and spent a very lonely and cheerless Christmas there, as the *Flores* points out.[77] He must have been deeply distraught at his sudden, shocking downfall, the betrayal of his wife and son, the deaths of Hugh Despenser and the others, the knowledge that few people had been willing to support him against the invaders, the awareness that he had so completely failed as a king and a leader. We can only imagine what thoughts went through his head at this time. Meanwhile, Isabella, Roger Mortimer and their allies spent Christmas at Wallingford. Edward of Windsor was of course also present, and his brother John of Eltham was brought there by a group of Londoners.[78]

Unsurprisingly, discussions about Edward II's fate dominated proceedings, though even at this late date it was unclear what should happen to the king. Many people, not least the pope, were also uneasy about the queen's failure to return to her husband.[79] But Isabella's rebellion, invasion and participation in the execution of the Despensers made it impossible that she and Edward could simply resume their marital relationship as if nothing had happened. Neither would Roger Mortimer have permitted her to; he had come far too close to power to allow Isabella to return to Edward, and his ambition required him to stay in her favour. And so Adam Orleton, bishop of Hereford, claimed that Edward carried a knife within his hose to kill Isabella, and if he had no other weapon he would crush her with his teeth; and therefore, the queen could never again live with her husband.[80] Edward indignantly refuted the allegation that he meant his wife any harm when he heard about it, and there is no other evidence that Edward was or wished to be violent towards his wife. Nor is there any reason to suppose that Isabella, despite her rebellion, wished Edward any physical harm, and it is unknown whether at Christmas 1326 she spoke in favour of his deposition or was, even now, reluctant to take this enormous step.[81] Perhaps, like her brother-in-law the earl of Kent, she had sought the destruction of the Despensers but not of her husband. The overwhelming success of the invasion must have taken everyone by surprise, even those who took part, and it may be that Isabella – and perhaps even some of her allies – had not anticipated or desired the king's humiliation. She sent Edward letters and gifts in 1327, and in April told a council meeting that she was ready and willing to visit him (they forbade it).[82] Whatever the queen's opinion, she must, like her allies, have come to the conclusion that allowing Edward to remain on the throne was impossible, whether they had originally planned this or not. And so finally the council decided that he should be deposed in favour of his son, not executed, but allowed to live in comfortable custody for the rest of his life.

The parliament during which Edward II was deposed began in London on 7 January 1327, though as Edward did not summon it, its legality was highly questionable. Whether Edward was deposed *in* this parliament or *by* this parliament is a question which has been frequently debated and need not concern us much here.[83] It is almost impossible to know what really happened in January 1327 and how Edward reacted to losing his throne, as we only know the official story which was allowed to come out, as with his handing over his Great Seal supposedly with pleasure some weeks before. The official version of events was that he piously and obediently, albeit with sighs and tears, consented to abdicate his throne to his son. What his real attitude was, we will never know. Early in January, Adam Orleton and others are said to have travelled to Kenilworth to persuade Edward to attend the parliament, but he 'cursed them contemptuously, declaring that he would not come among his enemies'.[84] One might question whether Edward really was asked to come to London or whether this story was a cover for the reality that Edward's enemies did not want him to appear before parliament and give him a chance to create sympathy for himself, and perhaps even, at this late stage, save his throne. No English king had ever been deposed and therefore it was entirely unclear how it should be done, and Roger Mortimer, the two bishops Adam Orleton and John Stratford and their allies were groping around in the dark. Ann Lyon has described the parliament of January 1327 as 'an attempt by what was a relatively small group of enemies of Edward II, most of its leaders motivated by personal grudges against him, to give an aura of legality to acts which were unprecedented and therefore illegal'.[85] Claire Valente points out that 'the new regime was also careful to conceal all evidence of opposition' to the deposition and that all but one chronicler, Rochester, associated with Bishop Hamo Hethe, 'recorded nothing but smooth sailing, one sign of a successful cover-up'.[86] Rochester is the only chronicle which records that William Melton, archbishop of York, and the bishops of Rochester, London and Carlisle openly spoke out for Edward and did not consent to his removal. Matters did not go as smoothly as the king's enemies had hoped: Adam Orleton made a speech on 12 January and asked whether the assembly would prefer to have Edward II as king or his son, and evidently the response was not nearly as enthusiastic as Orleton and others would have liked, which perturbed them.[87]

When parliament gathered again on the 13th, Thomas Wake was planted in the crowd to shout approval at appropriate moments during speeches by his cousin Mortimer, the bishops of Hereford and Winchester (Orleton and Stratford) and the archbishop of Canterbury (Walter Reynolds, formerly a friend of Edward), declaring that Edward had broken his coronation oath and should no longer be their king.[88] Swept up in the fervour of the moment and in the stage-managed piece of grand theatre it undoubtedly was, the gathering consented that Edward would be removed and his son crowned in his place, and a deputation of twenty-four men was sent to Kenilworth to inform Edward of the decision. They included William Trussell, Edward's nephew-in-law the earl of Surrey, who had switched sides to Isabella at some point, perhaps on hearing of the slow and bloody death of his brother-in-law Arundel, and the royal justice Geoffrey Scrope, also a former close ally of Edward.[89]

Many chronicles describe Edward's reaction to hearing the news, and they all depict it the same way. A penitent half-fainting Edward, in tears, reacts with patience and humble subservience, agrees that as things cannot be otherwise he is content that his son will succeed him, and blesses his son, who he hopes will find greater favour with the people than he has.[90] The Pipewell chronicle says that Edward begged his subjects' forgiveness on his knees, and *Flores* that he lamented his failings but could not be other than he was, though Adam Murimuth says that Edward's agreement was reported to parliament 'more fully than it was done', that is, his weeping and begging for forgiveness were exaggerated.[91]

According to the chronicle of Geoffrey le Baker decades later, but no one else, Edward was threatened that if he did not consent, his sons Edward and John would be passed over and the throne given to someone of non-royal birth, which has long been assumed to be a reference to Roger Mortimer (though Baker does not say this). This is an extremely unlikely story, and Mortimer, or anyone other than Edward of Windsor, would never have been accepted as king by the magnates and prelates or indeed by Isabella.[92] The official proclamation of the transfer of power declared that Edward had of his own free will decided that the governance of the realm should devolve to his son, and that this had been accepted by his magnates, prelates and the community of the realm. In short, it was presented not as Edward being made to accept his deposition, but his kingdom accepting his wish to abdicate.[93] Trussell formally withdrew the kingdom's allegiance from Edward, his steward Thomas le Blount ceremonially broke his staff of office, and Edward II's reign was over. His son's reign as Edward III, king of England, lord of Ireland, duke of Aquitaine, count of Ponthieu and earl of Chester, officially began on 25 January 1327, and the fourteen-year-old was crowned at Westminster on 2 February by Archbishop Reynolds. The other archbishop, Melton of York, refused to attend out of loyalty to Edward II, though evidently he became reconciled to the young king, as he performed the marriage ceremony of Edward III and Philippa of Hainault a year later. Melton's involvement in the former king's life was certainly not yet over, however.

Edward II was now merely Sir Edward of Caernarfon, and it was agreed that he would be housed in comfort for the rest of his days and treated with honour and respect as the king's father. Presumably he was informed about the Articles of the Deposition, a list of six charges intended to justify his removal: they included the statements that he had allowed himself to be governed by others who gave him bad counsel, that he had given himself up to improper pastimes and neglected the business of his kingdom, that he had left his kingdom and his people as lost, and because of his cruelty and his defects, he was incorrigible without hope of amendment.[94] It seems unlikely, given Edward's personality, that he really did react with such contrite acquiescence to the demands that he abdicate his throne, and far more likely that he spat utter rage at his subjects who had dared to behave in such a manner, and that he vowed revenge. Although this would not happen, the twists and turns of Edward II's extraordinary life continued beyond his deposition.

16

Four Conspiracies and a Funeral

The early months of 1327 passed uneventfully as far as Sir Edward of Caernarfon, formerly King Edward II of England, was concerned. He was free to wander around the gardens of Kenilworth Castle at will – though not to leave the castle, of course – and his cousin Henry of Lancaster treated him with courtesy and kindness. Once again Edward's state of mind remains unknown, and little evidence exists to tell us what his life at Kenilworth was like, though we know his son the new king sent him two tuns of wine.[1] Queen Isabella and Roger Mortimer, now ruling the kingdom in Edward III's name despite not being on the regency council appointed during his minority, did not trust Lancaster; they had needed his support after their invasion, but now they feared his enormous influence. With his vast income and lands and his large number of followers, Lancaster would always be far too powerful to ignore, and Mortimer and Isabella had seen first-hand how his brother Thomas had done more than anyone to ruin Edward II's reign. Henry's custody of the former king was a danger to them. The legality of the parliament which deposed Edward was uncertain; there remained the possibility that Edward might be able to overturn it and restore himself to the throne, if he attracted enough support. Lancaster's custody of Edward gave him leverage over Mortimer and Isabella, as he would always have the chance to hold Edward's possible return to the throne over their heads if they annoyed him, which they foolishly went out of their way to do. Lancaster, head of the regency council and Edward III's legal guardian, wielded little if any power in the government, while Isabella made sure that his access to his great-nephew the king was minimal.

Therefore, the former king had to be removed from Lancaster's custody and given to men whom Isabella and Mortimer could trust. The men they selected as Edward's new guardians were Thomas, Lord Berkeley, and Berkeley's brother-in-law, Sir John Maltravers, neither of whom had any reason to love Edward of Caernarfon. Berkeley, now probably in his early thirties and married to Mortimer's eldest daughter Margaret, had been imprisoned in 1322 and seen his lands given to Hugh Despenser and plundered, while his father died in prison as a Contrariant. Maltravers was about thirty-seven and had spent years in exile on the Continent after Boroughbridge with Mortimer, although his father of the same name stayed in England and remained loyal to Edward.

On 3 April 1327, custody of the former king of England was transferred to Berkeley and Maltravers, who were appointed as Edward's guardians with joint and equal responsibility for his safety.[2] The chronicler Henry Knighton suggested a few decades later that Lancaster gave up custody of Edward voluntarily, but it is most unlikely that he would willingly have surrendered such a powerful political weapon.[3] Although an indenture was drawn up on 21 March, the fact that Roger Mortimer waited near Kenilworth with an armed force during the transfer from Lancaster to Berkeley and Maltravers is telling, and the following year, Lancaster accused Mortimer of taking Edward from him by force.[4] It seems probable that Lancaster had been coerced, or tricked, or manipulated. There was another, perhaps even more pressing, reason to remove Edward from Kenilworth. Although the event is shrouded in obscurity, it seems that in March 1327, some supporters of Edward attempted to free him from Kenilworth Castle.[5] They failed, not surprisingly – Kenilworth was probably the most secure stronghold in the country – but this plot, combined with the doubts Mortimer and Isabella had over Henry of Lancaster, convinced them to move Edward. With a large armed escort, Thomas Berkeley and John Maltravers left Kenilworth and took Edward the few dozen miles to Berkeley's castle, in the Gloucestershire village of Berkeley.[6]

Geoffrey le Baker a few years later wrote a highly colourful and highly improbable account of Edward's journey to Berkeley, claiming that his captors tormented him by crowning him with hay, forcing him to shave with cold ditchwater and eat poisoned food, clothing him in rags despite the cold, not allowing him to sleep despite his exhaustion, jeering at him and trying to make him believe that he was mad. Baker's account of Edward's imprisonment at Berkeley in 1327 is well known and often repeated as certain fact: he claims that Edward was kept in a cell near a deep pit containing rotting animal corpses, his jailers hoping that the stench and the contagion would kill him.[7] It is impossible to take Baker's allegations seriously. (Unfortunately, many writers *have* taken them seriously.) Baker was not writing history, but hagiography; by the middle of the fourteenth century, when he wrote his chronicle, the popular, albeit highly implausible, campaign to have Edward canonised as a saint was well underway, and Baker's intention was to portray him as a Christlike figure nobly suffering the torments of lesser men, the 'satraps of Satan' as he memorably called them: the Passion of Edward of Caernarfon.[8]

Baker was keen to blame Isabella, whom he calls 'Jezebel' and 'the iron virago', for Edward's supposed torments, yet there is nothing to suggest that she would have allowed her husband to be subjected to such inhuman treatment. And although Edward III was only fourteen, he would grow up and one day take over the governance of his kingdom, and would not take kindly to allegations that his father's custodians had tortured and tormented him. In later years, Edward III neither accused Thomas Berkeley and John Maltravers of mistreating his father, nor Roger Mortimer of ordering the torment, as he surely would have done had Baker's stories had any substance in fact. It was stated that Edward would 'be looked after as was appropriate for such a lord' and 'honestly kept for the rest of his life, according to his estate', which means with all the respect and deference due to a man who was the son, grandson and father of kings, not abused and mistreated as a common criminal.[9]

All the available evidence suggests that Edward was in fact well treated during his incarceration at Berkeley. An entry on the Close Roll refers to the expenses of himself and his household, meaning that he had servants attending him, and castle records show that his custodians bought wine, cheese, capons, beef and eggs for him, and wax for his candles. He also had access to a chapel.[10] That Edward's guardians bought expensive wax, not the much cheaper tallow, is indirect proof that they were treating him well, and they would hardly have provided candles had they been intending to kill him by incarcerating him near a pit containing animal corpses, as Baker claims. Although we cannot prove conclusively that Edward received the items bought for him, there is no reason at all to think that he didn't.[11] Berkeley and Maltravers were given an enormous five pounds a day for Edward's upkeep, and on 15 May 1327 were given £500 for his expenses.[12] Adam Murimuth says that although Thomas Berkeley welcomed Edward kindly and treated him well, John Maltravers behaved with 'much harshness' towards him. As Murimuth believed, wrongly, that Maltravers was one of Edward's murderers, his testimony on this point is rather suspect, however. He also states that Berkeley and Maltravers switched custody of Edward, each man taking responsibility for a month, which may be true but is uncorroborated by other sources.[13] Jean Froissart, who visited Berkeley Castle in 1366 with Hugh Despenser's grandson Edward Despenser, says that Lord Berkeley 'was urged to take good care of him, with orders to give him all honourable service and attention and to place court officials round him who were familiar with their duties, but never to allow him to leave the castle precincts'.[14] Although Froissart is an unreliable source for Edward's reign, this account is borne out by other evidence. An anonymous fourteenth-century chronicle claims that carpenters working on the castle heard Edward moaning and groaning, which may indicate that he was being mistreated – but is far more likely to mean only that Edward, a highly emotional man at the best of times, was feeling the depths of despair at this, the worst of times.[15]

Isabella kept in touch with Edward at Berkeley, sending him affectionate letters enquiring after his health and comfort, and gifts of fine clothes, linen, delicacies and little luxuries.[16] This implies that she still had feelings for him; after all, there was no reason for her to write to Edward and send him gifts unless she wanted to. Geoffrey le Baker claims that Edward begged Isabella in tears to allow him to see his children, but she, 'whose heart was harder than stone ... that woman of iron', refused; however, Baker's hatred of Isabella and attempts to portray Edward as a long-suffering saint make his testimony unreliable. Even if the story is true, this does not automatically mean that Isabella acted out of cruelty towards her husband, but perhaps out of a desire to spare their children – who, Edward III excepted, were only ten, eight and five – the distress of seeing their once-powerful father cast so low.

At some unknown date in 1327, Thomas Berkeley appointed Thomas Gurney to share custody of Edward of Caernarfon with himself and John Maltravers. Gurney was a knight of Somerset and a distant cousin of the Berkeleys.[17] He had briefly been a household knight of Edward II in 1318, but held on to his connections with the Berkeleys: he took the side of the Marchers during the Despenser War, and was ordered to be arrested – with John Maltravers – in February 1322. He was imprisoned in the Tower of London then pardoned in return for a fine of £100, and his lands were restored.[18] Gurney petitioned Edward for permission to pay off his fine in ten-mark instalments, fought for him in Gascony, and in March 1326, was pardoned again for his adherence to the Contrariants.[19] Presumably, however, Gurney joined the invasion forces of Queen Isabella and Roger Mortimer in the autumn of 1326. Unlike the families of some other Contrariants, Gurney's wife and children were not imprisoned, and although he had no particular reason to love Edward of Caernarfon, neither did he have any reason to bear him deadly hatred.

A poem in French called 'The Lament of Edward II' dates to 1327 or shortly afterwards. Although once believed to have been written by Edward himself, this is unlikely, and it was most probably composed by one of his supporters soon after his deposition.[20] In the Lament, Edward shows much repentance for his many transgressions, and the poem also has him declaring, with reference to Isabella, 'God! How much I loved the fair one; but now the spark of true love is gone out, so that my joy is fled'. This may not, of course, represent Edward's true feelings, but it does show that, within months of his deposition, a writer saw nothing strange in portraying him as deeply in love with his wife and desperately unhappy at losing her. Geoffrey of Paris, who saw Edward and Isabella during their visit to France in 1313, also found nothing peculiar in stating that Edward loved and desired her. Their marriage of nearly twenty years was far more complex and interesting than it is usually depicted nowadays: as little more than a disaster from start to finish with an indifferent Edward constantly neglecting and punishing his long-suffering queen, who detests him and aims at his downfall and death for years on end.

While Edward languished comfortably at Berkeley Castle, Isabella and her favourite ruled England on behalf of the teenage Edward III. Having invaded England on a platform of liberating the country from greed and tyranny, Isabella granted herself the huge annual income of 20,000 marks, or £13,333, on the day of her son's coronation, the largest income anyone in England (kings excepted) received during the entire Middle Ages and more than 20 per cent higher than the income her enormously wealthy uncle Thomas of Lancaster had received from five earldoms. It amounted to a third of the entire annual royal revenue.[21] She also awarded herself cash grants of £31,843 between December 1326 and January 1327, supposedly to pay her debts abroad – which had in fact been paid already – and appropriated much of the inheritance which belonged to her uncle Henry of Lancaster and to which she had no right.[22] The cash grants amounted to seven years of her pre-September 1324 income. And the rapidity with which queen and Mortimer spent money is truly astonishing. Edward II left just under £62,000 in his treasury in November 1326, swollen by the forfeitures of the Despensers and the earl of Arundel to nearly £80,000.[23] By 1 December 1330, a few days after Mortimer's execution, a derisory forty-one pounds was left.[24]

The *French Chronicle of London* comments, 'The queen, Lady Isabel, and Sir Roger Mortimer, assumed to themselves royal power over many of the magnates of England and of Wales, and retained the treasures of the land themselves, and kept the young king wholly in subjection to themselves.' It further comments that Edward III realised that he had unwise counsel and that his realm was at the point of being lost, and the people too.[25] The *Brut* says, 'There was much loss and harm to all England; for the king and all the lords that should govern him were governed and ruled after [i.e. by] the king's mother Dame Isabel and by Sir Roger the Mortimer.' The chronicler also says that because of Isabella and Mortimer's counsel 'many harms, shames and reproofs have fallen unto the king' and criticises the way they wasted Edward II's treasure. Within a very short time, Isabella forfeited all her popularity of 1326: 'began the community of England to hate Isabel the queen, that so much loved her when she came to pursue the false traitors the Despensers from France', the *Brut* continues.[26] Isabella's toleration of her favourite's discourteous behaviour towards her son does not reflect well on her: she allowed Mortimer to remain seated in the king's presence, to walk ahead of him, and to tell Edward's friends that they owed loyalty to him rather than to the king. As Edward II had allowed his favourite Despenser to treat Isabella with disrespect, so she allowed her favourite Mortimer to treat her son with disrespect. As Despenser had persuaded Edward to confiscate Isabella's lands and reduce her income to lessen her political influence, so she kept her son short of money for the same reason. And as she had hidden her hatred of the Despensers, Edward III hid his hatred of Mortimer, while gathering about himself men with whom he could overthrow his mother's detested favourite. By 1330, most of Isabella and Mortimer's allies had turned from them in disgust: instead of the king and his ruthless greedy Marcher lord, the kingdom now suffered the queen and her ruthless greedy Marcher lord, hardly a great improvement. Edward III launched a coup against his mother and Mortimer at Nottingham Castle on 19 October 1330, shortly before his eighteenth birthday, and began ruling his kingdom himself, to the great relief of his subjects.

Whether Edward of Caernarfon, at Berkeley Castle, was aware that his wife and her favourite were sowing the seeds of their own destruction and repeating his mistakes is unknown. About Edward's state of mind during his imprisonment, or even how he passed his days, we have likewise no idea. As he lay in his room at Berkeley, Edward may or may not have known that outside the castle, he still had friends, men who had resolved to free him and restore him to the throne. The plot to remove him from Kenilworth in March had failed, but the men, fierce and fanatical supporters of the former king, were undeterred. Their leader was Thomas Dunheved, the Dominican friar whom the king had sent to the pope in 1324. Thomas was aided by his brother Stephen Dunheved, formerly lord of the manor of Dunchurch in Warwickshire – not another friar, as is often stated – who had been forced to abjure the realm, or voluntarily exile himself from England to avoid execution, after committing an unspecified felony. Stephen returned to England and had become a valet of Edward's chamber by mid-February 1322.[27] Stephen and Thomas Dunheved gathered about them a group of men equally determined to free him from Berkeley: Thomas 'travelled through England, not only secretly but even openly, stirring up the people of the south and north to rise for the deposed and imprisoned king and restore the kingdom to him'.[28] The *Brut* says that the Dominicans 'cast and ordained, both night and day, how they might bring him out of prison', and that Thomas Dunheved 'gathered a great company'.[29]

How Stephen and Thomas built their group cannot be known, but some former members of Edward II's household joined them, including three of his sergeants-at-arms, Roger atte Watre, Thomas de la Haye and John le Botiler.[30] The group's highest-profile member was Edmund Gascelyn, a knight, who witnessed grants of Hugh Despenser and his father on several occasions and is described in a petition of 1327 as a Despenser adherent.[31] Another member was Peter de la Rokele, under-sheriff of Buckinghamshire, another former adherent of Hugh Despenser and grandfather of William Langland (born *c.* 1325/30), one of the greatest poets of medieval England.[32] The group had a strong clerical element, including Robert Shulton, a Cistercian monk of Hailes Abbey in Gloucestershire; Henry de Rihale and John de Stoke, Dominican friars of Warwick; and John, a monk from the Cistercian abbey of Newminster. Edward II had stayed at Newminster, near Morpeth in Northumberland and 300 miles from Berkeley, on several occasions during his reign, the last time in August 1322. He must have made a powerful impression on John for the latter to leave his convent and travel to the other end of the country to fight for his former king, nearly five years after the last time he can have seen Edward. Other members included two parsons both called William Aylmer, and William Russell, parson of Huntley near Gloucester.

Roger Mortimer and Isabella got wind of the Dunheveds' plans, and as the fact that they were trying to free Edward of Caernarfon was too sensitive to commit to writing, ordered the known members of the group to be arrested on other charges – usually theft, breaking and entering, extortion and assault. The Patent Roll of March to July 1327 is full of entries accusing Dunheved adherents of these crimes, the important thing being to arrest and imprison them at all costs, as the thought of the former king of England wandering around freely in the company of men determined that he be free and perhaps even restored to the throne was too awful to contemplate.[33] At the beginning of May 1327, Stephen Dunheved and John de Stoke were to be arrested and 'taken to the king'. After early May, the gang disappeared for a month, then turned up in the North West, where Roger Mortimer and Isabella ordered the justice of Chester – Richard Damory, brother of Edward II's late favourite Roger – to arrest and imprison Thomas and Stephen Dunheved and other 'malefactors' gathering there who had 'perpetrated homicides and other crimes'.[34]

And the Dunheved group were not alone in plotting to restore Edward: his old friend Donald, earl of Mar 'returned to Scotland after the capture of the king, hoping to rescue him from captivity and restore him to his kingdom, as formerly, by the help of the Scots and of certain adherents whom the deposed king still had in England'.[35] Although Mar was in the north of England in the summer of 1327, leading one of the three columns of his uncle Robert Bruce's army against the new regime, his adherents gathered in the south-west of England and the Marches 'to do and procure the doing of what evils they can against the king [Edward III] and his subjects', that is, stirring up trouble on Edward of Caernarfon's behalf.[36] Mar, a great friend of Edward, was now described as the 'enemy and rebel' of his son, and Mortimer and Isabella ordered the arrest of two of his supporters in Staffordshire in August 1327 merely for sending letters to him.[37] On 14 July, they ordered the justice of Chester Richard Damory to imprison Richard le Brun, former mayor of the town, for adherence to Mar.[38] It is perhaps not a coincidence that the Dunheved brothers were in

Chester in June, and the town was a centre of disaffection in 1327, at least partly, perhaps, on Edward of Caernarfon's account: leading merchants were fined, and eighteen children imprisoned in the castle as hostages to ensure the citizens' good behaviour, at their own cost, as they had been 'disobedient and ill-behaved' towards Edward III.[39]

In the summer of 1327, Robert Bruce decided that the opportunity to take advantage of the political chaos in England was too good to resist: although Isabella and Mortimer sent envoys to negotiate a 'final peace' with him, the Scots launched an attack on England on 15 June, with Donald of Mar and Bruce's friends Thomas Randolph and James Douglas leading the three columns.[40] With Roger Mortimer, the most powerful man in England and Edward of Caernarfon's greatest enemy, safely out of the way hundreds of miles to the north, the Dunheved group could go ahead with their plan to liberate Edward. Probably in mid- to late June, they launched an attack on Berkeley Castle.

The truly astonishing thing is that the Dunheveds achieved their goal. This attack, which should have been a suicide mission with no chance of success, worked. The men managed to seize Edward, and even had time to plunder the castle before they fled into the Gloucestershire countryside, perhaps leaving a few dead bodies of their colleagues behind. Astonishing as this attack certainly was, we would have little knowledge of it were it not for the fortunate survival of a letter written by Thomas Berkeley on 27 July 1327 to John Hothum, chancellor of England, wherein Berkeley talks of 'some people indicted before me in the county of Gloucestershire, for coming towards the castle of Berkeley with an armed force, for having seized the father of our lord the king out of our keeping, and feloniously robbing the said castle'.[41] An entry on the Patent Roll five days later, granting Berkeley powers of arrest, names the same men as his letter, deeming them guilty of 'coming with an armed force to Berkeley Castle to plunder it, and refusing to join the king in his expedition against the Scots'.[42] Obviously the gang members had no intention of joining the Scottish expedition – and the clerics would never have been expected to – but this was a general accusation which would ensure that sheriffs would arrest them.[43] The writ judiciously omits any mention of Edward of Caernarfon.

What happened to Edward? It should be noted that Berkeley's letter does not explicitly state that the Dunheveds ever took him outside the castle, only that they managed to abduct him from Berkeley's custody. Although no direct evidence exists to confirm that Edward was ever recaptured, we may assume either that he was, or that the Dunheveds were forced to flee without him. Berkeley's letter betrays no alarm that Edward was wandering about freely, and while one might argue that he would not have dared commit such a sensitive fact to paper but would have ordered his messenger to inform Hothum orally, the tone of the letter is not what we would expect if he had been in a genuine panic that

Edward was at liberty. Also, more of Edward's friends conceived another plot to release him in early September, and they would surely have known if he were free.

Thomas Berkeley's letter also declares that 'I have heard from members of my household, who have seen and heard of it, that a great number of people have assembled in Buckinghamshire and other adjoining counties for the same cause'; that is, attempting to free Edward. This is unfortunately the only surviving evidence for this, the third (or part of the second, perhaps) plot to liberate him in 1327. However, Berkeley's letter states that two men whom he describes as 'great leaders of the company' were arrested in Dunstable, Bedfordshire – which borders Buckinghamshire – before the attack on Berkeley Castle, and 'are held there in prison'. They were John Norton, a clerk of Edward II, and John Redmere, formerly keeper of Edward's stud-farm, both of them Dominican friars. The Close Roll confirms that Norton and Redmere were in prison at Dunstable by 11 August 1327, and an order was issued on 21 October to send them and two other men held with them to the notorious Newgate prison in London.[44] Norton and Redmere petitioned Edward III, claiming that they had innocently been hearing Mass at the house of their order when the prior of Dunstable's bailiffs burst in, accused them of attempting to free Edward from Berkeley and threw them into prison, and that they were 'at point of death' as a result.[45] While Redmere subsequently vanishes from history, Norton's petition was successful: he was still alive in 1329.[46]

The *Annales Paulini* say that Thomas Dunheved, Dominican friar, was captured at Budbrooke near Warwick, 18 miles from his family home of Dunchurch, and taken to Isabella. Supposedly Thomas was caught while trying to escape from Pontefract Castle in Yorkshire, was thrown into a deep dungeon and died there in misery, though he may still have been alive in 1330.[47] His brother Stephen Dunheved fled to London, and the mayor and sheriffs were ordered to arrest him on 1 July 1327. He was captured and sent to Newgate, but escaped shortly before 7 June 1329.[48] Stephen reappears on record in 1330, when another order for his arrest was issued, this time for aiding the earl of Kent in his attempts to free the supposedly dead Edward II from prison. William Aylmer, parson of Deddington, was captured in Oxford shortly before 20 August 1327 and accused of 'consenting to and abetting the robbery of Berkeley Castle, and the taking of Edward of Carnarvan, the late king'.[49]

Most of the Dunheved gang were either dead, in prison or in hiding by the autumn of 1327 (Peter de la Rokele, for example, vanishes from the records for more than three years and reappears soon after Isabella and Mortimer's downfall).[50] And yet Edward still had supporters determined to free him, and in early September, they hatched yet another plot. The leader of this latest attempt was Rhys ap Gruffydd, formerly a squire of Edward's chamber, whom Edward appointed as an envoy to Isabella in

November 1326. Possibly, Donald of Mar also aided this latest attempt in person, and Sir Gruffydd Llwyd of North Wales, who had aided Edward during the Marcher campaign in 1322 and was a long-term ally of the king, also joined. The plot failed when it was betrayed to Roger Mortimer's deputy justice of Wales, William Shalford, on 7 September.[51] Roger Mortimer was in Wales at the time, and by 26 October had imprisoned thirteen conspirators at Caernarfon Castle, Edward's birthplace.[52] This plot is indirect proof that the Dunheveds had not succeeded in releasing Edward from Berkeley, or had done so only temporarily.

Although most of his kingdom had rejected him in 1326, and he had ended his reign wandering around Wales with a handful of supporters, the plots to free Edward of Caernarfon in 1327 show that he still had friends. The success of the Dunheveds' attack on Berkeley Castle demonstrates that this was no disorganised bunch of ruffians attracted by violence and plunder; the attack was well planned, well equipped and brilliantly executed. The number of arrest warrants issued, the warnings of malefactors gathering across numerous counties, Thomas Berkeley's statement that a 'large number of people' in Buckinghamshire and neighbouring counties were plotting on Edward's behalf, and the *Brut*'s comment that the Dunheveds had 'gathered a great company', suggest that there was a well-supported scheme to liberate Edward. The *Annales Paulini* even claim that 'certain magnates' supported the Dunheveds' plot to free Edward, though their identity is unknown.[53]

The latest plot to free Edward of Caernarfon convinced some men that he was too dangerous to be allowed to live. One of them, if we may believe the 1331 testimony of Hywel ap Gruffydd, one of Rhys ap Gruffydd's co-conspirators, was the deputy justice of Wales, William Shalford. Supposedly, Shalford sent a letter on 14 September 1327 to Mortimer. Hywel ap Gruffydd accused Shalford of complicity in the death of Edward II, and his testimony against Shalford runs:

> Rhys ap Gruffydd and others of his faction had assembled their power in South Wales and in North Wales, with the agreement of certain great lords of England, in order to forcibly deliver the said Lord Edward, father of our lord the king, who was then detained in a castle at Berkeley. And he [Shalford] also made clear in that letter that if the Lord Edward was freed, that Lord Roger Mortimer and all his people would die a terrible death by force and be utterly destroyed. On account of which the said William Shalford, like the traitor he is, counselled the said Roger that he ordain such a remedy in such a way that no one in England or Wales would think of effecting such deliverance.[54]

Again, we learn that 'certain great lords' supported Rhys's plot. In response to Shalford's letter, Mortimer allegedly sent a messenger, William Ockley, to Berkeley Castle to show Shalford's letter to Edward's custodians, and 'charged him to tell them to take counsel on the points contained in the letter and to quickly remedy the situation in order to avoid great peril'. Ockley, or Ockle or Ogle, was a man-at-arms and a rather obscure figure, convicted of the murder of Edward II in November 1330. He seems to have had connections in Ireland: in March 1326, he acted as attorney in Ireland for Stephen Ocle, probably his brother or cousin, and in 1327, lands in that country were restored to him.[55] Ockley is presumably the 'William de Okleye' who accompanied Roger Mortimer's wife Joan during her captivity in March 1322.[56]

Edward II is traditionally said to have been murdered at Berkeley Castle on 21 September 1327. Edward III heard the news of his father's death on the night of 23/24 September: the young king, not yet fifteen, sent a letter to his cousin the earl of Hereford informing him that 'my father has been commanded to God', and that he had heard the news the night before. The letter is dated at Lincoln on 24 September, and as we see, Edward III assumed the letter brought to him by Sir Thomas Gurney from Lord Berkeley was true and immediately began disseminating news of his father's demise.[57] A few days later, it was announced to parliament that Edward had died of natural causes – it is hard to imagine that anyone believed this – while the parliament of November 1330, the first one held after Isabella and Mortimer's downfall, gave the cause of Edward's death as murder for the first time. This later parliament convicted Thomas Gurney and William Ockley of the deed, but the parliamentary rolls say only that 'they falsely and treacherously murdered him'.[58] The method of the alleged murder was never stated. None of the murderers or anyone else involved with it ever spoke publicly about it, and no official government source ever stated the method, which leaves contemporary and later chronicles, none of whom knew the cause of death for certain. Gurney and Ockley, both sentenced to death in absentia, fled. Ockley was never heard of again; Gurney fled to Spain, where he was pursued by Edward III and where he died in 1333.[59] Roger Mortimer was also convicted of having had Edward of Caernarfon killed and on thirteen other charges, and Sir Simon Bereford was convicted of aiding Mortimer in all his felonies, including presumably Edward's murder. These two were executed. Edward II's custodian Thomas, Lord Berkeley was ultimately acquitted of any complicity in the former king's death and made a very curious speech to parliament, which we will examine later, and the other custodian Sir John Maltravers was never accused of any role in Edward's supposed murder either in 1330 or at any other point in his long life (he lived until 1364).

Fourteenth-century chronicles give a wide variety of causes for Edward's death, far more than one would guess nowadays from the almost inevitable statements by non-specialists that Edward was killed by having a red-hot poker inserted inside him.[60] This is emphatically not a certain historical fact. The *Annales Paulini* simply say that Edward died at Berkeley, the *Anonimalle* (whose author knew about the Dunheveds' plot to free Edward) says he died of an illness, and several continuations of the French Brut claim that he died *de grant dolour*, 'of great sorrow'.[61] Adam Murimuth thought at first that Edward had been murdered 'by a trick' and later wrote that he had been suffocated, and the Bridlington chronicler wrote that he did not believe the rumours which were current regarding Edward's death, presumably a reference to the infamous poker story.[62] *Lanercost* in the 1340s says that Edward died 'either by a natural death or by the violence of others', while the *Scalacronica* says, rather movingly, that Edward died 'by what manner was not known, but God knows it'.[63] A few chroniclers only say that Edward died at Berkeley, without further explanation; the *French Chronicle of London* says he was 'vilely murdered' but doesn't say how; the Wigmore chronicler was sure he died of natural causes; the Lichfield chronicler says he was strangled; and the Peterborough chronicler that he was well in the evening but dead by the morning.[64]

Chroniclers who give the 'red-hot poker' story include Ranulph Higden's *Polychronicon* of *c.* 1350 and the *Brut*, though the best-known account is Geoffrey le Baker's, of the 1350s:

> These cruel bullies, seeing that death by foetid odour would not overcome so vigorous a man, during the night of 22 [*sic*] September, suddenly seized hold of him as he lay on his bed. With the aid of enormous pillows and a weight heavier than that of fifteen substantial men they pressed down upon him until he was suffocated. With a plumber's red-hot iron, inserted through a horn leading to the inmost parts of the bowel, they burned out the respiratory organs beyond the intestines, taking care that no wound should be discernible on the royal body...[65]

Baker goes on to say that Edward's screams penetrated the walls of the castle to Berkeley village beyond, where many of the inhabitants fell to their knees and prayed on hearing the dreadful sound. The ludicrousness of this scenario – why bother with a red-hot poker when you have fifteen men and enormous pillows and could simply suffocate the victim? – did not stop writers of later decades repeating the story. Near the end of the fourteenth century, the writer John Trevisa, chaplain of Berkeley, translated the *Polychronicon* into English, and copied the poker story without comment. It is sometimes argued that Trevisa must have known this story was accurate, as he grew up in the village of Berkeley and was a small boy there at the time of Edward's death, served Edward's custodian Thomas, Lord Berkeley as chaplain and must have heard him confess to the murder, and would therefore not have translated the passage without comment had he known it to be untrue. This is all false. Trevisa came from Cornwall, and wasn't born until around 1342, fifteen years after Edward's alleged murder.[66] The Thomas, Lord Berkeley he served as chaplain was not Edward's custodian of 1327 but his grandson of the same name, who was born in 1353 and died in 1417. Trevisa did not arrive at Berkeley until 1388, long after the death of Edward's custodian and more than sixty years after Edward's supposed murder. He had no more knowledge about it than anyone else, and no more than Higden, author of the *Polychronicon*, who was a monk of Chester, 160 miles from Berkeley.

There are many reasons to reject the lurid, sensationalist story of the red-hot poker, despite its frequent repetition in the centuries since 1327. Firstly, the assumed reason for this grotesque method was to kill Edward without leaving a mark on his body – as stated by Baker and repeated numerous times ever since. Yet Baker also says that the villagers of Berkeley heard Edward's screams. It makes no sense to avoid leaving marks on Edward's body, yet ensure that the manner of death was so agonising that he screamed loudly, so that the nearby villagers would have known that he was being murdered. Secondly, it is not at all certain that this method would kill a person quickly; it might take hours or days for the victim to die. Thirdly, there was no reason for Gurney and Ockley to use such a pointlessly sadistic method which they couldn't have known beforehand would work, when much easier and tried and tested methods were at hand. Something as terrible as killing a king would surely have required them to use the easiest, quickest and most effective method they could devise. Roger Mortimer had escaped from the Tower in 1323 by drugging his guards, and knew how to procure sedatives. Gurney and Ockley could have drugged Edward and smothered him, or given him enough sedation that he would never wake up. It is doubtful that anyone would have recognised any signs of smothering on Edward's dead body. Strangulation would probably have left marks around the neck, but these could have easily been covered up. Fourthly, the red-hot poker story seems a bit too convenient, as a 'fitting' punishment for Edward's presumed sexual acts with men. In the late thirteenth and early fourteenth centuries, various manuscripts circulated about the death of Edmund Ironside (died 1016), who was supposed to have been murdered on the privy with a dagger inserted inside his bowels, and Edward's own brother-in-law the earl of Hereford had been killed at Boroughbridge with a pike thrust inside his anus.[67] These stories could have been seized on in the common imagination as a likely cause of the former king's death.

For a month, from 21 September to 20 October, Edward of Caernarfon's body lay in the chapel of Berkeley Castle guarded and looked after by only one man: a royal sergeant-at-arms named William Beaukaire, who was presumably a Frenchman, as Beaucaire is a town near Avignon. Beaukaire was a decidedly odd choice for the duty. Six months earlier, he had been one of the garrison who held out at Hugh Despenser's castle of Caerphilly against the queen for four months, for which he was pardoned with the rest in March 1327.[68] Among his comrades in the castle were former members of Edward II's household and Roger atte Watre of the Dunheved gang, also a royal sergeant-at-arms, by now probably dead, in prison or in hiding for his role in freeing the former king. Beaukaire seems to have arrived at Berkeley shortly before Edward's death.[69] Precisely why, of all people, a man who had been an adherent of Edward and Despenser arrived at Berkeley around the time Edward was supposedly murdered is uncertain, and why he was the only man watching the body for an entire month is also a difficult question to answer. Even if Beaukaire had completely renounced his former allegiance and was demonstrating his fervent loyalty to the new regime by participating in Edward's murder, it is odd that, of all the men who could have been sent to guard Edward of Caernarfon's body, a former presumed Despenser adherent should have been chosen.

Royal clerk and chronicler Adam Murimuth says that many knights, abbots, priors and burgesses of Bristol and Gloucester came to see Edward's body 'by invitation'.[70] Unfortunately, he doesn't give their names, specify what 'many' means – ten, fifty, a hundred? – whether they came all at once or individually or in small groups, whether they viewed the body at Berkeley Castle or after it had been moved to Gloucester a month later, or the motives for the invitation: to make sure that Edward was really dead, to identify the body as his, or merely as a ceremonial duty to mark the passing of a former king. We may assume that at least some of these men would have known Edward by sight. None of his own family, however, visited Berkeley to view the body. The Berkeley family historian John Smyth, writing in the early seventeenth century, claimed that Thomas Gurney returned from court with orders to keep Edward's death a secret locally until 1 November 1327.[71] Whether that is true or not, it is highly unlikely that Thomas Berkeley would have started circulating news of Edward's death until he knew the young king had been informed. This means that he had to wait for at least a week – Thomas Gurney returned to Berkeley Castle from Lincoln on or shortly before 29 September – before sending out messengers inviting the abbots, knights and others to Berkeley to view Edward's body. A week for Lord Berkeley to be sure that Edward III knew of the death, several days for messengers to ride to Gloucester and Bristol, several more days for the witnesses to receive the message and travel to Berkeley – assuming that is where the viewing took place – means that at least two weeks passed after Edward's death before any independent observer could have seen his body. Murimuth claims that the men saw the body whole (*integrum*), which seems unlikely, as it is reasonable to assume that Edward was embalmed soon after death, if only to prevent bodily decay; Edward III was embalmed immediately after death in 1377. We know for certain that Edward II's heart was removed during the embalming process, as Thomas Berkeley bought a silver casket in which to place it and send it to the queen, and it was not a royal physician who performed the embalming but a local woman, whose name is lost to history. (Heart removal was an entirely normal practice in royal burials at this time.) Payment for embalming materials appears on Thomas Berkeley's household rolls for the period ending 28 September.[72] Therefore, Edward's body was most probably not 'whole'. Adam Murimuth's most controversial statement, however, is that the knights, abbots and others observed (*conspexissent*) Edward's body superficially, *superficialiter*. Precisely what Murimuth was trying to convey with this statement is frustratingly unclear. Royal embalming involved covering the body with cerecloth, or wax-impregnated linen, including the face.[73] We cannot say for sure whether the men saw Edward's face, and 'superficially' implies they were only permitted a brief or distant glance at the body.

On 21 October 1327, Edward's body was taken in state on a black-covered carriage the fifteen miles from Berkeley Castle to Gloucester, where it had been decided that he would be buried. Other men stayed with the body from this time: one was the bishop of Llandaff, John Eaglescliff, a Dominican friar. Given Edward's great and reciprocated affection for the Dominican order, this was a thoughtful gesture, perhaps by Edward III or Isabella. Others were two royal knights, two chaplains, two royal sergeants and Andrew, a candle-maker, and William Beaukaire also stayed with the body until the day of the funeral.[74] Edward's body remained unburied at St Peter's Abbey (now Gloucester Cathedral) for two months. It originally lay on a hearse brought from London, but from 24 November was moved to a special one newly built, which had four gilded lions and standing figures of the four evangelists, and was decorated by eight incense-burners in the forms of angels and two more lions.[75] Eight hundred gold leaves were bought to gild a leopard decorating the cover lying over Edward's body, with more purchased to decorate leopards on to standards, banners and horse coverings.[76] The body lay in a coffin and was not visible to the public: a wooden image or effigy in Edward's likeness wearing a copper gilt crown and the robes he had worn to his coronation was used instead. Forty shillings was paid for the carving of the wooden image, and oak barriers were placed around the hearse to keep the crowds away.[77] The visitors did not and could not have seen Edward's face or body.

Very little is known about Edward's funeral of 20 December 1327 itself, as no details survive, except that it cost over £350.[78] The three-month delay since his death was normal: his father died on 7 July 1307 and was buried on 27 October, and his widow Isabella died on 22 August 1358 and was buried on 27 November. What was highly unusual was the use of the wooden effigy, the first time one is known to have been used in a royal burial in western European history.[79] Edward III, now fifteen, his mother Isabella and Roger Mortimer certainly attended. Edward II's younger half-brother Edmund of Woodstock, earl of Kent, and niece Elizabeth de Burgh, were there, and so presumably were his other half-brother Thomas of Brotherton, earl of Norfolk, his cousin Henry of Lancaster, many other magnates and prelates, and perhaps Edward's younger children John, Eleanor and Joan. Roger Mortimer had himself a new black tunic made for the occasion. Three years later, he would be dragged to his execution wearing it.[80] After Edward of Caernarfon's funeral, Edward III, Queen Isabella, Roger Mortimer and the court moved on to Worcester. In January 1328, Isabella summoned the woman who had embalmed her husband's body to her, though to what purpose and what the woman said to her is not known.

Normally, when a man's body lies in state for two months and his funeral takes place in the presence of dozens or hundreds of people, including his own family, we know that his life has ended and may bring our account of it to a close. But for Edward II, that most unconventional, complex and contradictory of men, nothing could ever be that simple.

Edward was not dead.

17

The Curious Case of the King Who Lived

On 14 January 1330, William Melton, archbishop of York and a long-term friend and ally of Edward II (whom he had known well since at least 1297), sent an extraordinary letter to the mayor of London, Simon Swanland.[1] Begging Swanland to keep what he wrote secret, Melton told him,

> We have certain news of our liege lord Edward of Caernarfon, that he is alive and in good health of body, in a safe place at his own wish [or command] ... We beg you as dearly as we trust in you that you procure for us a loan of £200 in gold, if you can have it, for the comfort of and in secret, taken to the said lord for us, and that you obtain two half cloths of different colours, good cloth and intimate clothing and good fur of miniver for six garments and three hoods of miniver, and two coverlets of different colours of the larger size, with the hangings, and two belts and two bags, the best that you can find for sale, and twenty ells of linen cloth, and send for his Cordovan leather so that we have six pairs of shoes and two pairs of boots, and have the above-mentioned things bundled up together ... and come to us as soon as you can to advise us how we will procure such a great sum of money for the said lord, as we wish that he may be helped as far as we and you are able to arrange...

The archbishop was so certain Edward of Caernarfon was alive that he ordered provisions for him, the focus on clothing explained by Swanland being a draper who had often supplied cloth to Edward's household. Melton was far from being the only person utterly convinced of the former king's survival years after his funeral. Edward's half-brother the earl of Kent was executed in March 1330 after admitting to parliament that he had attempted to free Edward from Corfe Castle in Dorset. Many men joined Kent's conspiracy and were either arrested or fled the country, and the plan had advanced far enough that arrangements had been made for Edward to be transferred by boat from Corfe along the coast to Kent's castle of Arundel in Sussex. In late 1329, Edward's Scottish friend Donald, earl of Mar, promised to come to England with an army to effect Edward's release. Some of the men who aided the earl of Kent and the archbishop of York's plans to free Edward sought refuge with Edward's nephew the duke of Brabant and plotted an invasion of England, intending to land near Scotland with Mar's help. Proclamations were issued declaring that anyone who stated that the former king was alive would be arrested, and half the country was wondering if it was true. Many people in Wales supported Rhys ap Gruffydd, one of the men who firmly believed that Edward was still alive, and the earl of Kent's adherents were thought to be particularly numerous in East Anglia. In short, many people in England, Wales, Scotland and on the Continent strongly believed that Edward of Caernarfon was alive years after his alleged death and were, in various ways, attempting to help him.

Exactly what happened to whom at Berkeley Castle in September 1327 will never be known for certain. A body was shown 'superficially' to a group of knights, abbots and burgesses, and was buried at Gloucester on 20 December 1327. The body was never visually displayed to the public, as the face was (almost certainly) covered in waxed cloth and the body encased in a coffin, with a covering decorated with a gilded leopard and a wooden effigy on top of it. Even at Edward's funeral, it seems apparent that his face was not uncovered, even to his family and friends, as his brother Kent and the archbishop of York were later completely convinced that he was alive.[2] It is reasonable to assume that Kent was not satisfied that anyone else had seen Edward's face and body closely enough to identify him properly either. As the earl, in attempting to free the supposedly dead king in 1329/30, must have known that he might suffer grave penalties for his actions (as he did; he was beheaded), he would hardly have acted the way he did without being entirely certain that neither he nor anyone else had seen Edward dead. The same applies to Archbishop Melton, and to knights of south-west England, such as Ingelram Berenger and Nicholas Dauney, who may have attended Edward's funeral in Gloucester and may have been among the men previously invited to see his body 'superficially', and who joined Kent and the archbishop in 1329/30.

William Melton's letter tantalises with the things he did not say: where Edward was, whether contact had been made with him directly, what happened at Berkeley in September 1327, how Edward was safe at his own wish or command, which implies that he somehow had control of his current situation. Probably Melton thought it imprudent to commit these details to parchment and told his messenger William Cliff – perhaps the man of this name who was once Hugh Despenser's attorney – to inform Swanland orally. His request to Swanland to have the £200 secretly 'taken to the said lord for us' implies that he knew how to gain access to Edward and that his messenger informed Swanland of the location. Melton must have had what he thought was extremely convincing evidence of Edward's survival to write such a letter, and he pledged the vast sum of £5,000 and declared that he would sell everything he owned, except for one vestment and one chalice, to help the former king. When interrogated in April 1330 about his part in the affair, Melton said that he had heard from a William Kingsclere on 10 October 1329 that Edward was alive. Kingsclere is hard to trace, and Melton did not state what proof he furnished, but obviously the archbishop found it plausible and compelling. The earl of Kent's confession as recorded by Adam Murimuth says that a friar who raised the devil informed him that Edward II was alive. *Lanercost* names this friar as none other than Thomas Dunheved.[3] It is impossible that men such as the bishop of London and the numerous others would have supported Kent on the strength of a devil-raising friar, so either this bizarre detail was inserted into the confession to discredit Kent, or he himself invented it to protect his real source.

Melton asking Swanland for £200 in gold, in limited circulation in England but useful on the Continent, indicates that the plan was not to try to restore Edward to the throne, at least not yet, but to send him somewhere abroad. Where this might have been is a matter for speculation: perhaps Ireland, where a letter of the 1330s claims he did in fact go after escaping from Berkeley; Castile, his mother's homeland; Scotland, where he could count on the support of Robert Bruce's nephew the earl of Mar; the papal court in Avignon, where the 1330s letter also says he went; or Brabant, where his sister Margaret still lived and his nephew ruled, and where some of the men plotting on his behalf in 1330 gathered. Duke John III of Brabant allowed Kent to meet two of his supporters in his chamber in Paris.[4] It is also unclear what the purpose was of sending Edward overseas: to keep him hidden away in secret, to give him an opportunity to raise an army, or to use his presence abroad to threaten Isabella and Mortimer in some way.

Kent believed his half-brother to be at Corfe Castle. It seems almost certain that Edward was indeed held at Corfe at some point. Adam Murimuth states 'Edward was secretly removed from Berkeley by night and taken to Corfe and other secret places'. The *Brut* author believed he was murdered at Corfe.[5] The association of Edward of Caernarfon with Corfe is very strong, and that Edward was outside Berkeley at some point is confirmed by the castle records, which say that one Henry Pecche was his guardian 'at Berkeley and elsewhere'. In September 1327, Edward's joint legal custodian John Maltravers was paid over £258 from Berkeley Castle accounts for 'services to the king's father in Dorset', and received letters from Lord Berkeley at Corfe.[6]

More than seventy named men aided the earl of Kent in his plot to free Edward of Caernarfon in 1329/30 and presumably shared his belief in Edward's survival, and the searches for his adherents across the south of England and Wales, recorded in the chancery rolls, indicate that the true number was far higher than this. Simon Swanland's role was never discovered, and Melton and his messenger William Cliff kept quiet about his involvement. Many others, however, were arrested between March and August 1330, or fled the country. They included the earl of Buchan, the bishop and a former sheriff of London, Edward's nephew Edward Monthermer, his great-nephew, Hugh Despenser's eldest son Huchon (in prison at Bristol Castle), numerous men who had been in Edward's household, former adherents of the Despensers including Hugh's confessor Richard Bliton, Rhys ap Gruffydd and Sir Gruffydd Llwyd's son Ieuan, lords, knights, sheriffs, clerks, squires, chaplains, friars, monks, merchants, and men so obscure they cannot be traced. Even Thomas Wake, who played a vital role in Edward II's deposition in January 1327, joined the plot and had fled from England by 4 April 1330. William la Zouche, one of the men who captured Edward and Hugh Despenser on 16 November 1326, was another Kent supporter, and told the earl that freeing Edward 'would be the greatest honour that ever befell him'.[7] The majority of the men, however, had once been close and loyal to Edward II, and thus it is likely that they genuinely believed in his survival and wanted to help him. The participation of Stephen Dunheved, a fanatical supporter of Edward imprisoned at Newgate prison for trying to rescue him in 1327, suggests he truly believed Edward was alive, as does the participation of Edward's close friend William, abbot of Langdon and many of his former servants and other friends, such as William Aune, Peter Bernard, John Harsik, Roger Audley, Adam Wetinhale, William Marenny, Giles of Spain, John de Toucestre and John Coupland. Kent has often unfairly been condemned as stupid and gullible by modern historians unable otherwise to explain his plot in the light of their certainty that Edward of Caernarfon was dead.[8] Kent was not stupid, and even if he were, Archbishop Melton, Bishop Stephen Gravesend of London, the earl of Mar and the countless others who shared his belief and acted on it were not.

Kent's supporter Ingelram Berenger, a Somerset knight pardoned for adherence to the Despensers in 1327, went to the earl to tell him that Sir John Pecche of Warwickshire would help the plot in any way he could.[9] This is highly significant, because Pecche was constable of Corfe Castle until replaced by John Maltravers on 24 September 1329. He also had links to Thomas and Stephen Dunheved's brother John.[10] Clearly Pecche was in an excellent position to know the truth of Edward of Caernarfon's incarceration at the castle, and would not have joined the earl of Kent's plot to free him, with his son Nicholas, had he not been entirely sure that Edward was alive there – something which was easily within in his power to check.

The men trying to free Edward in 1330 were punished when the plot came to light. The earl of Kent died for it. Archbishop Melton, Bishop Gravesend and others were indicted before King's Bench. Many men were imprisoned and their lands and goods seized; Sir William Cleydon died in prison, and John Pecche was one of those who lost all his lands and goods. Others fled the country and did not return until Edward III took over governance of his own kingdom. These men did not act on a whim, or because they were gullible and stupid; they were sure that the former king was alive and risked a great deal to free him. Donald of Mar was even willing to bring an army to England to help his friend, and promised the archbishop of York that he would raise 40,000 men, an impossibly large number (almost three times the size of Edward II's army at Bannockburn), but Mar's exaggeration demonstrates his determination to help Edward.[11]

If a large number of influential people firmly believed in Edward II's survival and acted on it despite the grave penalties they knew they would suffer in case of failure, then clearly there is an extremely high chance that Edward was indeed alive. A common modern explanation for the plot by writers convinced that he was dead by then is that the men who took part in it did not really believe he was alive, but were merely expressing their dissatisfaction with the regime of Queen Isabella and Roger Mortimer. They didn't need to pretend belief in the former king's survival to do that. Henry of Lancaster and many allies rebelled against the pair in late 1328 without using his cousin's name, and Richard Fitzalan, son of the executed earl of Arundel, attempted to raise an army against them in June 1330 also without mentioning Edward. William Melton's letter to Simon Swanland begged the latter not to reveal the startling news to 'any man or woman of the world', hardly the words of a man trying to start an uprising in the former king's name, and if everyone had known for sure that Edward II was dead, invoking his name in a rebellion – even if it perhaps provided a useful rallying call – would not have threatened Mortimer and Isabella. Henry of Lancaster was not tried for treason and executed or imprisoned in 1329 for raising an army and openly rebelling against the Crown, yet somehow the earl of Kent had to be beheaded for trying to free a dead man. Henry of Lancaster himself told the mayor of London John de Grantham on 5 November 1328 that Kent had told him certain things which he could not put into writing, but of which his messenger would inform the mayor orally.[12]

Kent's execution for a non-existent crime would make far more sense if the plot was real, Edward II was alive, and Kent, William Melton and the others really were on the brink of freeing him from Corfe Castle. The merciless speed with which the earl was tried and killed suggests that Isabella and Mortimer knew the plot was a genuine one and nearing fruition. The thought of the former king at liberty outside England, with powerful allies such as the duke of Brabant, the earls of Mar and Buchan and even the pope – Kent claimed to have the support of John XXII, whom he visited to discuss Edward's 'deliverance' in June 1329 – must have been extremely threatening to them. From the evidence we have, it is possible to work out how events were meant to unfold. Simon Swanland's men would try to gain access to Edward at Corfe and give him the money, clothes and shoes ordered by Melton from Swanland. It may be that Melton wrote to more men he trusted at this time to ask for other provisions to be taken to Edward as well, but the letters have not survived. It may also be that he had heard Edward's life at Corfe, though safe, was not comfortable, hence his wish to provide warm fur-lined clothes, coverlets and hangings for him, or perhaps these items were intended for the chilly sea journey from Dorset to Sussex in the late winter of 1330. John Gymmynges, another former Despenser adherent and valet of Edward II's chamber, and his cousin, a monk of Quarr Abbey on the Isle of Wight, were to provide three sailing vessels to take Edward and the earl of Kent to Kent's castle at Arundel. Kent evidently had it in mind to be present in person when Edward was freed. A writ to all the sheriffs of England declared that the earl 'had made alliance on both sides of the sea to assemble a force of men-at-arms'.[13] Perhaps he intended to take this armed force and either attack Corfe or, using his authority as a son, brother and uncle of kings, simply demand entry and leave with Edward. The three boats may have been intended to carry the men-at-arms as well as Kent and Edward. Kent's confession only says that after they had reached Arundel Castle, Edward would have been taken 'whithersoever should have been appointed', presumably in consultation with Melton, their other allies and of course Edward himself.[14] Unfortunately, Kent made the fatal error of asking his wife Margaret Wake to write a letter to his brother, telling him, 'I shall ordain for you that you shall soon come out of prison'. He was betrayed by John Deveril and Bogo de Bayouse of the Corfe garrison, who sent the letter to Roger Mortimer.[15] The earl, a brave honourable man, died on the scaffold in Winchester on 19 March 1330. He left his heavily pregnant widow Margaret and three small children, one of whom, Joan, was the mother of Richard II.

And there is other evidence which points to Edward II's survival past 1327. Sometime in the 1330s, an Italian papal notary called Manuel Fieschi, a nobleman by birth and appointed bishop of Vercelli in 1343, wrote a fascinating letter to Edward III. In it, he explained how Edward II escaped from Berkeley Castle in 1327, which story Fieschi claimed to have heard from the mouth of Edward himself. A servant, also called his custodian, told Edward that Thomas Gurney and Simon Bereford were coming to kill him. To save himself, Edward killed a sleeping porter, and, using the porter's keys to let himself out of the castle, fled with the unnamed servant and went to Corfe, where he stayed for a year and a half. Meanwhile, Edward said, the porter's body was buried as his at Gloucester. When at Corfe, he heard that his half-brother Kent had been executed, so he left there and went to Ireland, where he remained for nine months, that is, until Roger Mortimer's arrest and execution in late 1330. Dressed as a hermit, he briefly touched at Sandwich, from where he sailed to Normandy and travelled through France to Avignon, where he met John XXII and spent fifteen days with him, in secret. Edward then travelled to Brabant, Cologne and through Germany to Milan, to the hermitage of *Milasci* (probably Mulazzo in the Val di Magra); he stayed there for two years, and, finally, moved on to the hermitage of Cecima in the diocese of Pavia, where he remained for another two years.[16] Although the letter does not state directly that Edward II was still alive at the time of writing, neither does it say that he was dead.

In their belief that Edward died at Berkeley in 1327, many modern historians reject the contents of the letter, but have failed to explain adequately why an Italian churchman would have written such a letter to the king of England had he not firmly believed that his father was alive. Blackmail has been suggested as Fieschi's motive, but had Edward III known for certain that his father was dead, of course blackmail could never have been effective. Edward II himself, who certainly saw his father's body in July 1307, would never have been susceptible to a blackmail demand over Edward I still being alive. The mere existence of Fieschi's letter implies that that it was known to at least some people in Europe that there was doubt over Edward's death and that Fieschi knew Edward III had not properly seen his father's body. Even if we assume that Fieschi was deceived by a clever impostor, though his letter nowhere refers to the man he met as such – he calls him 'your father', i.e. Edward III's – this still implies his uncertainty about whether Edward had truly died in 1327 or not, and he must have had some reason for this doubt.

The letter contains a chronological error: Kent's execution followed two and a half years after Edward's supposed murder, not eighteen months as the letter states, though perhaps this is just a scribal error. The letter is in some ways problematic, for example the notion that Edward could escape from Berkeley simply by killing one man. After the Dunheveds successfully attacked the castle and seized Edward, it is most unlikely to have been guarded by only one porter, who moreover was asleep at the time. Edward's fleeing to Corfe Castle, and staying there for so long without the garrison noticing or recognising him, is also hard to explain. The letter names Thomas Gurney and Simon Bereford as Edward's would-be killers, though the November 1330 parliament found Gurney and William Ockley guilty. Then again, Simon Bereford was condemned to death at this parliament for aiding Roger Mortimer in all his felonies, including presumably the murder of Edward II. Edward knew Gurney and Bereford, who were knights, but surely had no idea who the man-at-arms Ockley was, and if we assume that Edward really did meet Manuel Fieschi, perhaps he heard that Gurney had been sentenced to death for his murder and that Bereford had been executed, and put two and two together. The detail in the early part of the letter, which describes Edward's attempt to sail from Chepstow in October 1326, being captured by Henry of Lancaster in Glamorgan and escorted to Kenilworth and later Berkeley, 'his' heart being sent to Isabella, John Maltravers being at Corfe in September 1327, is accurate and much of it could not have been known to an outsider. Edward's putting to sea at Chepstow on 20 October 1326, for example, is mentioned in no chronicle and is known only from his last chamber account, which fortunately still survives.[17] If the man who met Manuel Fieschi and told him this story was not Edward II, he must have been someone very close to him.

There is another Italian connection with Edward. When his son Edward III was in Koblenz, Germany, in September 1338, his wardrobe book records a payment to William le Galeys, 'who says he is the king's father' and who was taken to Edward III by Francisco the Lombard, i.e. of Lombardy in Italy. At Antwerp a few weeks later, the same man, now called Francekino Forcet or in modern spelling Francisco Forcetti, received money for his expenses looking after William le Galeys, who 'calls himself king of England and the father of the present king'. The name le Galeys means 'the Welshman', and Edward II was of course born in Wales.[18] As with the Fieschi letter, there is nothing in Edward III's wardrobe book which names le Galeys as an impostor or says that his claim to be the king's father was false, and the keeper of Edward III's wardrobe, William Norwell, had known Edward II well and served him from 1313 onwards.[19] At a time when royal pretenders were almost invariably executed, as with John of Powderham in 1318, William le Galeys met Edward III at the king's expense and spent time with him and perhaps Queen Philippa (Edward and Philippa's son Lionel was born in Antwerp in November 1338).[20] Almost certainly le Galeys was the same man who met John XXII and Manuel Fieschi. Two of Edward II's closest friends bore the name William, the archbishop of York and the abbot of Langdon, so if William le Galeys really was the former king, this might explain the name he took.

One final piece of evidence to consider in relation to Edward II's survival is the testimony to the November 1330 parliament of Thomas, Lord Berkeley, Edward's joint legal custodian at Berkeley Castle in 1327. Lord Berkeley's father-in-law Roger Mortimer was sentenced to death at this parliament, and executed on 29 November. Berkeley's brother-in-law and Edward's other custodian, John Maltravers, was sentenced to death in absentia for his role in the entrapment and execution of the earl of

Kent some months before, as were John Deveril and Bogo de Bayouse. Thomas Gurney and William Ockley were also condemned to death in absentia because they 'falsely and treacherously murdered' Edward II. Berkeley was asked how he wished to acquit himself of complicity in the king's death. His very odd reply, as recorded by a clerk in Latin, was: 'He never consented to his death, either by helping or by procuring it, and he never knew of his death until this present parliament.'[21] Lord Berkeley thus stated that he hadn't known Edward II was dead until he came to parliament, when the king was meant to have died in his own castle more than three years previously. Berkeley's words have often been translated and interpreted over-elaborately to make them fit into the notion that Edward was killed at Berkeley Castle: that Lord Berkeley really meant he didn't know Edward had been murdered, or that he didn't know the circumstances of his death. His words, however, simply mean 'he never knew of (or about) his death until the present parliament'. No more, no less.

It is true that no fourteenth-century chronicle says that Edward survived, and all say he died in 1327, giving a wide variation of causes of death, including that he died naturally or of illness or grief. This wide variation, in fact, demonstrates how little faith we should place in chronicle evidence for Edward's supposed death. None of them knew what happened at Berkeley and they were merely repeating stories they had heard or giving what they thought was a plausible explanation for the sudden death of a previously strong and healthy forty-three-year-old king. The people who knew about Edward's death or otherwise, Mortimer, Berkeley, Maltravers, Gurney, Ockley and probably Isabella, never spoke publicly about it, and chroniclers were as prone to believing and repeating mere rumour as anyone else, and frequently did so, especially near the end of Edward II's reign. Men who knew Edward well and cared about him, such as his half-brother Kent and his loyal friends, such as the archbishop of York, Stephen Dunheved, the earl of Mar and the abbot of Langdon, are a more reliable source for what happened to him than chroniclers who never saw him and in many cases were writing decades later and hundreds of miles away. Even Adam Murimuth, the only chronicler in the south-west of England in September 1327 (albeit almost a hundred miles away from Berkeley, in Exeter) changed his mind about the cause of death, saying at first somewhat cryptically that Edward died 'by a trick', then later that he was suffocated. Clearly Murimuth, though a clerk in royal service, had no more reliable information than anyone else, and also wrongly thought that Maltravers was one of Edward's killers. It was widely believed in 1327 and beyond that Edward was dead, as the information came from seemingly the most authoritative source there could be, his son the king himself. Yet the young Edward III immediately began spreading the news solely on the basis of Thomas Berkeley's letter, long before he could have sent anyone to Berkeley Castle to verify that it was true, and there is no evidence that he ever sent anyone there at all to see his father's body. And here came Thomas Berkeley to parliament three years later and announced that despite sending this letter, he had not previously known of the former king's death. As Ian Mortimer points out, 'the whole edifice of chronicle and record evidence that Edward II died was founded on a deception'.[22]

Having accepted in 1327 that his father was dead and spread the news without checking, having attended Edward II's funeral and marked the anniversary of his death every year, Edward III had no choice in 1330 but to continue the charade. To this end, Thomas Gurney and William Ockley were convicted in parliament of having killed him, but evaded execution. Roger Mortimer, also charged with Edward's murder, was hanged, but he was convicted on thirteen other charges which demonstrate Edward III's fury at his mother's favourite usurping his royal power. The young king was always going to execute Mortimer; adding the charge of killing Edward II made no difference, and confirmed in people's minds that the former king truly was dead. The last thing Edward III would have wanted was for him to be known to be alive, which might have resulted in civil war and the young king accused of treason, even forced to give up his throne to his father. Edward II's deposition was of very dubious legality and it was by no means impossible that he could have made himself king again, though whether he would have wanted to is another matter. Still, Edward III could not take the risk.

The main reason why Edward was murdered in 1327, so the argument goes, was that a deposed king is always dangerous, and that the plots to free him and perhaps restore him to the throne threatened Isabella and Mortimer, who thus had him killed to safeguard their position and that of Isabella's son. Edward II restored to power would certainly have had Mortimer cruelly executed and probably made strenuous attempts to have his marriage to Isabella annulled, so on the face of it they did have a strong motive to want him dead. The earl of Kent, however, knew Isabella (his sister-in-law and first cousin) and Mortimer very well, as did William Melton, and evidently they had good reasons for believing the pair had not had Edward killed. A motive to kill, or what we perceive with centuries of hindsight to be a motive, is not evidence, and when examining Edward II's deposition and presumed death we must remember that the murders of other deposed English kings, Richard II, Henry VI and Edward V, lay far in the future. Simply because we know that their successors had these later kings murdered to protect themselves does not necessarily mean that in 1327 anyone in England assumed Edward II should suffer the same fate. Edward's deposition was a new and revolutionary act in England, which we must not forget in the knowledge that it later became reasonably common. Henry IV had his cousin Richard II killed in 1400, and Edward IV his more distant cousin Henry VI killed in 1471, but Edward II was succeeded by his son, who was no patricide and who would be sure to punish anyone who hurt his father when he came of age.

Pretending that the king was dead gave Roger Mortimer and Isabella all the advantages of a truly dead king without the disadvantages of committing regicide and, in Isabella's case, the murder of her own husband. There is nothing to suggest that the queen, despite her rebellion against the Despensers and by extension Edward, desired his death, or that she was under Mortimer's thumb and would have stood by without protest as he had Edward murdered. It is far more probable that she refused to allow him to be killed and demanded that another solution be found.[23] Isabella was never accused of any role in it, and although it is understandable that Edward III might wish to draw a veil over his mother's complicity in his father's murder, her affectionately referring to Edward in 1325/26 as her 'very sweet heart' and her 'very dear and very sweet lord and friend', publicly grieving for the collapse of their marriage and avenging herself savagely on the man she held responsible for it, sending Edward gifts and wishing to visit him in 1327, suggest that she still loved him, not that she loathed him and wanted him dead. It is a huge step from anger and grief to having your husband and the father of your children killed in cold blood, and there is no evidence that she ever took this step. Isabella, daughter of two sovereigns, sister of three kings, who knew from the age of three that she would marry Edward and be his queen, was a woman with a profound and sacred sense of royalty, and it is hard to imagine how she could have tolerated the murder of a man as royal as she herself. After Isabella and Mortimer fell from power, her son Edward III treated her with every respect, and she lived an entirely conventional life as a dowager queen. She was not, as is still often stated today, locked up at Castle Rising and she did not go mad. She died at Hertford Castle in August 1358 and was buried at the Greyfriars church in London with the clothes she had worn at her wedding to Edward in 1308, and with his heart on her breast. It is merely a romantic myth that she chose to lie next to Roger Mortimer; he was buried in Coventry.[24]

The fact remains that a body was buried at Gloucester in December 1327, and if it was not Edward II's, whose was it? This is a question we unfortunately cannot answer; likewise, we cannot know whether the man standing in for the former king died naturally or not. Edward himself thought the sleeping castle porter he killed was buried in his place, but it seems unlikely that such a man would fortuitously resemble him closely enough to be passed off as him. Edward was tall and uncommonly strong. Then again, we know from tomb excavations that Hugh Despenser's nephew Hugh Hastings stood five feet ten inches, and Archbishop

William Melton, who came from a humble family in Yorkshire, was six feet tall.[25] Clearly men of such height were not unknown in England in the early fourteenth century, and not only among the nobility. As the body at Berkeley was almost certainly embalmed shortly after death and covered with waxed cloth, including the face, it need not have resembled Edward too closely as long as the height more or less matched. Even if the face was visible, pale and sunken in death it might still have fooled the visitors who only saw it superficially. Or perhaps it didn't. Perhaps one of the knights or abbots who saw it told the earl of Kent or others of his suspicions. For the first month after death, the sergeant-at-arms William Beaukaire, who had been pardoned at Hugh Despenser's castle of Caerphilly some months before, guarded the body, presumably to stop anyone examining it too closely, before it was carried on a funereal carriage to Gloucester.

In working out what might have happened to Edward II (though we can only speculate), we can try to combine the information given by William Melton and Manuel Fieschi in their letters. Melton claimed that Edward was in a safe place at his own wish or command, Fieschi that Edward escaped from Berkeley and went to Corfe with a servant, where he was received in the prisons there. It is hard to imagine that Lord Berkeley didn't send out search parties for Edward or that he could have remained at Corfe, which had a garrison and people often coming and going, without being spotted. And yet if Edward genuinely was alive, as so much evidence indicates, plans must have been made to fake his death, remove him from Berkeley and hide him elsewhere. We can try to reconcile the information given by Melton and Fieschi: a possible scenario is that Edward was allowed to 'escape', but himself genuinely thought he was escaping, so that the story he told Fieschi was true, so far as he knew. This could also explain Melton's belief that Edward was in a safe place by his own doing, which he had heard indirectly from Edward himself. Moving Edward through the countryside from Gloucestershire to Dorset with a large armed guard would be noticed, but his travelling in the company of only one man would attract little or no attention, so it may be that this was one reason for his 'escape' and that the unnamed servant mentioned in the Fieschi letter who helped him was in on the plot. The usual men on watch at Berkeley Castle would have been removed from duty, with only one porter remaining so that Edward would not be suspicious about being allowed to walk out of the castle too easily. Perhaps a man was intentionally chosen for his height, so that if he died during Edward's supposed escape, his body could be used in place of the king's. The servant would have instructions to take Edward to Corfe, perhaps by telling him he had supporters waiting there. At some point Edward heard of 'his' funeral held at Gloucester and that his heart had been sent to Isabella. Somehow the news that he was at Corfe got out and in 1328/29 reached the ears, by different information sources, of Edward's brother Kent, the archbishop of York and others. Although Edward thought he was free, in reality he was still under guard with the knowledge of some of the Corfe garrison, until Kent and others came close to freeing him in early 1330. At this point, Edward was taken to Ireland, and from there ultimately to Italy, as the rest of the Fieschi letter tells us. It is likely that at no point in his afterlife was Edward genuinely free, but always watched very closely, if not exactly incarcerated. He met the pope in Avignon in 1331 and his son in Koblenz in 1338, taken there by Francisco Forcetti, and at some point in around 1335 met Manuel Fieschi and told him his story.

Taken individually, all the pieces of evidence that Edward II survived past 1327 could be explained away, if we wish. Kent, Melton, Mar and their many supporters were misled by false information and, fond of Edward, carried away by their own wishful thinking. Manuel Fieschi was taken in by a well-informed impostor. Thomas Berkeley told parliament that he hadn't previously known that Edward was murdered and his words were written down confusingly. William the Welshman was a deluded subject of Edward III whom the king spent time with and magnanimously forgave for pretending to be his royal father. But taken as a whole, the pieces build a very strong picture that Edward II did not die at Berkeley in 1327. So, then, where did he die? Most probably in Italy, in the hermitage of Sant'Alberto di Butrio high in the hills near Cecima in the province of Pavia, where Manuel Fieschi says he lived. Both the Val di Magra where Edward first went or was taken (where Mulazzo is located) and the area around Cecima were then dominated by the Fieschi family, and the sergeant Francisco Forcetti also had ties to the Val di Magra.[26] An empty tomb in the hermitage of Sant'Alberto is claimed as Edward's to this day and shown to visitors, and it has long been accepted in Italy that Edward died in that country.[27] Or perhaps his body was returned to England and buried in his tomb at Gloucester after all, and his heart removed to be sent to Isabella for her to be buried with later. Edward III made a pilgrimage to Gloucester in March 1343, the first time he had visited since 1337.[28]. We cannot know for sure when Edward died, though Ian Mortimer has suggested 1341 or early 1342, as the early 1340s saw a flurry of Edward-related activity: Queen Isabella founded a chantry in Coventry in 1342 to pray for the soul of her husband; as noted, Edward III made a pilgrimage to Gloucester in 1343; and at the parliament of May 1343, the king passed on the title of prince of Wales, the one title his father had never given up to him, to his eldest son.[29] Edward of Caernarfon would then have been in his late fifties.

Objections to the idea that Edward lived on in Italy after his 'death' are usually rooted in incredulity. The red-hot poker story has been repeated as fact so many times that it can be difficult to grasp that it didn't happen. Throughout history there have been other tales of famous people living on secretly after their deaths, which understandably leads many people to the conclusion that Edward's story must likewise be a myth; but Edward's afterlife was testified to by an archbishop, bishops, earls and many others who knew him well. It is also hard for some to imagine that a king, especially one as extravagant as Edward, might have been able or willing to live in obscurity and as a hermit at that. But Edward was sincerely pious, he loved the outdoors, he loved spending time at monasteries: in 1300 when he was sixteen, he stayed at St Edmund's Abbey in Suffolk for a week longer than he had to, enjoying the daily routine, the food and the company of the monks. In 1318 a cleric complained that Edward spent too much time in religious houses, and he always enjoyed spending time with and befriending religious men.[30] Being king had brought Edward little but terrible unhappiness. He lost two men he loved dearly, Piers Gaveston and Hugh Despenser, and the company of his wife, his children, his beloved sister Mary and niece Eleanor, everyone else he loved. He had been rejected by his kingdom, humiliated at Bannockburn and elsewhere. Why would he have wanted to rule again? Although Edward was not a man given to critical self-reflection, even he must have realised in and after January 1327 that both he and his kingdom were much better off without him on the throne. Living out his years peacefully and contemplatively in a distant country, praying, working on the land and making the most of his physical strength, might well have appealed to him greatly. It is entirely fitting that the time, manner and place of death of this most unconventional man should be shrouded in mystery, though wherever his body may truly lie, his magnificent tomb in Gloucester with its canopy and alabaster effigy is one of the greatest treasures of medieval England.

Edward II was an exasperating and flawed man who failed as a king and as a war leader. Left an extremely difficult legacy by his mighty father, forced to try to fill a role he had little aptitude for or interest in, he lurched from one crisis to another until finally he became the first king of England forced to abdicate. Although Edward did have abilities when he chose to exercise them, the personal far too often dominated the political, and Edward the king was unable to put aside Edward the man. He was all too human, and his personality leaps off the pages of history and reaches us 700 years later. Although we must not forget his numerous failings and the misery inflicted on many of his subjects during his reign, especially in the north of England, we can bear in mind that he was born into his position, he did not choose it, and therefore try to judge him less harshly than his contemporaries and many historians have. He was not an evil man or one who set out to make anyone suffer; it was his misfortune and his kingdom's that he was born into a hereditary monarchy and had no other choice than to succeed his father. He gave England one of its greatest kings, his son Edward III, through whom he is the ancestor of a huge percentage of the English population alive today, and of millions of others around the world. Edward II's story is part of our collective story.

Notes

Abbreviations

AL: *Annales Londonienses 1195–1330*
Anonimalle: *The Anonimalle Chronicle 1307–1334*
AP: *Annales Paulini 1307–1340*
Baker: *Chronicon Galfridi le Baker de Swynbroke* (ed. Thompson)
BIHR: *Bulletin of the Institute of Historical Research*
'Brief Summary': Thomas Stapleton, 'A Brief Summary of the Wardrobe Accounts'
Bruce: G. W. S. Barrow, *Robert Bruce and the Community of the Realm of Scotland*
Brut: *The Brut or the Chronicles of England*
'Captivity': T. F. Tout, 'The Captivity and Death of Edward of Carnarvon'
CCR: Calendar of Close Rolls
CChR: Calendar of Charter Rolls 1300–1326
CCW: Calendar of Chancery Warrants 1244–1326
CDS: Calendar of Documents Relating to Scotland 1307–1357
CFR: Calendar of Fine Rolls
Chaplais, *Gaveston*: Pierre Chaplais, *Piers Gaveston: Edward II's Adoptive Brother*
CIM: Calendar of Inquisitions Miscellaneous 1308–1348
CMR: Calendar of Memoranda Rolls Michaelmas 1326–Michaelmas 1327
'Court': Michael Prestwich, 'The Court of Edward II' in *RENP*
CPL: Calendar of Papal Letters 1305–1341
CPR: Calendar of Patent Rolls
Croniques: *Croniques de London*
Doherty, *Death*: Paul Doherty, *Isabella and the Strange Death of Edward II*
EHR: English Historical Review
FCE: Fourteenth Century England
'First Journal': J. C. Davies, 'The First Journal of Edward II's Chamber'
Flores: *Flores Historiarum*, Vol. iii
Foedera: Foedera, Conventiones, Litterae, Vol. 2.1, 1307–1327
Gesta: *Gesta Edwardi de Carnarvon Auctore Canonico Bridlingtoniensi*
Guisborough: *The Chronicle of Walter Guisborough*
Haines, *Edward*: Roy Martin Haines, *King Edward II*
Hamilton, *Gaveston*: J. S. Hamilton, *Piers Gaveston, earl of Cornwall 1307–1312*
HMSO: Her/His Majesty's Stationery Office
Household Book: The Household Book of Queen Isabella of England

Intrigue: Ian Mortimer, *Medieval Intrigue: Decoding Royal Conspiracies*
Issues: Frederick Devon, *Issues of the Exchequer*
Itinerary: Elizabeth Hallam, *The Itinerary of Edward II and His Household*
JMH: Journal of Medieval History
Johnstone: Hilda Johnstone, *Edward of Carnarvon 1284–1307*
Lancaster: J. R. Maddicott, *Thomas of Lancaster 1307–1322*
Lanercost: *The Chronicle of Lanercost 1272–1346*
Livere: *Le Livere de Reis de Britanie e le Livere de Engletere*
Multitudo: Constance Bullock-Davies, *Menestrellorum Multitudo*
Traitor: Ian Mortimer, *The Greatest Traitor: The Life of Sir Roger Mortimer*
Murimuth: *Adae Murimuth Continuatio Chronicarum*
ODNB: Oxford Dictionary of National Biography
Opposition: J. C. Davies, *The Baronial Opposition to Edward II*
Perfect King: Ian Mortimer, *The Perfect King: The Life of Edward III*
Phillips: Seymour Phillips, *Edward II*
Place: T. F. Tout, *The Place of the Reign of Edward II in English History*
Polychronicon: *Polychronicon Ranulphi Higden*, Vol. 8
PROME: The Parliament Rolls of Medieval England
Register: Bullock-Davies, *A Register of Royal Domestic Minstrels*
RENP: *The Reign of Edward II: New Perspectives*, ed. Dodd and Musson
SAL MS: Society of Antiquaries of London, manuscript
Sardos: *The War of Saint-Sardos (1323-1325): Gascon Correspondence*
Scalacronica: *Scalacronica by Sir Thomas Gray of Heton, knight* (ed. Stevenson)
'Secular Musicians': Richard Rastall, 'Secular Musicians in Late Medieval England'
TNA: The National Archives (C: Chancery; DL: Duchy of Lancaster; E: Exchequer; SC: Special Collections)
Tout, Chapters: T. F. Tout, *Chapters in the Administrative History of England*
TRHS: Transactions of the Royal Historical Society
Trokelowe: *Johannis de Trokelowe et Henrici de Blaneforde Chronica et Annales*
Tyranny: Natalie Fryde, *The Tyranny and Fall of Edward II 1321–1326*
Valence: J. R. S. Phillips, *Aymer de Valence, earl of Pembroke 1307–1324*
Vita: *Vita Edwardi Secundi* (ed. Denholm-Young)

Introduction

1. *English Historical Documents 1189–1327*, Vol. iii, 287–8.
2. *Flores*, 235.
3. J. Mackinnon, *History of Edward III*, 1; May McKisack, *The Fourteenth Century 1307–1399*, 95; 'Captivity', 145; *Place*, 9; K. H. Vickers, *England in the Later Middle Ages*, 84; Richard Baker, *A Chronicle to the Kings of England*, 102.
4. The other is Edward's descendant Henry VI.

1 Heir to the Throne and Accession

1. *Lanercost*, 182.
2. *Foedera Vol. 1.2, 1272–1307*, 1018; *Guisborough*, 379, *Lanercost*, 182; *Vita*, 1.
3. *Itinerary*, 21; Johnstone, 125.
4. G. L. Haskins, 'Chronicle of the Civil Wars', 75; *Anonimalle*, 82; *Guisborough*, 380, 383; *Lanercost*, 184; *Vita*, 1.

5. *Brut,* 202–3; *Scalacronica,* 50.
6. *Vita,* 40.
7. Phillips, 33.
8. J. C. Parsons, 'Year of Eleanor of Castile's Birth', 246–9; Parsons, *Eleanor of Castile,* 9. Fernando was canonised in 1671.
9. Johnstone, 12.
10. Johnstone, 6–7; Phillips, 36. The story first appeared in 1584 in *The Historie of Cambria.*
11. Henry Gough, *Itinerary of King Edward the First, Vol. 1: 1272–1285,* 145–6.
12. Parsons, *Eleanor,* 33; Phillips, 40 note 45.
13. Johnstone, 10 note 4.
14. Johnstone, 64; Phillips, 38–9.
15. Parsons, 'Year of Birth', 248.
16. Marc Morris, *A Great and Terrible King,* 231.
17. Johnstone, 24; Phillips, 40.
18. Hilda Johnstone, *Letters of Edward, Prince of Wales 1304–5,* 70.
19. Johnstone, 15–17; Phillips, 53–7, 64–5; Phillips, 'Place of the Reign of Edward II', *RENP,* 221–6. It has often been unfairly assumed that Edward was stupid and badly educated, which Phillips refutes.
20. Phillips, 57, for Eleanor and Mary. Edward's half-brother the earl of Kent said in 1330 that his wife Margaret Wake had written a letter for him: *Murimuth,* 255.
21. *Trokelowe,* 98–9; *Sardos,* 143, 145.
22. Phillips, 62.
23. Johnstone, 26–7; Phillips, 48–9.
24. Johnstone, 27–8; Phillips, 41–2; *Issues,* 106–13.
25. *Issues,* 111.
26. Phillips, 45 note 76.
27. Morris, *Terrible King,* 307ff; Michael Prestwich, *Edward I,* 392ff; Prestwich, *Documents Illustrating the Crisis;* Phillips, 78ff.
28. *CChR 1300–26,* 6; Johnstone, 62; Phillips, 87.
29. *CPR 1301–7,* 424.
30. A list is given in *Multitudo,* 185–7.
31. Johnstone, 108.
32. Johnstone, 106–8.
33. *Multitudo,* 1–6.
34. *Multitudo,* xxv–xxvi.
35. *Lanercost,* 182–3; *Guisborough,* 379.
36. J. S. Hamilton, *Gaveston,* 37, 139.
37. Johnstone, 124; Hamilton, *Gaveston,* 35–6.
38. *Guisborough,* 382; Hannah Kilpatrick, 'Correction to Hoskins', 1–2.
39. Phillips, 46–7.
40. *Vita,* 40.
41. *Lanercost,* 222.
42. *Scalacronica,* 75.
43. *Polychronicon,* 298.
44. Nancy Goldstone, *Four Queens,* 6.
45. *Foedera,* 650.
46. *Polychronicon,* 299.
47. *Foedera,* 1; *Lanercost,* 183.
48. Phillips, 124; Prestwich, *Edward I,* 565–6.

2 The New King and His Favourite

1. *Vita*, 40; *Roll of Arms of Caerlaverock*, 18; *Polychronicon*, 299; *Scalacronica*, 45; *Gesta*, 91; *Anonimalle*, 80.
2. Prestwich, *Edward I*, 567; W. Mark Ormrod, *Edward III*, 578 and note 6.
3. Johnstone, *Letters of Edward*, 62.
4. *Foedera*, 2, 50. See also Phillips, 127, and Chaplais, *Gaveston*, 27–28.
5. Chaplais, *Gaveston*, 31; Hamilton, *Gaveston*, 37. TNA E 41/460 is the Cornwall charter.
6. K. B. McFarlane, *The Nobility of Later Medieval England*, 265.
7. For more information on Gaveston's family, see Hamilton, *Gaveston*, 19–28.
8. On 29 July 1304, Edward I granted Gaveston the wardship of Roger Mortimer (*CPR 1301–7*, 244), meaning Gaveston was at least twenty-one then; Hamilton, *Gaveston*, 21.
9. TNA SC/8/291/14546; *CDS 1272–1307*, 368; Johnstone, 89.
10. Hamilton, *Gaveston*, 30.
11. *Baker*, 4.
12. *CCR 1302–7*, 277 note 44, and 295 note 45; *Foedera 1272–1307*, 1010.
13. *Scalacronica*, 33.
14. *AP*, 255.
15. *Lanercost*, 184; *AP*, 259, 273; *Vita*, 7, 17, 28, 104; *Polistoire*, folio 232r, cited in Chaplais, *Gaveston*, 11; *AL*, 157. *Vita*, 28, and *AP*, 263, for the quotations.
16. Chaplais, *Gaveston*, 6–22.
17. *Vita*, 15.
18. Cited in Johnstone, 42.
19. Chaplais, *Gaveston*, 56, 67, 123.
20. *Brut*, 216–7.
21. Hamilton, *Gaveston*, 27.
22. F. D. Blackley, 'Bastard Son of Edward II', 76; Chris Given-Wilson and Alice Curteis, *Royal Bastards of Medieval England*, 8, 136; Phillips, 102.
23. Amie was a damsel of Edward II's daughter-in-law Philippa of Hainault.
24. 'Secular Musicians', 57; *Register*, 226.
25. Hamilton, *Gaveston*, 40.
26. Alison Weir, *Isabella*, 15.
27. As suggested in Doherty, *Death*, 42–3.
28. *Guisborough*, 383, *AP*, 257, *Lanercost*, 184–5; Beardwood, *Records of the Trial*, 1–2.
29. Morris, *Terrible King*, 349–50.
30. Jeffrey Denton, *Robert Winchelsey and the Crown*, 245–6.
31. *Foedera*, 11–12, 14, 17, 22, 25; *CPR 1307–13*, 13; *CCR 1307–13*, 7–9, 16–17.
32. From the early thirteenth century, the vast territory in France ruled by the English kings dwindled considerably, until only Gascony remained. However, although the kings of England no longer held the entire duchy, they continued to be called 'duke of Aquitaine'. Following contemporary practice, I refer to Edward II by his correct title, but use the word 'Gascony' in all other contexts.
33. H. M. Colvin, *History of the King's Works*, 2, 179–80; *Register*, 31.
34. *Foedera*, 8; Mary Saaler, *Edward II 1307–1327*, 38. Oljeitu or Öljaitü, also known as Muhammad Khodabandeh, was the great-great-great-grandson of Genghis Khan.
35. Prestwich, *Edward I*, 557.

36. *Issues*, 122–3; Phillips, 131 note 45.
37. *Vita*, 3.
38. Chaplais, *Gaveston*, 31–2.
39. *CCR 1307–1313*, 10.
40. The Gilbert de Clare who lived in Edward's household before his accession was not Gloucester, as often stated, but his cousin of the same name, who was lord of Thomond.
41. *Issues*, 119–20; Hamilton, *Gaveston*, 38, 140.
42. *Register*, 119; Hamilton, *Gaveston*, 38, 140.
43. *Issues*, 119.
44. Malcolm Barber, *The Trial of the Templars*, 85.
45. *Foedera*, 10, 16, 19, 24.
46. Barber, *Trial of the Templars*, 219; TNA SC 7/10/40.
47. *Foedera*, 23; *CCR 1307–13*, 48–9.
48. *CCR 1307–13*, 14.
49. *CCR 1307–13*, 90.
50. Evelyn Lord, *The Knights Templar in Britain*, 261.
51. *CPR 1307–13*, 21, 448.
52. *Foedera*, 17–18.
53. *Itinerary*, 26; *CPR 1307–13*, 13–26; *CCR 1307–13*, 9–13.
54. *Trokelowe*, 65; *AP*, 258–9.
55. *Vita*, 2.
56. *Vita*, 14–15.
57. *Murimuth*, 11.
58. *Gesta*, 33; *AP*, 259.
59. *AP*, 258; *Itinerary*, 26–7; *CPR 1307–13*, 29, 31; *CCR 1307–13*, 16; *Foedera*, 24–5; Jochen Burgtorf, 'With my Life', 37.
60. *Foedera*, 24; *CPR 1307–13*, 31.
61. *Vita*, 3.
62. *AP*, 260; Hamilton, *Gaveston*, 45–46; Chaplais, *Gaveston*, 34–42.
63. *CCR 1307–13*, 7–9, 16–17; *CPR 1307–13*, 13, 16.

3 Exile and Intrigue

1. *Itinerary*, 27. Edward had arranged to meet Philip on Sunday 21 January; *Foedera*, 25. There is no evidence that 'engrossed with Gaveston', he deliberately arrived late to insult the French, as suggested in Doherty, *Death*, 43.
2. Weir, *Isabella*, 8–9; Paul Doherty, 'Date of Birth of Isabella', 246–8.
3. Blanche, a niece of Louis IX of France, married firstly Enrique I of Navarre and secondly Edmund of Lancaster, younger brother of Edward I.
4. Weir, *Isabella*, 27.
5. Phillips, 134.
6. Phillips, 132; Elizabeth A. R. Brown, 'Political Repercussions of Family Ties', 576.
7. *AP*, 258.
8. Walter E. Rhodes, 'Inventory of the Jewels and Wardrobe', 518–21; Phillips, 135; Doherty, *Death*, 43–4.
9. *AP*, 258. See Burgtorf, 'With my Life', 45 and note 105: Gaveston received the gifts in his capacity as regent and there is no suggestion that Edward intended him to keep them, and Chaplais, *Gaveston*, 104: Edward was merely ensuring the safe delivery of the gifts.

10. *Lancaster*, 73; *Valence*, 25–9; Phillips, 138; Haines, *Edward*, 64.
11. *Traitor*, 35–6.
12. *Foedera*, 31; *Itinerary*, 28; *CPR 1307–13*, 45.
13. *CCR 1307–13*, 51; Phillips, 145 note 114.
14. Isabella and Richmond were both great-grandchildren of King Thibault I of Navarre.
15. Hamilton, *Gaveston*, 47, citing *Trokelowe*, 65; *Gesta*, 210.
16. *CFR 1307–19*, 14.
17. Burgtorf, 'With my Life', 46–7.
18. *Issues*, 122.
19. *AP*, 258–9.
20. *AL*, 152.
21. *AP*, 260.
22. For example, V. H. Galbraith, 'The Literacy of the Medieval English Kings', *Proceedings of the British Academy*, 21 (1935), 215: 'It was thus stupidity or laziness, and not want of opportunity to learn Latin, that made it necessary for Edward II to take his coronation oath in French.' Edward's son Edward III and great-grandson Richard II also took their coronation oaths in French in 1327 and 1377, and nobody has ever accused *them* of being stupid and lazy because of it. See Phillips, 54–6.
23. No record survives of Edward I's coronation oath in 1274, so it is possible that he also spoke French, and that it included the fourth clause.
24. *Issues*, 122.
25. *Flores*, 141–2.
26. Any details of the coronation not cited come from *AP*, 258–62.
27. *CPR 1307–13*, 47; *AP*, 258–9.
28. *Issues*, 121.
29. Phillips, 140.
30. Anthony Tuck, *Crown and Nobility 1272–1461*, 59; Michael Prestwich, *The Three Edwards*, 82.
31. TNA E/101/325/4.
32. *AL*, 260; Phillips, 145.
33. *AP*, 259.
34. Cited in Weir, *Isabella*, 40.
35. *AP*, 262; *Vita*, 15.
36. Edward and Isabella's first daughter Eleanor was an exception: born in June 1318, she bore her first child in May 1333, before she turned fifteen.
37. *Vita*, 4.
38. *Flores*, 151.
39. *Vita*, 1.
40. *Lanercost*, 186.
41. *Vita*, 4–5; F. C. Hingeston-Ralph, *The Register of Walter de Stapeldon, Bishop of Exeter 1307–1326* (1892), 11–12.
42. *Lancaster*, 83–4, 335–6.
43. *Lanercost*, 196; *Polychronicon*, 300.
44. Chaplais, *Gaveston*, 10.
45. *Lancaster*, 84.
46. *CPR 1307–13*, 51.
47. *CPR 1307–13*, 24; *Foedera*, 44; Tout, *Chapters*, Vol. 5, 277.
48. *Guisborough*, 382; Johnstone, 124–5.
49. TNA E 163/4/11; *Sardos*, 199–200.
50. *Vita*, 4; *Lanercost*, 187; *Traitor*, 39; Hamilton, *Gaveston*, 146.

51. *Foedera*, 44; CPR 1307–13, 71.
52. CPR 1307–13, 74, 78–9; Hamilton, *Gaveston*, 147; Chaplais, *Gaveston*, 47.
53. *Gesta*, 33–4; AP, 262–3; *Vita*, 5.
54. Haines, *Edward*, 61–2; *Lanercost*, 187.
55. *Foedera*, 51.
56. Chaplais, *Gaveston*, 45; CCW, 275.
57. *Foedera*, 49–51, 122–3.
58. Burgtorf, 'With my Life', 42–3.
59. CPR 1307–13, 83; *Foedera*, 51, 122–3, 129.
60. CFR 1307–19, 32.
61. *Bruce*, 249.
62. CPR 1307–13, 81–2.
63. *Foedera*, 63; Phillips, 152.
64. *Vita*, 6.
65. Hamilton, *Gaveston*, 41; Haines, *Edward*, 70.
66. *Vita*, 6.
67. AP, 264.
68. Andy King, 'Thomas of Lancaster's First Quarrel', 31–45; *Lancaster*, 92–4.
69. Johnstone, *Letters of Edward*, 61, 65, 107, 136, 122.
70. CPR 1307–13, 95, 96, 148, 453.
71. Phillips, 64–5.
72. *Livere*, 327; AP, 266.
73. AL, 157; AP, 267.
74. CPR 1307–13, 101, 156; *Foedera*, 69.
75. *Foedera*, 68.
76. Hamilton, *Gaveston*, 53–66.
77. CPR 1307–13, 102–3.
78. *Lancaster*, 95–102; Phillips, 155.
79. Sophia Menache, *Clement V* (1998), 260.
80. Phillips, 156–7; *Lancaster*, 97–8; Haines, *Edward*, 72; Tuck, *Crown and Nobility*, 57; *Place*, 76.
81. CCR 1307–13, 158–9.
82. AL, 157; *Vita*, 8.
83. CCR 1307–13, 225–6.
84. *Gesta*, 35; *Guisborough*, 384.
85. *Vita*, 7.

4 Another Exile

1. *Vita*, 16.
2. *Scalacronica*, 48; *Lanercost*, 194.
3. *Lanercost*, 194 (Warwick quotation), *Brut*, 207; *Flores*, 152; *Vita*, 8; *Place*, 12–13.
4. AL, 133.
5. Chaplais, *Gaveston*, 56, 67, 123.
6. *Vita*, 7.
7. *Vita*, 7–8.
8. Haskins, 'Chronicle of the Wars', 76; *Vita*, 1–3.
9. *Lanercost*, 184.
10. *Foedera*, 63, 71.
11. *Foedera*, 60.

12. Peter Linehan, 'English Mission of Cardinal Petrus Hispanus', 615–20; Johnstone, 120.
13. Peter Coss and Maurice Keen, *Heraldry, Pageantry*, 89; *Vita*, 40.
14. *CCR 1301–7*, 83.
15. *CCR 1307–13*, 224; *Foedera*, 78, 82–3.
16. *Foedera*, 85; *CDS*, 19.
17. *Foedera*, 74.
18. *CCR 1307–13*, 13, 42, 281; *Bruce*, 261.
19. *Foedera*, 79.
20. *Polychronicon*, 299.
21. Prestwich, *Edward I*, 111; Parsons, *Eleanor*, 50.
22. *Foedera*, 81.
23. *Vita*, 9; *Guisborough*, 384–5.
24. *Foedera*, 86, 98, 103; *CCR 1307–13*, 171, 173, 190, 270, 283, 291.
25. *CPR 1307–13*, 211.
26. *Foedera 1272–1307*, 995.
27. Yonge, *Flowers of History*, 585; *ODNB*.
28. *ODNB*.
29. *Vita*, 8.
30. *Foedera*, 102.
31. *Vita*, 9; *CPR 1307–13*, 206–07; *Foedera*, 103.
32. *AL*, 167–8.
33. *Opposition*, 359; *AL*, 169.
34. *AL*, 169–74.
35. *AL*, 170–71; Phillips, 166; *Opposition*, 357–93.
36. R. Graham, *The Register of Robert Winchelsey, Archbishop of Canterbury* (1956), Part 2, 1,043.
37. *CPR 1307–13*, 277.
38. Prestwich, *Three Edwards*, 81.
39. *Polychronicon*, 299; *Scalacronica*, 43.
40. SAL MS 122, 55, 63, 79.
41. *Vita*, 12.
42. *CDS*, 40–41, 48.
43. *CDS*, 33.
44. *CDS*, 39.
45. *Vita*, 40.
46. *CPR 1307–13*, 333; *Foedera*, 129; *AL*, 175; *AP*, 269.
47. Hamilton, *Gaveston*, 85; *Lancaster*, 115.
48. *Lanercost*, 192. J. S. Hamilton states that the story cannot be true, as Gaveston was only with Edward at Berwick in late March 1311, when the earl of Lancaster was in Leicester. Hamilton, *Gaveston*, 159 note 46; *Lancaster*, 342.
49. *CDS*, 40.
50. Phillips, 74, 174.
51. *CDS*, 41.
52. *AL*, 175–6.
53. *Itinerary*, 75–6; *Vita*, 17; *Register*, 76.
54. *Itinerary*, 76–7; *Vita*, 17. Queen Isabella went on pilgrimage to Canterbury in October 1311: *Household Book*, 143.
55. Hamilton, *Gaveston*, 91.
56. *Issues*, 124.
57. This and all following quotes from the Ordinance, and Edward's reaction to it, from *Vita*, 17–20.

58. *AP*, 270; *Trokelowe*, 67; *CCR 1307–13*, 439.
59. *Foedera*, 143.
60. *CCR 1307–13*, 441; *Foedera*, 144.
61. *CCR 1307–13*, 393, 441; *Foedera*, 144–5.
62. *Household Book*, 137.
63. Chaplais, *Gaveston*, 75–6.
64. *Vita*, 20.
65. *CPR 1307–13*, 26.
66. *AP*, 171; *AL*, 202; Philips, *Edward II*, 180.
67. *Itinerary*, 79; *CPR 1307–13*, 397–8; *CCR 1307–13*, 380–81, 441; *Foedera*, 148.
68. *CPR 1307–13*, 397.
69. *CPR 1307–13*, 397.
70. *CPR 1307–13*, 395, 398; *Household Book*, 209.
71. *Household Book*, 208; Chaplais, *Gaveston*, 75.
72. *Trokelowe*, 68–9; *Vita*, 21; *AP*, 271.
73. *CPR 1307–13*, 405; *Foedera*, 151.
74. *Vita*, 21.
75. Stones and Keil, 'Edward II and the Abbot of Glastonbury', 176–82; Chris Given-Wilson, *Chronicles: The Writing of History in Medieval England*, 73–4, 229. It is not entirely clear in which year this correspondence took place; possibly, it belongs to 1321/22, when Edward's friends the Despensers had also been banished from England, or to 1308/09, Gaveston's first exile.
76. *Foedera*, 149, 151; *CPR 1307–13*, 398; *CCR 1307–13*, 447.
77. Sayles, *Functions of Medieval Parliament*, 302.
78. *Vita*, 21.
79. 'Brief Summary ', 342.
80. *AL*, 202; *Gesta*, 41; *Vita*, 2; Hamilton, *Gaveston*, 93.
81. *Vita*, 21.

5 Death, Birth and Reconciliation

1. *Household Book*, 143.
2. *Itinerary*, 81; *CCW*, 382; Chaplais, *Gaveston*, 77–8.
3. *Gesta*, 42; Chaplais, *Gaveston*, 78–9; Hamilton, *Gaveston*, 93–4.
4. Chaplais, *Gaveston*, 77.
5. *CCR 1307–13*, 448–9; *Foedera*, 153; *AL*, 203.
6. Chaplais, *English Diplomatic Practice in the Middle Ages*, 128, 130; Tout, *Chapters*, Vol. 2, 199–200. Phillips, 'Place of the Reign', *RENP*, 221–3, discusses the 1317 letter, and earlier historians' insistence on Edward's alleged stupidity and illiteracy.
7. *Lanercost*, 196.
8. *Vita*, 22–4.
9. *Trokelowe*, 74–5; *Lancaster*, 124; Chaplais, *Gaveston*, 81.
10. *Register*, 50; *Household Book*, 17, 25.
11. *AL*, 203; *Lancaster*, 123.
12. *Vita*, 22–3.
13. *Register*, 143; 'Secular Musicians', 62.
14. *Register*, 167, 218.
15. *Register*, 116.
16. *Register*, 119.
17. *Household Book*, 25, 27, 137.

18. *Household Book*, 13.
19. *Traitor*, 49–50, 69–70, 87, 100–1, 305–9.
20. *Flores*, 149; *Vita*, 22.
21. Hamilton, *Gaveston*, 94.
22. 'Court', 66.
23. SAL MS 122, 21, 28, 45.
24. CCR *1307–13*, 581.
25. *Foedera*, 162.
26. Hamilton, *Gaveston*, 95.
27. CCR *1307–13*, 426; *Register*, 143; 'Secular Musicians', 63.
28. CPR *1307–13*, 454; CFR *1307–19*, 129.
29. *Foedera*, 163–4; CCR *1307–13*, 458.
30. *Foedera*, 169; *Lanercost*, 197; *Gesta*, 42; *Itinerary*, 85.
31. *Trokelowe*, 75–6.
32. Doherty, 'Isabella', 42, 92.
33. *Household Book*, xxv–xxvi: 'the story that Edward abandoned Isabella seems to be a most unlikely one'; Haines, *Edward*, 84: 'a fictitious tale'; Phillips, 482: Edward 'did not abandon the pregnant Isabella'; Doherty, *Death*, 51; Burgtorf, 'With my Life', 49. Weir (*Isabella*, 63–4) is one of the few modern writers who accepts the story.
34. *Household Book*, 55.
35. *Household Book*, xxvi, 15.
36. Doherty, *Death*, 51.
37. *Foedera*, 203–5; CPR *1307–13*, 554, 562.
38. *Vita*, 34–5.
39. *Gesta*, 42; *Lanercost*, 197–8; *Vita*, 24; *Lancaster*, 125; Phillips, 187–8.
40. *Vita*, 24.
41. CPR *1307–13*, 460; CCR *1307–13*, 460; *Foedera*, 169; *Valence*, 33.
42. *Gesta*, 42; *Trokelowe*, 76; *Vita*, 24.
43. *Flores*, 150–51.
44. Hamilton, *Gaveston*, 96; AL, 204–206.
45. AL, 204–06; *Vita*, 24.
46. *Vita*, 24.
47. *Vita*, 24.
48. *Valence*, 34; Hamilton, *Gaveston*, 97.
49. *Lancaster*, 127.
50. Vale, *Princely Court*, 180; *Foedera*, 170.
51. AL, 207, 236.
52. *Vita*, 25.
53. *Flores*, 152–3.
54. AL, 206–07.
55. *Vita*, 25.
56. *Trokelowe*, 77.
57. *Gesta*, 43–4.
58. *Vita*, 26.
59. *Vita*, 26–8.
60. *Vita*, 27, and see also: AL, 207; AP, 271; *Anonimalle*, 86; Baker, 5; *Gesta*, 44; *Flores*, 152; *Lanercost*, 198; *Murimuth*, 17–18; *Trokelowe*, 77.
61. AL, 207.
62. *Foedera*, 204.
63. AP, 262.
64. *Itinerary*, 86; *Household Book*, 45, 63, 221; CFR *1307–19*, 136–7; CCR

1307–13, 427–8; *CPR 1307–13*, 465; *Anonimalle*, 86, *Brut*, 207, *Vita*, 30, *Trokelowe*, 77.
65. *Vita*, 30.
66. *Vita*, 29–30; *Lanercost*, 198; *Anonimalle*, 86.
67. *Scalacronica*, 51.
68. T. Wright, *The Political Songs of England*, 258–61; *Vita*, 29.
69. Hamilton, *Gaveston*, 99.
70. *Lanercost*, 203; *Opposition*, 85.
71. *CPR 1307–13*, 497, 664.
72. *Itinerary*, 86; *Household Book*, 221.
73. 'Secular Musicians', 63; *Multitudo*, 143; *Register*, 63, 77, 218.
74. *AL*, 208–10.
75. *CPR 1307–13*, 489–90.
76. *Lanercost*, 199; *AL*, 216.
77. *Vita*, 31.
78. *Lanercost*, 198.
79. *Vita*, 30, 32.
80. *CPR 1307–13*, 490; *Foedera*, 178; *Vita*, 32–33.
81. *Vita*, 29.
82. *Vita*, 33–4.
83. *Vita*, 34.
84. *Vita*, 38.
85. *Foedera*, 191–2; *CPR 1307–13*, 517; *AL*, 221–25.
86. *Register*, 32; 'Secular Musicians', 64; Weir, *Isabella*, 69.
87. *Register*, 31–2; 'Secular Musicians', 64.
88. *CPR 1307–13*, p. 508; *Foedera*, 184. Isabella's will does not survive, and Edward himself never made one.
89. *Trokelowe*, 79–80; *Vita*, 36; *Perfect King*, 23.
90. *CPR 1307–13*, 516, 519.
91. *Vita*, 37.
92. *Perfect King*, 19–20.
93. *AL*, 220–21.
94. *Perfect King*, 23.
95. *CDS*, 58–9.
96. *Vita*, 48.
97. *Itinerary*, 94–5; Weir, *Isabella*, 73.
98. *Foedera*, 209.
99. *Foedera*, 203–05; Chaplais, *Gaveston*, 125–34; Hamilton, *Gaveston*, 119–127.
100. *Foedera*, 216.
101. *CCR 1307–13*, 537.
102. Chaplais, *Piers Gaveston*, 111–12.
103. *Itinerary*, 98; *Vita*, 39.
104. 'Secular Musicians', 64; *Register*, 122; quotation from Brown and Degalado, 'Le grant feste: Philip the Fair's Celebration', 59.
105. Brown and Degalado, 'Le grant feste', 60–63; Kathleen M. Ashley and Wim N. M. Hüsken, *Moving Subjects: Processional Performance in the Middle Ages and the Renaissance* (2001), 124.
106. *Chronique Métrique de Godefroy de Paris*, ed. J.-A. Buchon (1827), 194.
107. 'Le grant feste', 64, 66; Ashley and Hüsken, *Moving Subjects*, 134, 142.
108. *Register*, 9.
109. *Register*, 165; *Multitudo*, 51.
110. *Chronique Métrique*, 196 (also for the 'completely naked' quote).

111. 'Le grant feste', 64, 71–2.
112. Vale, *Princely Court*, 229, 280.
113. Trease, 'The Spicers and Apothecaries', 46.
114. *Trokelowe*, 80.
115. CPR 1313–7, 21–6, 35–6; *Foedera*, 230–3; AL, 222–9.
116. *Vita*, 43.
117. *Lanercost*, 203; *Vita*, 43.
118. *Livere*, 331.
119. *Vita*, 43–4.

6 Military Disaster and Famine

1.   *Flores*, 155–6; *Vita*, 45; *Gesta*, 45; *Melsa*, 329.
2.   *Lanercost*, 202–203; *Flores*, 155–6; *Vita*, 45–6.
3.   *Foedera*, 101.
4.   *Itinerary*, 109–10; *Trokelowe*, 82.
5.   Weir, *Isabella*, 96–8; Doherty, *Death*, p. 57.
6.   CPR 1313–7, 5, 38, 85–7.
7.   See Phillips, 222.
8.   *Trokelowe*, 83; CCR 1313–8, 38; CPR 1324–7, 193.
9.   *Trokelowe*, 83; *Historia Anglicana*, Vol. 1, 138–9; CCR 1313–8, 53.
10. *Foedera*, 258.
11. Weir, *Isabella*, 98.
12. *Lanercost*, 204; *Vita*, 48; *Bruce*, 274–9.
13. *Lanercost*, 202, 204; *Bruce*, 274, 277.
14. *Scalacronica*, 51–2; *Vita*, 48; *Lanercost*, 204; Haines, *Edward*, 481, note 118.
15. *Vita*, 49.
16. *Scalacronica*, 60.
17. *Bruce*, 336.
18. *Lancaster*, 162–3.
19. *Bruce*, 276–7; Nusbacher, *Bannockburn 1314*, 24–8; Reese, *Greatest Victory*, 52–3.
20. *Vita*, 50 (twenty leagues); Reese, *Greatest Victory*, 115–19, and Nusbacher, *Bannockburn 1314*, 85–114; Nusbacher, 89, for Hereford.
21. *Lanercost*, 206; *Flores*, 158.
22. Saaler, *Edward II*, 75.
23. Nusbacher, *Bannockburn 1314*, 89.
24. Vale, *Princely Court*, 221–2.
25. Derek Birley, *Sport and the Making of Britain* (1993), 32.
26. Kathleen Edwards, 'Political Importance of English Bishops', 324, 328.
27. *Baker*, 7.
28. Wright, *Political Songs*, 262–3.
29. *Vita*, 49.
30. For the battle, see Chris Brown, *Bannockburn 1314: A New History*; John Sadler, *Bannockburn: Battle for Liberty*; Aryeh Nusbacher, *Bannockburn 1314*; Peter Reese, *Bannockburn: Scotland's Greatest Victory*.
31. *Vita*, 52–3.
32. *Trokelowe*, 86.
33. *Scalacronica*, 54.
34. *Lanercost*, 208–9. See also AP, 276; AL, 230–1; *Gesta*, 46; *Vita*, 54–5.
35. Reese, *Greatest Victory*, 172; Nusbacher, *Bannockburn 1314*, 211–2.

36. *Issues*, 134; *CPR 1313–7*, 273; *CPR 1317–21*, 111; *CCR 1313–8*, 298, 497.
37. *Scalacronica*, 57; *Vita*, 55; Reese, *Greatest Victory*, 172–3.
38. *Baker*, 9.
39. Doherty, *Death*, 60.
40. Vale, *Princely Court*, 108–9.
41. *Anonimalle*, 88; *AL*, 231; *Lanercost*, 208.
42. *CCR 1313–8*, 71, 76; *CDS*, 63–4.
43. *Vita*, 54–5.
44. *Traitor*, 64.
45. *Vita*, 56.
46. *Trokelowe*, 87.
47. *Trokelowe*, 86.
48. *Lanercost*, 210–11.
49. *Foedera*, 254–5.
50. *CPR 1313–7*, 169; Sayles, *Functions*, 317.
51. *Place*, 93.
52. Weir, *Isabella*, 102–3.
53. Johnstone, 129–30; Johnstone, 'Eccentricities of Edward II', 264–67; Michael Prestwich, *Plantagenet England 1225–1360*, 180–1; Phillips, 277.
54. Phillips, 277–8.
55. *CPR 1313–7*, 160, 183; *Foedera*, 256; *CDS*, 71.
56. *CDS*, 59, 95.
57. *Lanercost*, 211.
58. *CCR 1313–8*, 131–8.
59. *CCR 1313–8*, 204.
60. Vale, *Princely Court*, 171, 245. There was a custom to choose a boy from a church or cathedral choir to act as 'boy-bishop'. Although he wasn't allowed to celebrate the Eucharist, he blessed people, gave at least one sermon, and gave out alms to the poor. The boy-bishop's 'reign' usually began on 6 December and ended on the 28th.
61. SAL MS 122, 62, 64, 75.
62. *Foedera*, 259; TNA E/101/375/15; E/101/376/2; E/101/375/16. The funeral took place either on 2 or 3 January 1315: Phillips, 241 note 21; Hamilton, *Gaveston*, 100; Chaplais, *Gaveston*, 110–11.
63. *Murimuth*, 17; C. F. R. Palmer, 'The Friar–Preachers of Kings Langley', *The Reliquary*, 23 (1882–3), 156.
64. Hamilton, *Gaveston*, 166, note 84.
65. Hamilton, *Gaveston*, 166, note 81.
66. *Vita*, 58.
67. *CCR 1313–8*, 139.
68. Hamilton, *Gaveston*, 100, 166–7.
69. Haines, *Edward*, 94; *Valence*, 83.
70. Alison Marshall, 'Childhood and Household', *RENP*, 204.
71. *Vita*, 123.
72. TNA C/81/90/3241; *Valence*, 132.
73. *AP*, 279.
74. *Vita*, 63–70.
75. *Foedera*, 263, 266; *Anonimalle*, 88.
76. *Vita*, 69; *Anonimalle*, 90.
77. *Anonimalle*, 90; *Lanercost*, 217; *Trokelowe*, 92.
78. *Trokelowe*, 93.
79. *Trokelowe*, 92.

80. *Vita*, 70; *Trokelowe*, 95.
81. *Trokelowe*, 95.
82. *Vita*, 70.
83. *Bruce*, 203; *Traitor*, 66–71, 80–81.
84. *Traitor*, 70–71; *CDS*, 89.
85. *Lanercost*, 213–6, and *Vita*, 61–2, for the siege (quotation from *Lanercost*, 215).
86. *Lanercost*, 216.
87. *CPR 1313–7*, 306–07; *CFR 1307–1319*, 248.
88. Walsingham, *Historia Anglicana*, i, 137.
89. *Vita*, 75–6.
90. *Issues*, 126.
91. *Scalacronica*, 65.
92. *Foedera*, 274–5; *CCR 1313–8*, 306; *AL*, 238–9.
93. Vale, *Princely Court*, 237, 307.
94. *Flores*, 173; Phillips, 252.
95. Johnstone, *Letters of Edward*, 7, 105; *Register*, 19.
96. Haines, *Edward*, 359, note 38.
97. TNA E 101/376/25; *CPR 1313–7*, 355–6.
98. Johnstone, 130.
99. *Flores*, 173; *Itinerary*, 132–7; *Foedera*, 277–83; *CPR 1313–7*, 352–79; *CCR 1313–7*, 248–62; *CCW*, 422–35, show that Edward was in the Fens in autumn.
100. *Croniques*, 35, for 1308/09; *AL*, 158, for 1309/10; also *AP*, 268.
101. Yonge, *Flowers of History*, 582; Derek Vincent Stern, *A Hertfordshire Demesne of Westminster Abbey: Profits, Productivity and Weather*, ed. Christopher Thornton (2000), 98–9.
102. *Issues*, 128–9.
103. *Register*, 147; 'Secular Musicians', 66.
104. *Scalacronica*, 65; *CCR 1323–7*, 440–1; *CPR 1313–7*, 422; Prestwich, 'Unreliability of Household Knights', 10.
105. *CPR 1313–7*, 372, 378, 384, 525, 598, 609, 615, etc; *CFR 1307–19*, 225, 294, 316–17.
106. *Flores*, 178.

7 Conflicts, Marriages and an Abduction

1. *PROME*.
2. McKisack, *Fourteenth Century*, 47.
3. *PROME*; Sayles, *Functions*, 353.
4. *CPR 1313–7*, 398.
5. *Issues*, 131.
6. 'Brief Summary', 342–3.
7. *Lanercost*, 217, and see also *Vita*, 69–70; *Gesta*, 48.
8. *Vita*, 66–7.
9. *Vita*, 67; *CPR 1313–17*, 384, 433; *Foedera*, 283.
10. *CCR 1313–18*, 274–5, 283.
11. *CCR 1313–18*, 419; *Foedera*, 334.
12. *Lancaster*, 184.
13. *CCW*, 436–7; *PROME*, 355–6; *Issues*, 131.
14. *Foedera*, 288.
15. *CCR 1313–18*, 462; *CCR 1318–23*, 187, 363, 525, 641, 699; *CCR 1323–7*, 353, 556.

16. *Issues*, 132.
17. *Lanercost*, 217.
18. J. S. Hamilton, 'Character of Edward II', *RENP*, 13–14.
19. *Foedera*, 271; *CCR 1313–18*, 301; *CPR 1313–17*, 332–3; *CCR 1313–18*, 454.
20. 'Brief Summary', 343.
21. *CPR 1307–13*, 272; *CPR 1313–17*, 360.
22. *Foedera*, 290.
23. 'Brief Summary', 343–4.
24. Chaplais, *English Medieval Diplomatic Practice*, Part 1, Vol. 2, 820.
25. 'Brief Summary', 319–20.
26. Prestwich, *Edward I*, 113; Prestwich, 'The Piety of Edward I', 125; Phillips, 71.
27. 'Court', 67.
28. *Itinerary*, 142–144; 'Brief Summary', 320.
29. *Lancaster*, 187.
30. 'Brief Summary', 322–3; *Issues*, 133; *CPR 1313–17*, 608.
31. *Foedera*, 293; *CPR 1313–17*, 527.
32. Edward gave a pound to the messenger who brought him news of John XXII's election on 17 August: 'Brief Summary', 321.
33. 'Brief Summary', 320; *Trokelowe*, 95.
34. *CCR 1313–8*, 430; *Foedera*, 296.
35. 'Brief Summary', 336; Phillips, 279.
36. *Flores*, 176–7.
37. *CPR 1313–17*, 621; 'Brief Summary', 320.
38. *Polychronicon*, 314.
39. *Register*, 144.
40. 'Brief Summary', 342; *Register*, 39. Philip was the grandson of Beatrice of Provence, sister of Edward's grandmother Eleanor of Provence.
41. *Place*, 315; *CPR 1313–17*, 609.
42. *CPR 1313–7*, 563–4; *Foedera*, 301 *Valence*, 106.
43. *Lancaster*, 188; *Valence*, 106.
44. *CPR 1301–7*, 308; *The Chronicle of Pierre de Langtoft*, ed. Thomas Wright, Vol. 2, pp. 368–9.
45. *CCR 1307–13*, 583.
46. Haines, *Edward*, 406, note 79; *CPR 1313–17*, 401, 434.
47. *CPR 1313–17*, 528–9.
48. 'Brief Summary', 341; *CPR 1313–17*, 12; *CCR 1313–18*, 45–6.
49. *Valence*, 110, 317.
50. *Foedera*, 304.
51. *Foedera*, 311–2.
52. *ODNB*.
53. 'Brief Summary', 342.
54. 'Brief Summary', 342.
55. *Foedera*, 308, 317.
56. *Foedera*, 320–1, 364; *CCR 1313–18*, 466.
57. *CPR 1313–17*, 614.
58. *CPL*, 11; *CPR 1281–92*, 137.
59. Mitchell, *Portraits of Medieval Women*, 108–13.
60. *Gesta*, 54; *Anonimalle*, 92; *Flores*, 178–9.
61. *Vita*, 80, 87.
62. *Foedera*, 322; TNA SC 7/24/10.
63. PROME.
64. *Opposition*, 432; *CPR 1313–7*, 609.

65. *CPR 1327–30*, 439–40.
66. Davies, *Opposition*, 433.
67. *CPR 1327–30*, 30; *CCR 1327–30*, 27; *Valence*, 149, 314; *Opposition*, 34.
68. C. M. Woolgar, *The Great Household in Late Medieval England*, 190.
69. *Vita*, 68.
70. 'Brief Summary', 338.
71. TNA SC 1/63/150.
72. Underhill, *Good Estate*, 18.
73. 'Brief Summary', 337–8.
74. *CPR 1313–7*, 644.
75. *CPR 1313–7*, 666.
76. *Issues*, 133.
77. Underhill, *Good Estate*, 18; *Issues*, 133–4.
78. Underhill, *Good Estate*, 17.
79. 'Brief Summary', 339.
80. *Trokelowe*, 98–9; Phillips, 296; Prestwich, *Plantagenet England*, 203.

8 Robbery, Holy Oil and an Impostor

1. *Vita*, 87; *Flores*, 178; *Valence*, 119.
2. *Vita*, 80; see also *Gesta*, 50; *Murimuth*, 271.
3. *Vita*, 80.
4. Sayles, *Functions*, 336–7.
5. *CPL*, 414, 430–1, 439.
6. *Vita*, 80.
7. *Vita*, 87; *Flores*, 176–7.
8. J. R. S. Phillips, 'The "Middle Party" and the Negotiating', 17.
9. Phillips, 297.
10. *Vita*, 80–1.
11. *Valence*, 119–20.
12. *Gesta*, 50–2; *Murimuth*, 271–6.
13. *Vita*, 29.
14. 'Brief Summary', 342–3; *Register*, 165.
15. *Foedera*, 333.
16. TNA SC 8/279/13911; *CPR 1313–47*, 672.
17. TNA SC/8/197/9804; *CCR 1313–18*, 463.
18. *CPL*, 434.
19. 'Brief Summary', 339–40.
20. W. W. Rouse Ball, *King's Scholars and King's Hall*, 3.
21. *Tyranny*, 69.
22. Trevor Henry Aston et al, *The Early Oxford Colleges* (1984), 195; *CPR 1317–21*, 75, 103–4, 168–9, 237; *CPR 1321–4*, 423.
23. Cobban, 'University of Cambridge', 49–78.
24. *Foedera*, 357.
25. Nicholas Orme, *From Childhood to Chivalry* (1984), 91; Susan Cavanaugh, 'Royal Books: King John to Richard II', 305–9; Johnstone, 18, 86.
26. McKisack, *Fourteenth Century*, 2.
27. Cavanaugh, 'Royal Books', 308–9.
28. *Register*, 8.
29. 'Court', 68; Johnstone, 29.
30. SAL MS 122, 51.

31. Prestwich, 'Court', 68.
32. Johnstone, 61.
33. Morris, *Terrible King*, 202; Phillips, 'Place of the Reign', 228, and *Edward II*, 70; *Place*, 283.
34. Ormrod, 'Personal Religion', 855–6; Prestwich, *Edward I*, 111–14; *Perfect King*, 109–13; *CPR 1327–30*, 440.
35. *Livere*, 333.
36. 'Brief Summary', 341.
37. *Valence*, 125.
38. Haines, *Edward*, 108; *Lancaster*, 208; *Valence*, 123.
39. *Valence*, 123–4.
40. *Vita*, 81 (both quotations).
41. *Flores*, 180; *Vita*, 82.
42. *Vita*, 81–2.
43. *Flores*, 180–1; *Lancaster*, 210; Haines, *Edward*, 109.
44. 'Brief Summary', 344; *Register*, 167.
45. Michael Prestwich, 'Gilbert de Middleton', 183.
46. Prestwich, 'Gilbert de Middleton', 189.
47. *CPL*, 431–2.
48. *Vita*, 83; 'Brief Summary', 328; *Lancaster*, 206.
49. *Foedera*, 342.
50. *Scalacronica*, 60; 'Brief Summary', 330.
51. *Livere*, 333–5; *Anonimalle*, 90–2; *Lanercost*, 218; *Scalacronica*, 60; *Vita*, 82–4.
52. *CPR 1317–21*, 46; *CCR 1313–8*, 575; *Foedera*, 345–6; 'Brief Summary', 329; *CIM*, 98–9.
53. *CFR 1307–19*, 225, 316.
54. *CFR 1307–19*, 346–7; *Foedera*, 345–346; *CCR 1313–1318*, 575.
55. *Lancaster*, 207–8; Haines, *Edward*, 107–8.
56. *CPR 1317–21*, 34, 46, 58.
57. *CFR 1307–19*, 350; T. B. Pugh, 'The Marcher Lords', 603, note 2.
58. *Valence*, 131; *Lancaster*, 224.
59. *Flores*, 219, 222, 228.
60. *Valence*, 139–47, 317–9; *Lancaster*, 211–12.
61. *Foedera*, 345.
62. 'Court', 73.
63. 'Brief Summary', 344.
64. Johnstone, 30; Daniel Hahn, *The Tower Menagerie* (2003), 41–2.
65. Johnstone, 86; *CDS 1272–1307*, 364–6.
66. *CCR 1313–8*, 4, 60, 124, 163, 249, 362–3, 389, 502.
67. Johnstone, *Letters of Edward*, 31, 117; Vale, *Princely Court*, 305; *CPR 1307–13*, 82, 204, 291, 437, 557, 643.
68. 'Brief Summary', 344.
69. 'Brief Summary', 344; 'Court' 66.
70. 'Brief Summary', 342.
71. 'Court', 66–7.
72. *Foedera*, 353.
73. *CPR 1327–30*, 439.
74. *CPR 1317–21*, 3, 8, 112, 223.
75. *CCR 1313–8*, 527.
76. *Foedera*, 360.
77. *Itinerary*, 165; 'Brief Summary', 337.
78. 'Brief Summary', 338.

79   Prestwich, *Three Edwards*, 161.
80. *Foedera*, 358, 388, 391; TNA SC 7/25/21; 'Brief Summary', 330.
81. 'Brief Summary', 330–1; *Bruce*, 341.
82. *Scalacronica*, 66; *Lanercost*, 219–20.
83. *CDS*, 113.
84. *Foedera*, 365.
85. *Lanercost*, 221; *Livere*, 335.
86. *Foedera*, 362, 364.
87. *Vita*, 89.
88. *Foedera*, 359, 360–1, 375, 384.
89. William Page, ed., *A History of the County of Hertford*, Vol. 4 (1971), 446.
90. *Foedera*, 361, 375, 384.
91. *CPR 1307–13*, 96, 148, 453, 515; *CPR 1313–7*, 295.
92. 'Brief Summary', 337.
93. *CFR 1307–19*, 389; *CPR 1327–30*, 163.
94. *Lanercost*, 221–6; Childs, 'Welcome my Brother'.
95. *Scalacronica*, 65; *Vita*, 86–7; *Gesta*, 55.
96. *Anonimalle*, 94.
97. *Vita*, 86.
98. *Anonimalle*, 94.
99. *Lanercost*, 222.
100. Childs, 'Welcome, my Brother', 153.
101. Phillips, 'Edward II and the Prophets', 196.
102. *CPL*, 436–7; Phillips, 'Edward II and the Prophets', 197–8; F. D. Blackley, 'The Holy Oil', 330–44; Phillips, 325–7, 340–2.
103. Phillips, 'Place of the Reign', 228; Phillips, 341–2.
104. Haines, *Edward*, 110.
105. Haines, *Edward*, 113.
106. *Foedera*, 370; *CCR 1318–23*, 112–4. For the Treaty, see: *Lancaster*, 213–29; *Valence*, 136–77; Haines, *Edward*, 109–17; Phillips, 318–21.
107. *Foedera*, 377; *Place*, 315, 350.
108. *Foedera*, 393.
109. *CCR 1307–1313*, 5; TNA E 101/369/11; *CPR 1301–07*, 443; *Chronicle of Pierre de Langtoft*, Vol. 2, 368–9.
110. *Baker*, 6.
111. *CDS*, 69; *CPR 1307–13*, 492; *CPR 1313–7*, 20, 540; *CFR 1307–19*, 181, 203, 223, 242, 278.
112. *CCW*, 308; *CFR 1307–19*, 54; *CCR 1307–13*, 198; *CIM*, 20; *AL*, 200, for the attack; Juliet Barker, *The Tournament in England*, 133.
113. For instance, *CPR 1307–13*, 528, 561, 571.
114. *CPR 1317–21*, 10, 45, 56.
115. *Tyranny*, 31.
116. *Vita*, 93, 111.

9 Household and Homage

1.   The original French text is printed in *Place*, 241–81.
2.   Woolgar, *Great Household*, 12.
3.   *Vita*, 75.
4.   *Vita*, 75.
5.   *Opposition*, 233.

6. Weir, *Isabella*, 150, makes this claim, but the men she names are frequently mentioned in Edward's chamber accounts of the 1320s as his valets.
7. SAL MS 122, 6, 19, 25, 63.
8. 'Court', 70.
9. Vale, *Princely Court*, 114–5.
10. Vale, *Princely Court*, 109–10.
11. 'First Journal', 676.
12. SAL MS 122, 41, 43, 60, 62–4, 79.
13. Frédérique Lachaud, 'Liveries of Robes', 290–1; Baines and Whatton, *History of the County Palatine of Lancaster*, 132–3.
14. CCR 1318–23, 118, 132; *Foedera*, 380–1; *Perfect King*, 403–4.
15. *Foedera*, 381, 405.
16. *Flores*, 192.
17. CCR 1318–23, 143.
18. CCR 1318–23, 141; *Foedera*, 400.
19. CPR 1317–21, 386, 415; TNA SC 8/294/14667; SAL MS 122, 9, 32, 62.
20. CCR 1318–23, 141.
21. *Foedera*, 402; *Itinerary*, 184–7.
22. Sayles, *Functions*, 337; ODNB.
23. *Vita*, 94; *Lancaster*, 246–7.
24. CDS, 124; *Lancaster*, 246–7.
25. *Lanercost*, 226.
26. Saaler, *Edward II*, 97.
27. Prestwich, *Edward I*, 115.
28. *Trokelowe*, 103.
29. Doherty, *Death*, 64.
30. *Vita*, 95–7.
31. Haskins, 'Chronicle of the Civil Wars', 77.
32. AP, 287–8; *Flores*, 188; Doherty, *Death*, 63–4; Phillips, 347.
33. *Trokelowe*, 104; *Gesta*, 57.
34. *Lanercost*, 227; *Livere*, 337; *Brut*, 211–12.
35. CCW, 570.
36. *Lancaster*, 248–9.
37. Cited in *Lancaster*, 249.
38. *Gesta*, 57.
39. *Vita*, 104; also *Flores*, 188.
40. Saaler, *Edward II*, 97.
41. *Trokelowe*, 104; *Itinerary*, 187.
42. *Walsingham*, 155–6; Phillips, 349.
43. *Flores*, 188; *Lancaster*, 247.
44. *Lanercost*, 227–8.
45. CPR 1317–21, 414, 416; *Foedera*, 409–11.
46. *Livere*, 337.
47. TNA C 47/22/12; *Flores*, 190–3.
48. *Foedera*, 412.
49. Rouse Ball, *King's Scholars*, 6–8.
50. Weir, *Isabella*, 124.
51. *Livere*, 337.
52. PROME.
53. *Foedera*, 417–8.
54. *Valence*, 189.
55. AP, 288.

56. *Foedera*, 20, 21, 43, 179, 355, 385.
57. Sayles, *Functions*, 360.
58. *Livere*, 337.
59. *Flores*, 193; *CCR 1327–30*, 4; SAL MS 122, 76.
60. 'Brief Summary', 334.
61. *CPR 1317–21*, 448–55.
62. 'Brief Summary', 332–3.
63. Morris, *Terrible King*, 43, 108.
64. E. Pole Stuart, 'Interview Between Philip V and Edward II', 412–15; the translation is from Vale, *Origins of the Hundred Years War*, 51, and see also Phillips, 358–9.
65. *Scalacronica*, 74–5.
66. 'Secular Musicians', 69; *Register*, 144.
67. *AP*, 290; *Foedera*, 428.
68. *Valence*, 190–1.
69. Chaplais, *English Medieval Diplomatic Practice*, Part 1, Vol. 1, 64–6.
70. *CCR 1318–23*, 326; *Foedera*, 433; 'Brief Summary', 338–9.
71. Cited in *PROME*.
72. Haines, *Edward*, 45.

10 The Despenser War

1. *Lanercost*, 230.
2. *Vita*, 115.
3. *AP*, 292; *Trokelowe*, 107; *Walsingham*, 252.
4. *Baker*, 11, translated by Haines, *Edward*, 124.
5. *AP*, 259.
6. *Brut*, 212.
7 *Anonimalle*, 92.
8. *Vita*, 115.
9. *Flores*, 194–6; *Lanercost*, 229; *Knighton*, 196.
10. *Scalacronica*, 70.
11. J. Goronwy Edwards, *Calendar of Ancient Correspondence*, 219–20.
12. *Vita*, 108–09.
13. *Place*, 124, calls the Marchers' privileges 'a dangerous anachronism'.
14. *CCR 1318–23*, 268, for Gower; *Vita*, 108, for the quote; see also *AP*, 293.
15. *CPR 1317–21*, 547–8.
16. *Vita*, 109.
17. *Polychronicon*, 298–300; *Scalacronica*, 75.
18. *Foedera*, 437.
19. *CCR 1318–23*, 365.
20. *Foedera*, 437.
21. *Issues*, 135.
22. Vale, *Princely Court*, 308.
23. Edwards, *Ancient Correspondence*, 219.
24. *CCR 1318–23*, 355.
25. *Brut*, 213; *Lancaster*, 267.
26. *Vita*, 111.
27. *CCR 1318–23*, 260, 285–6, 326; *CPR 1317–21*, 505.
28. *Vita*, 128–9.
29. *CCR 1318–23*, 260.

30. *CFR 1319–27*, 15, 18; *CFR 1307–19*, 103.
31. *CIM*, 245; TNA SC 8/160/7986.
32. *Valence*, 191.
33. *CPL 1342–62*, 164.
34. 'Brief Summary', 338.
35. *Foedera*, 444; *CCR 1318–23*, 363.
36. *CCR 1318–23*, 363–5; *Foedera*, 446.
37. *CCR 1323–27*, 359.
38. *Foedera*, 446.
39. *Lancaster*, 265.
40. *Vita*, 109.
41. *CCR 1318–23*, 367–8.
42. Stevenson, 'Letter of the Younger Despenser', 761.
43. Cited in *Lancaster*, 266, note 2.
44. 'Secular Musicians', 66; *Register*, 32–3.
45. *Vita*, 110.
46. *Brut*, 213; *Trokelowe*, 109; *AP*, 303.
47. Cited in *Lancaster*, 266, note 2.
48. *Foedera*, 449; 'Secular Musicians', 69.
49. *CCR 1318–23*, 541–3; *Flores*, 344–5; *Vita*, 110; *AP*, 293.
50. *CCR 1318–23*, 541–2; J. C. Davies, 'The Despenser War in Glamorgan', 55–6.
51. TNA SC 8/6/298; Davies, 'Despenser War', 58.
52. *CCR 1318–23*, 543–4; *CCR 1323–27*, 118.
53. *Vita*, 115. The author described the elder Despenser as 'brutal and greedy', and had no better opinion of the younger Hugh: *Vita*, 114–15.
54. Cited in Haines, *Edward*, 124.
55. 'Brief Summary', 335; Davies, 'Despenser War', 58.
56. *CPR 1321–4*, 167–8, 249.
57. *CCR 1318–23*, 541; *Flores*, 345.
58. TNA Arundell Deeds 215/1.
59. *Place*, 127.
60. *CPR 1317–21*, 591, 596–7.
61. *Valence*, 205–06.
62. *Tyranny*, 140.
63. 'Brief Summary', 338, 344–5; Vale, *Princely Court*, 308.
64. *Brut*, 213.
65. TNA SC 8/7/301.
66. TNA SC 8/92/4561; *Trokelowe*, 108; *Walsingham*, 160.
67. *Brut*, 213–4; *Lancaster*, 272–7.
68. *CFR 1319–27*, 68.
69. Tebbit, 'Royal Patronage and Political Allegiance', 206.
70. *Foedera*, 452.
71. *CPR 1321–24*, 23.
72. *CPR 1327–30*, 163.
73. *CCR 1313–8*, 477; *Foedera*, 453.
74. *AP*, 294.
75. *Vita*, 112; *AP*, 294–6.
76. *Lancaster*, 283–5; *PROME*.
77. *AP*, 296–7.
78. *Vita*, 113.
79. Haines, *Edward*, 128–9.
80. *AP*, 297.

81. *CCR 1318–23*, 494; *Vita*, 113; *AP*, 297; *Anonimalle*, 100.
82. *Murimuth*, 33; *Baker*, 11; Haines, *Edward*, 129.
83. *Murimuth*, 33.
84. *Vita*, 121.
85. *CCR 1318–23*, 492–494, 541–3; *PROME*.
86. *CPR 1321–24*, 15–21; *Foedera*; 454; TNA DL 10/234; *PROME*.
87. *Vita*, 116.
88. *PROME*; Phillips, 394.

11 The King's Revenge

1. *Brut*, 214; *Anonimalle*, 100.
2. *Vita*, 115–6, for the quote, and also *Brut*, 214; *AP*, 300; *Anonimalle*, 100; *Croniques*, 42; *Flores*, 198; *Trokelowe*, 110; *Scalacronica*, 70; G. A. Holmes, 'Judgement on the Younger Despenser, 1326', 264.
3. *Foedera*, 941.
4. *CPR 1324–7*, 130.
5. *Murimuth*, 33.
6. *CCR 1318–23*, 477–8.
7. *AP*, 298; TNA SC 8/17/833.
8. *Valence*, 216.
9. *AP*, 299.
10. Weir, *Isabella*, 134.
11. *Anonimalle*, 102–4; *Calendar of Letter-Books of London 1314–1337*, 155. See also *AP*, 298–9; *Baker*, 11–12; *Flores*, 199–200; *Livere*, 339; *Murimuth*, 35; *Trokelowe*, 110–11; *Vita*, 116.
12. *Tyranny*, 51.
13. *Vita*, 117.
14. *Murimuth*, 34; *Scalacronica*, 67.
15. *Anonimalle*, 102.
16. *CFR 1319–27*, 76; *Anonimalle*, 102; *Croniques*, 43; *AP*, 299.
17. Donald Matthew, *King Stephen* (2002), 80.
18. *Vita*, 116.
19. *CCR 1313–23*, 505–6; *Foedera*, 459.
20. *Lancaster*, 300.
21. *Livere*, 339.
22. *Lancaster*, 304.
23. *CPR 1321–4*, 37; *CCR 1318–23*, 410, 510–11.
24. Haines, *Edward*, 134.
25. *CCR 1318–23*, 510–11.
26. *Livere*, 339.
27. *Vita*, 116.
28. *Flores*, 192–3.
29. *CPR 1321–4*, 40.
30. *CPR 1321–4*, 45.
31. *Letters of the Kings of England*, 23–4.
32. *Vita*, 117.
33. *Trokelowe*, 111; *AP*, 301; Vale, *Princely Court*, 309.
34. *CCR 1318–23*, 510–11; *Foedera*, 470.
35. Mark Buck, *Politics, Finance and the Church*, 138–9; Edwards, 'Political Importance', 339.

36. *CCR 1318–23*, 516; Scott L. Waugh, 'Profits of Violence', 850.
37. Waugh, 'Profits of Violence', 850; Haines, *Edward*, 135.
38. *CPR 1321–4*, 47; *Lancaster*, 306.
39. *Foedera*, 471; *CPR 1321–4*, 47.
40. *Vita*, 118; see also *Gesta*, 74.
41. *CCR 1318–23*, 511–14; *Foedera*, 471.
42. *Vita*, 121.
43. Tebbit, 'Household Knights', 90.
44. *CPR 1321–4*, 202, 307.
45. *CPR 1321–4*, 47–8, 51; *Foedera*, 472.
46. *Vita*, 119.
47. *Croniques*, 43; *Vita*, 119.
48. TNA SC 8/6/255.
49. *CPR 1321–4*, 62, 77; *CCR 1318–23*, 418, 422, 519.
50. *Vita*, 119; Haines, *Church and Politics*, 142.
51. Vale, *Princely Court*, 309.
52. *CFR 1319–27*, 91.
53. *CCR 1318–23*, 525–6; *Foedera*, 474, and see also 459, 463, 472.
54. *Bruce*, 343.
55. *CCR 1318–23*, 515–16.
56. *Lancaster*, 307.
57. *CCR 1318–23*, 516; *Foedera*, 474.
58. *CPR 1321–4*, 64; *AP*, 301.
59. *CCR 1318–23*, 521–2; *Foedera*, 474–5.
60. *CCR 1318–23*, 525–6.
61. *CCR 1318–23*, 524.
62. *CCR 1318–23*, 525.
63. *Gesta*, 75.
64. *CFR 1319–27*, 100.
65. *Livere*, 341.
66. Haines, *Edward*.
67. *Opposition*, 218, 233.
68. *CPR 1338–40*, 102–3.
69. George Sayles, 'Formal Judgements on the Traitors', 58.
70. *Lanercost*, 235; *Croniques*, 44. See also *Gesta*, 74–5; *Baker*, 13; *Flores*, 346; *Livere*, 340; *Murimuth*, 36. For Elizabeth's statement, see G. A. Holmes, 'A Protest Against the Despensers', 210.
71. *Vita*, 123.
72. *Lancaster*, 310.
73. *Brut*, 217.
74. *Flores*, 346.
75. Hamilton, *Gaveston*, 39.
76. For the battle, see: *Brut*, 215–20; *Lanercost*, 231–3; *Flores*, 204–05; *Gesta*, 74–6.
77. *Foedera*, 479; *CIM*, 130.
78. *Vita*, 124–5.
79. *CCR 1318–23*, 535; *CIM*, 131.
80. *CIM*, 129–134.
81. *Brut*, 216– 21.
82. *Vita*, 125.
83. *Anonimalle*, 106.
84. Phillips, 408; *Lancaster*, 311–12.

85. *Vita*, 126.
86. *Brut*, 222; *Vita*, 126; *Livere*, 341–2.
87. *Lanercost*, 234; *Anonimalle*, 108; *Brut*, 222.
88. *Vita*, 126.
89. *Brut*, 223; *Vita*, 126.
90. *Scalacronica*, 67.
91. *Brut*, 223; *Lanercost*, 234; *AP*, 302–03; *Baker*, 14; *Gesta*, 77; *Trokelowe*, 112–24.
92. *Anonimalle*, 108; *Brut*, 228; *Lancaster*, 329.
93. *Lancaster*, 329.
94. *CPR 1321–4*, 148–9; *CCR 1318–23*, 673; Sayles, 'Formal Judgement', 60.
95. *Trokelowe*, 109.
96. *Scalacronica*, 67; *Gesta*, 78; *Anonimalle*, 108–10; *Lanercost*, 237; *AP*, 303; *Foedera*, 536–7; *Vita*, 119–20. For a full list of the men executed, see http://edwardthesecond.blogspot.com/2009/06/edward-iis-executions-of-1322.html
97. *Brut*, 221; *CPR 1338–40*, 209; Sayles, 'Formal Judgement', 60.
98. Haskins, 'Chronicle of the Civil Wars', 83; *Lanercost*, 62; *Vita*, 100.
99. *CFR 1319–27*, 280; *CCR 1323–7*, 202–03.
100. *CFR 1319–27*, 154–71.
101. Buck 'Reform of Exchequer', 247–8.
102. *Tyranny*, 63.
103. Phillips, 412, note 7; Morris, *Terrible King*, 190.
104. *Anonimalle*, 80; *Lanercost*, 235; *Flores*, 200, cited in Phillips, 412.
105. *CPR 1321–4*, 249; see also *Anonimalle*, 110; *Opposition*, 565.
106. *CPR 1321–4*, 93; *Foedera*, 481.
107. *CChR*, 441–53; *CPR 1321–4*, 183, 327; *Foedera*, 491; *CCR 1323–7*, 335; *Tyranny*, 107–18, 228–32.
108. *CDS*, 140.
109. *Foedera*, 481; *CPL*, 448; TNA SC 7/25/14. Doherty, *Death*, 74, claims without citing a source that John XXII 'intervened and begged the King to show some restraint' regarding the executions. I have been unable to find this.
110. *Brut*, 225.

12 Tyranny, Miracles and an Escape

1. *Vita*, 136.
2. *Brut*, 220; *Scalacronica*, 70.
3. Holmes, 'Judgement', 265.
4. *CIM*, 200–01.
5. Underhill, *Good Estate*, 31–3.
6. Holmes, 'Protest Against the Despensers', 211.
7. *Scalacronica*, 70.
8. *Tyranny*, 107, 232.
9. E. B. Fryde, 'Deposits of Hugh Despenser', 348.
10. 'First Journal', 676.
11. TNA E 372/171, mem. 41; *CPR 1324–7*, 172, 278, 325; *CPR 1327–30*, 168–9.
12. John Carmi Parsons, 'Intercessory Patronage', 153–5.
13. *Opposition*, 97; SAL MS 122, 43.
14. Claire Sponsler, 'The King's Boyfriend', 147; *Polychronicon*, 314.
15. *CFR 1319–27*, 124; *CCR 1318–23*, 529–34, 556–9.
16. *Lanercost*, 237–8.

17. *CCR 1318–23*, 577–8; *CPR 1321–4*, 184.
18. Gunnar Tilander, *La Venerie de Twiti* (1956).
19. Weir, *Isabella*, 170.
20. Blackley, 'Bastard Son', 76–7.
21. *Foedera*, 497; *CCR 1318–23*, 680.
22. Graham Bell, *Robert the Bruce's Forgotten Victory*, 114; *Bruce*, 345–6.
23. *Flores*, 224–5.
24. *Anonimalle*, 112. See also *Lanercost*, 240, and *CDS*, 147.
25. *Foedera*, 498.
26. *Gesta*, 79.
27. *Flores*, 210; *Lanercost*, 240.
28. *Croniques*, 45.
29. *Scalacronica*, 69–70.
30. *Flores*, 218; *Tyranny*, 69–105.
31. Holmes, 'Judgement', 265.
32. *CDS*, 146.
33. *Bruce*, 346.
34. Haines, *Edward*, 84 and 394, note 142; Weir, *Isabella*, 146–7; Doherty, *Death*, 75–8.
35. Doherty, *Death*, 75, says the Despensers 'decided once again to place the Queen in danger'. His account of subsequent events in fact contradicts this.
36. Weir, *Isabella*, 146; Saaler, *Edward II*, 116.
37. *CPL*, 457.
38. 'First Journal', 678.
39. *CPR 1321–4*, 227, 229.
40. *CCR 1318–23*, 597; *CPR 1321–4*, 206.
41. *CPR 1321–4*, 215, 221–2, 254; *CCR 1318–23*, 622, 685; 'First Journal', 680.
42. 'First Journal', 678; *Vita*, 128.
43. *Vita*, 128.
44. *Flores*, 212; *CPR 1321–4*, 232.
45. Phillips, 428–9.
46. Phillips, 429.
47. 'Secular Musicians', 70; 'First Journal', 675–6.
48. *Livere*, 347; *Brut*, 228.
49. 'First Journal', 676, 678; TNA E 101/379/17.
50. 'First Journal' 677; E 101/379/17.
51. 'First Journal', 677–8; E 101/379/17.
52. *CCR 1318–23*, 687, 690.
53. Saaler, *Edward II*, 116.
54. TNA E 101/379/17, 4.
55. Isabella's letter: TNA SC 1/37/45; Eleanor's: SC 1/37/4.
56. *Opposition*, 96–7; E 101/379/7. *La Alianore* appears to have been a different ship from *La Despenser*.
57. Phillips, 363–4, note 222, and 483, note 169; Haines, *Edward*, 43, 375, note 93; 'Court', 71.
58. 'Court', 71.
59. *Flores*, 229; 'Court', 71.
60. *Knighton*, 434.
61. Doherty, *Death*, 100–2, suggests that Despenser sexually harassed Isabella or that 'wife-swapping' was involved; Weir, *Isabella*, 149, that Despenser raped the queen. No evidence is offered except the 'dishonour'.
62. 'First Journal', 678.

63. 'First Journal', 679.
64. *CCR 1323–7*, 168, 327; *CPR 1321–4*, 341; *CPR 1324–7*, 52; TNA E 40/4880; Fryde, 'Deposits', 348, 351.
65. *Lanercost*, 241.
66. *Foedera*, 502; *CDS*, 148.
67. *CCR 1318–23*, 692; *CPR 1321–4*, 234.
68. 'First Journal', 678.
69. *Lanercost*, 242 (quotation); *Foedera*, 504.
70. *Lanercost*, 243–4.
71. *CPR 1321–4*, 260; *Lanercost*, 245; *Brut*, 227–8; *Foedera*, 509.
72. *Brut*, 228.
73. *Lanercost*, 245; *Gesta*, 81–4; *AP*, 303–4; *Trokelowe*, 127.
74. *CCR 1327–30*, 404.
75. *Lanercost*, 242.
76. *CDS*, 152.
77. *CCR 1318–23*, 697; *Foedera*, 506.
78. 'First Journal', 679; TNA E 101/379/7, mem. 3.
79. TNA E 101/379/7, mem. 3.
80. *Vita*, 129–31; *Trokelowe*, 138–9.
81. *Livere*, 347, and see also *Brut*, 231, and *Trokelowe*, 138–9.
82. *CPR 1321–4*, 234; *Vita*, 130.
83. *CPR 1321–4*, 257, 314, 349.
84. *Foedera*, 507.
85. *CCR 1318–23*, 697. Sanchia and Richard of Cornwall's only child Edmund died childless in 1300, leaving Edward I and then Edward II as his heirs.
86. *CCR 1323–7*, 136; *Foedera*, 531, 534.
87. *CCR 1318–23*, 697.
88. *Foedera*, 517–20, 524–9.
89. *Foedera*, 527; Haines, *Archbishop John Stratford*, 139.
90. *CCR 1323–7*, 147–8; *CCW*, 546.
91. *CCR 1323–7*, 147–8; *CCW*, 546.
92. *Foedera*, 464.
93. Haines, *Church and Politics*, 138.
94. *CCR 1323–7*, 325.
95. Edwards, 'Political Importance', 336; Haines, *John Stratford*, 139.
96. *CPL*, 468–9.
97. Edwards, 'Political Importance', 340.
98. Malcolm Vale, 'Ritual Ceremony', 27; Teofilo F. Ruiz, *The City and the Realm 1080–1492* (2004), 144.
99. *CCR 1318–23*, 701; *Foedera*, 510.
100. *Lancaster*, 329–30.
101. *Tyranny*, 153.
102. *CIM*, 528–9.
103. *Brut*, 230.
104. *CCW*, 543.
105. *CPR 1321–4*, 278; *CDS*, 150; *Valence*, 230–1.
106. *CPR 1321–4*, 277–9; *Foedera*, 510–11, 521–3; *Gesta*, 84; *Flores*, 215–16; *Lanercost*, 246–7.
107. *CCR 1318–23*, 713–4.
108. *Sardos*, 16.
109. 'Secular Musicians', 71; *CPR 1321–4*, 333; *Foedera*, 531.
110. *CCR 1323–7*, 13.

111. *CCR 1323–7*, 132.
112. *CPR 1321–4*, 335; Phillips, 459.
113. *CCR 1323–7*, 133.
114. *Scalacronica*, 72; *Lanercost*, 251; *Anonimalle*, 116; *AP*, 305–6; *Croniques*, 46–7; *Livere*, 349–51; *Trokelowe*, 145–6.
115. Gransden, *Historical Writing*, 20, citing *Flores*, 217, citing Acts 16, 22–28, and Acts 12, 6–11.
116. *Brut*, 231; *Murimuth*, 40.
117. F. D. Blackley, 'Isabella and the Bishop of Exeter', 221.
118. *Traitor*, 130–31.
119. *CCR 1323–7*, 137–8, 140–1.
120. *CPR 1321–4*, 349; *CCR 1323–7*, 134–5.
121. *CPR 1327–30*, 17, 28, 31, 42, 57, 60, 70, 125; *AP*, 311.
122. *CPR 1321–4*, 443, 449.
123. *CCR 1323–7*, 87–8, 106.
124. *Sardos*, 22, 103.
125. Haines, *Church and Politics*, 49–52, 139–53; Haines, *Edward*, 152–7.
126. *Lancaster*, 319.
127. *Vita*, 136–8.
128. *AP*, 306; *Opposition*, 561–2.
129. Tout, *Chapters*, Vol. 2, 277.
130. Sayles, *Functions*, 328, for the quote.
131. *Sardos*, 176–7.
132. *Sardos*, 180.
133. *Sardos*, 5; *CCW*, 548.
134. *CCR 1323–7*, 322.
135. *CCR 1323–7*, 21–2, 58, 156, 171–3.
136. *CCW*, 549–50.
137. 'Secular Musicians', 71.
138. J. P. Toomey, *Records of Hanley Castle* (2001), xx. The castle has long since disappeared.
139. Martyn Lawrence, 'Secular Patronage', 92–3.
140. *CCR 1323–7*, 72; *Foedera*, 546; *Murimuth*, 43; *AP*, 306.
141. *CPR 1321–4*, 426.
142. *Sardos*, 189.
143. *Sardos*, 188–90; *Foedera*, 547.

13 Catastrophe in Gascony

1. *Tyranny*, 162–4.
2. *CPL*, 461.
3. *CCR 1323–7*, 171.
4. *CCR 1323–7*, 175–6. Alfonso XI, born August 1311, was a great-great-grandson of Edward's grandfather Fernando III. Juan Manuel was also a grandson of Fernando III. Felipe was the son of Sancho IV and brother of Fernando IV, and Juan el Tuerto was the son of Juan (died 1319), son of Edward's uncle Alfonso X.
5. *Place*, 283–4; Prestwich, 'Piety of Edward I', 126.
6. Hamilton, *Gaveston*, 167, note 85.
7. *Flores*, 222; *Valence*, 233.
8. *Brut*, 232.

9.   *CCR 1318–23*, 563–4.
10.   *Valence*, 234–6.
11.   *Sardos*, 131–2, 191.
12.   *Tyranny*, 143.
13.   Morris, *Terrible King*, 268; *Baker*, 15.
14.   *Sardos*, 64.
15.   *Sardos*, 61–3, 92.
16.   *Sardos*, 50, note 1; *Foedera*, 570.
17.   *Sardos*, 52–3; *Tyranny*, 143.
18.   *CCR 1323–7*, 313–4.
19.   *CPR 1324–7*, 32.
20.   *CCR 1323–7*, 358–9.
21.   *CCR 1323–7*, 516–7.
22.   *CPR 1324–7*, 104.
23.   *CPR 1324–7*, 103–4; *Sardos*, 140–2.
24.   *CCR 1323–7*, 254, 344.
25.   *CPR 1324–7*, 104.
26.   *CCR 1323–7*, 556–7. Like Alfonso XI of Castile, Afonso IV of Portugal was the great-great-grandson of Fernando III of Castile. Queen Beatriz was yet another of Edward's Castilian cousins, daughter of Sancho IV and sister of Fernando IV.
27.   Haines, *Edward*, 323.
28.   *CCR 1323–7*, 344–5.
29.   *Sardos*, 76, 80.
30.   *Sardos*, 118–19, 145.
31.   *Sardos*, 130.
32.   *Sardos*, 59, 72–3.
33.   Fryde, 'Deposits', 361–2; *Tyranny*, 145.
34.   Sardos, 59–61; *Tyranny*, 145.
35.   *CFR 1319–27*, 300–2, 308; *CCR 1323–7*, 223, 260; *Foedera*, 569.
36.   *Lanercost*, 249, is one of the chronicles which gives Isabella's income as a pound a day; see Buck, 'Reform of the Exchequer', 251; *Place*, 140; and Tout, *Chapters*, Vol. 5, 274, for her real income.
37.   Menache, 'Isabelle of France', 110.
38.   Tout, *Chapters*, Vol. 3, 275.
39.   *CPR 1317–21*, 38, 46, for the seizure of Marguerite's lands.
40.   *CCR 1323–7*, 204, 206–7, 209–11, 216.
41.   *Sardos*, 128, 130.
42.   *CCR 1323–7*, 260; *CPR 1324–7*, 88, 157, 243; SAL MS 122, 81; *Notes and Queries*, 7th series (September 1886), 258. The girls lived sometimes in Pleshey, Essex, and sometimes in Marlborough, Wiltshire. One of them stayed for a while with the prioress of Ankerwick, Buckinghamshire, in or before May 1325 (SAL MS 122, 2, 78).
43.   Underhill, *Good Estate*, 40–41.
44.   TNA E 101/382/12: expenses; SAL MS 122, 66.
45.   Paul Doherty in his 1977 doctoral thesis about Isabella claimed that Edward removed the queen's children from her at the same time as he confiscated her lands in September 1324. The source Doherty cites for this, TNA E 403/201, is an issue roll of Edward's wardrobe department from 8 July 1322 to 7 July 1323.
46.   *CPR 1292–1301*, 592, 606; Benz St John, *Three Medieval Queens*, 109–110.
47.   Ormrod, 'Royal Nursery', 400–11.
48.   Marshall, 'Childhood and Household', *RENP*, 191–2.

49. *Lanercost*, 249; *Flores*, 226.
50. *Household Book*, 19, 127–9.
51. Haines, *Edward*, 43, 375.
52. PROME; *Sardos*, 95–7.
53. *Sardos*, 59, 214, 224, 233–4. There are many other such examples.
54. *Sardos*, 104, 217–8. Despenser, although about a dozen years older than Kent, was his nephew by marriage: Kent was the youngest son of Edward I, and Despenser's wife was Edward's eldest granddaughter.
55. *Sardos*, 143, 145.
56. *Sardos*, 143, 145.
57. *Scalacronica*, 70.
58. *Sardos*, 76.
59. CPR 1324–7, 6; CDS, 155–6; *Foedera*, 561, 578.
60. *Vita*, 131–4.
61. 'Secular Musicians', 72; Emma Griffin, *Blood Sport: Hunting in Britain since 1066* (2007), 81.
62. CIM, 326.
63. Vale, 'Ritual Ceremony', 25, citing TNA E 101/380/4, folio 24v.
64. 'Secular Musicians', 72.
65. CPR 1317–21, 387, 582.
66. CPR 1324–7, 88, 157, 243.
67. CPR 1324–7, 335; CMR, 32. John was the eldest son of the earl of Hereford killed at Boroughbridge in 1322.
68. Haines, *Archbishop John Stratford*, 156, says that neither Charles IV, Isabella nor anyone else 'had the slightest inkling of the extraordinary outcome of the policy they were advocating. Only in retrospect could the imaginative discern an overall scheme' to deprive Edward of his throne.
69. Sponsler, 'King's Boyfriend', 153, 163; Saaler, *Edward II*, 123.
70. Menache, 'Isabelle of France', 115.
71. *Sardos*, 42–3.
72. *Sardos*, 195–6.
73. *Baker*, 19.
74. CPL, 458, 462, 465, 467–8.
75. *Foedera*, 599.
76. *Vita*, 135.
77. *Lanercost*, 249; AP, 337.
78. CPL, 474; Blackley, 'Bishop of Exeter', 226.
79. *Croniques*, 50; *Anonimalle*, 120; *Brut*, 233.
80. Blackley, 'Bishop of Exeter', 226.
81. *Sardos*, 196.
82. CCR 1323–7, 353.
83. *Sardos*, 267.
84. Blackley, 'Bishop of Exeter', 228; *Tyranny*, 96.
85. *Vita*, 143.
86. *Sardos*, 199–200.
87. CPL, 466.
88. CCR 1323–7, 352; *Foedera*, 591, 595.
89. CCR 1323–7, 353.
90. *Sardos*, 114.
91. *Place*, 298, 315.
92. CCR 1323–7, 500.
93. *Foedera*, 601.

94. SAL MS 122, 4, 16, 19.
95. SAL MS 122, 19.
96. *CCR 1327–30*, 143–4, 147–8; *CIM*, 245–7; TNA SC 8/169/8443, SC 8/169/8437 etc.
97. Fryde, 'Deposits', 361–2.
98. SAL MS 122, 21.
99. *CCR 1323–7*, 385; *Foedera*, 602–3.
100. *Tyranny*, 148.
101. Buck, *Politics, Finance*, 156, note 199.
102. *Vita*, 140.
103. Parsons, *Eleanor*, 13.
104. *CPL*, 466; *Foedera*, 603.
105. *CCR 1323–7*, 496; SAL MS 122, 26, 31.
106. *CPR 1324–7*, 161–2, 166–8; *CCR 1323–7*, 503.
107. *Tyranny*, 96.
108. *CPR 1324–7*, 171.
109. *CPR 1324–7*, 171.
110. *CCR 1323–7*, 399; *CPR 1324–7*, 171.
111. *CPR 1324–7*, 167–70, 173–5.
112. *Foedera*, 607; *Sardos*, 195, 241.
113. *Murimuth*, 44; Denholm-Young, 'Edward of Windsor and Bermondsey Priory', 433. Phillips, 67, says that Abbot William was one of Edward's close personal friends.
114. SAL MS 122, 20–22.
115. *CCR 1323–7*, 577–8.
116. *Anonimalle*, 120; *Murimuth*, 44; *Vita*, 138.

14 The Queen Takes a Favourite

1. Denholm-Young, 'Bermondsey Priory', 433–4; *Foedera*, 609.
2. *Sardos*, 243; *CCR 1323–7*, 507; *CPR 1324–7*, 175.
3. SAL MS 122, 27.
4. Saaler, *Edward II*, 124.
5. SAL MS 122, 27.
6. *CCW*, 569.
7. SAL MS 122, 28.
8. *Itinerary*, 277; SAL MS 122, 29.
9. SAL MS 122, 28, 34, 38.
10. *CCR 1323–7*, 526; *Foedera*, 612–3.
11. SAL MS 122, 29, 34.
12. SAL MS 122, 38,
13. *AP*, 310, saying that Kent married Margaret around the time that Charles of Valois died, i.e. 16 December.
14. *CCR 1323–7*, 464.
15. Blackley, 'Bishop of Exeter', 230–5; Buck, *Politics, Finance*, 156–8.
16. *Vita*, 142–3; *Croniques*, 49.
17. Haines, *Edward*, 170; Phillips, 491.
18. SAL MS 122, 40ff.
19. *Livere*, 354–5; *CCR 1323–7*, 593; *CFR 1319–27*, 418.
20. Haines, *Archbishop John Stratford*, 166.
21. Blackley, 'Bishop of Exeter', 231; Carla Lord, 'Isabella at the Court', 46.

22. CCR 1323–7, 552; CFR 1319–27, 383, 388; *Foedera*, 630.
23. *Vita*, 143–4.
24. *Vita*, 144–5.
25. CPR 1324–7, 171, 193; CCR 1323–7, 505–6, 508, 527–8, 540–1, 569.
26. Vale, *Princely Court*, 159, 339.
27. *Foedera*, 617–8; CPL, 260.
28. CCR 1323–7, 543.
29. CCR 1323–7, 578–9.
30. *Lanercost*, 266–7; *Vita et Mors*, 307, cited in Haines, *Edward*, 169.
31. *Murimuth*, 45–6.
32. CCR 1323–7, 578–9.
33. Haines, *Edward*, 216 and 462, note 214; Burgtorf, 'With my Life', 40; *Scalacronica*, 72; *Croniques*, 61.
34. CPR 1324–7, 213.
35. Isabella's letter is cited in Phillips, 491, and Blackley, 'Bishop of Exeter', 234. Weir, *Isabella*, 196, claims the queen's 'profound revulsion' but cites no evidence.
36. CCR 1323–7, 580–82.
37. CCR 1323–7, 579–80.
38. SAL MS 122, 40, 43.
39. SAL MS 122, 45.
40. SAL MS 122, 46–7.
41. *Tyranny*, 186; Alison Marshall, 'Thomas of Brotherton', 81–6; SAL MS 122, 81.
42. SAL MS 122, 48–9, 54.
43. CPR 1317–21, 235; CPR 1321–4, 189.
44. *Livere*, 353–5.
45. CPR 1324–7, 238, 250, 283–4, 286; CCR 1323–7, 550–1; CCW, 575.
46. For the Folvilles, see Ian Mortimer, *Time-Traveller's Guide*, 240–2.
47. Aston, *Early Oxford Colleges*, 237–8; CChR, 481–2, 485–6.
48. Haines, *John Stratford*, 166.
49. Haines, *Edward*, 443, note 218; CCR 1323–7, 540–1; *Foedera*, 618.
50. CCR 1323–7, 556–7; *Foedera*, 625–6.
51. CPR 1324–7, 215.
52. SAL MS 122, 50, 65; *Notes and Queries* (September 1886), 258.
53. SAL MS 122, 50, 58.
54. CCR 1323–7, 545–7; *Foedera*, 619.
55. CCR 1323–7, 535–7, 542, 552, 638–40, etc; *Foedera*, 616, 636, 642.
56. CCR 1323–7, 543; *Foedera*, 619.
57. CCR 1323–7, 547; *Foedera*, 619; SAL MS 122, 51.
58. SAL MS 122, 50 (*q'nt le Roi sist enp's son lit vn poi deuant la mynoet*).
59. SAL MS 122, 21, 69, 78, 81.
60. *Place*, 254.
61. SAL MS 122, 51, 53, 56–8.
62. SAL MS 122, 55.
63. SAL MS 122, 53, 55.
64. CPR 1324–7, 285–6.
65. For example, *Trokelowe*, 110, and *Croniques*, 49.
66. CCR 1323–7, 551.
67. *Lanercost*, 250.
68. *Foedera*, 625l; CCR 1323–7, 543, 650.
69. *Brut*, 252–3.
70. CPR 1324–7, 286.
71. CCR 1323–7, 578–9.

72. *Vita*, 140.
73. *Perfect King*, 45.
74. SAL MS 122, 49, 59, 60, 68, 75, etc.
75. SAL MS 122, 49, 59, 60, 68, 75, etc.
76. *CCR 1323–7*, 471–2, 557.
77. *CCR 1323–7*, 569.
78. SAL MS 122, 62, 75, 92–3.
79. Lord, 'Isabella at the Court', 50.
80. *CCR 1323–7*, 576–8.
81. SAL MS 122, 62–4, 66, 70.
82. *CPL*, 473.
83. Haines, *Archbishop John Stratford*, 168.
84. *CPR 1324–7*, 269; *CCR 1323–7*, 563–4; Chaplais, *English Medieval Diplomatic Practice*, Part 1, Vol. 2, 314–5.
85. *AP*, 312; *Croniques*, 41; *CPL*, 478.
86. SAL MS 122, 65: *iewer a pelot*, 'playing at ball'.
87. Haines, *John Stratford*, 167–8; PROME.
88. *CPL*, 475, 477–8.
89. *CPL*, 476, 479, 481–3.
90. *CPL*, 482.
91. SAL MS 122, 65–6.
92. SAL MS 122, 66; Phillips, 496–8.
93. Haines, 'Bishops and Politics', 605–6.
94. Phillips, 498; Haines, *Edward*, 276; *CDS*, 160.
95. *Perfect King*, 59; Weir, *Isabella*, 200–01.
96. *Foedera*, 632–3, 637–8, 640–1.
97. *Tyranny*, 182; Jonathan Sumption, *Trial by Battle*, 101.
98. Sumption, *Trial by Battle*, 102; SAL MS 122, 70.
99. *ODNB*; Sumption, *Trial by Battle*, 102.
100. SAL MS 122, 66.
101. *CPR 1324–7*, 281.
102. SAL MS 122, 75, 77.
103. SAL MS 122, 75, 77.
104. *AP*, 312–3; SAL MS 122, 78–9.
105. *AP*, 312.
106. *CCR 1323–7*, 452, 533; *CPR 1324–7*, 206, 258.
107. SAL MS 122, 80–81.
108. SAL MS 122, 81.
109. *Brut*, 234–5.
110. *Flores*, 231; Haines, *Edward*, 173; Phillips, 500.
111. *CFR 1319–27*, 404, 410; *CCR 1323–7*, 636, 642; *CPR 1324–7*, 296.
112. *CCR 1323–7*, 556, 643.
113. *CCR 1323–7*, 640–5 (p. 642, 'malice'); SAL MS 122, 83 (*la Dorre*); Fryde, *Tyranny*, 184–5; Haines, Edward, 172.
114. Fryde, 'Deposits', 348, 350.

15 Invasion, Abdication and Imprisonment

1. Phillips, 501–02.
2. Phillips, 504; Ormrod, *Edward III*, 42; *Perfect King*, 48.
3. SAL MS 122, 87; *Foedera*, 643.

4. *CCR 1327–30*, 189, 249.
5. *CCR 1323–7*, 650–51.
6. *Foedera*, 645–6; Phillips, 509–10.
7. For the accusations of sodomy, see *Intrigue*, 47–50; for Orleton, Haines, *Edward*, 179, and Haines, *Church and Politics*, 165.
8. *Perfect King*, 49.
9. *Tyranny*, 188.
10 *CFR 1319–27*, 418, 421. Edward's chamber accounts call Hugh Huchon; the *Anonimalle*, 132, Hughelyn.
11. *CPR 1324–7*, 328, 335; *CCR 1323–7*, 650–51.
12. *CPR 1324–7*, 325–7.
13. Bloom, 'Simon de Swanland and King Edward II', 2.
14. SAL MS 122, 92.
15. *CCW*, 582.
16. Haines, *Edward*, 178.
17. Phillips, 506.
18. Buck, *Politics, Finance*, 220–21; Haines, *John Stratford*, 173; *Croniques*, 52.
19. *Croniques*, 56; *AP*, 321.
20. Haines, *Edward*, 179; Phillips, 507.
21. Phillips, 98.
22. SAL MS 122, 88–90.
23. SAL MS 122, 89.
24. *CCR 1327–30*, 9.
25. *CPR 1321–4*, 62–3, 78, 97, 358, 396; *CCR 1323–7*, 125.
26. *CCR 1323–7*, 638; *CPR 1324–7*, 304.
27. *CFR 1327–37*, 43; *CCR 1327–30*, 182.
28. *Murimuth*, 257; *CCR 1330–3*, 77.
29. *CCR 1323–7*, 517.
30. TNA SC 8/32/1572.
31. *CCR 1323–7*, 622.
32. TNA SC 8/307/15309.
33. *CFR 1319–27*, p. 421; *CPR 1324–7*, 336.
34. Dryburgh, 'Last Refuge of a Scoundrel?', *RENP*, 119, 134–5, 139; Phillips, 510–12; *Anonimalle*, 130. Arundel's whereabouts at this time are unclear.
35. *Lanercost*, 253.
36. SAL MS 122, 90; *Itinerary*, 290.
37. Claire Sponsler, 'The King's Boyfriend', 162, note 9.
38. *Foedera*, 646; *CCR 1323–7*, 655.
39. Ormrod, *Edward III*, 44, note 70, for Zouche; Edward's generosity to Wateville, which included giving him gifts of forty marks twice and forty pounds, visiting him at his house in London and paying his expenses when he was ill, is recorded in SAL MS 122, 9, 50, 64–5, 75, 77, 89.
40. SAL MS 122, 90.
41. Winchester was born on 1 March 1261: *CFR 1272–1307*, 149, 152; *Calendar of Inquisitions Post Mortem, Vol. 2, 1272–1307*, Nos 101, 389.
42. *AP*, 317–18; *Brut*, 240; Haines, *Edward*, 181; Phillips, 513.
43. *Gesta*, 87.
44. *CFR 1319–27*, 422.
45. Rees, *Caerphilly Castle*, pp. 109–121.
46. *CFR 1319–27*, 430; *CFR 1327–37*, 12–13; *CPR 1324–7*, 341, 344; *CPR 1327–30*, 12, 14, 18, 37–9.
47. SAL MS 122, 90; Phillips, 514, note 363.

48. SAL MS 122, 90.
49. *CPR 1327–30*, 37–9, has a list of the Caerphilly garrison, who included Edward's chamber staff Wat Cowherd, Peter Plummer, Henry Hustret, Rodrigo de Medyne, John Edriche, John Pope and others.
50. *CCR 1327–30*, 26.
51. *Lanercost*, 253.
52. *CPR 1324–7*, 335–6.
53. *CPR 1324–7*, 336.
54. *CFR 1329–27*, 422; *CPR 1324–7*, 337; Phillips, 514.
55. Phillips, 515.
56. *AP*, 319; *Murimuth*, 49; *Flores*, 234.
57. *AP*, 319; *Anonimalle*, 130.
58. *CCR 1323–7*, 655.
59. Haines, *Edward*, 185.
60. *Brut*, 240; *Anonimalle*, 130; *Croniques*, 56.
61. *Tyranny*, 77, 191–3, claims that Reading was one of Despenser's closest friends, his marshal and loyal knight; Doherty, *Death*, 106, says he was Despenser's 'principal henchman'. I have found no evidence to support this. Reading was not a knight but a royal sergeant-at-arms, as SAL MS 122 makes clear.
62. *Murimuth*, 50. Michael Burtscher, *The Fitzalans*, 24.
63. *ODNB*; Burtscher, *Fitzalans*, 24–5; *Lanercost*, 252.
64. *Murimuth*, 50, wrongly gives Micheldever's first name as Thomas, but it was certainly Robert: TNA SC 8/17/835; *CFR 1327–37*, 8; *CPR 1327–30*, 22.
65. SAL MS 122, 9; *CPR 1324–7*, 206, 258, 283; *CFR 1319–27*; 101.
66. *CPR 1324–7*, 339.
67. *Brut*, 339–40; *Froissart*, 43–4; Haines, *Edward*, 185; *Traitor*, 241.
68. Holmes, 'Judgement', 261–7, prints them in the French original, and see my translation at http://edwardthesecond.blogspot.com/2009/04/charges–against–hugh–despenser–younger.html.
69. Haines, *Edward*, 185.
70. *Brut*, 240; *Anonimalle*, 130; *AP*, 320; *Froissart*, 43–4; *Gesta*, 87; *Traitor*, 162; Phillips, 518; Sponsler, 'The King's Boyfriend', 152ff; Danielle Westerhof, 'Deconstructing Identities', 92–4.
71. *CCR 1330–3*, 175.
72. *CPR 1324–7*, 339–40.
73. *CCR 1323–7*, 624.
74. Underhill, *Good Estate*, 39–40.
75. I am grateful to Jules Frusher for bringing this point to my attention.
76. *English Historical Documents 1189–1327*, Vol. iii, 288.
77. *CPR 1324–7*, 337; Phillips, 518, note 384; *Flores*, 235.
78. *Anonimalle*, 132.
79. *CPL 1305–41*, 482.
80. Haines, *Death of a King*, 32; Haines, 'Stamford Council', 145, points out that there is no evidence for the allegation.
81. Doherty, *Death*, 108–9, 133, claims that Isabella 'had murder in her heart' regarding her husband and called for his execution at Wallingford, and that in her eyes he became a 'non-person'. No evidence is cited in support of these unlikely statements.
82. Haines, 'Stamford Council', 143, Phillips, 521.
83. Edward's deposition is discussed at length in Claire Valente, 'Deposition and Abdication of Edward II', 852–81; Phillips, 524–39; Haines, *Edward*, 188–94.
84. *Lanercost*, 254.

85. Lyon, *Constitutional History of the UK*, 95.
86. Valente, 'Deposition and Abdication', 869.
87. Valente, 855–6.
88. Phillips, 527–9; Valente, 859.
89. Phillips, 533–4; Valente, 860–1.
90. *Murimuth*, 51; *Scalacronica*, 74; *English Historical Documents*, 288; *Flores*, 235, etc.
91. Rothwell, *English Historical Documents*, 287–8; *Flores*, 235; *Murimuth*, 51; Valente, 870.
92. Next in line after Edward's sons Edward of Windsor and John of Eltham were his half-brothers Norfolk and Kent and their sons, then his cousin Lancaster.
93. *Foedera*, 683; Valente, 870–71.
94. *Foedera*, 650.

16 Four Conspiracies and a Funeral

1. Phillips, 541.
2. *PROME*, November 1330 parliament; *CCR 1327–30*, 77.
3. *Chronicon Henrici Knighton*, I, ed. J. R. Lumby (1889), 444.
4. *Traitor*, 173–4, 288, note 26; *Perfect King*, 58.
5. 'Captivity', 153, 157–8.
6. *AP*, 333; *Baker*, 31; 'Captivity', 158–9.
7. *Baker*, 30–31.
8. *Baker*, 31.
9. *PROME*.
10. *CCR 1327–30*, 77; 'Captivity', 155; Haines, Edward, 225–6.
11. As suggested in Doherty, *Death*, 120.
12. *CCR 1327–30*, 77, 86.
13. *Murimuth*, 52.
14. Froissart, 44.
15. Cited in Doherty, *Death*, 123.
16. *Murimuth*, 52.
17. For Gurney's family, see Haines, *Death of a King*, 150.
18. *Valence*, 262; *CPR 1321–4*, 53; *CPR 1324–7*, 5; *CCR 1323–7*, 202–3.
19. TNA SC 8/232/11592; *CCR 1323–7*, 554.
20. Claire Valente, 'Lament of Edward II', 422–39.
21. *Murimuth*, 52.
22. Doherty, *Death*, 113; Weir, *Isabella*, 256–7.
23. *Tyranny*, 209.
24. *Tyranny*, 209, 212–16, 223–4.
25. *Croniques*, 61–3.
26. *Brut*, 254–5, 257–9.
27. *CFR 1319–27*, 95, 101, 185.
28. *Lanercost*, 258–9.
29. *Brut*, 249.
30. *CPR 1321–4*, 50; *CPR 1324–7*, 326, 336; *CPR 1327–30*, 38.
31. *CCR 1323–7*, 169, 532; SC 8/98/4856.
32. ODNB; *CCR 1323–1327*, 101, 120; *CPR 1321–4*, 168, 372, 378; *CPR 1327–30*, 100; SC 8/47/2308.
33. *CPR 1327–30*, 74–99.
34. *CPR 1327–30*, 99.

35. *Lanercost*, 257.
36. *Bridlington*, 96; *Lanercost*, 256–7; CCR *1327–30*, 212 (quotation); CPR *1327–30*, 139, 180, 183, 191, and CCR *132–30*, 157, 212.
37. CCR *1327–30*, 157.
38. CCR *1327–30*, 142; CPR *1327–30*, 183.
39. CCR *1327–30*, 169, 187–8, 273, 278.
40. CPR *1327–30*, 95.
41. F. J. Tanqueray, 'Conspiracy of Thomas Dunheved, 1327', 119–24.
42. CPR *1327–30*, 156–7.
43. Doherty, *Death*, 218–19.
44. CCR *1327–30*, 156, 179.
45. TNA SC 8/69/3444.
46. CCR *1327–30*, 241, 566; CPR *1327–30*, 360.
47. *AP*, 337; *Brut*, 249; *Lanercost*, 259, 264–5.
48. CCR *1327–30*, 146, 549.
49. CCR *1327–30*, 158; *Foedera*, 714.
50. CCR *1330–3*, 178, 181, 274.
51. 'Captivity', 165.
52. CCR *1327–30*, 182.
53. *AP*, 337.
54. 'Captivity', 165, 182–190.
55. CPR *1324–7*, 249; Haines, *Death of a King*, 138.
56. CPR *1321–4*, 77.
57. TNA DL 10/253; *Intrigue*, 68.
58. *PROME*, November 1330 parliament.
59. Haines, *Death of a King*, 90–95, 138, 146; Hunter, 'Measures Taken', 274ff.
60. For thorough accounts of the chronicle evidence for Edward's death, see *Intrigue*, 55–8; Phillips, 560–65.
61. *AP*, 337–8; *Anonimalle*, 134; Phillips, 561, note 238.
62. *Murimuth*, 53–4; *Gesta*, 97–8.
63. *Lanercost*, 259; *Scalacronica*, 74.
64. Phillips, 561–2.
65. Cited in Haines, *Death of a King*, 49.
66. David C. Fowler, *The Life and Times of John Trevisa, Medieval Scholar* (1995), 9, 16, 23.
67. Chaplais, *Piers Gaveston*, 112–13.
68. CPR *1327–30*, 37.
69. Mortimer, 'Death of Edward II' in *Intrigue*, 66.
70. Haines, *Death of a King*, 53.
71. *Intrigue*, 68.
72. *Intrigue*, 68.
73. *Intrigue*, 67.
74. Moore, 'Documents Relating to the Death', 217.
75. Moore, 'Documents', 221; Phillips, 553; *Intrigue*, 67.
76. Moore, 'Documents', 221.
77. Moore, 'Documents', 221–2; *Intrigue*, 67, 69; Phillips, 553.
78. Ormrod, 'Personal Religion of Edward III', 870, note 120, citing TNA E 101/383/2.
79. Ernst Kantorowicz, *The King's Two Bodies* (new ed., 1997), 420.
80. *Traitor*, 240.

17 The Curious Case of the King Who Lived

1. The letter is held at Warwickshire County Record Office, CR136/C2027. It is printed in French in Haines, 'Sumptuous Apparel', 893–4, and in English in *Intrigue*, 154–5 (my translation differs slightly).

2. *CCR 1330–3*, 132, states that Kent attended Edward's funeral 'with other magnates of the realm'. There is no direct evidence that Melton was present, but it is extremely likely that he was, given that he was a high-ranking prelate and had for many years shown great loyalty to and affection for Edward.

3. *Murimuth*, 255–6; *Lanercost*, 264–5; Phillips, 566–7, *Intrigue*, 161. Kingsclere, oddly, was arrested in 1332 by Giles of Spain (an adherent of Kent in 1330) on suspicion of involvement in Edward II's death.

4. *Intrigue*, 155, 161; Kathryn Warner, 'Adherents of Edmund of Woodstock', 804 note 150; *Murimuth*, 256.

5. *Murimuth*, 52–4; *Brut*, 253.

6. *Intrigue*, 75.

7. Warner, 'Adherents', 782–4, 799.

8. For a refutation of the accusation of stupidity, see *Intrigue*, 83–4, 153–4.

9. *Murimuth*, 256.

10. Mortimer, *Intrigue*, 86–7, 140. John Dunheved acknowledged in 1317 and 1329 that he owed a debt of £1,000 to Pecche, and mortgaged his manor of Dunchurch to him: *CCR 1313–8*, 572; *CCR 1323–7*, 201; *CCR 1327–30*, 543.

11. *Intrigue*, 161; Phillips, 567.

12. *Calendar of Plea and Memoranda Rolls of London 1323–64*, ed. A. H. Thomas, 72. For detailed accounts of Melton and Kent's plot, its timing and the men who supported them, see Mortimer, 'The Plot of the Earl of Kent, 1328–30' in *Intrigue*, 153–173, and my 'Adherents', 779–805.

13. *CCR 1330–3*, 24, 132.

14. *Murimuth*, 256.

15. *Brut*, 263–7; *PROME*.

16. The Fieschi letter has been reprinted, discussed and interpreted numerous times since its discovery in 1877. See e.g. Cuttino and Lyman 'Where is Edward II?', 522–43; Phillips, 582–94; *Traitor*, 251–62; *Intrigue*, 182–9; *Tyranny*, 203–6; Doherty, *Death*, 192–215; Haines, *Death of a King*, 100–8. For *Milasci*, see *Intrigue*, 197–8, and *Perfect King*, 414–5.

17. See *Traitor*, 258. Phillips, 591, states Fieschi is incorrect in saying that the earl of Arundel was still with Edward and Despenser, but I know of no evidence which definitely places Arundel elsewhere, and he may well have still been with the king on 20 October at Chepstow. It is unclear when and where Arundel was captured, only that he was killed in Hereford on 17 November. The Fieschi letter correctly states that Edward was captured with Despenser and Robert Baldock, and not Arundel.

18. *Intrigue*, 178–82, 188–9, 202, 205; Phillips, 594–6.

19. *Intrigue*, 181, 221, note 29; *Perfect King*, 152–3, 412.

20. A notable exception is Richard de Neueby, who met Edward II in 1313, claiming to be his brother, and received a generous gift of money. As we have no record of him being punished and the entry also does not say 'falsely claiming', he may genuinely have been an illegitimate son of Edward I, or at least convinced Edward II that he was.

21. *PROME: dicit quod ipse nunquam fuit consentiens, auxilians, seu procurans, ad mortem suam, nec unquam scivit de morte sua usque in presenti Parliamento isto.*

22. *Intrigue*, 69.
23. Isabella's reputation was far worse centuries after her death than in her own lifetime, when it doesn't seem as though she was viewed as a notorious adulteress and murderess (except by Geoffrey le Baker). The 'she-wolf' nickname was first given to her in 1757, in a poem by Thomas Gray.
24. Blackley, 'Cult of the Dead', 26–9.
25. *ODNB*; Dixon and Raine, *Lives of the Archbishops of York*, Vol. 1, 436.
26. *Intrigue*, 197–202, 226–7; *Perfect King*, 414–5; Phillips, 586–8.
27. Sant'Alberto's official website has a section in Italian and English on Edward II and the mysteries surrounding his death. His afterlife in Italy is discussed at length in Appendix 3 of Ian Mortimer's *Perfect King* and in much of his *Intrigue*, which includes a long chapter on the Fieschi family and their connections to Edward II and III. The 2011 film *Uncertain Proof*, made by Bristol Films, deals with Edward's afterlife in Italy, as does Ivan Fowler's 2013 novel *Auramala: The King Lives*.
28. *Perfect King*, 201.
29. *Perfect King*, 201, 417.
30. Saaler, *Edward II*, 17; *Vita*, 75; Phillips, 66.

Select Bibliography

Primary Sources

Adae Murimuth Continuatio Chronicarum, ed. E. M. Thompson (London: Eyre and Spottiswoode, 1889).

Annales Londonienses 1195–1330, in W. Stubbs, ed., *Chronicles of the Reigns of Edward I and Edward II*, Volume 1, Rolls Series, 76 (London: Rolls Series, 76, 1882).

Annales Paulini 1307–1340, in Stubbs, *Chronicles*, Volume 1.

The Anonimalle Chronicle 1307 to 1334, from Brotherton Collection MS 29, ed. W. R. Childs and J. Taylor (Yorkshire Archaeological Society Record Series 147, 1991).

The Brut or the Chronicles of England, Part 1, ed. F. W. D. Brie (London: Early English Text Society, 1906).

Calendar of Chancery Warrants, Vol. 1, 1244–1326 (London: HMSO, 1927).

Calendar of the Charter Rolls, Vol. 3, 1300–1326 (London: HMSO, 1908).

Calendar of the Close Rolls, eleven vols, 1272–1333 (London: HMSO, 1898–1906).

Calendar of Documents Relating to Scotland Vol. 3, 1307–1357, ed. Joseph Bain (Edinburgh: H. M. General Register House, 1887).

Calendar of Entries in the Papal Registers Relating to Great Britain and Ireland: Papal Letters, Vol. 2, 1305–1341.

Calendar of the Fine Rolls, four vols, 1272–1334 (London: HMSO, 1911–13).

Calendar of Inquisitions Miscellaneous (Chancery) Vol. 2, 1308–1348 (London: HMSO, 1916).

Calendar of the Patent Rolls, eleven vols, 1272–1334 (London: HMSO, 1891–1903).

Calendar of Memoranda Rolls (Exchequer): Michaelmas 1326–Michaelmas 1327 (London: HMSO, 1968).

Croniques de London Depuis l'An 44 Hen III Jusqu'à l'An 17 Edw. III, ed. G. J. Aungier (London: Camden Society, 1844).

Davies, James Conway, 'The First Journal of Edward II's Chamber', *English Historical Review*, 30 (1915).

Devon, Frederick, *Issues of the Exchequer: Being A Collection of Payments Made Out of His Majesty's Revenue* (London: John Murray, 1837).

Edwards, J. Goronwy, *Calendar of Ancient Correspondence Concerning Wales* (Cardiff: University Press Board, 1935).

Edwards, J. Goronwy, *Calendar of Ancient Petitions Relating to Wales* (Cardiff: University of Wales Press, 1975).

English Historical Documents, Vol. 3, 1189–1327, ed. Harry Rothwell (London: Eyre and Spottiswoode, 1975).

Flores Historiarum, ed. H. R. Luard, Vol. iii (London: Eyre and Spottiswoode for HMSO, 1890).

The Flowers of History, especially such as relate to the affairs of Britain. From the beginning of the world to the year 1307, ed. C. D. Yonge (London: Henry G. Bohn, 1853).

Froissart: Chronicles, ed. Geoffrey Brereton (London: Penguin, 1978).

The Chronicle of Geoffrey le Baker of Swinbrook, translated by David Preest (Woodbridge: Boydell and Brewer, 2012).

Chronicon Galfridi le Baker de Swynebroke, ed. E. M. Thompson (Oxford: Clarendon Press, 1889).

Gesta Edwardi de Carnarvon Auctore Canonico Bridlingtoniensi, in W. Stubbs, ed., *Chronicles of the Reigns of Edward I and Edward II*, Volume 2 (London: Rolls Series, 76, 1883).

The Chronicle of Walter Guisborough, ed. Harry Rothwell (London: Butler and Tanner (Camden Society, third series, Vol. 89) 1957).

Haskins, G. L., 'A Chronicle of the Civil Wars of Edward II', *Speculum*, 14 (1939).

Historia Anglicana, Vol. 1, ed. H. T. Riley (London: Longman, Green, 1863).

The Household Book of Queen Isabella of England: For The Fifth Regnal Year Of Edward II, 8th July 1311 To 7th July 1312, ed. F. D. Blackley and G. Hermansen (Edmonton: University of Alberta Press, 1971).

Hallam, Elizabeth, *The Itinerary of Edward II and His Household, 1307–1327* (London: List and Index Society, 1984).

Johannis de Trokelowe et Henrici de Blaneforde Chronica et Annales, ed. H. T. Riley (London: Longman, Green, 1866).

The Chronicle of Lanercost 1272–1346, ed. Herbert Maxwell (Glasgow: James Maclehose and Sons, 1913).

Letters of the Kings of England, Vol. 1, ed. J. O. Halliwell (London: Henry Colburn, 1848).

Le Livere de Reis de Britanie e le Livere de Reis de Engletere, ed. John Glover (London: Longman, Green, 1865).

The National Archives: Chancery, Duchy of Lancaster, Exchequer and Special Collection records, especially E 101/379/17, E 101/624/24, E 101/379/11, E 101/376/15, E 101/379/7 (account books of the chamber in the 1320s).

Polychronicon Ranulphi Higden, monachi Cestrensis, Vol. 8, ed. J. R. Lumby (London: Longman, Green, 1865).

The Parliament Rolls of Medieval England, ed. Chris Given-Wilson et al, CD-ROM edition (Scholarly Editions, 2005).

Records of the Trial of Walter Langeton, Bishop of Coventry and Lichfield 1307–1312, ed. Alice Beardwood (London: Camden Fourth Series, 6, 1969).

Rhodes, Walter E., 'The Inventory of the Jewels and Wardrobe of Queen Isabella (1307–8)', *EHR*, 12 (1897).

Foedera, Conventiones, Litterae et Cujuscunque Generis Acta Publica, Vol. 2.1, 1307–1327 (London: Thomas Rymer, 1818).

Roll of Arms of Caerlaverock, ed. T. Wright (London: John Camden Hotten, 1864).

Scalacronica: The Reigns of Edward I, Edward II and Edward III as Recorded by Sir Thomas Gray of Heton, knight, ed. Herbert Maxwell (Glasgow: James Maclehose and Sons, 1907).

Scalacronica: By Sir Thomas Gray of Heton, knight. A Chronicle of England and Scotland from A.D. MLXVI to A.D. MCCCLXII, ed. J. Stevenson (Edinburgh: Maitland Club, 1836).

Society of Antiquaries of London MS 122 (Edward's chamber account of 1325/26)

Stapleton, Thomas, 'A Brief Summary of the Wardrobe Accounts of the tenth, eleventh, and fourteenth years of King Edward the Second', *Archaeologia*, 26 (1836)

Vita Edwardi Secundi Monachi Cuiusdam Malmesberiensis, ed. N. Denholm-Young (London: Thomas Nelson and Sons, 1957).

The War of Saint-Sardos (1323–1325): Gascon Correspondence and Diplomatic Documents, ed. Pierre Chaplais (London: Camden Third Series, 87, 1954).

Warwickshire County Record Office, CR 136/C2027 (letter of January 1330).

Wright, T., *The Political Songs of England* (London: Camden Society, 1839).

Secondary Sources: Articles, Essays and Dissertations

Blackley, F. D., 'Adam, the Bastard Son of Edward II', *BIHR*, 37 (1964).

Blackley, F. D., 'Isabella and the Bishop of Exeter', in T. A. Sandqvist and M. R. Powicke, eds., *Essays in Medieval History Presented to Bertie Wilkinson* (Toronto: University of Toronto Press, 1969).

Blackley, F. D., 'Isabella of France, Queen of England (1308–1358) and the Late Medieval Cult of the Dead', *Canadian Journal of History*, 14 (1980).

Bloom, J. Harvey, 'Simon de Swanland and King Edward II', *Notes and Queries*, 11th series, 4 (1911).

Brown, Elizabeth A. R., 'The Political Repercussions of Family Ties in the Early Fourteenth Century: The Marriage of Edward II and Isabelle of France', *Speculum*, 63 (1988).

Brown, Elizabeth A. R., 'The Marriage of Edward II of England and Isabelle of France: A Postscript', *Speculum*, 64 (1989).

Brown, Elizabeth A. R., 'Diplomacy, Adultery and Domestic Politics at the Court of Philip the Fair: Queen Isabelle's Mission to France in 1314', in J. S. Hamilton, ed., *Documenting the Past: Essays in Medieval History Presented to George Peddy Cuttino* (Woodbridge: Boydell Press, 1989).

Brown, Elizabeth A. R., and Degalado, Nancy Freeman, '*Le grant feste*: Philip the Fair's Celebration of the Knighting of His Sons in Paris at Pentecost of 1313', in Barbara Hanawalt and Kathryn Reyerson, eds., *City and Spectacle in Medieval Europe* (Minneapolis: University of Minnesota Press, 1994).

Buck, Mark, 'The Reform of the Exchequer, 1316–1326', *EHR*, 98 (1983).

Burgtorf, Jochen, 'With my Life, his Joyes Began and Ended: Piers Gaveston and King Edward II of England Revisited', *FCE V*, ed. Nigel Saul (Woodbridge: Boydell and Brewer, 2008).

Cavanaugh, Susan, 'Royal Books: King John to Richard II', *The Library*, 5th series, 10 (1988).

Childs, W. R., 'Welcome, My Brother: Edward II, John of Powderham and the Chronicles, 1318', in I. Wood and G. A. Loud, eds., *Church and Chronicle in the Middle Ages: Essays Presented to John Taylor* (London and Rio Grande: Hambledon Press, 1991).

Childs, W. R., 'England in Europe in the Reign of Edward II', *RENP*.

Cobban, A. B., 'Edward II, Pope John XXII, and the University of Cambridge', *Bulletin of the John Rylands Library*, 47 (1964–65).

Cuttino, G. P., and Lyman, T. W., 'Where is Edward II?', *EHR,* 53 (1978).

Davies, James Conway, 'The Despenser War in Glamorgan', *TRHS*, third series, 9 (1915).

Denholm-Young, N., 'Edward III and Bermondsey Priory', *EHR*, 48 (1933).

Dobrowolski, Paula, 'Women and Their Dower in the Long Thirteenth Century 1265–1329', *Thirteenth-Century England VI*, ed. Michael Prestwich, R. H. Britnell and Robin Frame (Woodbridge: Boydell and Brewer, 1997).

Doherty, Paul, 'The Date of Birth of Isabella, Queen of England', *BIHR*, 48 (1975).

Dryburgh, Paul, 'The Last Refuge of a Scoundrel? Edward II and Ireland, 1321–7', *RENP*.

Dryburgh, Paul, 'The Career of Roger Mortimer, first Earl of March (*c.* 1287–1330)', Univ. of Bristol PhD thesis, 2002.

Edwards, Kathleen, 'The Personal and Political Activities of the English Episcopate During the Reign of Edward II', *BIHR*, 16 (1938).

Edwards, Kathleen, 'The Political Importance of the English Bishops During the Reign of Edward II', *EHR*, 59 (1944).

Edwards, J. G., 'Sir Gruffydd Llwyd', *EHR*, 30 (1915).

Frame, Robin, 'Power and Society in the Lordship of Ireland, 1272–1377', *Past and Present*, 76 (1977).

Fryde, E. B., 'The Deposits of Hugh Despenser the Younger with Italian Bankers', *Economic History Review*, 2nd series, 3 (1951).

Gibbs, V., 'The Battle of Boroughbridge and the Boroughbridge Roll', *Genealogist*, 21 (1905).

Haines, Roy Martin, 'Bishops and politics in the reign of Edward II: Hamo de Hethe, Henry Wharton, and the 'Historia Roffensis', *Journal of Ecclesiastical History*, 44 (1993).

Haines, Roy Martin, 'Sir Thomas Gurney of Englishcombe, Regicide?', *Somerset Archaeological and Natural History*, 147 (2004).

Haines, Roy Martin, 'The Stamford Council of April 1327', *EHR*, 122 (2007).

Haines, Roy Martin, 'Roger Mortimer's Scam', *Transactions of the Bristol and Gloucestershire Archaeological Society*, 126 (2008).

Haines, Roy Martin, 'Sumptuous Apparel for a Royal Prisoner: Archbishop Melton's letter, 14 January 1330', *EHR*, 124 (2009).

Hallam, Elizabeth, 'Royal Burial and the Cult of Kingship in France and England, 1066–1330' *JMH*, 8 (1982).

Hamilton, J. S., 'The Uncertain Death of Edward II', *History Compass*, 6, 5 (2008).

Hamilton, J. S., 'Charter Witness Lists for the Reign of Edward II', *Fourteenth Century England I*, ed. Nigel Saul (Woodbridge: Boydell and Brewer, 2000).

Hamilton, J. S., 'Some Notes on 'Royal' Medicine in the Reign of Edward II', *Fourteenth Century England II*, ed. Chris Given-Wilson (Woodbridge: Boydell and Brewer, 2002).

Hamilton, J. S., 'The Character of Edward II: The Letters of Edward of Caernarfon Reconsidered', *RENP*.

Hamilton, J. S., 'A Reassessment of the Loyalty of the Household Knights of Edward II', *Fourteenth Century England VII*, ed. Mark Ormrod (Woodbridge: Boydell and Brewer, 2012).

Haskins, G. L., 'The Doncaster Petition of 1321', *EHR*, 53 (1938).

Haskins, G. L., 'Judicial Proceedings Against a Traitor after Boroughbridge', *Speculum*, 12 (1937).

Holmes, G. A., *The Estates of the Higher Nobility in Fourteenth-Century England* (1957).

Holmes, G. A., 'The Judgement on the Younger Despenser, 1326', *EHR*, 70 (1955).

Holmes, G. A., 'A Protest Against the Despensers, 1326', *Speculum*, 30 (1955).

Hunter, Joseph, 'Measures Taken for the Apprehension of Sir Thomas de Gurney, One of the Murderers of Edward II', *Archaeologia*, 27 (1838).

Hunter, Joseph, 'Journal of the Mission of Queen Isabella to the Court of France and of her long residence in that Country', *Archaeologia*, 36 (1855).

Johnstone, Hilda, 'Isabella, the She-wolf of France', *History*, 21 (1936).

Johnstone, Hilda, 'The Eccentricities of Edward II', *EHR*, 48 (1933).

Johnstone, Hilda, 'The Parliament of Lincoln, 1316', *EHR*, 36 (1921).

Johnstone, Hilda, 'The County of Ponthieu, 1279–1307', *EHR*, 29 (1914).

Kilpatrick, Hannah, 'Correction to Hoskins' 'Chronicle of the Civil Wars of Edward II'', *Notes and Queries*, 58 (2011).

King, Andy, ''Pur Salvation du Roiaume': Military Service and Obligation in Fourteenth-Century Northumberland', *FCE II*.

King, Andy, 'Bandits, Robbers and *Schavaldours*: War and Disorder in Northumberland in the Reign of Edward II', *Thirteenth-Century England IX*, ed. Michael Prestwich, Richard Britnell and Robin Frame (Woodbridge: Boydell and Brewer, 2003).

King, Andy, 'Thomas of Lancaster's First Quarrel with Edward II', *Fourteenth Century England III*, ed. W. M. Ormrod (Woodbridge: Boydell and Brewer, 2004).

Lachaud, Frédérique, 'Liveries of Robes in England, c.1200–c.1330', *EHR*, 61 (1996).

Lawne, Penny, 'Edmund of Woodstock (1301–1330): A Study of Personal Loyalty', in *Fourteenth Century England VI*, ed. C. Given-Wilson (Woodbridge: Boydell and Brewer, 2010).

Lawrence, Martyn, 'Rise of a Royal Favourite: the Early Career of Hugh Despenser the Elder', *RENP*.

Lawrence, Martyn, 'Secular Patronage and Religious Devotion: the Despensers and St Mary's Abbey, Tewkesbury', *Fourteenth Century England V*, ed. Nigel Saul (Woodbridge: Boydell and Brewer, 2008).

Lawrence, Martyn, 'Power, Ambition and Political Rehabilitation: the Despensers, c. 1281–1400', Univ. of York DPhil thesis, 2005.

Linehan, Peter, 'The English Mission of Cardinal Petrus Hispanus, the Chronicle of Walter of Guisborough, and news from Castile at Carlisle (1307)', *EHR*, 117 (2002).

Lord, Carla, 'Queen Isabella at the Court of France', *FCE II*.

Lucas, H. S., 'The Great European Famine of 1315, 1316 and 1317', *Speculum*, 5 (1930).

Lumsden, Andrew, 'The fairy tale of Edward II', *The Gay and Lesbian Review Worldwide*, March/April 2004.

Maddicott, J. R., 'Thomas of Lancaster and Sir Robert Holland: a Study in Noble Patronage', *EHR*, 86 (1971).

Marshall, Alison, 'The Childhood and Household of Edward II's Half–Brothers, Thomas of Brotherton and Edmund of Woodstock', *RENP*.

Marshall, Alison, 'Thomas of Brotherton, Earl of Norfolk and Marshal of England: A Study in Early Fourteenth-Century Aristocracy', Univ. of Bristol PhD diss., 2006.

Moore, S. A., Documents Relating to the Death and Burial of Edward II', *Archaeologia*, 50 (1887).

Menache, Sophia, 'Isabelle of France, Queen of England – A Reconsideration', *JMH*, 10 (1984).

Mortimer, Ian, 'The Death of Edward II in Berkeley Castle', *EHR*, 489 (2005) (reprinted in his *Medieval Intrigue*).

Mortimer, Ian, 'Sermons of Sodomy: A Reconsideration of Edward II's Sodomitical Reputation', *RENP* (reprinted in his *Medieval Intrigue*).

Nicholson, R., 'The Last Campaign of Robert Bruce', *EHR*, 77 (1962).

Ormrod, W. M., 'The Personal Religion of Edward III', *Speculum*, 64 (1989).

Ormrod, W. M., 'The Royal Nursery: A Household for the Younger Children of Edward III', *EHR*, 120 (2005).

Ormrod, W. M., 'The Sexualities of Edward II', *RENP*.

Parsons, John Carmi, 'The Intercessory Patronage of Queens Margaret and Isabella of France', *Thirteenth-Century England VI*, ed. Michael Prestwich, R. H. Britnell and Robin Frame (Woodbridge: Boydell and Brewer, 1997).

Parsons, John Carmi, 'The Year of Eleanor of Castile's Birth and Her Children by Edward I', *Mediaeval Studies*, 46 (1984).

Phillips, J. R. S., 'The "Middle Party" and the Negotiating of the Treaty of Leake, August 1318: A Reinterpretation', *BIHR*, 46 (1973).

Phillips, J. R. S., 'Edward II and the Prophets', *England in the Fourteenth Century: Proceedings of the 1985 Harlaxton Symposium*, ed. W. M. Ormrod (Woodbridge: Boydell Press, 1986).

Phillips, J. R. S., '"Edward II" in Italy: English and Welsh Political Exiles and Fugitives in Continental Europe, 1322–1364', *Thirteenth Century England X*, ed. Prestwich, Britnell and Frame (Woodbridge: Boydell and Brewer, 2005).

Phillips, J. R. S., 'The Place of the Reign of Edward II', *RENP*.

Prestwich, Michael, 'The Court of Edward II', *RENP*.

Prestwich, Michael, 'The Unreliability of Royal Household Knights in the Early Fourteenth Century', *FCE II*.

Prestwich, Michael, 'An Everyday Story of Knightly Folk', *Thirteenth-Century England IX*, ed. Prestwich, Britnell and Frame (Prestwich, Michael, Britnell, Richard, and Frame, Robin, eds., *Thirteenth-Century England X* (Woodbridge: Boydell and Brewer, 2001).

Prestwich, Michael, 'Gilbert de Middleton and the Attack on the Cardinals, 1317', *Warriors and Churchmen in the High Middle Ages: Essays Presented to Karl Leyser*, ed. T. Reuter (London and Rio Grande: Hambeldon Press, 1992).

Prestwich, Michael, 'The Piety of Edward I', *England in the Thirteenth Century: Proceedings of the 1984 Harlaxton Symposium*, ed. W. M. Ormrod (Woodbridge: Boydell Press, 1985).

Prestwich, Michael, 'English Castles in the Reign of Edward II', *JMH*, 8 (1982).

Pugh, T. B., 'The Marcher Lords of Glamorgan and Morgannwg, 1317–1485', *Glamorgan County History, III: The Middle Ages*, ed. T. B. Pugh (1971).

Rastall, Richard, 'Secular Musicians in Late Medieval England', Univ. of Manchester PhD thesis, (1968).

Saul, Nigel, 'The Despensers and the Downfall of Edward II', *EHR*, 99 (1984).

Sayles, George Osborne, 'The Formal Judgements on the Traitors of 1322', *Speculum*, 16 (1941).

Smith, J. B., 'Edward II and the Allegiance of Wales', *Welsh History Review*, 8 (1976).

Sponsler, Claire, 'The King's Boyfriend', in Glenn Burger and Steven F. Kruger, eds., *Queering the Middle Ages* (Minneapolis: University of Minnesota Press, 2001).

Stevenson, W. H., 'A Letter of the Younger Despenser on the Eve of the Barons' Rebellion, 21 March 1321', *EHR*, 12 (1897).

Stones, E. L. G., and Keil, I. J. E., 'Edward II and the Abbot of Glastonbury: A New Case of Historical Evidence Solicited from Monasteries', *Archives*, 12 (1976).

Stuart, E. Pole, 'The Interview Between Philip V and Edward II at Amiens in 1320', *EHR*, 41 (1926).

Tanqueray, Frédéric J., 'The Conspiracy of Thomas Dunheved, 1327', *EHR*, 31 (1916)

Taylor, A. J., 'The Birth of Edward of Caernarvon and the Beginnings of Caernarvon Castle', *History*, 35 (1950).

Taylor, John, 'The Judgement on Hugh Despenser the Younger', *Medievalia et Humanistica*, 12 (1958).

Tebbit, Alistair, 'Royal Patronage and Political Allegiance: The Household Knights of Edward II 1314–1321' in *Thirteenth-Century England X*.

Tebbit, Alistair, 'Household Knights and Military Service under the Direction of Edward II', *RENP*.

Tout, T. F., 'The Captivity and Death of Edward of Carnarvon', *Collected Papers of T. F. Tout*, Vol. iii (Manchester: Manchester University Press, 1934).

Trease, G. E., 'The Spicers and Apothecaries of the Royal Household in the Reigns of Edward I and Edward II', *Nottingham Medieval Studies*, 3 (1959).

Vale, Malcolm, 'Ritual Ceremony and the 'Civilising Process': The Role of the Court, *c.* 1270–1400', in Steven J. Gunn and A. Janse, eds., *The Court as a Stage* (Woodbridge: Boydell and Brewer, 2006).

Valente, Claire, 'The Deposition and Abdication of Edward II', *EHR*, 113 (1998).

Valente, Claire, 'The "Lament of Edward II": Religious Lyric, Political Propaganda', *Speculum*, 77 (2002).

Warner, Kathryn, 'The Adherents of Edmund of Woodstock, Earl of Kent, in March 1330', *EHR*, 126 (2011).

Waugh, Scott L., 'For King, Country and Patron: The Despensers and Local Administration 1321–1322', *The Journal of British Studies*, 22 (1983).

Waugh, Scott L., 'The Profits of Violence: the Minor Gentry in the Rebellion of 1321–22 in Gloucestershire and Herefordshire', *Speculum*, 52 (1977).

Westerhof, Danielle, 'Deconstructing Identities on the Scaffold: the Execution of Hugh Despenser the Younger, 1326', *JMH*, 33 (2007).

Wilkinson, Bertie, 'The Sherburn Indenture and the Attack on the Despensers', *EHR*, 63 (1948).

Secondary Sources: Books

Altschul, Michael, *A Baronial Family in Medieval England: the Clares, 1217–1314* (Baltimore: Johns Hopkins University Press, 1965).

Barber, Malcolm, *The Trial of the Templars* (Cambridge: Cambridge University Press, second edition, 2006).

Barker, Juliet R. V., *The Tournament in England 1100–1400* (Woodbridge: Boydell Press, 1986).

Barrow, G. W. S., *Robert Bruce and the Community of the Realm of Scotland* (Edinburgh: Edinburgh University Press, second edition, 1976).

Bell, Graham, *Robert the Bruce's Forgotten Victory: The Battle of Byland 1322* (Stroud: Tempus Publishing, 2005).

Benz St John, Lisa, *Three Medieval Queens: Queenship and the Crown in Fourteenth-Century England* (New York: Palgrave Macmillan, 2012).

Bingham, Caroline, *The Life and Times of Edward II* (1973).

Boswell, J., *Christianity, Social Tolerance and Homosexuality* (Chicago: University of Chicago Press, 1980).

Brown, Chris, *Bannockburn 1314: A New History* (Stroud: The History Press, 2009).

Brown, Michael, *Bannockburn: The Scottish War and the British Isles 1307–1323* (Edinburgh: Edinburgh University Press, 2008).

Buck, Mark, *Politics, Finance and the Church in the Reign of Edward II: Walter Stapeldon, Treasurer of England* (Cambridge: Cambridge University Press, 1983).

Bullock-Davies, Constance, *Menestrellorum Multitudo: Minstrels at a Royal Feast* (Cardiff: University of Wales Press, 1978).

Bullock-Davies, Constance, *A Register of Royal and Baronial Domestic Minstrels 1272–1327* (Woodbridge: Boydell Press, 1986).

Burtscher, Michael, *The Fitzalans: Earls of Arundel and Surrey, Lords of the Welsh Marches (1267–1415)* (Woonton Almeley: Logaston Press, 2008).

Chaplais, Pierre, *English Medieval Diplomatic Practice, Part 1: Documents and Interpretation,* 2 vols (London: HMSO, 1982).

Chaplais, Pierre, *Piers Gaveston: Edward II's Adoptive Brother* (Oxford: Clarendon Press, 1994).

Chaplais, Pierre, *English Diplomatic Practice in the Middle Ages* (London: Bloomsbury, 2003).

Colvin, H. M., *History of the King's Works*, Vol. 2 (London: HMSO, 1976).

Coss, Peter R. and Keen, Maurice Hugh, *Heraldry, Pageantry and Social Display in Medieval England* (Woodbridge: Boydell Press, 2003).

Davies, James Conway, *The Baronial Opposition to Edward II: Its Character and Policy* (Cambridge: Cambridge University Press, 1918).

Denton, Jeffrey H., *Robert Winchelsey and the Crown 1294–1313* (Cambridge: Cambridge University Press, 2002).

Dixon, W. H., and Raine, J., *Lives of the Archbishops of York*, Vol. 1 (London: Longman, Green, 1863).

Dodd, Gwilym, and Musson, Anthony, eds., *The Reign of Edward II: New Perspectives* (York: York Medieval Press, 2006).

Doherty, Paul, *Isabella and the Strange Death of Edward II* (London: Constable and Robinson, 2003).

Frame, Robin, *English Lordship in Ireland, 1318–1361* (Oxford: Oxford University Press, 1982).

Fryde, Natalie, *The Tyranny and Fall of Edward II 1321–1326* (Cambridge: Cambridge University Press, 1979).

Given-Wilson, Chris, ed., *Fourteenth Century England II* (Woodbridge: Boydell and Brewer, 2002).

Given-Wilson, Chris, and Curteis, Alice, *The Royal Bastards of Medieval England* (London: Routledge and Kegan Paul, 1984).

Given-Wilson, Chris, *Chronicles: The Writing of History in Medieval England* (London: Bloomsbury, 2004).

Goldstone, Nancy, *Four Queens: The Provençal Sisters Who Ruled Europe* (New York: Viking, 2007).

Gransden, Antonia, *Historical Writing in England II: c. 1307 to the Early Sixteenth Century* (London: Routledge, 1982).

Griffiths, John, *Edward II in Glamorgan* (London: W. H. Roberts, 1904).

Haines, Roy Martin, *King Edward II: His Life, His Reign, and Its Aftermath, 1284–1330* (Montreal: MacGill-Queen's University Press, 2003).

Haines, Roy Martin, *Death of a King* (Lancaster: Scotforth Books, 2002).

Haines, Roy Martin, *The Church and Politics in Fourteenth-Century England: the Career of Adam Orleton, c. 1275–1345* (Cambridge: Cambridge University Press, 1978).

Haines, Roy Martin, *Archbishop John Stratford: Political Revolutionary and Champion of the Liberties of the English Church, ca. 1275/80–1348* (Toronto: Pontifical Institute of Mediaeval Studies, 1986).

Hamilton, J. S., *Piers Gaveston, Earl of Cornwall 1307–1312: Politics and Patronage in the Reign of Edward II* (Detroit: Wayne State University Press, 1988).

Hutchison, Harold F., *Edward II: The Pliant King* (London: Eyre and Spottiswoode, 1971).

Johnstone, Hilda, *Edward of Carnarvon 1284–1307* (Manchester: Manchester University Press, 1946).

Johnstone, Hilda, *Letters of Edward, Prince of Wales 1304–5* (Cambridge: Roxburghe Club, 1931).

Lord, Evelyn, *The Knights Templar in Britain* (London: Pearson, 2004).

Lyon, Ann, *Constitutional History of the UK* (London: Cavendish, 2003).

Maddicott, J. R., *Thomas of Lancaster 1307–1322: A Study in the Reign of Edward II* (Oxford: Oxford University Press, 1970).

McFarlane, K. B., *The Nobility of Later Medieval England* (Oxford: Clarendon Press, 1973).

McKisack, May, *The Fourteenth Century 1307–1399* (Oxford: Clarendon Press, 1959).

Mitchell, Linda E., *Portraits of Medieval Women: Family, Marriage and Politics in England 1225–1350* (New York: Palgrave Macmillan, 2003).

Moor, Charles, *Knights of Edward I*, (London: Harleian Society 81–84, 1929–32).

Morris, Marc, *A Great and Terrible King: Edward I and the Forging of Britain* (London: Hutchinson, 2008).

Mortimer, Ian, *The Greatest Traitor: The Life of Sir Roger Mortimer, Ruler of England 1327 to 1330* (London: Pimlico, 2003).

Mortimer, Ian, *The Perfect King: The Life of Edward III* (London: Vintage, 2006).

Mortimer, Ian, *The Time-Traveller's Guide to Medieval England* (London: The Bodley Head, 2008).

Mortimer, Ian, *Medieval Intrigue: Decoding Royal Conspiracies* (London: Continuum, 2010).

Nusbacher, Aryeh, *Bannockburn 1314* (Stroud: Tempus, 2005).

Ormrod, W. M., ed., *Fourteenth-Century England III* (Woodbridge: Boydell and Brewer, 2004).

Ormrod, W. M., *Edward III* (New Haven and London: Yale University Press, 2011)

Oxford Dictionary of National Biography, online edition.

Parsons, John Carmi, *Eleanor of Castile: Queen and Society in Thirteenth-Century England* (Basingstoke: Macmillan, 1995).

Perry, R., *Edward the Second: Suddenly, at Berkeley* (Wotton-under-Edge: Ivy House Books, 1988).

Phillips, J. R. S., *Aymer de Valence, earl of Pembroke 1307–1324: Baronial Politics in the Reign of Edward II* (Oxford: Clarendon Press, 1972).

Phillips, Seymour, *Edward II* (New Haven and London: Yale University Press, 2010).

Prestwich, Michael, *Plantagenet England 1225–1360* (Oxford: Clarendon Press, 2005).

Prestwich, Michael, *Edward I* (London: Methuen, 1988).

Prestwich, Michael, *The Three Edwards: War and State in England 1272–1377* (London: Routledge, 1980).

Prestwich, Michael, *Documents Illustrating the Crisis of 1297–98 in England* (London: Camden Fourth Series, 24, 1980).

Prestwich, Michael, Britnell, Richard, and Frame, Robin, eds., *Thirteenth-Century England X* (Woodbridge: Boydell and Brewer, 2003).

Rees, William, *Caerphilly Castle and Its Place in the Annals of Glamorgan* (Caerphilly: D. Brown and Sons, new edition, 1974).

Reese, Peter, *Bannockburn: Scotland's Greatest Victory* (Edinburgh: Canongate Books, 2003).

Richardson, Douglas, *Plantagenet Ancestry: A Study in Colonial and Medieval Families* (Baltimore: Genealogical Publishing Company, 2004).

Roberts, R. A., *Edward II, the Lords Ordainers and Piers Gaveston's Jewels and Horses (1312–1313)* (London: Camden Miscellany, xv, 1929).

Rouse Ball, W. W., *The King's Scholars and King's Hall* (printed privately, 1917).

Saaler, Mary, *Edward II 1307–1327* (London: Rubicon, 1997).

Sadler, John, *Bannockburn: Battle for Liberty* (Barnsley: Pen and Sword Military, 2008).

Saul, Nigel, ed., *Fourteenth Century England 1* (Woodbridge: Boydell and Brewer, 2000).

Sayles, George Osborne, *The Functions of the Medieval Parliament of England* (London: Bloomsbury, revised edition, 1988).

Sumption, Jonathan, *The Hundred Years War 1: Trial by Battle* (London: Faber and Faber, 1999).

Tout, T. F., *The Place of the Reign of Edward II in English History* (Manchester: Manchester University Press, second edition, 1936).

Tout, T. F., *Chapters in the Administrative History of England* (Manchester: Manchester University Press, six vols, 1920–1937).

Tuck, Anthony, *Crown and Nobility 1272–1461* (London: Fontana, 1985).

Underhill, Frances A., *For Her Good Estate: The Life of Elizabeth de Burgh* (New York: St Martin's Press, 1999).

Vale, Malcolm, *The Princely Court: Medieval Courts and Culture in North-West Europe* (Oxford: Oxford University Press, 2001).

Vale, Malcolm, *The Origins of the Hundred Years War: The Angevin Legacy 1250–1340* (Oxford: Clarendon Press, 1990).

Ward, Jennifer C., *English Noblewomen in the Later Middle Ages* (London and New York: Longman, 1992).

Weir, Alison, *Isabella, She-Wolf of France, Queen of England* (London: Pimlico, 2005).

Woolgar, C. M., *The Great Household in Late Medieval England* (New Haven and London: Yale University Press, 1999).

Websites

My Edward II site at http://edwardthesecond.blogspot.com/ has many hundreds of articles about Edward, his life, his family, his reign and its aftermath, going back to 2005.

http://www.ianmortimer.com/ includes essays about Edward II and his survival, and history in general.

http://www.ladydespensersscribery.com/ is an excellent resource for the Despensers, Edward and the fourteenth century.

The archives of http://susandhigginbotham.blogspot.com/ contain many great articles about Edward.

https://theauramalaproject.wordpress.com/ discusses the possibilities of Edward's survival in Italy.

http://www.british-history.ac.uk/

https://www.nationalarchives.gov.uk/

Index

Also available from Amberley Publishing

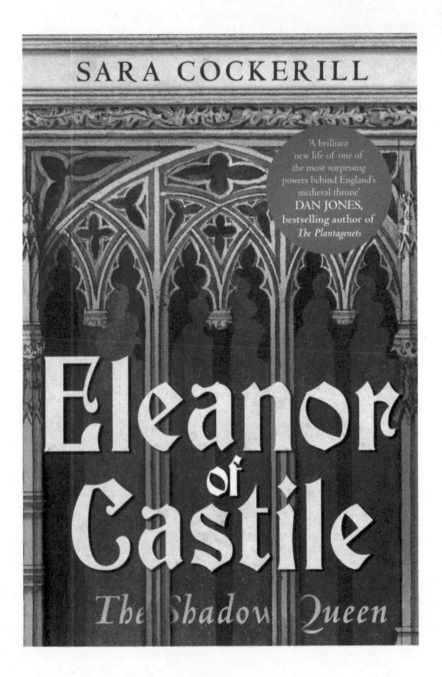

SARA COCKERILL

'A brilliant
new life of one of
the most surprising
powers behind England's
medieval throne'
DAN JONES,
bestselling author of
The Plantagenets

Eleanor
of
Castile

The Shadow Queen

Available from all good bookshops or to order direct
Please call **01453-847-800**
www.amberleybooks.com